MT. PLEASANT LIBRARY
PLEASANTVILLE, NY

D1557061

THE POINT OF NO RETURN

The Point of No Return

American Democracy at the Crossroads

Thomas Byrne Edsall

PRINCETON UNIVERSITY PRESS

PRINCETON AND OXFORD

Chapters 1–44 copyright © 2015–2022 by Thomas Edsall and The New York Times Company. All rights reserved.

All other material copyright © 2023 by Princeton University Press

Princeton University Press is committed to the protection of copyright and the intellectual property our authors entrust to us. Copyright promotes the progress and integrity of knowledge. Thank you for supporting free speech and the global exchange of ideas by purchasing an authorized edition of this book. If you wish to reproduce or distribute any part of it in any form, please obtain permission.

Requests for permission to reproduce material from this work should be sent to permissions@press.princeton.edu

Published by Princeton University Press
41 William Street, Princeton, New Jersey 08540
99 Banbury Road, Oxford OX2 6JX

press.princeton.edu

All Rights Reserved

ISBN 9780691164892
ISBN (e-book) 9780691247564

Library of Congress Control Number: 2022945385

British Library Cataloging-in-Publication Data is available

Editorial: Bridget Flannery-McCoy, Alena Chekanov
Jacket Design: Karl Spurzem
Production: Erin Suydam
Publicity: James Schneider, Kathryn Stevens
Copyeditor: Ashley Moore

This book has been composed in Adobe Text Pro and Gotham.

Printed on acid-free paper. ∞

Printed in the United States of America

10 9 8 7 6 5 4 3 2 1

I dedicate this book to my wife, Mary; to my daughter, Alexandra; to her husband, Bob; and to my two grandchildren, Thomas Edsall Victor and Lydia Edsall Victor. Their love has sustained me.

CONTENTS

ACKNOWLEDGMENTS

I have been lucky over the years to work with some legendary editors—Ben Bradlee at the *Washington Post*, Bob Silvers at the *New York Review of Books*, Michael Kinsley and Frank Foer at *The New Republic*. I am deeply grateful to Nick Lemann, who in 2006 appointed me to the Joseph Pulitzer II and Edith Pulitzer Moore Chair at the Columbia Graduate School of Journalism.

I owe thanks as well to Elaine B. Gin and Reid Dobell for their invaluable assistance in preparing this manuscript.

First among equals, however, is my brilliant, erudite, talented, and tireless *New York Times* editor, Aaron Retica, who oversaw the columns in this volume. My debt to him is incalculable.

THE POINT OF NO RETURN

Introduction

The years following the passage of the Civil Rights Act of 1964 and the Voting Rights Act of 1965 saw the abandonment of the Democratic Party by the white American South. That partisan realignment led slowly but directly to the arrival of Donald Trump, a supremely dangerous man—an enemy of racial justice—at the pinnacle of American power, where despite his narrow loss in 2020 he still lodges.

Many of the conflicts dividing Americans today have their roots in the civil rights movement and broader rights revolutions of the 1960s and 1970s—and in the reactionary response to those revolutions. Progressive insurgencies granted full citizenship to African Americans, empowered previously marginalized populations, and diversified the Democratic Party. They also mandated legal and constitutional protections for women, ethnic and racial minorities, criminal defendants, the poor, homosexuals, the handicapped, and the mentally ill.

The strategy that Trump, ever the opportunist, adopted when he launched his bid for the presidency was the white supremacist position that had been unambiguously articulated nearly six decades earlier by archconservative *National Review* editor William F. Buckley in his August 1957 essay "Why the South Must Prevail": "The issue is whether the White community in the South is entitled to take such measures as are necessary to prevail, politically and culturally, in the areas in which it does not predominate numerically. The sobering answer is Yes." Buckley argued that this is "because, for the time being, it is the advanced race." The question, then, "as far as the White community is concerned, is whether the claims of civilization supersede those of universal suffrage." Buckley's answer: "The *National Review* believes that the South's premises are correct. If the majority wills what is socially atavistic, then to thwart the majority may be, though undemocratic, enlightened."

By the late 1960s it had become uncommon for people to explicitly express racially insensitive views. Buckley soon renounced his own editorial, and Republicans in general swiftly shifted to code words and phrases, such as "law and order," "the silent majority," and "welfare queens."

Still, the rights revolutions had given political conservatives a powerful tool to mobilize voters—especially lower- and middle-income non-college-educated whites who felt the Democratic Party had abandoned them. In 1964 many of these Southern voters supported Barry Goldwater, who carried Louisiana, Mississippi, Georgia, Alabama, and South Carolina. By January 1976, Ronald Reagan picked up the racist mantle and regaled his Asheville, North Carolina, audience on the campaign trail with this oft-disputed anecdote: "In Chicago, they found a woman who holds the record. She used 80 names, 30 addresses, 15 telephone numbers to collect food stamps, Social Security, veterans' benefits for four nonexistent deceased veteran husbands, as well as welfare." "In fact," Reagan added, "her tax-free cash income alone has been running at $150,000 a year."[1]

By the time of Reagan's 1980 victory, the Republican Party had become the home of racial reaction.

Fueling the conservative response to the civil rights revolution of the mid-1960s was the onset of a surge in immigration to the United States following enactment of the Immigration and Nationality Act of 1965.

According to the official House of Representatives description of the law, "Congress erected a legal framework that prioritized highly skilled immigrants and opened the door for people with family already living in the United States. The popular bill passed the House, 318 to 95. The law capped the number of annual visas at 290,000, which included a restriction of 20,000 visas per country per year. But policymakers had vastly underestimated the number of immigrants who would take advantage of the family reunification clause."[2]

In 1970, 4.7 percent of this country's population was foreign born; by 2019, that had shot up to 13.7 percent. In actual numbers, there were 9.6 million immigrants in 1970; in 2019, there were 44.9 million, a 263 percent increase, with most of the new immigrants coming from Latin America, Asia, and Africa rather than the countries of northern, western, eastern, or southern Europe.[3]

For Trump, it has been a simple matter to focus native discontent on the surge in foreign-born low-wage workers competing for jobs and—in the view of his partisans—transforming American culture. He has demonized immigrants in countless ways, including by disparaging countries with majority-Black populations and supporting participants in the August 2017 Unite the Right rally in Charlottesville.[4]

Understanding the role of increasing racial and ethnic diversity in empowering the contemporary conservative movement is crucial to understanding contemporary American politics—but there is more to American politics than that. These developments are explored in my 1992 book, *Chain Reaction: The Impact of Race, Rights, and Taxes on American Politics*, and in my May 1991 *Atlantic* article, "When the Official Subject Is Presidential Politics, Taxes, Welfare, Crime, Rights, or Values . . . the Real Subject Is Race."[5]

The post-1964 Democratic Party quickly became a biracial coalition—and more recently a multiracial, multiethnic coalition. An increasingly influential upscale wing has also emerged as growing numbers of white, college-educated voters abandoned the Republican Party and, supporting more liberal politics, became Democrats.

The knowledge class in the post–World War II era has shaped, and was shaped by, the human rights, civil rights, antiwar, feminist, and gay rights movements, as well as by the broader sexual and information revolutions. Members of this class—academics, artists, editors, human relations managers, lawyers, librarians, architects, journalists, psychologists, social workers, teachers, and therapists, as well as those in engineering, the sciences, finance, and other technology-focused domains—have had their lives upended by the legalization of contraception and abortion, by no-fault divorce, feminism, new behavioral norms, the effective disappearance of censorship, and the abolition of mandatory military service.

In the context of this ongoing state of flux are concerns among the growing numbers of college-educated voters who are preoccupied with reproductive rights, the environment, self-actualization, nonviolence, aesthetic fulfillment, racial and gender equality, and the administration of justice. This upscale cohort within the Democratic coalition is intensely hostile to agendas of imposed moral orthodoxy—often to religious observance itself—and particularly to the agenda of the socially conservative Right. The interests of these voters do not necessarily, or reliably, coincide with the priorities of the less privileged, and they often conflict with the values and religiosity of millions of middle- and working-class voters—many of them low wage, with only high school educations—who often find themselves disempowered, annoyed by, and resentful of contemporary cultural trends.

Across both parties, one's identity as a man or woman; as a heterosexual, homosexual, or transgender person; as white, Black, or Hispanic; as a feminist; as a Southerner; as a Christian; as tolerant or a disciplinarian; as an individualist or collectivist; as a pacifist or militarist; as a cosmopolitan or provincial; as an egalitarian—these and more have become a part of one's being as a liberal or Democrat on one side or as a conservative or Republican on the other.

Contemporary partisan schisms are far deeper and more irresolvable than past conflicts that positioned economic liberals and the Democratic Party against free market advocates and the Republican Party. Particularistic identities across the spectrum have now become consistent and coherent, what political scientists call "sorted"—into two competing and increasingly hostile identities, progressive or conservative, Democrat or Republican. One's sense of self has become deeply entwined with one's partisan allegiance, escalating the stakes for both sides.

The subordination of economic to cultural and racial issues as the prime factors in elections has imposed significant consequences on those least equipped to bear the costs. In effect, the internal realignment of the Democratic Party has left without effective representation the broad class interests of those in the bottom half of the income distribution—those millions, of all races and ethnicities, without college degrees and with household incomes in the 25th to 65th percentile—just when the need for a strong political voice has intensified, especially for those left behind by the exacerbation of global competition that began in the early 1970s. Over subsequent decades, American corporations have cut pay and benefits for many workers in order to compete with low-wage producers in foreign countries, abandoning the post–World War II concord between labor and management and outsourcing production to factories abroad, while automation continues to transform the need for skills that used to be the province of human beings alone.

Artificial intelligence, argued MIT economist Daron Acemoglu in a September 2021 essay, "Harms of AI," is "being used and developed at the moment to empower corporations and governments against workers and citizens."[6] If the deployment of artificial intelligence remains on this trajectory, in Acemoglu's view, it will likely "produce various social, economic and political harms. These include damaging competition, consumer privacy and consumer choice; excessively automating work, fueling inequality, inefficiently pushing down wages, and failing to improve worker productivity; and damaging political discourse, democracy's most fundamental lifeblood."

The fracturing of the Left means there is no counterbalancing political force to reroute the thrust of AI more constructively. Beyond that, a weakened economic Left gives the Right what amounts to an open field to shape tax legislation, deregulation, and spending policies favoring the interests of those at the top. From roughly 1968 to the present, policy-making has been driven by the top quintile of the income distribution and by corporate America.

Not only have economic conservatives benefited from a wounded adversary, but the most powerful economic forces—global competition, outsourcing, an accelerating digital revolution, the ability of corporations to move capital and operations across borders—have worked to their advantage, and to the disadvantage of workers.

Liberal theorists have repeatedly called for a wide range of structural reforms, some of which might have spread more evenly the costs and benefits of the ongoing postindustrial upheaval. These include a stronger safety net; a higher minimum wage; expanded health care, childcare, and prescription drug coverage; more generous provision for the disabled and the aged; sharply increased spending on worker training (especially in community colleges); tax reform; trade policies with worker protections; and a complete revision of the National Labor Relations Act to account for globalization and robotization. No matter what their merits, these options have not had a chance while the balance of economic power has been tilted so far to the right.

The labor-left Economic Policy Institute, in *The State of Working America*, correctly points to the growing tension between wages and productivity:

> A key feature of the labor market since 1973—one that was not present in prior decades—has been the stunning disconnect between the economy's potential for improved pay and the reality of stunted pay growth, especially since 2000. Productivity grew 80.4 percent between 1973 and 2011, when, as noted, median worker pay grew just 10.7 percent. Since 2000, productivity has grown 22.8 percent, but real compensation has stagnated across the board, creating the largest divergence between productivity and pay in the last four decades. Stagnant wage and benefit growth has not been due to poor overall economic performance; nor has it been inevitable. Rather, wage and benefit growth stagnated because the economy, as structured by the rules in place, no longer ensures that workers' pay rises in tandem with productivity.[7]

The question remains: Why do the contemporary rules of the economy not ensure pay raises in proportion to improved productivity?

There are global forces beyond national reach driving some of these trends, but insofar as the rules are set domestically, the issue is political power. And at the moment, those who would benefit from policies encouraging shared rewards from growing productivity are split between two political parties, unable to effectively promote their material interests.

Evidence of the shift in emphasis from economic to cultural politics can be found in the contrast between voting in some of the nation's poorest white counties, on the one hand, and voting in affluent suburbs, on the other. Take 96.2 percent white McDowell County, West Virginia, where the median household income in 2020 was $25,997, compared with the national median of $67,340, and the poverty rate was 31.9 percent, compared with a national rate of 11.9 percent. In 1964, the county voted 83 percent to 17 percent for Lyndon Johnson over Barry Goldwater. In 2020, the county voted 78.9 percent to 20.4 percent for Trump over Joe Biden. Or take the entire state of West Virginia, which ranks forty-sixth in median household income. In 1964, fifty-one of the state's fifty-five counties voted Democratic. In 2020 and 2016, all fifty-five of the state's counties cast majorities for Trump.

In the 2020 election, nine of the ten counties in the United States with the highest median household income voted for Biden, including all of the top five, Loudon and Fairfax Counties in Virginia, Santa Clara and San Mateo Counties in California, and Los Alamos County in New Mexico.

The Democratic Party, once the party of working men and women, is currently dominated by issues of race, gender, and sexuality. In recent elections, these issues have overridden economic divisions. State voting patterns are defined by the degree to which residents have entered into what has been called a "second demographic transition" (SDT). This transition, according to Ron J. Lesthaeghe, of the Vrije Universiteit of Brussels, has two components: "The *first* principal component or factor describes typical SDT features such as the postponement of marriage, greater prevalence of cohabitation and same-sex households, postponement of parenthood, sub-replacement fertility, and a higher incidence of abortion. By contrast, the *second* principal component captures the family variables that generally lead to greater vulnerability of young women and children, such as teenage marriage and fertility, subsequent divorce, single-parent households, and children residing in the households of grandparents."[8]

Lesthaeghe elaborates further: "The SDT starts in the 1960s with a series of multifaceted revolutions. First, there was the contraceptive revolution, with the introduction of hormonal contraception and far more efficient IUDs; second, there was the sexual revolution, with declining ages at first sexual intercourse; and third, there was the gender revolution, questioning the sole breadwinner household model and the gendered division of labor that accompanied it."[9]

———

This demographic transition has transformed the Democratic Party, transferring agenda-setting power to the knowledge class. And this ascendant constituency is most concerned with protecting and advancing recently democratized rights—notably reproductive rights, the right to privacy, and women's rights—as well as a comprehensive commitment to cultural, ethnic, and racial diversity.

These trends were apparent as early as the 1996 presidential campaign when two of Bill Clinton's top advisers, Dick Morris and Mark Penn, reported that one of the most effective ways of predicting voter behavior was from answers to five questions: Do you believe homosexuality is morally wrong? Do you ever personally look at pornography? Would you look down on someone who had an affair while married? Do you believe sex before marriage is morally wrong? Is religion very important in your life?

How did this come about?

Figures 0.1 and 0.2 compare the elections of 1976 (between two centrist candidates, Jimmy Carter and Gerald Ford) and 2016 (pitting Donald Trump against Hillary Clinton). The horizontal axis measures the percentage of each state's vote cast for the Republican candidates (including Evan McMullin in 2016), and the vertical axis measures the degree to which the population of a given state has entered the SDT.[10]

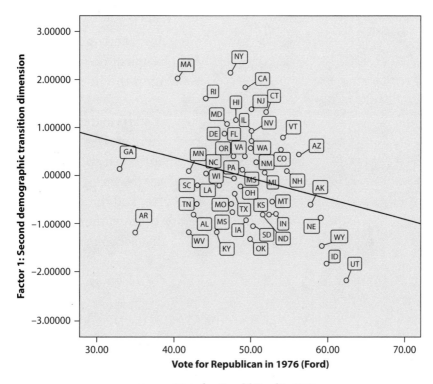

FIGURE 0.1. Vote for Gerald Ford in 1976.

In this country, individual states have moved into the SDT at very different rates. Those rates have, in turn, become increasingly correlated with how each state votes in presidential elections. What figure 0.1 shows is that as recently as 1976, the correlation between a state's ranking in the SDT and its partisanship in presidential elections was modest at best. States are scattered all over the plot. A host of states from Massachusetts to Utah are nonconforming outliers, placed far from the axis.

Figure 0.2 shows how, in a matter of forty years, the SDT becomes powerfully correlated with state voting. Instead of the scattergram seen in figure 0.1, the states in 2016 form a neat line along the axis, with virtually no deviance from the overall pattern.

In many respects, Lesthaeghe's SDT can be linked to the emergence of "postmaterialism" and the value of self-expressive individualism, first described by the late Ronald Inglehart, professor of political science at the University of Michigan, in his 1971 paper

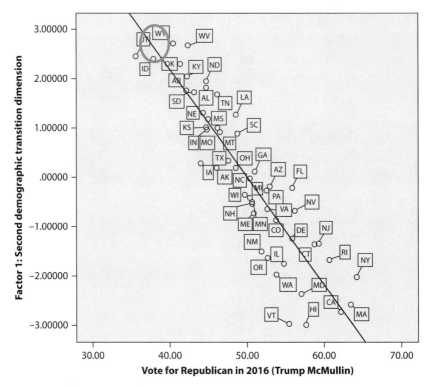

FIGURE 0.2. Relationship between the SDT factor and the vote for Trump and McMullin in 2016, US 50 states ($r = -.909$).
Source: Ron J. Lesthaeghe and Lisa Neidert, "Spatial Aspects of the American 'Culture War': The Two Dimensions of US Family Demography and the Presidential Elections, 1968–2016." From The New York Times. © 2017 The New York Times Company. All rights reserved. Used under license.

"The Silent Revolution in Europe: Intergenerational Change in Post-industrial Societies."[11] In three subsequent books, *The Silent Revolution* (1977), *Culture Shift* (1989), and *Cultural Evolution* (2018), Inglehart described the movement to postmaterialism, which included the following:

- "[A] shift in child-rearing values, from emphasis on hard work toward emphasis on imagination and tolerance as important values to teach a child."
- "An environment of trust and tolerance, in which people place a relatively high value on individual freedom and have

activist political orientations—attributes that, the political culture literature has long argued, are crucial to democracy."
- "[A] shift away from deference to all forms of external authority. Submission to authority has high costs: the individual's personal goals must be subordinated to those of others."
- "Tolerance of diversity and rising demands [among citizens] to have a say in what happens to them."
- "[The young are] more tolerant of homosexuality than their elders, and they are more favorable to gender equality and more permissive in their attitudes toward abortion, divorce, extramarital affairs, and euthanasia."
- "The feminization of society and declining willingness to fight for one's country."
- "[A] systematic erosion of religious practices, values and beliefs."[12]

When Lesthaeghe and Inglehart first explored the SDT and post-materialist values, an underlying assumption was that these were beneficent trends reflecting growing affluence: that as scarcity diminished, new generations would inevitably shift their focus from economic survival to matters of lifestyle—including the environment and the breakdown of racial and gender barriers. In the words of Inglehart and Pippa Norris, a professor at Harvard's Kennedy School, in their 2017 paper, "Trump and the Populist Authoritarian Parties: *The Silent Revolution* in Reverse," "During the postwar era, the people of developed countries experienced peace, unprecedented prosperity and the emergence of advanced welfare states, making survival more secure than ever before. Postwar birth cohorts grew up taking survival for granted, bringing an intergenerational shift toward Postmaterialist values."[13]

In the mid-1970s, however, the postwar era of sustained, shared growth came to a halt, and the liberal order, and the economic security that accompanied it, began to fray. As foreign producers became competitive, globalization started to impose costs on American corporations and workers. Instead of shared prosperity, median salaries stagnated while those at the top grew rapidly, driving new levels of inequality. A high school diploma lost its status as a sufficient credential for a middle-class job. Before long, big-box stores (Walmart, Target, and Costco) and, by the turn of the century, online commerce (Amazon) had begun to devastate small businesses and to decimate small towns.

Faced with growing challenges at home and abroad, American corporations abandoned paternalistic employment policies that carried the implicit promise of employment for life; the corporate view of unions changed from ally to adversary, with worker demands seen as leading to dangerous increases in bottom-line costs.

By the late 1970s, with the emergence of simultaneous inflation and stagnation—"stagflation"—and the threat to American industry from abroad, corporate America, joined by an ascendant conservative political movement, produced a powerful antitax, antiregulatory movement. In order to regain strength in a globally competitive environment, business abandoned past obligations to workers, the state, and the community. Environmental and workplace safety rules, seniority protection, unions, pensions, health insurance, and loyalty to workers were abruptly viewed as unsustainable costs that allowed European and Asian companies to undercut domestic producers.

These shifts in corporate employment policies coincided with a massive surge in immigration to the United States following the liberalizing policies of the Immigration and Nationality Act of 1965. For Trump, it was a simple matter to focus native discontent on the surge in foreign-born low-wage workers competing for jobs and—in the view of his partisans—transforming American culture.

The net effect of the two revolutions that have dominated American society for the past five decades—first, the social and cultural revolution, and second, the technological and economic revolution that transformed employment, corporate business models, and market expectations—imposed what was often viewed as a survival-of-the-fittest ethos on the working and middle classes. Members of the upper-middle class survived and often prospered under the new sink-or-swim regime, but the less well-off, especially those without college degrees, were ill-equipped to cope. It was at this stage that many liberals and the Democratic Party became preoccupied with the expanding cultural revolution, the plight of minorities, and various manifestations of identity politics, effectively forsaking the past commitment to class politics that had animated the Left through the New Deal and Fair Deal eras.

Emerging social-cultural movements—rooted in racial, sexual, religious, and gender, as opposed to class, identities—produced a series of conservative and right-wing countercultural revolutions over the course of the next five decades. These included Nixon's silent majority, the Christian Right, the Reagan Democrats, the angry white men, and the Tea Party and culminated most recently in the Trump Revolution. Each development was opposed, in part or in whole, to a greater or lesser degree, to the temper of the SDT, to postmaterialist values, to racial and ethnic diversity, to secularization, to reproductive rights, and to rapidly transforming gender roles.

The Republican Party capitalized on the dislocation and conflict generated by rapid cultural modernization, exploiting "wedge" issues like abortion and gay marriage which pushed voters' "anger points" and motivated turnout.

In the conservative-wave elections of 1980, 1994, 2010, and 2014, postmaterialism, noted Inglehart and Norris, "became its own gravedigger."[14] As liberalism shifted from advocacy on behalf of the economic have-nots to an agenda of racial integration and personal fulfillment, policies of redistribution, legal protection of unions, and the defense of the material interests of the working class were subordinated. "This, plus large immigration flows from low-income countries with different cultures and religions, stimulated a reaction in which much of the working class moved to the right, in defense of traditional values," wrote Inglehart and Norris. "The classic economic issues did not disappear. But their relative prominence declined to such an extent that non-economic issues became more prominent than economic ones in Western political parties' campaign platforms."[15] For white working-class voters experiencing lost jobs, the hegemony of alien cultures, and the steady deterioration of their communities, the new, value-laden, antimaterialist liberal agenda amounted to an insult.

Ironically, these trends, which benefit Democrats, are arguably also fostering inequality. The late Princeton sociologist Sara McLanahan, in "Diverging Destinies: How Children Are Faring under the Second Demographic Transition," wrote that while children "born to the most-educated women are gaining resources, in terms of parents' time and money, those who were born to the least-educated women are losing resources. The forces behind these changes include feminism, new birth control technologies, changes in labor market opportunities, and welfare-state policies. I contend that Americans should be concerned about the growing disparity in parental resources and that the government can do more to close the gap between rich and poor children."[16]

As sociocultural and identity issues displace an ideology based on economic class, not only do the incentives for liberalism and the Democratic Party to address class-based problems of mobility and inequality diminish, but the center-left becomes vulnerable to economic special-interest pressures. Lobbies and trade associations focused on the legislative process as a means to commercial goals— tax breaks, regulatory change, subsidies, and so forth—can more readily apply pressure through campaign contributions and grass-roots mobilization to members of the House and Senate who lack a broad ideological commitment to those in the bottom three quintiles of the income distribution. In a parallel development, Democratic incumbents have become increasingly dependent on the votes of the affluent to win elections, making these politicians reluctant to threaten the interests of their upscale constituents.

There are few better examples of Democratic susceptibility to special-interest pressure than the continued preservation of the carried interest tax break through four years of Democratic control of Congress—from 2006 to 2010 and again after the 2020 election. The carried interest break provides an estimated $18 billion annually to wealthy hedge fund operators and beneficiaries of investment funds.[17]

For a Democrat seeking election, the easiest path to capitalize on Republican social and moral extremism had been to stress threats to reproductive rights, to the teaching of evolution, to gay marriage, and to the protection of transgender people. In many respects, this was until recently a successful strategy: in seven of the last eight presidential elections, the Democratic candidate has won the popular vote.[18]

As the January 2021 insurrection in the US Capitol and the relentless, ongoing Republican efforts to have Trump illegitimately declared the winner of the 2020 election demonstrate, however, Democrats now face Republican adversaries who are determined not only to pare back the liberal state but to sabotage democracy itself, to overturn the will of the voters, to overthrow majority control, and to attack the legitimacy of election outcomes, undermining the very essence of American democracy.

At the same time, the Democratic Party's shift to postmaterialist values has left millions of white working-class voters with no perceived choice except the Republican Party.

For Republicans, the prospect of losing has become what political scientists describe as a "normative threat"[19]—a danger to the moral order underpinning society. Many liberals and Democrats saw and see Trump and the Republican Party as a fully comparable existential threat. Victory for the opposition, in each case, raises the specter of moral collapse.

———

There has been a precipitous and accelerating decline of the United States on measures of freedom and democracy. From 2010 to 2020 Freedom House, which ranks countries based on an analysis of the electoral process, political pluralism and participation, the functioning of the government, freedom of expression and of belief, associational and organizational rights, the rule of law, personal autonomy and individual rights,[20] demoted the United States from seventh worldwide to eighteenth, just below Croatia, Argentina, and

Romania. "The erosion of US democracy is remarkable, especially for a country that has long aspired to serve as a beacon of freedom for the world," the authors of the Freedom House study reported. "The downward trend accelerated considerably over the last four years, as the Trump administration trampled institutional and normative checks on its authority, cast aside safeguards against corruption, and imposed harsh and discriminatory policies governing immigration and asylum."[21]

In a ranking by the *Economist* magazine,[22] the United States fell from sixteenth in 2006 to twenty-sixth in 2020, "based on five categories: *electoral process and pluralism, functioning of government, political participation, political culture,* and *civil liberties.*" The United States was described as a "flawed democracy"—as opposed to a full democracy. Twenty-two countries achieved "full democracy" status, led by Norway, New Zealand, and Finland. Among the fifty-three flawed democracies, the United States ranked just below France, Israel, Spain, and Chile, and just above Estonia and Portugal.

These downward trends culminated in Trump's election in 2016 and, despite his defeat in 2020, in his continuing power over a majority of Republican voters.

———

The collection that follows of *New York Times* opinion columns from 2015 onward provides a real-time account of how and why Trump managed to prevail and an enlarged understanding of the forces that enabled his rise. The Trump era is not over yet—forewarned is forearmed.[23]

2015–2016

On June 16, 2015, when he announced his presidential bid, no one
except perhaps Donald Trump himself anticipated not only that he
would win the nomination and the presidency but that he would lead
a revolution within the Republican Party, crushing the dominant
establishment wing while empowering the legions of white working-
class voters whose ballots had produced victories but whose voices
had remained peripheral. Singlehandedly, Trump demonstrated the
weakness of the network of donors, party officials, lobbyists, and
politicians who for decades had picked the party's nominees. In one
of the ironies of politics, Trump democratized the Republican Party
just as he turned it into an authoritarian institution.

The columns that follow document the start of an abrupt and
unexpected outcome in American politics, the emergence of an anti-
Democratic president who converted the Republican Party into a
reflection of his own image.

1

The Not-So-Silent White Majority

Between Richard Nixon's election by the silent majority in 1968 and Donald Trump's stunning victory in 2016, there have been six conservative waves that swept Republicans into office. Disaffected white voters without college degrees have been the driving force in all of them.

This is surprising not only because these voters were once the backbone of the Democratic coalition but because they have steadily declined as a share of the electorate. The percentage of white voters without college degrees fell from 83 percent in 1960 to 36 percent in 2012. It was 34 percent this year.

So why did they matter as much as they did in 2016? For one thing, Trump's 39-point lead among less well-educated whites surged past Mitt Romney's 25-point margin. This was enough to make up for the fact that Trump's margin of victory among whites with college degrees, at 4 points (49 percent to 45 percent), was well behind Romney's. (Romney carried college-educated whites by 14 points, 56 percent to 42 percent.)

Despite their declining share of the electorate, non-college-educated white voters continue to exercise an outsize influence: as

This article first appeared in *The New York Times* on November 16, 2016. Copyright © 2016 by Thomas Edsall and The New York Times Company. All rights reserved.

the silent majority of 1968 and 1972, the Reagan Democrats of 1980, the angry white men of 1994, the Tea Party insurgents of 2010, and now the triumphant Trump Republicans of 2016.

Let's take a look at the history of this trend.

In 1968, these white voters—often low or moderate income, disproportionately male, and clustered in exurban and rural areas, then as now—were crucial to the birth of the modern conservative coalition.

That year, famously, Southern whites angered by enactment of the 1964 Civil Rights Act and the 1965 Voting Rights Act abandoned the Democratic Party in droves, and they were soon joined by many Northern whites opposed to court-ordered busing.

The Democratic Party's commitment to civil rights prompted millions of white voters to cast ballots either for Richard Nixon, running as the Republican nominee, or for George Wallace, the segregationist Dixiecrat and former governor of Alabama, running as the nominee of the American Independent Party.

Together, Nixon and Wallace won 56.9 percent of all votes in 1968 and more than six out of every ten white votes, laying the groundwork for the conversion of the segregationist wing of the Democratic Party into a key component of the modern Republican Party. Democrats have made inroads into this coalition a few times, either by running more centrist Southerners like Jimmy Carter or Bill Clinton or through the campaign magic of Barack Obama, who promised to transcend the red-blue divide. But this white Republican coalition has proved remarkably enduring.

In the two elections before 1968, John F. Kennedy and Lyndon B. Johnson, both Democrats, averaged 55 percent of the white working-class vote. According to Ruy Teixeira, then a senior fellow at the pro-Democratic Center for American Progress, Hubert Humphrey and George McGovern, both Democrats, averaged 35 percent of that vote, in 1968 and 1972. Since that time, many Republican candidates have tapped into anti-Black bias without running as overt segregationists.

"The Republicans suddenly became the party of the white working class," Teixeira wrote on his blog.

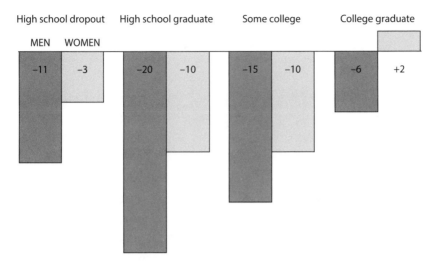

FIGURE 1.1. WHITE FLIGHT. Change, in percentage points, in Democratic support in congressional races by white voters from 1992 to 1994 by education levels.
Source: Ruy Teixeira and Joel Rogers, "America's Forgotten Majority." From The New York Times. © 2016 The New York Times Company. All rights reserved. Used under license.

The election of Ronald Reagan in 1980 further strengthened the commitment of the white working class to Republican presidential candidates, especially in the North.

It was not, however, until 1994, with the so-called Gingrich revolution, that the Republican Party was able to finally rupture the continuing commitment of lower- and moderate-income whites to Democratic congressional candidates. Figures 1.1 and 1.2, derived from the 2000 book *America's Forgotten Majority* by Teixeira and Joel Rogers, show how the bottom fell out in 1994 for white working-class Democratic congressional support.

Gingrich claimed responsibility for his party's 1994 victories. Bill Clinton's initial abandonment of the themes that he campaigned on in 1992 was, in fact, more important.

In his first presidential run, Clinton promised welfare reform, a middle-class tax cut, and the commitment of his presidency to the "ideal that if you work hard and play by the rules you'll be rewarded." Clinton's first two years in office, however, were dominated by the

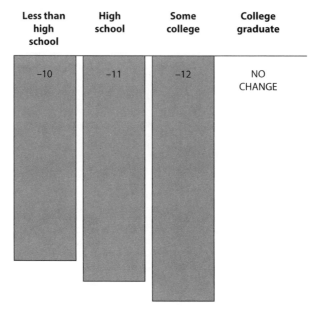

FIGURE 1.2. LOST GROUND. Change, in percentage points, in Democratic support in congressional races from 1992 to 1994 by voters' education levels.
Source: Ruy Teixeira and Joel Rogers, "America's Forgotten Majority." From The New York Times. © 2016 The New York Times Company. All rights reserved. Used under license.

issues of gays in the military, health care reform, and his attempt to make good on his vow to pick a cabinet that "looks like America."

The changed agenda proved disastrous for Democratic members of the House and Senate.

Stanley Greenberg, Clinton's 1992 campaign pollster, wrote in the 1999 book *The New Majority: Toward a Popular Progressive Politics* that "the 1994 congressional debacle should be a reminder of what happens when Democrats lose touch with the lives of working people. Bill Clinton's election was accompanied by great hopes in the country, but over the next two years those hopes turned to disappointment. On the eve of the off-year elections Clinton seemed like a culturally liberal president who could not deliver."

Greenberg continued, "The 1994 election was a disaster produced by a downscale, working-class revolt against the Democrats. Support for congressional Democrats among high school graduates dropped 12 points to only 46 percent. Among white male high school graduates, support for the Democrats fell off a cliff, careening 20 points downward from 57 percent to 37 percent."

The march of working- and middle-class whites toward the Republican Party took another giant step forward in the Tea Party election of 2010, when they voted against Democratic congressional candidates by 30 points (65 percent to 35 percent), providing crucial ballast for the Republicans as they gained sixty-three seats in the House.

For many analysts and Democratic operatives, Obama's two victories in 2008 and 2012 marked the final collapse of the conservative coalition. Even the Republican Party, notably in the so-called Autopsy Report produced in 2013 by Reince Priebus—soon to be Trump's chief of staff—acknowledged that a white-dominated conservative alliance was doomed to defeat unless the party opened its doors in general and to Hispanics in particular.

Which brings us to 2016.

On one level, demographic change was moving in Hillary Clinton's direction. The overall white share of the electorate, which was 91 percent in 1960, continued to decline, falling to 72 percent in 2012 and 70 percent in 2016.

How, then, is it possible that this supposedly fading constituency played such a decisive role in 2016?

Two reasons.

First, while Trump barely improved on Romney's margin among whites generally, the whites who did vote for Trump were significantly different from those who voted for Romney. Trump won non-college-educated whites by 14 points more than Romney, a modern-day record. Just as important, the working-class voters Trump carried by such huge margins were heavily concentrated in the Rust Belt states of Wisconsin, Ohio, Michigan, Iowa, and Pennsylvania—all states carried by Obama in 2012 and lost by Clinton in 2016. Together, these states cast seventy Electoral College votes.

Trump's voters were situated in a way that allowed them to exercise far more influence on the outcome in the Electoral College than their overall numbers would suggest, enabling Trump to sweep across the Rust Belt to victory.

This apostasy among white voters has certainly not gone unnoticed, and party strategists have long debated what, if anything, could be done to bring these voters back into the Democratic fold, particularly since the landslide defeat of 1984.

In 1985, Democrats conducted two major studies of white working-class discontent, one by Greenberg, which looked at white workers and retirees who were members of the United Automobile Workers in Macomb County, Michigan, the other of thirty-three focus groups nationwide conducted by CRG, a marketing and polling firm.

Greenberg found that for these voters, "Blacks constitute the explanation of their vulnerability and for almost everything that has gone wrong in their lives." This "special status of blacks is perceived by almost all of these individuals as a serious obstacle to their personal advancement. Indeed, discrimination against whites has become a well-assimilated and ready explanation for their status, vulnerability and failures."

The CRG study was equally brutal. These voters "have a whole set of middle-class economic problems today, and their party is not helping them. Instead it is helping blacks, Hispanics and the poor. They feel betrayed."

CRG found that in the view of the white working class, the "Democrats are the giveaway party and 'giveaway' means too much middle class money going to blacks and the poor."

The struggle to revive Democratic support among low- and moderate-income white voters has more recently become a regular subject on the Democratic Strategist, a website run by the Democratic activist Ed Kilgore, who was once the vice president for policy at the Democratic Leadership Council. Kilgore also publishes a newsletter, the *White Working Class Roundtable*. In the first issue of the newsletter, Kilgore wrote, "It has become increasingly clear that progressives and Democrats have no alternative except to challenge the hold that conservative [*sic*] and the GOP have established over white working Americans."

In a direct counter to Kilgore, Lee Drutman, a senior scholar at the New America Foundation, argued in a November 11 essay in *Foreign Policy* that the Democrats need to give up on appeals to working-class whites. The headline of his article reads, "The GOP Has Become the Party of Populism. Now the Democrats Have to Build a New Party of Multicultural Cosmopolitanism."

Drutman argues that "if Democrats define themselves as the party that is opposed to Republicans (as they must), they will soon find themselves as the party of fiscal responsibility (as opposed to the Republicans, who will again run huge deficits), as the party of international responsibility (as opposed to the more isolationist and nationalist Republicans), and as the party of global business (as opposed to the protectionist Republicans). They will continue to be the party of environmentalism (the stakes of this will get even greater soon) and the party of diversity and tolerance."

At the policy level, there are substantial objections to the full-scale emergence of a Democratic Party along these lines. It would mean that neither party would represent the economic interests of the bottom half of the income distribution—regardless of race or ethnicity—on crucial issues of tax and spending policies.

There is, however, growing evidence that the wheels of electoral politics have made the developments Drutman describes increasingly likely.

A comparison of 2004 exit polls and 2016 exit polls shows the changing relevance of income to voting.

In 2004, those with incomes under $30,000 voted Democratic by 20 points; in 2016, these voters voted Democratic by 12 points, a 40 percent decline.

At the upper end, voters with household incomes from $100,000 to $200,000 voted Republican in 2004 by 15 points. In 2016, they voted Republican by 1 point. Voters making more than $200,000 in 2004 voted Republican by 28 points; in 2016, they also voted Republican by 1 point.

As Drutman points out, "With a President Trump, there is now a change agent to accelerate these forces."

In another postelection analysis, published on November 15, Teixeira argues that the conservative victory on Election Day will prove short-lived: "In the end, the race will be won by change—as it always is."

By 2032, Teixeira writes, "we are far more likely to view the 2016 election as the last stand of America's white working class, dreaming of a past that no longer exists."

Maybe.

In 2002, Teixeira and John Judis published the classic book *The Emerging Democratic Majority*, only to see the reelection of George W. Bush two years later and the election of Donald Trump fourteen years later.

Judis, whose most recent book is *The Populist Explosion*, is less confident than Teixeira. He argues that in this year's election, either John Kasich or Marco Rubio "could have beaten Clinton, but the coalition would have looked different," adding in an email, "What I would say, if someone put a gun to my head, is that there is still a stalemate between the two parties in spite of Trump's and the Republicans' success. Trump could fail, the Dems could come back, and then the G.O.P. or Trump could thread the needle and win two terms. Not clear what will happen. But politically—leave aside the Census Bureau—the Dems are in disarray."

White tribalism or ethnocentrism—whatever you want to call it—is undeniably a powerful force. But so are the identities, loyalties, and resentments of those who have their own competing racial and ethnic commitments. The American experiment, which gives all these interests participatory roles in a dynamic democracy, has long been under strain. Over the next four years, it will now be openly tested. The outcome may well be wrenching.

2

The Great Trump Reshuffle

A general election that pits Hillary Clinton against Donald Trump will produce a decisively more affluent and better-educated Democratic presidential electorate and a decidedly less affluent and less educated Republican one than in any previous election going back as far as 1976.

It is no secret that Trump is the driving force behind this year's reconfigured coalition on the right. He has successfully appealed to middle- and lower-income white voters motivated by opposition to liberalized attitudes and social norms on matters of race, immigration, and women's rights.

Public Opinion Strategies, a Republican polling firm, analyzed a survey conducted in April by NBC and the *Wall Street Journal*. Respondents were asked to choose between Clinton and Trump, and the results demonstrate that there will be substantial shifts in the income and education levels of Democratic and Republican voters, at least as far as this presidential election is concerned.

One of the largest shifts is among college-educated voters, who are expected to defect from the Republican Party by the millions if Trump is the nominee. In 2012, President Barack Obama lost

This article first appeared in *The New York Times* on May 4, 2016. Copyright © 2016 by Thomas Edsall and The New York Times Company. All rights reserved.

college-educated voters by four points; this year, according to Public Opinion Strategies' analysis, Clinton will win them by 29 points.

In addition, the NBC/*WSJ* poll reveals that Clinton should make substantial gains among voters from households earning in excess of $100,000. While Obama lost these affluent voters in 2012 by 10 points, the NBC/*WSJ* survey shows Clinton carrying them by 12 points.

There are two groups among whom Trump will gain and Clinton will lose: voters making less than $30,000 and voters with only high school degrees. Both less affluent groups are expected to increase their level of support for the Republican nominee over their 2012 margins, by 13 and by 17 points, respectively.

For the Democratic presidential coalition in 2016, the net effect of this shift will be to further reverse the working-class tilt of the party, which has been trending upscale since 1992. The Republican coalition of 2016, in fact, will look increasingly like the Democratic Party of the 1930s.

A Trump-versus-Clinton contest will deepen the partisan divisions that have set those who support the social and cultural revolutions of the past five decades on race, immigration, women's rights, gender equality, and gay rights—as well as the broader right to sexual privacy—against those who remain in opposition.

First, let's take race.

Michael Tesler, a political scientist at the University of California, Irvine, examined answers to "racial resentment" questions in a Presidential Election Panel Survey conducted by the RAND Corporation in December and January to see how the responses correlated with presidential voting intentions.

The racial resentment scale is based on favorable or unfavorable responses to survey prompts like these: "Irish, Italian, Jewish and many other minorities overcame prejudice and worked their way up. Blacks should do the same without any special favors"; "Generations of slavery and discrimination have created conditions that make it difficult for blacks to work their way out of the lower class"; "Over the past few years, blacks have gotten less than they deserve"; and "It's really a matter of some people not trying hard enough; if blacks would only try harder they could be just as well off as whites."

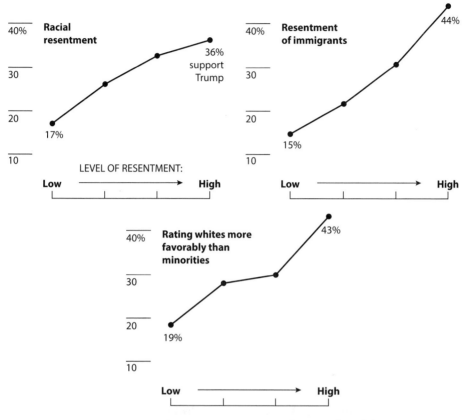

FIGURE 2.1. RESENTING OTHERS, LIKING TRUMP. A survey found that support for Donald J. Trump among Republican primary voters rose in tandem with disapproval of other groups.
Source: Analysis of RAND Corp. survey data by Michael Tesler, University of California–Irvine, and John Sides, George Washington University. From The New York Times. © 2016 The New York Times Company. All rights reserved. Used under license.

In addition, the RAND survey sought to measure "ethnocentrism" by asking respondents to rank their own racial or ethnic group on a seven-point scale for "lazy or hardworking," "intelligent or unintelligent," and "trustworthy or untrustworthy." The respondents were then asked to rate other groups by the same measures. Those ranking their own race or ethnic group higher than others ranked high on ethnocentrism.

Tesler's findings are illustrated in figure 2.1. There was a dose effect: the higher you scored on racial resentment, the more likely you were to support Trump; the more you resented immigrants or professed your white ethnocentrism, the likelier you were to plan to vote for Trump.

On March 3, Tesler and John Sides, a political scientist at George Washington University, published an article in the *Washington Post*: "How Political Science Helps Explain the Rise of Trump: The Role of White Identity and Grievances." Using data collected by the American National Election Studies, Tesler and Sides ranked white respondents by their level of "white racial identity"—determined by asking white respondents questions like, "How important is being white to your identity?"; "How important is it that whites work together to change laws that are unfair to whites?"; and "How likely is it that many whites are unable to find a job because employers are hiring minorities instead?"

Trump's level of support in the survey rose in direct proportion to respondents' level of agreement with each of these statements.

Trump has also recruited strong support from those who have not come to terms with the women's rights, reproductive rights, and gay rights movements.

Ron Lesthaeghe and Lisa Neidert of the University of Michigan's Population Studies Center have done pioneering work that sheds more light on Trump's success so far. They have ranked all 3,140 counties in the United States by their level of entry into what researchers call the "second demographic transition" (SDT).

"The Second Demographic Transition: A Concise Overview of Its Development," by Lesthaeghe, summarizes this concept: "The SDT starts in the 1960s with a series of multifaceted revolutions. First, there was the contraceptive revolution, with the introduction of hormonal contraception and far more efficient IUDs; second, there was the sexual revolution, with declining ages at first sexual intercourse; and third, there was the gender revolution, questioning the sole breadwinner household model and the gendered division of labor that accompanied it."

These revolutions have reordered much of society. Lesthaeghe continues, "These three 'revolutions' fit within the framework of an overall rejection of authority, the assertion of individual freedom of

TABLE 2.1. Trump Nation at Home

Researchers have ranked every American county by its position between these two sets of social norms. In the first stage, traditional rules from religious and other authorities dominate; after the "second demographic transition" people lean liberal, secular, and for individual choice. Trump does best among the former.

First stage	Second demographic transition (SDT)
MARRIAGE	
• Rise in proportions marrying, declining ages at first marriage.	• Fall in proportions married, rising ages at first marriage.
FERTILITY	
• Declining marital fertility via reductions at older ages, lowering mean ages at first childbearing.	• Fertility postponement, increasing mean ages at parenthood.
• Declining illegitimate fertility.	• Rising nonmarital fertility, parenthood outside marriage.
SOCIETAL BACKGROUND	
• Preoccupation with basic material needs: income, work conditions, housing, children and adult health, schooling, social security; solidarity a prime value.	• Rise of higher order needs: individual autonomy, expressive work/socialization values, self-actualization, grassroots democracy; tolerance a prime value.
• Strong normative regulation by churches and state, first secularization wave.	• Retreat of the state, second secularization wave, sexual revolution, refusal of authority.
• Segregated sex roles, family-centered policies, "embourgeoisement" of the family with the breadwinner model at its core.	• Rising symmetry in sex roles, rising female education levels, greater female economic autonomy.

Source: Ron Lesthaeghe and Lisa Neidert of the University of Michigan Population Studies Center

By The New York Times

choice (autonomy), and an overhaul of the normative structure. The overall outcome of these shifts with respect to fertility was the postponement of childbearing: mean ages at first parenthood rise again, opportunities for childbearing are lost due to higher divorce rates, the share of childless ever-partnered women increases, and higher parity births (four or more) become rare."

Table 2.1 summarizes the key cultural and social transformations put into effect by this demographic transition.

Measured by these criteria, the top-ranked counties were cosmopolitan centers, with a larger percentage of affluent, highly educated residents: New York City; the District of Columbia; Pitkin County, Colorado (where Aspen is); San Francisco; and Marin County, California. The counties at the bottom tended to be small, white, rural, poor, and less educated, and they were located in the South and the Mountain West: Millard County, Utah (population 12,662); Loup County, Nebraska (pop. 576); Perry County, Mississippi (pop. 12,131); and Roberts County, Texas (pop. 831).

To see where Trump has been getting his strongest support in terms of the Lesthaeghe-Neidert measures, it is useful to look at county-level results from the Republican presidential primaries in four states: Ohio, Michigan, Florida, and Tennessee. With rare exceptions, the same pattern emerged in all four states: the lower the SDT ranking, the higher Trump's votes compared with his statewide average; the higher the SDT level, the lower Trump's votes. In many cases, the spread was 10 percentage points or more.

Take Manhattan. In these rankings, it is the highest of the 3,140 counties in the United States. Trump won the entire state of New York with 60.4 percent of the primary vote. In Manhattan, however, Trump lost to John Kasich, the more moderate candidate, 41.8 percent to 45.2 percent.

Or take two Virginia counties, Arlington and Alexandria, which rank high on the SDT list at seventh and eighth. Trump carried all of Virginia with about 35 percent of the vote (Marco Rubio came in second, with about 32 percent), but in Alexandria and Arlington, Trump won only 18.8 percent and 16.8 percent, respectively.

Compare that with two Texas counties, Tyler and San Augustine, which rank near the bottom in the SDT ratings. Trump lost Texas to his former opponent, Ted Cruz, 43.8 percent to 26.7 percent. In San Augustine, Trump outperformed his statewide results, winning 39.6 percent of the county's votes, a 12.9 point improvement. In Tyler, Trump received 35.9 percent, 9.2 points better than his statewide average.

Similarly, in Ohio, Trump exceeded his statewide average in fifteen out of eighteen counties ranked near the bottom on the Lesthaeghe-Neidert scale, while falling well below his statewide percentage in four metropolitan counties—Franklin, Delaware, Cuyahoga, and Hamilton—near the top of the rankings.

The nomination of Trump will sharpen and deepen the Republican Party's core problems. Trump gains the party ground among declining segments of the population—less well-educated, less well-off whites—and loses ground with the growing constituencies: single women, well-educated men and women, minorities, the affluent, and professionals.

This is especially true in the case of Trump's dependence on support from communities at the bottom of the Lesthaeghe-Neidert SDT scale. Not only are more and more Americans adopting the practices and values described by Lesthaeghe and Neidert—self-expressiveness, gender equality, cohabitation, same-sex couples, postponed marriage and childbearing—but so too is much of the developed world.

This transition has effectively become the norm in much of Europe, and as Lesthaeghe points out, it is gaining ground in regions as diverse as East Asia and Latin America.

In this country, the transition has led to partisan schism. For decades now, the Republican Party has been conducting a racial and cultural counterrevolution. It proved a successful strategy from 1966 to 1992. Since then, as the percentage of Americans on the liberal side of the culture wars has grown steadily, the counterrevolutionary approach has become more and more divisive.

In this respect, Trump is not, as many charge, violating core Republican tenets. Instead, he represents the culmination of the rear-guard action that has characterized the party for decades. There is a chance that Trump will bring new blood into a revitalized Republican coalition. It's also possible that he will accelerate the Republican Party's downward spiral into irrelevance.

3

Why Trump Now?

The economic forces driving this year's nomination contests have been at work for decades. Why did the dam break now?

The share of the gross national product going to labor as opposed to capital fell from 68.8 percent in 1970 to 60.7 percent by 2013, according to Loukas Karabarbounis, an economics professor at the University of Chicago's Booth School of Business.

Even more devastating, the number of manufacturing jobs dropped by 36 percent, from 19.3 million in 1979 to 12.3 million in 2015, while the population increased by 43 percent, from 225 million to 321 million.

The postwar boom, when measured by the purchasing power of the average paycheck, continued into the early 1970s and then abruptly stopped (figure 3.1).

In other words, the economic basis for voter anger has been building over forty years. Starting in 2000, two related developments added to worsening conditions for the middle and working classes.

First, that year marked the end of net upward mobility. Before 2000, the size of both the lower and middle classes had shrunk,

This article first appeared in *The New York Times* on March 1, 2016. Copyright © 2016 by Thomas Edsall and The New York Times Company. All rights reserved.

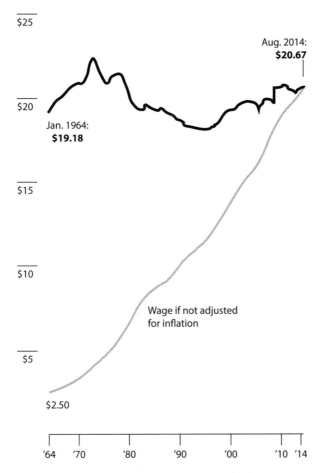

FIGURE 3.1. STILL STAGNANT AFTER ALL THESE YEARS.
Adjusted for inflation, the average hourly wage increased
$1.49 from 1964 to 2014. Seasonally adjusted data for
production and non-supervisory employees on private,
non-farm payrolls.
Sources: Bureau of Labor Statistics; Pew Research Center.
From The New York Times. © 2016 The New York Times
Company. All rights reserved. Used under license.

while the percentage of households with inflation-adjusted incomes
of $100,000 or more grew. Americans were moving up the ladder.

After 2000, the middle class continued to shrink, but so did the
percentage of households making $100,000 or more. The only group
to grow larger after 2000 was households with incomes of $35,000

or less. Americans were moving down the ladder. (This downward shift can be seen in figure 3.2.)

The second adverse trend is that trade with China, which shot up after China's entry into the World Trade Organization in December 2001, imposed far larger costs on American workers than most economists anticipated, according to recent studies. And the costs of trade with China have fallen most harshly on workers on the lower rungs of the income ladder.

In their January 2016 paper "The China Shock," David Autor, David Dorn, and Gordon Hanson, economists at MIT, the University of Zurich, and the University of California–San Diego, respectively, found that

> if one had to project the impact of China's momentous economic reform for the U.S. labor market with nothing to go on other than a standard undergraduate economics textbook, one would predict large movements of workers between U.S. tradable industries (say, from apparel and furniture to pharmaceuticals and jet aircraft), limited reallocation of jobs from tradables to non-tradables, and no net impacts on U.S. aggregate employment. The reality of adjustment to the China shock has been far different. Employment has certainly fallen in U.S. industries most exposed to import competition. But so too has overall employment in local labor markets in which these industries were concentrated. Offsetting employment gains either in export-oriented tradables or in non-tradables have, for the most part, failed to materialize.

High-wage workers find it relatively easy to adjust and "do not experience an earnings loss," argue Autor and his colleagues. Low-wage workers, in contrast, "suffer large differential earnings loss, as they obtain lower earnings per year both while working at the initial firm and after relocating to new employers."

This is why Donald Trump's charge that China has gotten the better of the United States has gained traction.

When I asked Hanson what factors provoked the populist insurgencies in both parties in this particular election cycle, he emailed back, "The recipe for populism seems pretty clear: take a surge in

Percentage of households in the United States by income range, 1967–2013:

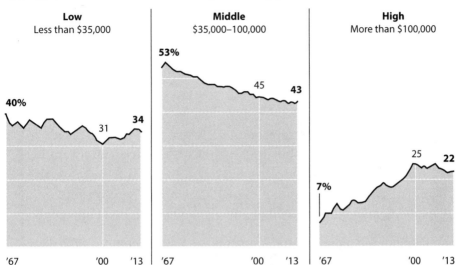

FIGURE 3.2. THE SHRINKING MIDDLE CLASS. Over about the past half-century, the middle class has shrunk consistently. Before 2000, this was primarily because more Americans moved up the income ladder. But since 2000, more have fallen down.
Sources: U.S. Census Bureau; Minnesota Population Center/Ipums. From The New York Times. © 2016 The New York Times Company. All rights reserved. Used under license.

manufacturing imports from China and continued automation in the US workplace and add a tepid macroeconomy. The result is a combustible stew sure to sour the stomach of party leaders nationwide."

The stew, to continue Hanson's metaphor, began to boil over with the cataclysmic financial collapse in September 2008, which many people left and right felt was caused by reckless financial engineering on Wall Street. The collapse and the destruction it left in its wake were, without question, the most important economic and political events in recent years.

"It was the financial crisis, what it revealed about government–Wall Street links, and the fumbling of the response to it that put the nail in the coffin of trust in government," Daron Acemoglu, an economist at MIT, wrote in reply to my questions. "Once trust in government was destroyed, those that had not benefited from the previous boom years became particularly easy pickings for populist rhetoric."

On October 3, 2008, Congress enacted, and President George W. Bush signed, the Troubled Asset Relief Program. TARP funds bailed out major investment banks and were also used, as the Federal Reserve Bank of St. Louis put it, "to make loans and direct equity investments to select auto industry participants, backstop credit markets, provide a lifeline to the American International Group (AIG) and provide ongoing support for government housing initiatives"—but in addition, TARP insulated the very institutions and executives that caused the collapse and the disastrous recession that followed.

"I don't think you can overestimate or overemphasize the impact of the bailout," Norm Ornstein, a scholar at the American Enterprise Institute, a center-right Washington think tank, told me in an email: "The widespread sense that all the elites in Washington and New York conspired to bail out the miscreants who caused the disaster and then gave them bonuses, while the rest of us lost our houses or saw their value, the biggest and often only asset of Americans, plummet, lost our jobs or saw them frozen and stagnant, and then saw gaping inequality grow even more, is just palpable."

On January 10, 2010, the Supreme Court granted those in upper-income brackets additional privileges in its *Citizens United* decision (buttressed by subsequent lower-court rulings) that allowed wealthy individuals, corporations, and unions to make unlimited political contributions. By opening the door to the creation of super PACs (political action committees) and giving Wall Street and other major financial sectors new ways to buy political outcomes, the courts gave the impression, to say the least, that they favored establishment interests over those of the less well off.

A Bloomberg poll last September found that 78 percent of voters would like to see *Citizens United* overturned, and this view held across a range of partisan loyalties: Republicans at 80 percent; Democrats at 83 percent; and independents at 71 percent.

In March 2010, two months after *Citizens United* was decided, President Barack Obama signed the Affordable Care Act, a.k.a. Obamacare, a program many in the white middle and working classes perceived as reducing their own medical care in order to provide health coverage to the disproportionately minority poor.

By the midterm elections of 2010, voter dissatisfaction among whites found expression in the Tea Party movement, which produced the sweeping defeat of Democrats in competitive congressional districts as well as of moderate and center-right Republicans in primary contests.

Voter anger was directed at two targets—the "undeserving rich" and the "undeserving poor."

The 2010 election pattern was repeated in the 2014 midterms.

To many of those who cast their ballots in anger in 2010 and 2014, however, it appeared that their votes had not changed anything. Obamacare stayed in place and Wall Street and corporate America grew richer while the average worker was stuck going nowhere.

Already disillusioned with the Democratic Party, these white voters became convinced that the mainstream of the Republican Party had failed them, not only on economic issues but on cultural matters as well.

A September 2015 Ipsos survey asked voters if they agreed or disagreed with the statement, "More and more, I don't identify with what America has become." Of surveyed Republicans, 72 percent concurred, compared with 58 percent of independents and 45 percent of Democrats. Two-thirds of Republicans, 62 percent, agreed with the statement, "These days I feel like a stranger in my own country," compared with 53 percent of independents and 37 percent of Democrats. Here is one place where Trump's scathing dismissal of political correctness found fertile ground.

Jared Bernstein, a senior fellow at the Center for Budget and Policy Priorities, described in blunt terms the consequences of disillusionment with old-guard Republicans: "The intersection of inequality driven by real wage/income stagnation and the fact that the folks perceived to have blown the damn economy up not only recovered first, but got government assistance in the form of bailouts to do so. If you're in the anxious middle and that doesn't deeply piss you off, you're an unusually forgiving person."

In these circumstances, Bernstein wrote, the logic supporting the traditional Republican Party fell apart: "The core theme of Republican establishment lore has been to demonize not unregulated finance or trade or inequality, but 'the other'—e.g., the immigrant or minority taking your job and claiming unneeded government support. And yet, none of their trickle down, deregulatory agenda helped ameliorate the problem at all. So they lost control."

Just as animosity to Republican power brokers in Washington intensified, the Republican Party began to splinter.

I asked Nathan Persily, a Stanford law professor, "Are party establishments now fictions, no longer able to exercise control?" Persily responded, "This election has demonstrated that there is no Republican Party organization, per se. The Republican Party exists as an array of allied groups, incumbent office holders, media organizations, and funding vehicles (e.g., SuperPACs, 501(c)(4)s, and the like). When people ask why the 'establishment' or 'the party' has not done anything to stop Trump, it is not exactly clear who they mean."

On Super Tuesday, Trump won a majority of the dozen states that were up for grabs. He collected far more delegates than Ted Cruz or Marco Rubio.

The tragedy of the 2016 campaign is that Trump has mobilized a constituency with legitimate grievances on a fool's errand.

If he is shoved out of the field somehow, his supporters will remain bitter and enraged, convinced that a self-serving and malign elite defeated their leader.

If he prevails, a constituency that could force politicians to confront the problems of the working and middle class will waste its energies on a candidate incompetent to improve the lives of the credulous men and women lining up to support him.

4

How the Other Fifth Lives

For years now, people have been talking about the insulated world of the top 1 percent of Americans, but the top 20 percent of the income distribution is also steadily separating itself—by geography and by education as well as by income.

This self-segregation of a privileged fifth of the population is changing the American social order and the American political system, creating a self-perpetuating class at the top, which is ever more difficult to break into.

Figure 4.1, taken from "The Continuing Increase in Income Segregation," a March 2016 paper by Sean F. Reardon, a professor of education at Stanford, and Kendra Bischoff, a professor of sociology at Cornell, demonstrates the accelerating geographic isolation of the well-to-do—the upper-middle and upper classes (a pattern of isolation that also applies to the poor, with devastating effect).

In hard numbers, the percentage of families with children living in very affluent neighborhoods more than doubled between 1970 and 2012, from 6.6 percent to 15.7 percent.

At the same time, the percentage of families with children living in traditional middle-class neighborhoods with median incomes

This article first appeared in *The New York Times* on April 27, 2016. Copyright © 2016 by Thomas Edsall and The New York Times Company. All rights reserved.

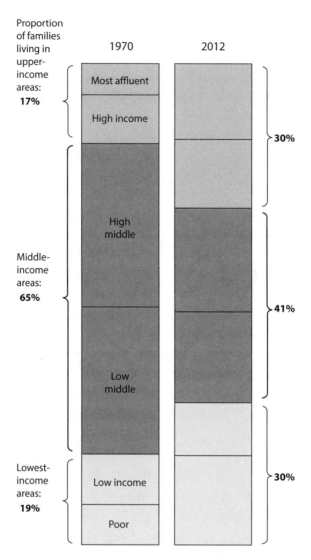

FIGURE 4.1. THE CHANGING SHAPE OF AMERICAN
NEIGHBORHOODS. Numbers do not add up to
100 percent because of rounding. Neighborhoods are
in metropolitan areas with more than 500,000 people.
Source: Sean F. Reardon and Kendra Bischoff, Stanford
Center for Education Policy Analysis. From The New
York Times. © 2016 The New York Times Company.
All rights reserved. Used under license.

between 80 and 125 percent of the surrounding metropolitan area fell from 64.7 percent in 1970 to 40.5 percent.

Reardon and Bischoff write, "Segregation of affluence not only concentrates income and wealth in a small number of communities, but also concentrates social capital and political power. As a result, any self-interested investment the rich make in their own communities has little chance of 'spilling over' to benefit middle- and low-income families. In addition, it is increasingly unlikely that high-income families interact with middle- and low-income families, eroding some of the social empathy that might lead to support for broader public investment in social programs to help the poor and middle class."

Geographic segregation dovetails with the growing economic spread between the top 20 percent and the bottom 80 percent: the top quintile is, in effect, disengaging from everyone with lower incomes.

Timothy Smeeding, a professor of public affairs and economics at the University of Wisconsin, has explored how the top quintile is pulling away from the rest of society. In an essay published earlier this year, "Gates, Gaps, and Intergenerational Mobility: The Importance of an Even Start," Smeeding finds that the gap between the average income of households with children in the top quintile and households with children in the middle quintile has grown, in inflation-adjusted dollars, from $68,600 to $169,300—that's 147 percent.

In an earlier paper, Smeeding and two coauthors wrote that "we have seen a threefold increase between 1972 and 2007 in top-decile spending on children, an increase that suggests that parents at the top may be investing in ever more high-quality day care and babysitting, private schooling, books and tutoring, and college tuition and fees."

The bottom line, Smeeding wrote in an email, is this: "The well-to-do are isolated from the day to day struggles of the middle class and below to provide these key services (health, education, job search and other opportunities) to aid the upward mobility of their children. But the upper middle class are happy to take advantage of tax subsidies for their own housing, preschool for their kids, and saving for college which benefit them."

Political leverage is another factor separating the top 20 percent from the rest of America. The top quintile is equipped to exercise much more influence over politics and policy than its share of the electorate would suggest. Although by definition this group represents 20 percent of all Americans, it represents about 30 percent of the electorate, in part because of high turnout levels. Figure 4.2, which shows voting patterns by income in the 2012 and 2014 elections, illustrates this phenomenon (it was created by Sean McElwee, a policy analyst at Demos, a liberal think tank).

Equally or perhaps more important, the affluent dominate the small percentage of the electorate that makes campaign contributions.

In a September 2015 essay, "The Dangerous Separation of the American Upper Middle Class," Richard Reeves, a senior fellow at Brookings, writes, "The top fifth have been prospering while the majority lags behind. But the separation is not just economic. Gaps are growing on a whole range of dimensions, including family structure, education, lifestyle, and geography. Indeed, these dimensions of advantage appear to be clustering more tightly together, each thereby amplifying the effect of the other."

The same pattern emerges in the case of education. Reeves cites data showing that 56 percent of heads of households in the top quintile have college or advanced degrees, compared with 34 percent in the third and fourth quintiles and 17 percent in the bottom two quintiles.

Similar patterns emerge in the percentage of married households.

"Family structure, as a marker and predictor of family stability, makes a difference to the life chances of the next generation," Reeves writes. "To the extent that upper middle class Americans are able to form planned, stable, committed families, their children will benefit—and be more likely to retain their childhood class status when they become adults."

Using 2013 census data, Reeves finds that 83 percent of affluent heads of household between the ages of thirty-five and forty are married, compared with 65 percent in the third and fourth income quintiles and 33 percent in the bottom two.

As the top 20 percent becomes more isolated and entrenched, reforms designed to open opportunities for those in the middle

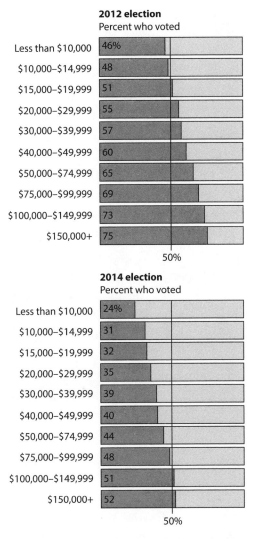

FIGURE 4.2. PEOPLE WITH MORE MONEY VOTE MORE. Percent of voters turning out in two elections, by family income.
Source: Analysis of Census Bureau data by Demos. From The New York Times.
© 2016 The New York Times Company. All rights reserved. Used under license.

and on the bottom "can all run into the solid wall of rational, self-interested upper middle class resistance," Reeves argues.

At the same time that lifestyle and consumption habits of the affluent diverge from those of the middle and working classes, wealthy voters are becoming increasingly Democratic, often motivated by their culturally liberal views. A comparison of exit poll data from 1984 and 1988 with data from the 2008 and 2012 elections reveals the changing partisan makeup of the top quintile.

In the 1980s, voters in the top ranks of the income ladder lined up in favor of Republican presidential candidates by two to one. In 1988, for example, George H. W. Bush crushed Michael Dukakis among voters making $100,000 or more by an impressive 34 points, 67 percent to 33 percent.

Move forward to 2008 and 2012. In 2008, voters from families making $100,000 to $200,000 split their votes 51 percent to 48 percent in favor of John McCain, while those making in excess of $200,000 cast a slight majority of 52 percent to 46 percent for Barack Obama.

In his first term, Obama raised taxes on the rich and criticized excessive CEO pay. As a result, he lost ground among the well-to-do but still performed far better than earlier Democrats had done, losing among voters making $100,000 or more by 9 points, 45 percent to 54 percent.

In other words, Democrats are now competitive among the top 20 percent. This has changed the economic makeup of the Democratic Party and is certain to intensify tensions between the traditional downscale wing and the emergent upscale wing.

The Republican Party in 2016 is an example of what can happen when the dominant wing fails to address the concerns of the majority. The rebellion against the Republican establishment is on the verge of producing the nomination of a man who is anathema to the majority of elected officials and party activists, a candidate with the potential to drag the party into minority status for years to come.

The "truly advantaged" wing of the Democratic Party—a phrase coined in this newspaper by Robert Sampson, a sociologist at Harvard—has provided the Democratic Party with crucial margins of victory where its candidates have prevailed. These upscale Democrats have helped fill the gap left by the departure of white working-class voters to the Republican Party.

At the same time, the priorities of the truly advantaged wing—voters with annual incomes in the top quintile, who now make up an estimated 26 percent of the Democratic general election vote—are focused on social and environmental issues: the protection and advancement of women's rights, reproductive rights, gay rights, and transgender rights, as well as climate change, and less on redistributive economic issues.

The tension within the current Democratic coalition is exemplified in, of all places, a 2012 poll of students and faculty at Phillips Exeter Academy in New Hampshire, a prestigious private boarding school founded in 1781. As Democrats have entered the ranks of the top quintile, their children have effectively realigned the student bodies of prep schools in New England and other northeastern states.

The Exeter survey found decisive majority support in the student body for Obama over Mitt Romney, but the more interesting finding was that among Exeter students old enough to vote, nine out of ten identified themselves as liberal on social issues.

In the case of economic policy, however, these students were split, 30 percent conservative, 33 percent liberal, and the rest moderate or unwilling to say.

"Morally, I am a Democrat," one of the participants commented, "but my wallet says I am a Republican."

A Democrat whose wallet tells him he is a Republican is unlikely to be a strong ally of less well-off Democrats in pressing for tax hikes on the rich, increased spending on the safety net, or a much higher minimum wage.

Bernie Sanders has tried to capitalize on this built-in tension within the Democratic primary electorate, but Hillary Clinton has so far been able to skate over intraparty conflicts. In the New York primary, for example, she did better among voters making $100,000 or more than among the less affluent, while simultaneously carrying African Americans and moderate Democrats of all races by decisive margins.

For years, Grover Norquist, a leader of the antitax movement, boasted that the Right has built a rock-solid "leave us alone coalition," only to see Trump crack it wide open this year.

Sanders is unlikely to do the same to the center-left coalition. His support is heavily concentrated among young, well-educated, white, very liberal, independent voters and it is not broad enough to defeat Clinton, as Tuesday's primary results demonstrated.

Anticipating this development, Tad Devine, a top adviser to Sanders, said on Saturday, "If we think we have to, you know, take a different way or re-evaluate, you know, we'll do it then."

Sanders's extraordinary performance to date, however, points to the vulnerability of a liberal alliance in which the economic interests of those on the top—often empowered to make policy—diverge ever more sharply from those in the middle and on the bottom.

As the influence of affluent Democratic voters and donors grows, the leverage of the poor declines. This was evident in the days leading up to the New York primary when, as Ginia Bellafante of the *Times* reported, both Clinton and Sanders, under strong pressure from local activists, agreed to tour local housing projects. Bellafante noted that their reluctance reflects how "liberal candidates on the national stage view public housing as a malady from which it is safest to maintain a distance."

The lack of leverage of those on the bottom rungs can be seen in a recent Pew survey in which dealing with the problems of the poor and needy ranked tenth on a list of public priorities, well behind terrorism, education, Social Security, and the deficit. This tenth-place ranking is likely to drop further as the gap widens between the bottom and the top fifth of voters in the country.

It turns out that the United States has a double-edged problem—the parallel isolation of the top and bottom fifths of its population. For the top, the separation from the middle and lower classes means less understanding and sympathy for the majority of the electorate, combined with the comfort of living in a cocoon.

For those at the bottom, especially the families who are concentrated in extremely high-poverty neighborhoods, isolation means bad schools, high crime, high unemployment, and high government dependency.

The trends at the top and the bottom are undermining cohesive politics, but more important, they are undermining social interconnection as they fracture the United States more and more into a class and race hierarchy.

5

Whose Neighborhood Is It?

On June 25, 1974, suburban residents of Detroit won their four-year battle to overturn court-ordered busing of Black city students across county lines into their schools.

In a key five-to-four Supreme Court decision, *Milliken v. Bradley*, Chief Justice Warren Burger declared that forty-one white suburban governments had not committed "significant violations" of the Constitution.

Burger wrote, "No single tradition in public education is more deeply rooted than local control over the operation of public schools; local autonomy has long been thought essential both to the maintenance of community concern and support for public schools and to quality of the educational process."

The victory in *Milliken* was based on the assumption that African Americans would be bused in, not that they would be living next door. What was not anticipated was a Black exodus from Detroit as African Americans capitalized on new housing laws to move away from the decaying city. The white response to this migration? Flight from inner-ring suburbs.

This article first appeared in *The New York Times* on September 19, 2015. Copyright © 2015 by Thomas Edsall and The New York Times Company. All rights reserved.

Southfield, Michigan, for example, which had been 0.7 percent Black in 1970, by 2010 had become 70.3 percent Black, and its schools nearly 95 percent Black. Over the same time period, Ecorse, a suburb southwest of Detroit, went from 0.4 percent Black to 44.5 percent, and its school system to 72 percent Black; Oak Park from 0.6 percent to 57.4 percent, and its school system to 95 percent Black; Harper Woods from 0.3 percent to 45.6 percent, and its school system to 88 percent Black.

"In *Milliken*, the Supreme Court had in effect told whites that it was safe to flee and that it would protect them," Myron Orfield, a professor of law at the University of Minnesota, writes in a 2015 *UCLA Law Review* article. Since then, however, many of "these communities have faced a wave of migrants from neighborhoods far more troubled than they were in 1972, a wave that will grow as Detroit continues to depopulate."

These suburban Detroit communities provide a case study in what has come to be called the "tipping point," the point at which whites begin to leave a residential locale en masse as African Americans or other minorities move in.

This phenomenon puzzled Thomas Schelling, a professor emeritus of economics at Harvard and a Nobel Laureate, who was struck by the lack of stable integrated communities. In 1971, he began work on a mathematical theory to explain the prevalence of racial segregation in a paper titled "Dynamic Models of Segregation," published in the *Journal of Mathematical Sociology*.

Schelling's famous thesis has been carefully summarized by Junfu Zhang, an economist at Clark University. Zhang writes, "Schelling's most striking finding is that moderate preferences for same-color neighbors at the individual level can be amplified into complete residential segregation at the macro level. For example, if every agent requires at least half of her neighbors to be of the same color—a preference far from extreme—the final outcome, after a series of moves, is almost always complete segregation."

In other words, residential segregation can emerge even if initial preferences are very slight.

According to Schelling, Zhang writes,

> In an all-white neighborhood, some residents may be willing to tolerate a maximum of 5 percent black neighbors; others may tolerate 10 percent, 20 percent, and so on.
>
> The ones with the lowest tolerance level will move out if the proportion of black residents exceeds 5 percent. If only blacks move in to fill the vacancies after the whites move out, then the proportion of blacks in the neighborhood may reach a level high enough to trigger the move-out of the next group of whites who are only slightly more tolerant than the early movers. This process may continue and eventually result in an all-black neighborhood.
>
> Similarly, an all-black neighborhood may be tipped into an all-white neighborhood, and a mixed-race neighborhood can be tipped into a highly segregated one, depending on the tolerance.

In the years since 1971, scholars have followed up on the Schelling argument with empirical studies.

David Card, a Berkeley economist, working with Alexandre Mas and Jesse Rothstein, both Princeton economists, studied neighborhood change from 1970 to 2000, and found that "most major metropolitan areas are characterized by a city-specific 'tipping point,' a level of the minority share in a neighborhood that once exceeded sets off a rapid exodus of the white population."

The tipping point, Card and his collaborators note, has been slowly but steadily rising, from an 11.9 percent minority share in the period from 1970 to 1980, to 13.5 percent in 1980–90, to 14.5 percent in 1990–2000.

A tipping point in the 13–15 percent range means that "a neighborhood can remain stable with a moderate minority share," according to Card. He and his coauthors conclude "that tipping points are semi-stable, and that neighborhoods can retain an integrated character so long as they remain below the tipping point."

Neither Schelling nor Card addresses the specific question of integrating poor African Americans into middle-class, majority-white neighborhoods.

The percentage of people living in neighborhoods of high concentrated poverty—census tracts where the federal poverty rate is 40 percent or more—has been growing steadily over the past two decades. Moving the poorest residents out of such neighborhoods would involve finding homes for nearly 13.8 million people.

"We are witnessing a nationwide return of concentrated poverty that is racial in nature," writes Paul A. Jargowsky, a fellow at the Century Foundation, in his August 11 essay "Architecture of Segregation: Civil Unrest, the Concentration of Poverty, and Public Policy."

There is wide agreement among scholars that these neighborhoods are harmful to the children who live in them, who suffer disproportionately from impaired cognitive abilities, increased behavioral problems, and fragile family structures. In August, Margery Austin Turner, a scholar at the Urban Institute, summarized the problem this way: "Young people from high-poverty neighborhoods are less successful in school than their counterparts from more affluent communities; they earn lower grades, are more likely to drop out, and are less likely to go on to college. Neighborhood environments influence teens' sexual activity and the likelihood that girls will become pregnant as teenagers. And living in disadvantaged neighborhoods significantly increases the risk of disease and mortality among both children and adults."

Who actually lives in very poor neighborhoods? According to the Century Foundation, 25.2 percent of African Americans, 17.4 of Hispanics, and 7.5 percent of whites (figure 5.1).

Black children under the age of six are the likeliest to live in high-poverty neighborhoods; 28 percent of African American children of that age live in them.

At the same time, the evidence of the benefits to children of living in better-off (low-poverty) neighborhoods is growing, according to the latest findings from the Moving to Opportunity experimental project.

These benefits—in improved school performance for poor Black children, higher college attendance rates, increased marriage rates, and greater future annual income—have put liberal advocates of

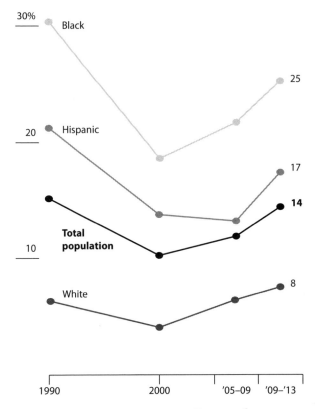

FIGURE 5.1. PROGRESS REVERSED. Percent of poor
Americans living in high-poverty neighborhoods (those
where 40 percent or more are impoverished).
Sources: Census Bureau; The Century Foundation. From
The New York Times. © 2015 The New York Times
Company. All rights reserved. Used under license.

integration on a political collision course with white communities
with their own anxieties about tipping points.

In the case of white suburban Detroit, Orfield, of the University of
Minnesota, points out that just "as racial integration was temporary
in Detroit neighborhoods, so it appears to be in its suburbs. Half of
the suburbs that were racially diverse in 2000 had become predominantly nonwhite in 2010, and most of the integrated suburbs in 2010
were in the process of resegregation."

In other words, in the case of the Detroit metropolitan area, moving poor children out of high-poverty communities into less poor

sections that are themselves on a path to greater poverty is at best a stopgap measure.

"Our highly dispersed and profoundly unequal distribution of housing is not inevitable," Jargowsky of the Century Foundation writes. He argues that there are two major changes "that need to occur," both "simple to state, but hard to bring about."

"First, the federal and state governments must begin to control suburban development," Jargowsky argues, in order to prevent excessive construction that leads to accelerated abandonment of existing housing: "New housing construction must be roughly in line with metropolitan population growth. Second, every city and town in a metropolitan area should be required to ensure that the new housing built reflects the income distribution of the metropolitan area as a whole."

These two policy initiatives, along with others requiring aggressive intervention, are hard to bring about in the absence of a national consensus. Without concerted action, the more likely prospect is the continued growth of neighborhoods with high concentrations of poverty.

The reality is that integration of the nation's public schools—despite notable if modest successes with elite exam schools—has been on a steady downward path since 1988, the high point. That year, 43.5 percent of Black students attended majority-white schools. By 2011, the percentage had fallen to 23.2.

In the case of residential segregation, Daniel T. Lichter, director of the Cornell Population Center, writing in the *American Sociological Review* with Domenico Parisi and Michael C. Taquino, sociologists at Mississippi State University, provides evidence that segregation is growing "between places: city-to-suburb segregation and suburb to suburb." Lichter said in a phone interview that Ferguson, Missouri, "is illustrative of the new place-based segregation, where some communities are becoming more diverse (Black, Asian or Hispanic), in part because whites are moving farther out into white suburbs or moving back to the city."

William Frey, a Brookings demographer, does not dispute Lichter, but argues that when you look at census data at the neighborhood level—

as opposed to data at the level of city and county jurisdictions—there is actually a trend toward lessened segregation: "The average white person today lives in a neighborhood that includes more minorities [27 percent] than was the case in 1980, when such neighborhoods were nearly 90 percent white. Moreover, each of the nation's major minority groups lives in neighborhoods that are at least one-third white."

There may be a trend, then, toward a growing number of stable, middle-class, integrated communities. But that does not mean that these middle-class communities will unambiguously open their doors to the minority poor.

Even residents of Marin County in California, a bastion of Democratic liberalism, have protested proposals to build affordable housing. In May 2014, the California Assembly passed legislation reducing the obligation of Marin County to build low- and moderate-income housing.

If Marin County—as one writer put it a couple of years ago, "the most beautiful, bucolic, privileged, liberal, hippie-dippie place on the earth"—is having a hard time accepting affordable housing, the path out of impoverished neighborhoods for substantial numbers of Black children will be arduous.

Residential and public school integration remain an immense challenge. Affordable housing, one piece of the integrative process, got a boost from a favorable Supreme Court decision in June, *Texas Department of Housing*, that further empowers plaintiffs in housing discrimination cases. A second boost came from new Department of Housing and Urban Development regulations issued in July requiring local governments "to take significant actions to overcome historic patterns of segregation, achieve truly balanced and integrated living patterns, promote fair housing choice, and foster inclusive communities."

Government action has often been resisted but, over time, it has pulled millions of Blacks into the mainstream of American life. From 1940 to 2014, the percentage of African Americans ages twenty-five to twenty-nine with high school degrees rose from 6.9 percent to 91.9 percent. Over the same period, the percentage of Blacks with college degrees grew from 1.4 percent to 22.4 percent. From 1963 (a year before enactment of the Civil Rights Act of 1964) to 2015, the percentage of Blacks employed in management, professional, and related occupations more than tripled, from 8.7 percent to 29.5 percent.

Although progress toward racial and ethnic integration has been sporadic—frequently one step forward, two steps back—credible progress has been made over the last seventy-five years. We have not come to the end of the story, but there are grounds for optimism.

6

Purity, Disgust, and Donald Trump

What has Donald Trump tapped into that other Republican candidates are missing? I posed this question to some of my best sources.

Jonathan Haidt, the author of *The Righteous Mind*, emailed me his response.

Many American voters, Haidt wrote, "perceive that the moral order is falling apart, the country is losing its coherence and cohesiveness, diversity is rising, and our leadership seems to be suspect or not up to the needs of the hour. It's as though a button is pushed on their forehead that says 'in case of moral threat, lock down the borders, kick out those who are different, and punish those who are morally deviant.'"

Haidt, a professor at New York University's Stern School of Business, argues that Trump "is not a conservative, and is not appealing to classical conservative ideas. He is an authoritarian, who is profiting from the chaos in Washington, Syria, Paris, San Bernardino, and even the chaos on campuses, which are creating a more authoritarian electorate in the Republican primaries."

In other words, the segment of the electorate drawn to Trump is especially receptive to mobilization at times of perceived disorder—to

This article first appeared in *The New York Times* on January 6, 2016. Copyright © 2016 by Thomas Edsall and The New York Times Company. All rights reserved.

a belief in looming external threats, from the Islamic State to Syrian refugees to illegal immigration from Latin America.

Noting that conservatives are preoccupied with notions of purity and disgust, Haidt also offers an explanation for some of the more remarkable oddities of Trump's political approach in an online post:

> If morality is about how we treat each other, then why did so many ancient texts devote so much space to rules about menstruation, who can eat what, and who can have sex with whom? There is no rational or health-related way to explain these laws. The emotion of disgust seemed to me like a more promising explanatory principle. The book of Leviticus makes a lot more sense when you think of ancient lawgivers first sorting everything into two categories: "disgusts me" (gay male sex, menstruation, pigs, swarming insects) and "disgusts me less" (gay female sex, urination, cows, grasshoppers).

Jesse Graham, a professor of psychology at the University of Southern California, elaborated on the purity-disgust dimension of this year's political campaign: "More than any other Republican presidential nominee, Donald Trump has been appealing to a particular combination of in-group loyalty and moral purity concerns. On the purity side, he often expresses disgust, often toward women and women's bodies (e.g., Clinton's bathroom break during a Democratic debate). But his purity appeals are most commonly in the context of group boundaries, like building walls on our national borders to prevent contamination by outsiders, who are cast as murderers and rapists, both morally and physically dirty."

These themes, in Graham's view, have laid the groundwork for Trump's popularity with explicitly racist and fascist groups: "The National Alliance and National Vanguard spawned *The Turner Diaries*, which imagined a dystopian future where America is ruled by lazy and corrupt Jews and Blacks, until a morally pure white resistance group nukes the Pentagon. Trump of course is not advocating anything like these horrors, but the moral intuitions he's playing on can lead in this direction if unrestrained by other moral concerns, such as injustice and the suffering of out-group members."

According to Graham, Trump's personal style attracts voters, including current and former Democrats, who are drawn to authoritarian leaders: "Trump is more domineering than the other candidates, bullying opponents and reporters alike, calling them losers, refusing to ever apologize for anything. This could indeed appeal to those high in social-dominance orientation and authoritarianism, particularly those who mistake such domineering for actual authority."

John Jost, a professor of psychology at New York University, picks up some of the same themes as Haidt and Graham. In an email he writes that Trump "is tapping into and indeed amplifying anger and fear, primarily among white citizens who are older and less educated than the average Republican voter. He is answering that anger and fear with tremendous self-confidence and 100 percent certainty, which some people find impressive and reassuring."

Alan Abramowitz, a political scientist at Emory, was emphatic in placing authoritarianism first in describing Trump's current success.

Abramowitz is one of a number of scholars who see Trump as posing a significant danger to American democracy. He wrote in an email that Trump "is very clearly, in my view, advancing a modern American version of fascism. A lot of the coarse language, harsh personal attacks and misogyny play into the theme of 'strong leadership' and willingness to say things that are 'politically incorrect' no matter who doesn't like it."

Trump's campaign style, his bullying and his pointed insults of competitors, fits into the psychological research concept of "social dominance orientation." The level of an individual's social dominance orientation is determined by agreement or disagreement with a series of statements. Those with a social dominance orientation agree strongly with such statements as, "Some groups of people are simply inferior to other groups"; "It's O.K. if some groups have more of a chance in life than others"; and "To get ahead in life, it is sometimes necessary to step on other groups."

And they disagree with such statements as, "It would be good if groups could be equal"; "We should do what we can to equalize conditions for different groups"; and "No group should dominate in society."

Jim Sidanius, a professor of sociology at Harvard and one of the originators, in the 1990s, of the concept of social dominance orientation, said in a phone interview that Trump had captured "the resentment and sense of loss" in a large segment of the white electorate: "These folks have lost a lot with the hollowing out of the middle and working class; if you combine that with floating xenophobia, you get this kind of reaction."

Sidanius argues that Trump's supporters have been receptive to this kind of appeal since Barack Obama's victory in 2008 and his reelection in 2012, but until now, "nobody was there to exploit it, to pick out the marketing opportunity. This is Trump's genius."

Nowhere has Trump's appeal been better captured than in a focus group of twenty-nine supporters conducted in Alexandria, Virginia, on December 9 by the Republican pollster Frank Luntz. A portion of Luntz's transcript read,

> "He is saying things that he knows the mainstream media will grab and throw gasoline on. And it goes really big," an unidentified man said. Clarissa joined in: "We want someone to take a stand, we want someone who says 'yes, O.K., here's what we're going to do.'"

Luntz asked the group if Trump acted presidential when he said he "would bomb the BLEEP out of ISIS." The twenty-nine participants replied in unison, "Yes, yes!"

For these voters, Trump's transgression of conventional boundaries is a selling point, not a liability:

> Matthew: "We've seen a lot of bad things that Trump has done. We've seen a lot of bad things that he's said. However, we've got a lot more problems in this country that I feel he is more qualified to handle." Scott: "Yeah he makes mistakes. He's human. He says things that are off color, that I'm embarrassed by occasionally, but I still think he's a leader."

Stephen Ansolabehere, a political scientist at Harvard, elaborated on Trump's popularity in an email: "Trump has been much more

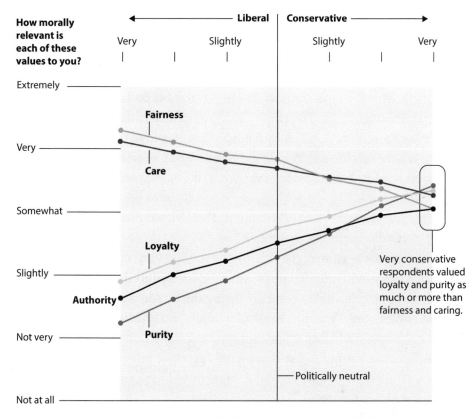

FIGURE 6.1. THE VALUES GAP. A poll of more than 187,000 people found a gap in relevance of these five values among liberals—a gap that disappears in the most conservative people.

Source: Bill Marsh, YourMorals.org poll of 187,471 people between 2007 and 2014. From The New York Times. © 2016 The New York Times Company. All rights reserved. Used under license.

effective in getting his message through, and that makes him more distinctive. He appears to be leading the dialogue. Because of the distinctiveness of his presentation, he gets more coverage, and that further reinforces the image of leading the discourse, and of being the alpha in the pack."

Graham and Haidt have found in their research that for the most conservative voters, the two "values" with the strongest appeal are authority and purity.

Figure 6.1, adapted from their 2009 paper "Liberals and Conservatives Rely on Different Sets of Moral Foundations," shows how this works: for the most conservative voters, the emphasis on the importance of the values of authority and purity increases while the stress placed on fairness and the avoidance of harm declines.

The strong appeal of purity to committed conservatives helps explain why Trump's supporters are not put off by his compulsive focus on disgust. On December 22, Trump described his reaction to a bathroom break taken by Clinton during a debate.

"Where did she go? Where did Hillary go?" he asked at a rally in Grand Rapids. "I know where she went, it's disgusting, I don't want to talk about it."

He then continued to talk about it: "No, it's too disgusting. Don't say it, it's disgusting, let's not talk."

Earlier in the campaign, Trump also revealed a striking obsession with disgust when he famously attacked Megyn Kelly, the anchor-woman who had challenged him during the Fox News debate. Kelly had confronted Trump: "You call women you don't like 'fat pigs,' 'dogs,' 'slobs' and 'disgusting animals,'" asking if Trump was fueling the "war on women." Explaining his response later, Trump said, "You could see there was blood coming out of her eyes, blood coming out of her wherever."

As my *Times* colleague Frank Bruni noted, Trump has a "bizarre obsession with, and objection to, body fluid," especially "the fluids of women."

Mark Schaller and Justin Park, psychologists at the Universities of British Columbia and Bristol, developed an intriguing evolutionary explanation of strong disgust responses in their 2011 paper "The Behavioral Immune System."

Schaller and Park found in experiments (and by comparing countries culturally) that higher levels of disease or pathogen threat increase "emphasis on conformity to existing cultural traditions and norms," while lower threat levels encourage individualism "defined in part by a tolerance for (and even encouragement of) deviance."

In our conversation, Sidanius posed a key question concerning Trump: Does he represent a growing constituency on the right that will become increasingly powerful, or will the Trump phenomenon eventually dissipate?

The truth is that Trump has already left an indelible imprint on the political system. He has inflicted tremendous damage on the Republican establishment, as he hoped he would, but he has done much more. By setting a populist agenda that appeals to millions of Republicans and to substantial numbers of Democrats and independents as well, Trump has opened the door to a reshaping of the traditional two-party coalition.

As everything shifts and we question previously sacrosanct boundaries, Trump and his supporters embody conflicts that the American political system will be hard pressed to resolve. Whatever happens next, he has remade the landscape on which these conflicts will be fought—for better or, more likely, for worse.

7

Donald Trump's Alt-Reality

Since Election Day there has been an abundance of liberal hyperbole about the dangers of a Trump administration.

Michael Kinsley wrote in the *Washington Post* that "Donald Trump is actually a fascist." Jonathan Chait warned in *New York Magazine* of "the step-by-step acceptance of the unthinkable as normal." Masha Gessen, a Russian journalist known for her opposition to Vladimir Putin who is also a colleague, primed Americans on what to expect from a Trump administration in an essay in the *New York Review of Books*: "Autocracy: Rules for Survival."

Some on the right dismiss these arguments as over the top— "articles about the Left's freakout over Donald Trump are getting a little stale," Jonah Goldberg wrote on *National Review*'s website—and it's possible that Kinsley, Chait, and Gessen will be proved wrong.

There is, however, a good chance that they are dead right.

Trump proved throughout his campaign and in the month since he won not only that he would lie repeatedly but that he could get away with it. As Glenn Kessler, who writes the Fact Checker column for the *Washington Post*, pointed out on November 4, "Donald Trump has amassed such a collection of Four-Pinocchio

This article first appeared in *The New York Times* on December 15, 2016. Copyright © 2016 by Thomas Edsall and The New York Times Company. All rights reserved.

ratings—59 in all—that by himself he's earned as many in this campaign as all other Republicans (or Democrats) combined in the past three years."

Trump's fifty-nine totally false "whoppers," in the Kessler rating system, compared with seven awarded to Hillary Clinton.

Trump's success in winning the presidency despite a modern-day record of lying suggests that for the moment he has been empowered by a large segment of the electorate to redefine the past, present, and future to suit his agenda. He has been unconstrained by facts.

We don't yet know if Trump will take full advantage of this free pass or how much leeway Congress, the courts, and the public will grant him. But once established, this command over reality has an appeal that is difficult, if not impossible, to let go. Trump has shown no signs of doing so. Indeed, he brings to mind George Orwell's observation that totalitarianism demands "the continuous alteration of the past, and in the long run probably demands a disbelief in the very existence of objective truth."

Trump, in a notorious tweet on November 27, asserted, "In addition to winning the Electoral College in a landslide, I won the popular vote if you deduct the millions of people who voted illegally."

Appearing December 11 on *Fox News Sunday*, Trump, despite losing the popular vote by 2.84 million, continued to describe his win as "one of the great victories of all time," arguing that Democrats "suffered one of the greatest defeats in the history of politics in this country" and that "we had a massive landslide victory."

Trump's adamant rejection of the CIA's finding that Russia intervened in the election in order to help him has become the focus of partisan warfare, putting Trump in conflict not only with Democratic congressional adversaries but with Republican critics like Senators John McCain and Lindsey Graham.

On December 9, the *Washington Post* published a story on the CIA's assessment that American intelligence agencies had "identified individuals with connections to the Russian government who provided WikiLeaks with thousands of hacked emails from the Democratic National Committee and others, including Hillary Clinton's campaign chairman, according to U.S. officials. Those officials described the individuals as actors known to the intelligence community and part of a wider Russian operation to boost Trump and hurt Clinton's chances."

The Trump transition team quickly attacked the credibility of the CIA in a prepared statement: "These are the same people that said Saddam Hussein had weapons of mass destruction. The election ended a long time ago in one of the biggest Electoral College victories in history. It's now time to move on and 'Make America Great Again.'"

The pushback against Trump was swift. Michael V. Hayden, director of the National Security Agency and later the CIA under George W. Bush, told the *Times*, "To have the president-elect of the United States simply reject the fact-based narrative that the intelligence community puts together because it conflicts with his a priori assumptions—wow."

The ongoing conflict over the CIA's analysis of Russian involvement has become the first major test of Trump's alt-reality vision.

John McCain, the Arizona Republican who chairs the Senate Armed Services Committee, flatly contradicted Trump last Sunday during an appearance on *Face the Nation*: "The facts are stubborn things. They did hack into this campaign."

On December 12, Mitch McConnell, the Senate majority leader, endorsed a formal inquiry into the allegations. In doing so, McConnell set the stage for a confrontation between the congressional and executive branches even before Trump takes office.

There is method to Trump's madness. Despite the nine lives he has demonstrated, he seems eager to avoid a damaging challenge to his legitimacy as the nation's chief executive, intent on defining his election as "a massive landslide victory" and "one of the great victories of all time."

Studies conducted before and during the election found that support for Trump correlated with voters' desire for what they see as authoritative leadership. Marc Hetherington, a political scientist at Vanderbilt, described such voters as having what he calls a "fixed worldview," as opposed to those with a "fluid worldview." Hetherington notes that those with a fixed view score high on tests of authoritarianism and those with a more fluid view score low.

In an essay published in October in *PS: Political Science and Politics*, "Authoritarian Voters and the Rise of Donald Trump," Matthew C. MacWilliams, a teaching associate at the University of Massachusetts–Amherst, found that "Trump's rise is in part the result of authoritarian voters' response to his unvarnished, us-versus-them rhetoric" and that "uniformity and order are authoritarian watch words. Authoritarians obey. They seek order. They follow authoritarian leaders. They eschew diversity, fear 'the other,' act aggressively toward others, and, once they have identified friend from foe, hold tight to their decision."

Based on survey data collected in the course of this year's Republican primaries, MacWilliams found a strong relationship between support for Trump and voters' support for authoritarian values.

The power and depth of this kind of support have freed Trump from the normal obligation to avoid making statements that are verifiably untrue. His loyalists are strongly inclined to believe what he says, and to forgive falsehoods that they see as harmless exaggerations.

"One thing that's been interesting this campaign season to watch is that people that say facts are facts—they're not really facts," Scottie Nell Hughes, a Trump supporter, said on *The Diane Rehm Show* on November 30. Her remarks caused a ruckus, but Hughes also laid bare Trump's basic method, which got lost in the kerfuffle: "There's no such thing, unfortunately anymore, as facts. And so Mr. Trump's tweets, among a certain crowd—a large part of the population—are truth. When he says that millions of people illegally voted, he has some facts—among him and his supporters—and people believe they have facts to back that up. Those that do not like Mr. Trump, they say that those are lies and there's no facts to back it up."

Or as Corey Lewandowski, Trump's former campaign manager and current adviser, puts it, "This is the problem with the media. You guys took everything that Donald Trump said so literally. The American people didn't."

This willingness to suspend disbelief "gives Trump not only license but incentive to spin fantasy, because no one expects him to tell the truth," Rob Stutzman, a Republican consultant who worked for Jeb Bush, told the *Los Angeles Times*. "They believe they're getting lied to constantly, so if their hero tells lies in order to strike back, they don't care."

Ownership of this phenomenon is not the exclusive property of the Right. Democrats, liberals, and academics have made significant, if unknowing, contributions to the credulity of Trump's supporters.

In a November 15 essay, "Straight Talk on Trade," Dani Rodrik, an economist at Harvard, poses the question, "Are economists partly responsible for Donald Trump's shocking victory in the US presidential election?"

Proponents of globalization, Rodrik argues, have in recent decades downplayed the costs of trade on the "implicit premise" that "there are barbarians on only one side of the trade debate. Apparently, those who complain about World Trade Organization rules or trade agreements are awful protectionists, while those who support them are always on the side of the angels."

The result is that many in the economics profession "have consistently minimized distributional concerns, even though it is now clear that the distributional impact of, say, the North American Free Trade Agreement or China's entry into the World Trade Organization were significant for the most directly affected communities in the United States."

Eduardo Porter, a *Times* colleague, raised the same basic issue in a column earlier this week, "Where Were Trump's Votes? Where the Jobs Weren't." Porter wrote that "less-educated white voters had a solid economic rationale for voting against the status quo—nearly all the gains from the economic recovery have passed them by."

Since November 7, 2007, according to Porter, Hispanics have gained nearly five million jobs, African Americans and Asian Americans have each gained over two million jobs, but whites have lost nearly one million jobs. Those job losses were heavily concentrated in those Rust Belt and, relatively speaking, more rural states where Trump racked up his Electoral College win.

The credibility of the Democratic Party generally among Trump voters is at an all-time low, as Democratic candidates discovered on November 8.

This Democratic vulnerability was explored in depth by Katherine Cramer, a political scientist at the University of Wisconsin, in a book on voters in that state, *The Politics of Resentment*, which came out in March. In her study, Cramer described the three elements of "rural consciousness": "First, a belief that rural areas are ignored by decision makers, including policy makers, second, a perception that rural areas do not get their fair share of resources, and third a sense that rural folks have fundamentally distinct values and lifestyles, which are misunderstood and disrespected by city folks."

The result, she argues, is the creation of a rural identity "infused with a sense of distributive injustice," much of it focused on liberal policies directing tax dollars to urban racial minorities.

These rural voters, and others in the Trump coalition, are more than willing to give Trump the benefit of the doubt. Their deep feeling that, whatever else he was, he was on their side permitted him to shrug off criticism as emanating from malevolent political elites.

Trump's attempt to subvert truth is a major challenge to democratic governance. In this context, it may be wise to listen to the predictions of Gessen. "Despite losing the popular vote, Trump has secured as much power as any American leader in recent history," she writes in the *New York Review of Books* essay I mentioned earlier. "He will want to maintain and increase it—his ideal is the totalitarian-level popularity numbers of Vladimir Putin."

Having watched in frustration as Trump ran roughshod over the party establishment and all of its candidates, Republicans are actually more likely than Democrats to recognize the potential threat posed by the president-elect. Because of this—in the strange pathways of politics—the hearings on alleged Russian hacking will become not only an inquiry into cyber espionage but also a forum for Republican leaders to put Trump in his place and to set limits on his presidency.

2017

During the first year of Donald Trump's presidency, three things became clear: the threat to democracy, the extremism of Trump loyalists, and the emphasis conservative, evangelical churches placed on the acquisition of power. In 2011, just 30 percent of evangelicals, the smallest percentage of any denomination, agreed that "an elected official who commits an immoral act in their personal life can still behave ethically and fulfill their duties in their public and professional life." By October 2016, with Trump as the Republican presidential nominee, the percentage of white evangelicals who said a politician who commits an immoral act could fulfill their public and professional duties shot up to 72 percent, higher than the percentage of any other denomination, including Catholics and white mainline Protestants. Trump and the voters he mobilized reflected the steady conversion of the Republican Party from the party that freed the slaves to the party that capitalized on white resentment and finally to the party with disregard for the basic tenets of democracy.

8

Reaching Out to the Voters
the Left Left Behind

The devastating recession that began at the end of 2007 and officially ended in June 2009 was the most severe downturn since World War II.

The political, social, and even medical consequences of this recession have been duly noted, but even so, the depths of its effects are only now becoming clear. One we're still learning more about is how the rural, less populated regions of the country (known among demographers as nonmetropolitan counties), which already suffered from higher-than-average poverty rates, recovered from the recession at a far slower pace than more populous metropolitan counties.

The fact that people living outside big cities were battered so acutely by the recession goes a long way toward explaining President Donald Trump's victory in the last election.

In Luzerne County, in northeast Pennsylvania, population 316,383 and falling, the unemployment rate in February 2017 was 6.7 percent, substantially higher than it had been at the start of the

This article first appeared in *The New York Times* on April 13, 2017. Copyright © 2017 by Thomas Edsall and The New York Times Company. All rights reserved.

recession (it was at 4.6 percent in October 2007). The total number of people in the county labor force declined by 2,544.

In 2016, Luzerne County, which had twice previously cast majorities for Barack Obama, supported Trump 57.9 percent to 38.6 percent.

Similarly, in Defiance County in northwest Ohio, population 38,158, the unemployment rate rose from 5.3 percent in August 2007 to 5.9 percent in February 2017. The local labor force shrank over this period by 1,379 workers.

In 2016, Defiance became much more Republican than it had been: while voters there had supported Mitt Romney over Obama 55.5 percent to 42.2 percent, they supported Trump over Hillary Clinton 63.7 percent to 29.3 percent.

Compare Luzerne and Defiance counties with the Los Angeles–Glendale–Long Beach metropolitan area. There, not only did the unemployment rate fall from 5.6 percent in July 2007 to 4.8 percent in February 2017, but total employment grew from 4.68 million to 4.84 million.

The greater Los Angeles region—like other densely populated metropolitan areas such as Clark County, which includes Las Vegas, and Dallas County in Texas—recovered strongly and swiftly and supported the Democratic Party in November 2016, from candidates for local office to the president.

Trump lost to Clinton in Los Angeles County by 48 points, a substantially larger margin than the 39.5 points by which Romney lost the county to Obama in 2012.

The diverging fortunes of metropolitan counties and virtually all nonmetro regions of the country are graphically displayed in figure 8.1, produced by the Department of Agriculture's Economic Research Service.

The figure shows that since the bottom of the recession in the fourth quarter of 2009, metropolitan areas have fully bounced back and are now significantly above their prerecession employment levels. In contrast, employment in nonmetro areas remains well below its prerecession level.

Trump won majorities in counties with populations under one million, and his margin of victory rose as the population numbers

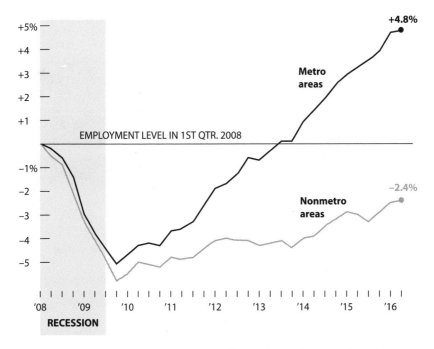

FIGURE 8.1. A VERY UNEVEN RECOVERY. Change in employment since the start of the Great Recession.
Source: Bill Marsh, U.S.D.A. Economic Research Service. From The New York Times. © 2017 The New York Times Company. All rights reserved. Used under license.

got smaller. In counties with fewer than 2,500 people, Trump won 70.6 percent to 25.1 percent.

From another vantage point, Trump did best in regions where economic growth was the worst—where jobs are disappearing and where middle-aged white men and women are dying at younger ages.

The crucial role of the financial meltdown and its aftermath in shaping regional politics is also on display in figure 8.2, produced by the Economic Innovation Group, a bipartisan think tank.

In the period from 1992 to 1996, communities of one hundred thousand or less were engines of growth, producing 27 percent of the nation's new jobs. The large metropolitan areas with populations of over one million produced 16 percent.

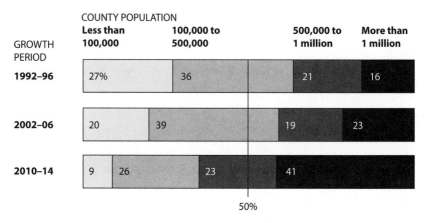

FIGURE 8.2. MORE JOBS IN THE BIG CITY. Share of U.S. job creation by size of county in three periods of economic growth. Because of rounding, not all figures add up to 100 percent.
Source: Economic Innovation Group. From The New York Times. © 2017 The New York Times Company. All rights reserved. Used under license.

By 2010 to 2014, the share of new jobs in the lowest-population counties shrank to 9 percent, while the share produced in the largest counties grew from 16 percent to 41 percent.

Put still another way, counties with populations below one million have seen their share of job creation drop from 84 percent of the national total in 1992–96 to 78 percent in 2002–6—and then abruptly plummet to 59 percent in 2010–14.

The pattern of net new business creation (new firms minus firms going out of business) reveals an even sharper reversal of fortune. In 1992–96, counties with fewer than one hundred thousand people produced 32 percent of new enterprises, while the biggest counties produced 13 percent.

By 2010–14, very rural counties saw zero net growth in new firms, while the biggest counties boomed with 58 percent of new firms. All counties with populations under a million created 87 percent of the nation's new businesses from 1992 to 1996, but the number was 42 percent in 2010–14.

In other words, the centuries-long shift of economic activity from country and small-town areas to populous urban regions has sharply accelerated over the past ten years. The result is that "America faces a small-county crisis of dire proportions," as Mark Muro, a senior fellow at Brookings, put it, "and a period of opportunity in cities, the bigger the better."

There is a combination of forces driving these trends, according to Muro, most especially the growing importance of the high-tech and digital industries. "Urbanization," he wrote me, "has become a major trend in the last decade or so, driven by the clustering of workers and firms in larger cities. The increased digitization of the economy has accelerated this dynamic, and ensured that changing skills demands have changed what places are best valued."

By 2015, 74 percent of all high-tech jobs were located in the one hundred largest counties, "where the universities, technology innovation assets, supply chains, STEM workers, and industry clusters on which the sector depends reside," Muro wrote in a paper in August 2016 with two Brookings colleagues, David M. Hart and Siddharth Kulkarni.

At the same time, Muro noted by email, "rural America has been hammered by the end of the immediate post-crisis commodity boom and now there is precious little relief there: Agricultural prices are low, coal prices and automation are hammering coal country, natural gas prices are suffering from glut conditions, and meanwhile, no subdivision of the economy is suffering from more moribund employment growth."

The rural crisis, according to Muro, "isn't just economic but is now compounded by the rising mortality rates" described in detail by the economists Anne Case and Angus Deaton.

In their most recent published work, "Mortality and Morbidity in the 21st Century," a Brookings paper, Case and Deaton, who teach at Princeton, update their earlier studies to provide "a more complete picture of midlife mortality—by sex and education group, over the full age range of midlife, using shorter age windows, over time, by cause, and by small geographic areas."

The Case-Deaton description of rising midlife mortality—especially an increase of "deaths of despair" from alcohol, opioids, and suicide—is, in effect, a demographic portrait of many of Trump's

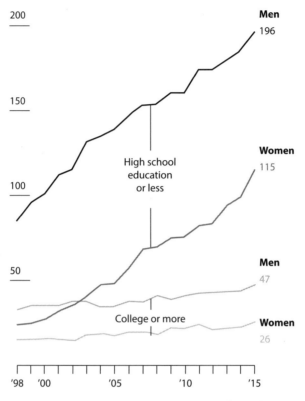

FIGURE 8.3. WHITE "DEATHS OF DESPAIR." Deaths per 100,000 non-Hispanic whites aged 50 to 54 from suicide, alcohol, or other drugs, by education level. *Source*: Brookings Papers on Economic Activity. From The New York Times. © 2017 The New York Times Company. All rights reserved. Used under license.

core supporters: whites with a high school degree or less living in rural to medium-sized towns and cities.

Case and Deaton show that from 1999 to 2015 mortality rates among non-college-educated whites rose in every age group, most especially among younger whites aged twenty-five to thirty-four.

Figure 8.3 shows the rising "deaths of despair" rates for whites without college degrees, compared with the virtually unchanging rates for whites with degrees.

Case and Deaton found that mortality rates for whites were stable or declining in all counties with populations of one million or more—the counties, in other words, that voted decisively for Clinton. Conversely, white mortality rates rose by roughly 1 percent a year in all counties of less than a million—the counties that voted for Trump.

Bill Bishop, coauthor of the book *The Big Sort* and a founder of the Daily Yonder, makes the case that the political split in America is not an urban-rural divide. Instead, he argues, it is between the largest cities and the rest of America.

In an email, Bishop noted that "outside of cities of a million or more—and really outside of the 56 central city counties of these large metros—Democrats lose."

This applies not only to presidential races but to the House of Representatives as well. In a piece for the Daily Yonder, Bishop wrote that "Democrats don't have a 'rural problem.' They have an 'everywhere-but-big-cities problem.'" He provided data on the pattern of partisan victory in 2014 House races on a scale from super urban to very rural. Democrats won a majority of districts only in the most urban counties, while Republicans won two out of every three in very rural districts.

Bishop argued in his email to me that "the split isn't just about politics. It's about lifestyle and identity." Increasingly, where you live "is tied into lifestyle and lifestyle aligns with politics. Politics, like lifestyle, is one way we construct our identities."

The accelerated shift toward urban prosperity and exurban-to-rural stagnation reinforces polarizing disagreements between city and country on matters ranging from family values to education to child-rearing practices to religious faith.

The two maps in figure 8.4 show results by county in 1992, when Bill Clinton first won the presidency, and in 2016, when Trump did. The maps demonstrate the strategic hurdles currently confronting both parties. In 1992, Bill Clinton won 1,519 counties, compared with 1,582 carried by George H. W. Bush. In 2016, Hillary Clinton won majorities in 490 counties, compared with Trump victories in 2,622. Obama won 875 counties in 2008 and 693 in 2012.

FIGURE 8.4. CLINTON VS. CLINTON. Two presidential votes, by the candidates who carried each county.
Source: Matthew Bloch, Dave Leip's *Atlas of U.S. Presidential Elections*. From The New York Times. © 2017 The New York Times Company. All rights reserved. Used under license.

Much attention has been paid to one daunting task facing Republicans: the need to prevent liberal values and ideas from seeping beyond large, urban counties into red counties and states.

As the last election demonstrated, the compact geographical distribution of Democratic voters with liberal or progressive ideologies in states that were already blue allowed Trump to win in the Electoral College despite a sizable Democratic victory in the popular vote.

Democrats, in turn, must figure out a way to extend their reach beyond the mega-population centers located mostly on the coasts, where cosmopolitan, globalist, and postmaterialist values dominate.

Jeff Spross, the economics correspondent for the *Week*, wrote in an April 3 essay, "The Dark Side of Cities," "Trump supporters' politics may be filtered through the perverse lenses of racial anxiety and cultural reaction. But they are not wrong to look upon cities as distant and alien metropolises that have benefited at rural America's expense."

"So what's the fix?" Spross asks. "Return to the old ways of robust public investment, antitrust enforcement, and tax and regulatory policy to force money back down the income ladder. Stop treating deficit reduction as a goal in itself; rather whatever deficit level maintains full employment is the right one."

The technological revolution poses a major problem for Democrats seeking ways to make economic outcomes more equitable by geography and class.

In a June 2015 joint interview with the *Harvard Business Review*, Erik Brynjolfsson and Andrew McAfee, authors of *The Second Machine Age*, argue that it's "time to start tackling the economic downside of new technologies." They voice a mixture of pessimism and optimism.

McAfee noted that, given current trends, "we'll continue to see the middle class hollowed out and will see growth at the low and high ends. Really good executives, entrepreneurs, investors, and novelists— they will all reap rewards. Yo-Yo Ma won't be replaced by a robot anytime soon, but financially, I wouldn't want to be the world's 100th-best cellist."

Brynjolfsson argued, however, that the economic consequences of technological advance can be shaped by policy:

> Our one confident prediction is that digital technologies will bring the world into an era of more wealth and abundance and less drudgery and toil. But there's no guarantee that everyone will share in the bounty, and that leaves many people justifiably apprehensive. The outcome—shared prosperity or increasing inequality—will be determined not by technologies but by the choices we make as individuals, organizations, and societies. If we fumble that future—if we build economies and societies that exclude many people from the cycle of prosperity—shame on us. Technological progress is an extraordinarily powerful force, but it's not destiny. It won't lift us into utopia or carry us into an unwanted future. The power to do that rests with us human beings. Technologies are merely our tools.

For the moment, the Democratic Party is forced to stand by and watch the Trump spectacle, unable to enact policies to address the issues Spross, Brynjolfsson, and McAfee raise. Would better candidates help to enlarge the electorate to appeal to voters whose primary concerns are economic?

One place to look toward is the West, where such Democratic governors as Jay Inslee of Washington, John Hickenlooper of Colorado, and Steve Bullock of Montana preside.

All three have been elected and reelected in competitive states where to survive politically they have had to balance urban and non-metro bread-and-butter interests.

Shifting the focus of attention onto politicians like these would be a modest first step, but for a party struggling to regain its foothold, a modest first step would be a major achievement. The question going forward is whether Democrats can compete more effectively and more efficiently for the votes of those who have been left behind. They should set themselves this challenge.

9

Democracy, Disrupted

As the forces of reaction outpace movements predicated on the ideal of progress, and as traditional norms of political competition are tossed aside, it's clear that the internet and social media have succeeded in doing what many feared and some hoped they would: they have disrupted and destroyed institutional constraints on what can be said, when and where it can be said, and who can say it.

Even though in one sense President Donald Trump's victory in 2016 fulfilled conventional expectations—because it prevented a third straight Democratic term in the White House—it also revealed that the internet and its offspring have overridden the traditional American political system of alternating left-right advantage. They are contributing—perhaps irreversibly—to the decay of traditional moral and ethical constraints in American politics.

Matthew Hindman, a professor of media and public affairs at George Washington University and the author of *The Myth of Digital Democracy*, said in a phone interview that "if you took the label off, someone looking at the United States would have to be worried about democratic failure or transitioning toward a hybrid regime."

This article first appeared in *The New York Times* on March 2, 2017. Copyright © 2017 by Thomas Edsall and The New York Times Company. All rights reserved.

Such a regime, in his view, would keep the trappings of democracy, including seemingly free elections, while leaders would control the election process, the media, and the scope of permissible debate. "What you get is a country that is de facto less free."

Scott Goodstein, the CEO of Revolution Messaging, has run online messaging for both the Obama and Sanders campaigns. When I spoke to him in a phone interview, he argued that the internet has been "a great thing for getting additional layers of transparency. It was true for Donald Trump as it was for Bernie Sanders; the internet ended smoke-filled back rooms, deal-cutting moved from back room to a true campaign, with a more general population. Maybe an unwashed population, but that's the beauty of American politics with 350 million people."

Goodstein noted, however, "a horrible development on the internet" last year: "In this cycle you saw hate speech retweeted and echoed, by partisan hacks, the Jewish star used in neo-Nazi posts. There is no governing body, so I think it's going to get worse, more people jumping into the gutter."

The use of digital technology in the 2016 election "represents the latest chapter in the disintegration of legacy institutions that had set bounds for American politics in the postwar era," Nathaniel Persily, a law professor at Stanford, writes in a forthcoming paper, "Can American Democracy Survive the Internet?"

According to Persily, the Trump campaign was "totally unprecedented in its breaking of established norms of politics." He argues that "this type of campaign is only successful in a context in which certain established institutions—particularly, the mainstream media and political party organizations—have lost most of their power, both in the United States and around the world."

The Trump campaign is the most recent beneficiary of the collapse of once-dominant organizations:

The void these eroding institutions have left was filled by an unmediated, populist nationalism tailor-made for the internet age. We see it in the rise of the Five Star Movement in Italy and the Pirate Party in Iceland. We see it in the successful use of social media in the Brexit referendum, in which supporters were seven times more numerous on Twitter and five times more active on Instagram. And we see it in the pervasive fears of government leaders throughout Europe, who worried well before the American election that Russian propaganda and other internet tactics might sway their electorates.

The influence of the internet is the latest manifestation of the weakening of the two major American political parties over the past century, with the civil service undermining patronage, the rise of mass media altering communication, campaign finance law empowering donors independent of the parties, and the ascendance of direct primaries gutting the power of party bosses to pick nominees.

In a forthcoming paper, "Outsourcing Politics: The Hostile Takeovers of Our Hollowed Out Political Parties," Samuel Issacharoff, a law professor at New York University, writes about how the erosion of political parties played out in 2016: "Neither party appeared to have a mechanism of internal correction. Neither could muster the wise elders to steer a more conventional course. Neither could use its congressional leadership to regain control of the party through its powers of governance. Neither could lay claim to financial resources that would compel a measure of candidate loyalty. Neither could even exert influence through party endorsements."

The result: "The parties proved hollow vehicles that offered little organizational resistance to capture by outsiders. And what was captured appeared little more than a brand, certainly not the vibrant organizations that are heralded as the indispensable glue of democratic politics."

Issacharoff expressed even more concern about the future of democratic politics in a talk, "Anxieties of Democracy," that he gave in February at the University of Texas Law School.

"We are witnessing a period of deep challenge to the core claims of democracy to be the superior form of political organization of civilized peoples," he told his audience. "The current moment of democratic uncertainty draws from four central institutional challenges, each one a compromise of how democracy was consolidated over the past few centuries. First, the accelerated decline of political parties and other institutional forms of engagement; second, the weakness of the legislative branches; third, the loss of a sense of social cohesion; and fourth, the decline in democratic state competence."

In a phone interview, Issacharoff cited the emergence of internet-based methods of communication as a major contributing factor in the deterioration of political parties.

"Technology has overtaken one of the basic functions you needed political parties for in the past, communication with voters," he said. "Social media has changed all of that, candidates now have direct access through email, blogs and Twitter," along with Facebook, Instagram, Snapchat, and other platforms.

Two developments in the 2016 campaign provided strong evidence of the vulnerability of democracies in the age of the internet: the alleged effort of the Russian government to secretly intervene on behalf of Trump, and the discovery by internet profiteers of how to monetize the distribution of fake news stories, especially stories damaging to Hillary Clinton.

In an email, Samuel Greene, the director of the Russia Institute at King's College London, described his "best estimate" of Russian cyber hacking under Putin's guidance: "Teams of hackers, operating with varying levels of resources and at various distances from the central chain of command, had a lot of license to poke and prod and see what they could come up with. Some of these people found it easier to do certain kinds of things—like break into Podesta's emails—than they had expected. Having obtained a windfall, they were then given license to push it even further."

The question now is, Who benefits more from the digital revolution and the ubiquity of social media, the Left or the Right?

Andreas Jungherr, an expert in social and computer science at the University of Konstanz in Germany, argues that the internet is particularly helpful to opposition movements. He emailed me, "It seems to me this is not a question about ideological placement but more about organizational or movement strategy. As long as I am in opposition, the payoff is higher in investing in digital infrastructure and thereby channeling the activities and enthusiasm of my supporters than when in power. So I would expect a re-emergence of political activity, for example in the form of alternative news sources, on the liberal side in the coming years."

Along parallel lines, Cristian Vaccari, a reader in politics at Royal Holloway, University of London, argued in an email that social media have contributed to the sudden emergence of candidates and parties running the ideological gamut:

> By qualitatively expanding the pool of participants, social media may thus be substantially contributing to some of the vivid examples of political disruption that we have witnessed over the past few years across and beyond the Western world: from the spread of protest movements to the sudden rise of new parties such as the Five Star Movement in Italy and Podemos in Spain, from the ascent of populist leaders all across Europe to electoral upheavals such as the Brexit referendum and the surge of Bernie Sanders and Donald Trump in the United States 2016 Presidential elections.

Clay Shirky is a professor in the Interactive Telecommunications Program at New York University. In a 2009 TED talk—the full political significance of which has only become clear over the past eight years—he described some of the implications of the digital revolution: "The internet is the first medium in history that has native support for groups and conversation at the same time. Whereas the phone gave us the one-to-one pattern, and television, radio, magazines, books, gave us the one-to-many pattern, the internet gives us the many-to-many pattern."

Shirky continues,

> The second big change is that, as all media gets digitized, the internet also becomes the mode of carriage for all other media, meaning that phone calls migrate to the internet, magazines migrate to the internet, movies migrate to the internet. And that means that every medium is right next door to every other medium. Put another way, media is increasingly less just a source of information, and it is increasingly more a site of coordination,

because groups that see or hear or watch or listen to something can now gather around and talk to each other as well.

And the third big change, according to Shirky, is that members of the former audience "can now also be producers and not consumers. Every time a new consumer joins this media landscape a new producer joins as well, because the same equipment—phones, computers—let you consume and produce. It's as if, when you bought a book, they threw in the printing press for free; it's like you had a phone that could turn into a radio if you pressed the right buttons."

There is good reason to think that the disruptive forces at work in the United States—as they expand the universe of the politically engaged and open the debate to millions who previously paid little or no attention—may do more to damage the Left than strengthen it. In other words, just as the use of negative campaign ads and campaign finance loopholes to channel suspect contributions eventually became routine, so too will be the use of social media to confuse and mislead the electorate.

Of course, this problem goes much deeper than the internet. Sam Greene of King's College London put it this way in an email:

Our politics are vulnerable to nefarious influences—whether of the Kremlin variety or the Breitbart variety—not because our information landscape is open and fluid, but because voters' perceptions have become untethered from reality. For reasons that are both complex and debatable, very many voters have stopped seeing government as a tool for the production of the common good, and have instead turned to politicians (and others) who at least make them feel good. Thus, the news we consume has become as much about emotion and identity as about facts. That's where the vulnerability comes in, and its roots are in our politics—not on the internet.

10

Democracy Can Plant the Seeds of Its Own Destruction

Will President Donald Trump's assault on the norms underpinning constitutional democracy permanently alter American political life?

On a daily basis, Trump tests the willingness of the public to accept a president who lies as a matter of routine. So far, Trump has persuaded a large swath of America to swallow what he feeds them.

Asked whether the media makes up stories about Trump, nearly half the population of the United States, 46 percent, now says yes, according to a Politico / Morning Consult poll conducted October 12–16. Compare this with 37 percent who say that the media does not fabricate material about the president. While Republicans and Democrats diverge in the directions you would expect, a plurality of independents, 44 percent, says that the media produces false stories; 31 percent say the media is accurate.

Trump has flourished at a time when trust in basic institutions— organized religion, banks, medical services, Congress, the media,

This article first appeared in *The New York Times* on October 19, 2017. Copyright © 2017 by Thomas Edsall and The New York Times Company. All rights reserved.

government, you name it—has eroded. His presidency is a product of this erosion, but it is also proving to be an accelerant of the process.

Eight days after Trump was elected, Clare Malone, a senior political writer for the website FiveThirtyEight, put it this way: "Trump did not so much conjure a dark view of America's direction as tap into reserves that have lain deep and been sporadically voiced."

Or, as Roberto Stefan Foa and Yascha Mounk write in the July 2016 issue of the *Journal of Democracy*, "Even as democracy has come to be the only form of government widely viewed as legitimate, it has lost the trust of many citizens who no longer believe that democracy can deliver on their most pressing needs and preferences."

The danger, they argue, cannot be underestimated: "As democracies deconsolidate, the prospect of democratic breakdown becomes increasingly likely—even in parts of the world that have long been spared such instability."

Trump is the most prominent of the right-wing populist politicians continuing to gain strength both here and in Europe (despite some electoral setbacks), but because the viewpoint he represents is now so widespread, he is in one sense personally irrelevant—a symptom rather than a cause.

As Sasha Polakow-Suransky, the author of *Go Back to Where You Came From: The Backlash against Immigration and the Fate of Western Democracy*, warns in the *New York Review of Books*, "Liberal democracies are better equipped than authoritarian states to grapple with the inevitable conflicts that arise in diverse societies, including the threat of terrorist violence. But they also contain the seeds of their own destruction: if they fail to deal with these challenges and allow xenophobic populists to hijack the public debate, then the votes of frustrated and disaffected citizens will increasingly go to the anti-immigrant right, societies will become less open, nativist parties will grow more powerful, and racist rhetoric that promotes a narrow and exclusionary sense of national identity will be legitimized."

The threat to democracy posed by the current outbreak of populist nationalism has become a matter of concern for both scholars and ordinary citizens. The central topic at a conference at Yale earlier this month was "How do democracies fall apart?" and the subject will be taken up again in November at a Stanford conference called "Global Populisms: A Threat to Democracy?"

I contacted several of the participants at the Yale gathering and was struck by their anxiety over the future prospects of democratic governance.

One of the most insightful was Adam Przeworski, a political scientist at New York University, who has written, but not yet published, his own analysis of current events under the title "What's Happening."

First and foremost, Przeworski stresses, "there is nothing 'undemocratic' about the electoral victory of Donald Trump or the rise of anti-establishment parties in Europe."

These parties and candidates, he points out, "do not advocate replacing elections by some other way of selecting rulers. They are ugly—most people view racism and xenophobia as ugly—but these parties do campaign under the slogan of returning to 'the people' the power usurped by elites, which they see as strengthening democracy. In the words of a Trump advertisement, 'Our movement is about replacing a failed and corrupt political establishment with a new government controlled by you, the American people.'"

In support of Przeworski's argument, it is clear that the success of the Trump campaign in winning the Republican nomination was the result of a classic democratic insurgency: the Republican electorate's rejection of its party's establishment.

The danger in the United States, in Przeworski's view, is the possibility that the Trump administration will use the power of the presidency to undermine the procedures and institutions essential to the operation of democracy: "that the incumbent administration would intimidate hostile media and create a propaganda machine of its own, that it would politicize the security agencies, that it would harass political opponents, that it would use state power to reward sympathetic private firms, that it would selectively enforce laws, that it would provoke foreign conflicts to monger fear, that it would rig elections."

Przeworski believes that "such a scenario would not be unpre-cedented. The United States has a long history of waves of political repression: the 'Red Scare' of 1917–20, the internment of Japanese citizens during World War II, the McCarthy period, the Nixon presidency."

Along similar lines, Anna Grzymala-Busse, a political scientist at Stanford, replied by email to my inquiry, "My big worry is not sim-ply that formal institutions have been eroded, but that the informal norms that underpin them are even more important and even more fragile. Norms of transparency, conflict of interest, civil discourse, respect for the opposition and freedom of the press, and equal treat-ment of citizens are all consistently undermined, and without these the formal institutions become brittle."

Trump, in Grzymala-Busse's assessment, "articulates a classic populist message that we see in Europe: the elite establishment is a collusive cartel uninterested in the problems of 'the people,'" and, she continued, he has begun to follow the path of European populist leaders: "Much of Trump's language and actions are also familiar: there is a standard authoritarian populist template, developed in Hungary and faithfully followed in Poland and in Turkey: first, go after the courts, then the media, then the civil society, churches, universities."

The attacks on the courts, media, and universities "are not simply the ravings of a lunatic, but an established strategy for undermining democratic oversight and discrediting the opposition."

Margaret Levi, another political scientist at Stanford, wrote me that she was "not sure Trumpism per se will survive Trump. But I do think it is the current embodiment of a right-wing populism that is likely to remain the basis of internal opposition within the Republican Party or be the basis of a split in the Party, leading to two new parties."

Some form of right-wing populism, Levi argued, "is already a competitive force in general elections. And it is once again a force in competitive elections in democracies world-wide."

She added that there was no guarantee that right-wing populism "will not transform into the fascist and Nazi forms."

Unless the Democratic Party in this country and moderate parties in the rest of the world "find a way to address the populace's
underlying economic insecurity and deterioration in the perceived
(and actual in many cases) standard of living, the possibility for
irreparable damage does exist," Levi wrote. "Otherwise, both confidence in democratic government, measured by the extent it is a
reliable provider of needed goods and services, including domestic
and international security, and its legitimacy, the normative belief in
its right to rule, will decline significantly and dangerously—perhaps
even to the point of no return."

While white identitarianism, anger over immigration, and economic dislocation are often cited as causes of the emergence of right-
wing populism, another argument is that there is a growing segment
of the electorate that is alienated from cultural norms they see as
imposed on them by a ruling elite—a repressive elite; politically
correct and socially remote.

In a research paper published in the current issue of the *Journal
of Democracy*, "Eroding Norms and Democratic Deconsolidation,"
Paul Howe, a political scientist at the University of New Brunswick,
Canada, describes the increasing size of the nihilistic segment of the
American electorate.

This constituency of the disengaged and profoundly alienated
provides a base of support in the United States and Europe for
populist leaders who, in Howe's view, fit the Trump mold: "They
compete in the democratic process, yet with words and actions that
convey disregard for core democratic principles such as the rule of
law, minority rights, and checks and balances on executive power.
At the same time, a number of these individuals are prone to brazen,
dubious, and sometimes aggressive behaviors that suggest outsized
egos, scant respect for others, and a degree of contempt for social
norms."

Looking at data from World Values Surveys in recent decades,
Howe finds that in the United States, "the rise of antidemocratic
sentiment has less to do with dysfunction in the political arena than
with corrosive changes that have reshaped the social and cultural
landscape more generally."

These corrosive changes include an increase in the number of citizens who say it is OK to "claim government benefits to which one is not entitled; take a bribe in the course of one's duties; cheat on taxes; and avoid a public-transit fare."

When answers to these questions were correlated with political attitudes, Howe found that "indifferent feelings toward democracy are interlaced with a broader set of self-interested and antisocial attitudes that are present among a substantial minority of the U.S. population."

He then argues that the "broader constellation of transgressive and antisocial attitudes among a subsection of the public is an important force behind rising disregard for democratic norms."

Clearly, a sense of isolation, actual isolation, the breakdown of the family, the rise of opiates, the disappearance of associations, a nation "bowling alone" and "coming apart," have all played a role in creating an antisocial constituency. This very constituency has produced some of the strongest Trump supporters and backing for the so-called alt-right. As Howe writes, "Those with a high-school education or less are substantially more likely than those with a college degree to express skeptical views about democracy as well as tolerance of various antisocial behaviors, by variances that range from 5 to 30 percentage points across the questions."

Few people have looked at these issues as long and as hard as Ronald Inglehart, a political scientist at the University of Michigan. In "The Danger of Deconsolidation: How Much Should We Worry?" (published alongside the Foa-Mounk essay in the July 2016 issue of the *Journal of Democracy*), Inglehart raises this question:

What makes the United States so distinctive? One reason may be that in recent years U.S. democracy has become appallingly dysfunctional. It suffers from 1) virtual paralysis at the top, as exemplified by the willingness of Congress to shut down the federal government, regardless of the damage to the country's credit, after failing to get its way via normal procedures in a budget standoff with the White House; 2) massive increases in income inequality—greater than those found in any other established democracy, with most of the population's real income declining during the past few decades despite substantial economic growth; and 3) the disproportionate and growing political influence of billionaires, as money plays a greater role in U.S. politics than in almost any other democracy.

The economic boom in the post–World War II years "produced rising security and an intergenerational shift toward self-expression values," Inglehart wrote, but "in recent decades most advanced industrial societies have experienced economic stagnation, rising unemployment coupled with massive immigration, and the worst recession since the Great Depression of the 1930s."

The resulting "high levels of existential insecurity," Inglehart argues, "are conducive to authoritarianism, xenophobia, and rejection of new cultural norms. The economic stagnation and rising inequality of recent decades have led to increasing support for authoritarian, xenophobic political candidates, from Marine le Pen in France to Donald Trump in the United States."

While the contemporary explosion of right-wing populism is a recent phenomenon, its roots go deeper, best captured by Daniel Bell in his 1972 essay "The Cultural Contradictions of Capitalism," which foreshadowed the Trump era.

American capitalism, Bell wrote, "has lost its traditional legitimacy which was based on a moral system of reward, rooted in a Protestant sanctification of work. It has substituted in its place a hedonism which promises a material ease and luxury, yet shies away from all the historic implications which a 'voluptuary system'—and all its social permissiveness and libertinism—implies."

The conflict between "the principles of economics and economizing" and a culture "rooted in a return to instinctual modes" has produced a "disjunction which is the historic crisis of Western society. This cultural contradiction, in the long run, is the deepest challenge to the society."

For the moment, the Republican Party has become the main battleground for the struggle over authoritarianism, xenophobia, and the erosion of received standards.

At the Yale conference, Daniel Ziblatt, a professor of government at Harvard, warned that Trump and other right-wing leaders have breached traditional political boundaries that serve as "the soft guardrails of democracy." The two "master norms," in Ziblatt's view, are mutual toleration—that is, the acceptance of "the basic legitimacy of our opponents"—and institutional forbearance, or the responsible exercise of power by those in office.

Both Trump's detractors and his supporters recognize that he has flouted countless rules—and revels in doing so. On Monday, Senator John McCain, awarded the Liberty Medal by the National Constitution Center in Philadelphia, challenged Trump on this score: "To fear the world we have organized and led for three-quarters of a century, to abandon the ideals we have advanced around the globe, to refuse the obligations of international leadership and our duty to remain 'the last best hope of earth' for the sake of some half-baked, spurious nationalism cooked up by people who would rather find scapegoats than solve problems is as unpatriotic as an attachment to any other tired dogma of the past that Americans consigned to the ash heap of history."

Mounk and Ziblatt, writing for Vox in March 2016, made the case that "Trump isn't a fascist; he's a demagogue." Their conclusion, however, was that Trump's demagoguery does not make him any "less dangerous." Instead, Trump and politicians like him are "a profound threat to the survival of democratic politics."

Politicians in the Trump mold "wreck the informal rules of civility that democracies require to survive. Once voters are activated along violent lines and fervently believe the myths propagated by the demagogue, the dam is broken; the ordinary rules of democratic politics no longer apply, and there is no telling what might come next."

Timothy Snyder, a historian at Yale and the author of *Bloodlands* and *Black Earth* (and also a contributor to the *New York Times*), was a participant at the conference at Yale. He introduces his most recent book, *On Tyranny*, this way: "The Founding Fathers tried to protect us from the threat they knew, the tyranny that overcame ancient democracy. Today, our political order faces new threats, not unlike the totalitarianism of the twentieth century. We are no wiser than the Europeans who saw democracy yield to fascism, Nazism, or communism. Our one advantage is that we might learn from their experience. Now is a good time to do so."

Writing in 2012, well before the advent of Trump, three economists, Luigi Guiso, Helios Herrera, and Massimo Morelli, argued that the populist political tradition itself is based, first, on "promises of redistribution to the masses" and, second, on "concealment of government budget constraints from the voters." Promising redistribution to the masses and concealing government budget constraints was the essence of Trump's campaign strategy, as he promised to build a multibillion-dollar wall "which Mexico will pay for"; to repeal Obamacare and replace it with "health care which will expand choice, increase access, lower costs & provide better care"; to preserve Medicare; and to enact a gigantic tax cut for the middle class. So far, Trump has failed to fulfill any of these promises, boxed in by the reality of "government budget constraints."

Paul Waldman, writing in the *Washington Post* on October 17, summed up Trump's approach to veracity and to reality itself: "Trump takes his own particular combination of ignorance, bluster and malice, and sets it off like a nuclear bomb of misinformation. The fallout spreads throughout the country, and no volume of corrections and fact checks can stop it. It wasn't even part of a thought-out strategy, just a loathsome impulse that found its way out of the president's mouth to spread far and wide."

Trump's recklessness is disturbing enough on its own. But what makes it especially threatening is that much of the public—well beyond the 40 percent of the electorate that has shown itself to be unshakable in its devotion to the president—seems to be slowly accommodating itself to its daily dose of the Trump reality show, accepting the rhetorical violence that Trump inflicts on basic standards of truth as the new normal.

11

President Trump Is the Enemy of Their Enemies

The political success or failure of the Trump administration will be determined in large part by the answer to a simple question: Is Donald Trump's ability to give voice to the anger and resentment of his constituents adequate to offset his broken promises and what his enemies trumpet as his failure to improve the lives of those who voted for him?

No one is more aware of this issue than President Trump himself. His strategy for dealing with it was on full display last week after Congress delayed action on his bill to replace Obamacare—a prime example of legislation that will inflict costs on his own supporters.

At an open-air rally in Harrisburg, Pennsylvania, on Saturday that was timed as a counterstrike to the White House Correspondents' Association dinner, Trump pounded home his core message—that no matter what he does and no matter what Washington tries to do to him, he and he alone is on the people's side.

"A large group of Hollywood celebrities and Washington media are consoling each other in a hotel ballroom in our nation's capital

This article first appeared in *The New York Times* on May 4, 2017. Copyright © 2017 by Thomas Edsall and The New York Times Company. All rights reserved.

right now," Trump said. Looking out at his audience, with its Make America Great Again caps and its Deplorable Lives Matter T-shirts, Trump made the contrast between his people and Washington's even more direct: "I could not possibly be more thrilled than to be 100 miles away from Washington's swamp, spending my evening with all of you and with a much, much larger crowd and much better people."

His goal, of course, was not only to ally himself with the crowd against the black-tie-wearing media celebrating at the Washington Hilton but to goad and troll his opponents.

Many liberal Democrats think that Trump's taunting rhetoric will soon wear thin. According to this view, as decent jobs increasingly demand college degrees, as automation continues to decimate manufacturing employment, and as voters lose key benefits of the liberal welfare state (pared-down health coverage under a new Republican program, for example), support for Trump will fade away.

"Trump campaigned as a champion of rural America and small and midsize Rust Belt cities, but—much like his proposed Obamacare repeal—his budget brings the hammer down on the very people who put him in office," Tim Murphy wrote on March 16 in *Mother Jones*.

Murphy may be proved prescient. But there are a number of ways for Trump to maintain support among his voters without delivering the tangible economic or social benefits he promised.

First of all, the bulk of Trump's supporters have nowhere else to go, nor do they want to go anywhere. They experience themselves as living in a different world from liberals and Democrats.

Their animosity toward the Left, and the Left's animosity toward them, is entrenched.

Trump's basic approach—speaking the unspeakable—is expressive, not substantive. His inflammatory, aggressive language captures and channels the grievances of red America, but the specific grievances often feel less important than the primordial, mocking incivility with which they are expressed. In this way, Trump does not necessarily need to deliver concrete goods because he is saying with electric intensity what his supporters have long wanted to say themselves.

"President Trump reminds distrustful citizens of liberal institutions' disinterest in, and disrespect for, challenges in their own lives," Arthur Lupia, a political scientist at the University of Michigan, wrote in response to my inquiry about Trump's appeal.

In a paper that was published last month, Alan Abramowitz and Steven Webster, political scientists at Emory, describe just how much ideological enmity is driving the mutual dislike of Republicans and Democrats for each other.

Instead of the type of conflict "largely based off of tribal affiliations," Abramowitz and Webster find that "the rise of negative affect and incivility in American politics is closely connected with the rise of ideological polarization among the public as well as among political elites. Democrats and Republicans dislike each other today because they disagree with each other about many issues and especially about the fundamental question of the role of government in American society. It is very hard to disagree without being disagreeable when there are so many issues on which we disagree and the disagreements on many of these issues are so deep."

More succinctly, they write, "Rational dislike of the other party may be more difficult to overcome than irrational dislike."

In a recent paper, "Voter Decision-Making with Polarized Choices," Jon C. Rogowski, a political scientist at Harvard, found that the extremity of Trump's language and stances effectively helps ensure continued support from Republican voters: "When the candidates are relatively divergent, there is virtually no chance that partisans will cross party lines and vote for the candidate of the opposite party."

The near certainty that partisans will not switch to the opposition gives Trump an unexpected level of freedom in his policy choices. As Rogowski put it, "High levels of ideological conflict lead partisan voters to make decisions that place increased emphasis on their partisan ties, and less emphasis on the relative degree of congruence between their policy views and the candidates' platforms."

In an email, Rogowski elaborated: "Most Americans are sorted into one of the two major-party camps, and their party membership is an important part of their identities. For Americans who identify as

Republicans, voting for a Democratic candidate would be inconsistent with their identity—and the same goes for Democratic-identifiers considering a vote for a Republican candidate."

In this environment, Rogowski continued, "Trump can more or less count on continued support from Republican identifiers and has some freedom of choice on policy issues."

In other words, Trump can go either left or right as he betrays his campaign promises—as long as his followers believe that he is standing with them and is against what they're against.

There are also more subtle changes working to Trump's advantage.

Just as partisan ideological divisions and animosities are starker and starker, so too are divisions in the ways that men and women conduct their daily lives in red and blue regions of the United States.

Trump has capitalized on a cultural schism that has long been the focus of the work of Ron Lesthaeghe and Lisa Neidert, demographers at the University of Michigan Population Studies Center. They recently extended their demographic research into the 2016 election.

In "Spatial Aspects of the American 'Culture War': The Two Dimensions of US Family Demography and the Presidential Elections, 1968–2016," the authors write, "The map of the American 'Culture War' is not only in evidence in the local voting patterns, but just as markedly so in its family demography."

Voting for Democratic presidential candidates, Lesthaeghe and Neidert found, correlates with a number of key demographic variables: an increase in the percentage of white, non-Hispanic women between the ages of twenty-five and thirty-four who have never married; abortions per one thousand live births; older mothers (age at first birth of twenty-eight or over); and the percentage of households with same- or different-sex cohabitants.

Democratic states and counties are further along in the "second demographic transition" (SDT) described in an earlier paper by Lesthaeghe, which I have cited before.

Lesthaeghe writes,

The SDT starts in the 1960s with a series of multifaceted revolutions. First, there was the contraceptive revolution, with the introduction of hormonal contraception and far more efficient IUDs; second, there was the sexual revolution, with declining ages at first sexual intercourse; and third, there was the sex revolution, questioning the sole breadwinner household model and the gendered division of labor that accompanied it. These three "revolutions" fit within the framework of an overall rejection of authority, the assertion of individual freedom of choice (autonomy), and an overhaul of the normative structure. The overall outcome of these shifts with respect to fertility was the postponement of childbearing: mean ages at first parenthood rise again, opportunities for childbearing are lost due to higher divorce rates, the share of childless ever-partnered women increases, and higher parity births (four or more) become rare.

The demographic constituency described by Lesthaeghe is the liberal, urban, cosmopolitan, well-educated elite, embodied, in many respects, not only by Hillary Clinton but by much of official Washington—the attendees at the White House Correspondents' Association dinner so conspicuously shunned by Trump.

At the end of their recent essay, Lesthaeghe and Neidert ask, "Can we conclude that an era of conservative backlash has been inaugurated by the election of Trump?"

Their answer is that it's too early to tell. They note that while issues change with each election, "the relative positions of states have been very stable since the mid-1990s and very predictable on the basis of the SDT pattern at the onset. Very much the same holds for counties."

The "composite SDT index" has been "the best predictor of the presidential voting outcomes at the county level" for the last five campaigns, as figure 11.1, which provides data for the fifty states, shows.

There is a negative correlation between the advance of the SDT and the percentage voting Republican. The strength of this correlation grew steadily from −0.149 in 1968 when Nixon was the candidate to −0.830 in 2016 when Trump was the candidate.

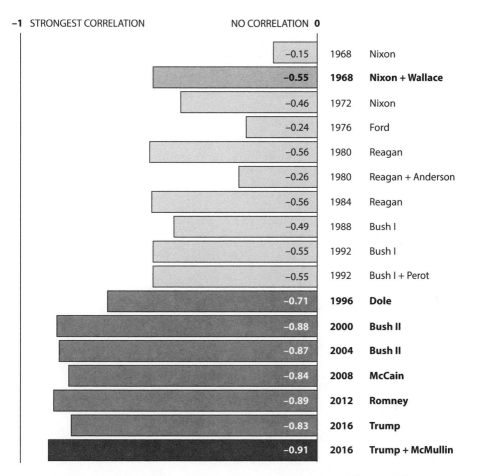

−1 STRONGEST CORRELATION   NO CORRELATION **0**

−0.15	1968	Nixon
−0.55	**1968**	**Nixon + Wallace**
−0.46	1972	Nixon
−0.24	1976	Ford
−0.56	1980	Reagan
−0.26	1980	Reagan + Anderson
−0.56	1984	Reagan
−0.49	1988	Bush I
−0.55	1992	Bush I
−0.55	1992	Bush I + Perot
−0.71	**1996**	**Dole**
−0.88	**2000**	**Bush II**
−0.87	**2004**	**Bush II**
−0.84	**2008**	**McCain**
−0.89	**2012**	**Romney**
−0.83	**2016**	**Trump**
−0.91	**2016**	**Trump + McMullin**

FIGURE 11.1. CONSERVATIVE VALUES DOMINATE. In the 1990s, the Republican electorate began moving sharply toward conservative family values. Researchers find an increasingly strong negative correlation between the Republican electorate and a more liberal approach to family values and practices. The most conservative third-party candidates, when paired with the Republican candidate, heighten the effect.
Source: Ron Lesthaeghe and Lisa Neidert, University of Michigan Population Studies Center. From The New York Times. © 2017 The New York Times Company. All rights reserved. Used under license.

Figure 11.2 shows the actual lineup of states in 2016, from reddest (Utah and Wyoming) at the top to bluest (Massachusetts) at the bottom.

What can we learn about Trump and the persistence of his appeal from research about intensified partisan animosity, the divide over

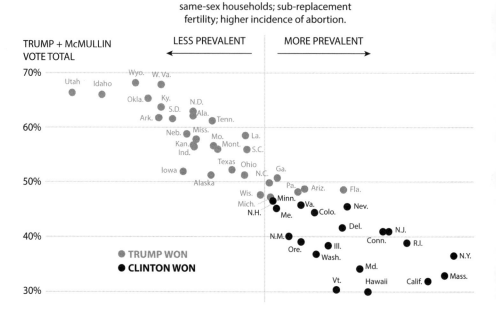

FIGURE 11.2. THE CULTURAL DIVIDE AND THE VOTE. The lower the prevalence of post-1960s family values and practices in a state, the more likely the state's voters were to support either Trump or the fringe anti-Trump Republican Evan McMullin in 2016.
Source: Ron Lesthaeghe and Lisa Neidert, University of Michigan Population Studies Center. From The New York Times. © 2017 The New York Times Company. All rights reserved. Used under license.

the SDT, Trump's fervid rally audiences, the White House Correspondents' Association dinner, and political identity?

Over the past fifty years, overarching and underlying conflicts about morality, family, autonomy, religious conviction, fairness, and even patriotism have been forced into two relatively weak vessels, the Democratic Party and the Republican Party. The political system is not equipped to resolve these social and cultural conflicts, which produce a gamut of emotions, often outside our conscious awareness. Threatening issues—conflicts over race, immigration, sexuality, and many other questions that cut to the core of how we see ourselves and the people around us—cannot be contained in ordinary political speech, even as these issues dominate our political decision-making.

It is Trump's willingness to violate the boundaries of conventional discourse that has granted him immunity to mainstream criticism. Pretty much everything he does that goes overboard helps him. He is given a free hand by those who feel in their gut that he is fighting their fight—that he is their leader and their defender. As the enemy of their enemies, President Trump is their friend.

12

The End of the Left and the Right as We Knew Them

By now it has become quite clear that conservative parties in Europe and the United States have been gaining strength from white voters who have been mobilized around issues related to nationalism—resistance to open borders and to third-world immigration. In the United States, this development has been exacerbated by ongoing conservative recruitment on issues of race that has reinforced opposition to immigration. On the liberal side, the Democratic Party and the center-left European parties have been allied in favor of globalization, if we define globalization as receptivity to open borders, the expansion of local and nationalistic perspectives, and support for a less rigid social order and for liberal cultural, immigration, and trade policies. In recent decades, these parties, both in Europe and in the United States, have begun to include and reflect the views of large numbers of well-educated elites—relatively affluent knowledge- or creative-class workers—in alliance with predominantly nonwhite minority constituencies of the less well off.

This article first appeared in *The New York Times* on June 22, 2017. Copyright © 2017 by Thomas Edsall and The New York Times Company. All rights reserved.

Ewald Engelen, a social scientist at the University of Amsterdam, argues that the old paradigm of a Left arguing for strong government intervention and a Right preferring market solutions to social problems has been replaced. "Today," he told *Al Jazeera*, "we see that the dominant dichotomy has become globalism versus nationalism."

Stewart Patrick, the director of the International Institutions and Global Governance Program at the Council on Foreign Relations, elaborated on these trends in an email: "The most salient political division today is not between conservatives and liberals in the United States or social democrats in the United Kingdom and France, but between nationalists and globalists. The victory of the Leave campaign in Britain, the triumph of Donald Trump, and the unprecedented success of Marine Le Pen's National Front (albeit in a losing effort) were underpinned by economic and cultural anxiety that transcended traditional ideological lines—and a rejection of conventional parties and a political establishment that had too long ignored those concerns."

In the United States, Sean McElwee, a policy analyst at the liberal think tank Demos, and Jason McDaniel, a professor of political science at San Francisco State University, examined data from American National Election Studies and reported in the *Nation* that "Trump accelerated a realignment in the electorate around racism, across several different measures of racial animus—and that it helped him win. By contrast, we found little evidence to suggest individual economic distress benefited Trump. The American political system is sorting so that racial progressivism and economic progressivism are aligned in the Democratic Party and racial conservatism and economic conservatism are aligned in the Republican Party."

In their essay, McElwee and McDaniel graphed data documenting their findings, which is reproduced in figure 12.1. White voters who supported Trump were decidedly strong on measures of anti-Black affect and hostility to the integration of immigrants into the population of the United States.

Elections over the past two years here and in Britain, Austria, France, and the Netherlands have demonstrated the depth of this

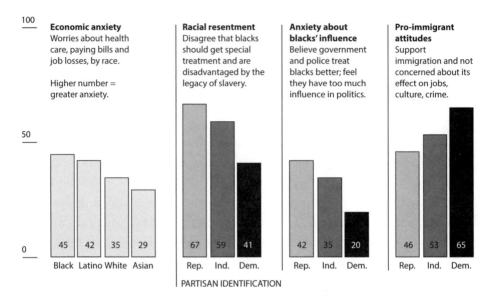

FIGURE 12.1. DID RACIAL BIAS TIP THE PRESIDENTIAL ELECTION? A national survey of voting-age Americans found that racial resentment, more than economic anxiety, influenced the presidential election. The survey period was both before and after the election; respondents' average answers are shown here on a scale from zero to 100.
Source: Bill Marsh, Analysis of the American National Election Studies 2016 survey by Jason McDaniel and Sean McElwee. From The New York Times. © 2017 The New York Times Company. All rights reserved. Used under license.

transformation of the organized Left and the organized Right. Whatever the outcome of the voting in a particular country, a clear pattern appears. The emerging or nascent partisan divide has a strong cultural subtext: for or against "traditional values"; young versus old; rural versus urban; the college educated versus those without degrees; blue collar versus white collar; us versus them; whites versus nonwhites; immigrant versus native born; European versus non-European.

The rise of an affluent Left—sometimes triumphant, sometimes not—can be seen in the victories of Emmanuel Macron and his new La République en Marche (Republic on the Move) party in France; in the surprise showing of Jeremy Corbyn's Labour Party in the June 8 parliamentary elections in Britain; in the composition of the electorate that unsuccessfully backed Hillary Clinton; and in the victories of Alexander Van der Bellen, president of Austria, and of Mark Rutte's People's Party for Freedom and Democracy in the Netherlands.

In much of Europe, although not in Britain, the growth of the populist Right has devastated once-powerful labor and social democratic parties on the left. In the Austrian presidential election, for example, the success of the far-right Freedom Party resulted in a fourth-place showing for the Social Democratic candidate. In the French parliamentary elections this month, the ruling Socialist Party saw its 280 seats dwindle to 29 out of 577. In the Netherlands, the number of seats held in Parliament by the Dutch Labor Party fell from 38 to 9 after the March election.

On the surface, the success of the British Labour Party in the elections two weeks ago would appear to stand apart. But Labour's gains were not based on improved margins in traditionally Labour-leaning constituencies. Corbyn's Labour Party actually lost ground on its home turf, but it more than made up for those setbacks by prevailing in Conservative constituencies.

The *Financial Times* has documented a steady decline in class-based voting in Britain. In 1987, the British middle class voted for the Conservative Party by 40 points more than the national average, while the working class voted for the Labor Party by 32 points more than the national average—a 72-point spread. By 2017, the spread had dropped to 15 points. Once a Tory stronghold, the British middle class now splits its vote evenly.

A parallel voting pattern emerged in the case of education, as Labour Party gains were strongest in districts with high percentages of voters with college and advanced degrees. The outcome of the contest for a parliamentary seat in the Kensington section of London has become a symbol of the election. "Labour wins Kensington—UK's richest constituency—for first time," declared the June 9 *New Statesman* headline.

In other words, the Labour Party in England can no longer be considered a labor party in the traditional sense of representing the working class. In this respect, there is a growing demographic convergence between the Democratic Party, the Labour Party in England, Macron's En Marche in France, the voters who elected Van der Bellen president of Austria, and those who voted for the People's Party for Freedom and Democracy in the Netherlands.

In France, Macron's margin of victory over Marine Le Pen grew larger as the average income and average level of education in a community rose—as the average percentage of working-class voters declined. The *Financial Times* noted that the pattern in France was echoed in the 2016 Brexit referendum, in the presidential election here, and in the recent Dutch election: "In each of these plebiscites, education emerged as the strongest predictor of votes for a right populist option, where the less educated chose it more often than those with degrees."

The *Financial Times* could have added Austria to this list. The presidential election there in May 2016 pitted Van der Bellen, the center-left candidate, against the hard-right populist Norbert Hofer. Polls showed that Van der Bellen won decisively among the well educated and the better paid, while Hofer won workers and the less well educated in a landslide. The election in the Netherlands was also emblematic of the disruption of traditional partisan divisions. Koen Damhuis, a Dutch sociologist at the European University Institute in Florence, said in an interview with *Al Jazeera* that this new dichotomy has been problematic for all traditional parties—"some of them haven't decided yet how they want to position themselves"—but especially so for labor: "They are visibly confused."

According to Stewart Patrick of the Council on Foreign Relations, globalization and the Great Recession of 2007–9 have resulted in a "pervasive anxiety" that provides "fertile grounds for populists who promise a reassertion of control and national sovereignty, including over borders, as well as a renewed focus on those left behind in the global economy."

Patrick shares with a number of internationalists the hope that Macron and En Marche represent a viable political solution to contemporary conflicts that could be applied in other countries:

"Macron's genius has been to argue that he can thread the political needle, by embracing globalization and reinforcing social protections to compensate those exposed to its downside. In the process, he has obliterated traditional parties of the left and the right, while promising a synthesis tailor made for the twenty-first century. If he can bring it off, he will become a model for other leaders to follow—including in the United States."

In the 2016 election, as issues of race and immigration became more salient, the percentage of Trump and Clinton support among voters making more than $50,000 was virtually the same. If anything, those at the top making $200,000 or more tilted slightly to Clinton.

Even more striking, among all voters, Clinton won 52 percent to 42 percent among the college educated, while Trump carried those without degrees 51 percent to 44 percent.

There is no question that in the days after Trump's victory, Bernie Sanders's call on *CBS This Morning* to revive the New Deal origins of the Democratic Party—"I come from the white working class, and I am deeply humiliated that the Democratic Party cannot talk to the people where I came from"—was powerful. A candidate making that appeal, however, and seeking to build a broad majority biracial coalition, must in fact have broad biracial appeal. As of now, Sanders is far from personifying broad majority biracial appeal. Worse, existing Democratic candidate recruitment and nomination processes have paid insufficient attention to the selection of candidates who are competent to build bridges across America's immense cultural gaps.

Instead of trying to bridge these gaps, as two of my *Times* colleagues, Alexander Burns and Jonathan Martin, wrote earlier this week, there is a "growing tension" between the Democratic Party's "ascendant militant wing and Democrats competing in conservative-leaning terrain."

The "ascendant militant wing"—a colorful, if controversial, description of the Sanders-Warren wing of the party—has the moral high ground within Democratic ranks, but the votes they want the party to seek are those of some of the least reachable constituencies—white men and women whose views on immigration, race, and political correctness are in direct conflict with liberal idealism. It would be an extraordinary challenge to get these particular voters to join with minorities and progressive activists.

Peter Beinart, writing in the *Atlantic*, addresses the way this plays out. He argues that party leaders have to draw the line on issues dear to the heart of the Left: "Liberals must take seriously Americans' yearning for social cohesion. To promote both mass immigration and greater economic redistribution, they must convince more native-born white Americans that immigrants will not weaken the bonds of national identity."

In practical terms, Beinart writes, "it means celebrating America's diversity less, and its unity more."

The hard part "is backing tough immigration enforcement so that path to citizenship doesn't become a magnet that entices more immigrants to enter the U.S. illegally."

Beinart cites Karen Stenner's 2005 book, *The Authoritarian Dynamic*, in which she wrote, "Exposure to difference, talking about difference, and applauding difference—the hallmarks of liberal democracy—are the surest ways to aggravate those who are innately intolerant, and to guarantee the increased expression of their predispositions in manifestly intolerant attitudes and behaviors. Paradoxically, then, it would seem that we can best limit intolerance of difference by parading, talking about, and applauding our sameness."

Americans, Beinart contends, "know that liberals celebrate diversity. They're less sure that liberals celebrate unity. And Obama's ability to effectively do the latter probably contributed to the fact that he—a black man with a Muslim-sounding name—twice won a higher percentage of the white vote than did Hillary Clinton."

What we are seeing now is the replacement of class-based politics, a trend apparent in the United States and Europe. This gives us a more racialized and xenophobic politics, on one hand, and a politics capitalizing on increasing levels of education and open-mindedness in the electorate, on the other. If the building of a viable left coalition is possible, it is likely to require some thoughtful and humane co-optation in the form of deference to our limits and boundaries.

13

Trump Says Jump. His Supporters Ask, How High?

In the Donald Trump era, Republicans have been revising their views on right and wrong.

In 2011, the Public Religion Research Institute (PRRI) asked voters if "an elected official who commits an immoral act in their personal life can still behave ethically and fulfill their duties in their public and professional life."

White evangelical Protestants were the least forgiving. Sixty-one percent said such a politician could not "behave ethically," twice the 30 percent who felt that such a politician could manage it (figure 13.1).

Every other religious group was less judgmental. Catholics: 49 percent no, 42 percent yes; white mainline Protestants: 44 percent no, 38 percent yes; the religiously unaffiliated: 26 percent no, 63 percent yes.

Are the moral convictions of white evangelical Protestants writ in stone? Apparently not.

Five years later, in October 2016, PRRI asked the same question. The percentage of white evangelical Protestants who said that a poli-

This article first appeared in *The New York Times* on September 14, 2017. Copyright © 2017 by Thomas Edsall and The New York Times Company. All rights reserved.

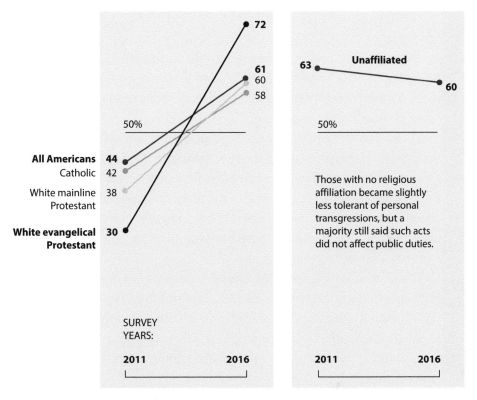

FIGURE 13.1. POLITICIANS' PERSONAL TRANSGRESSIONS? Moving On from That. In just five years, Americans, particularly evangelicals, became much more accepting of immoral personal behavior by politicians. Above are the percentages who said private immoral conduct did not prevent elected officials from fulfilling their public duties.
Source: PRRI. From The New York Times. © 2017 The New York Times Company. All rights reserved. Used under license.

tician who commits an immoral act in their personal life could still behave ethically shot up from 30 percent to 72 percent. The percentage saying such a politician could not serve ethically plunged from 63 percent to 20 percent.

"In a head-spinning reversal," Robert P. Jones, the CEO of PRRI, wrote in the July 2017 issue of the *Atlantic*, "white evangelicals went from being the least likely to the most likely group to agree that a candidate's personal immorality has no bearing on his performance in public office."

What happened in the interim? The answer is obvious: the advent of Trump.

There is more to this phenomenon than evangelical hypocrisy. Many Republican voters, including self-identified strong conservatives, are ready and willing to shift to the left if they're told that that's the direction Trump is moving.

Michael Barber and Jeremy C. Pope, political scientists at Brigham Young University, reported in their recent paper "Does Party Trump Ideology? Disentangling Party and Ideology in America" that many Republican voters are "malleable to the point of innocence, and self-reported expressions of ideological fealty are quickly abandoned for policies that—once endorsed by a well-known party leader—run contrary to that expressed ideology."

Those most willing to adjust their positions on ten issues ranging from abortion to guns to taxes are firm Republicans, Trump loyalists, self-identified conservatives, and low-information Republicans.

The Barber-Pope study suggests that, for many Republicans, partisan identification is more a tribal affiliation than an ideological commitment.

Many partisans are, in effect, more aligned with the leader of their party than with the principles of the party. (Although Barber and Pope confined their study to Republicans, they note that Democrats may "react in similar ways given the right set of circumstances.")

President Trump's ability to slide his supporters to the left or right will face a major challenge if he lives up to what Democratic congressional leaders described on Wednesday night as the beginnings of an agreement to prevent the deportation of nearly eight hundred thousand undocumented young immigrants and to strengthen border security without building a wall.

Barber and Pope's paper expands on recent work by David E. Broockman and Daniel M. Butler, "The Causal Effects of Elite Position-Taking on Voter Attitudes," which was published in the *American Journal of Political Science*. Broockman and Butler, who are political scientists at the Stanford Graduate School of Business and the University of California–San Diego, respectively, found that "voters often adopted the positions legislators took, even when legislators offered little justification. Moreover, voters did not evaluate their legislators more negatively when representatives took positions these voters had previously opposed, again regardless of whether legislators provided justifications. The findings are consistent with theories suggesting voters often defer to politicians' policy judgments."

Along similar lines, Christopher Achen and Larry Bartels, political scientists at Princeton and Vanderbilt, respectively, reject traditional views of democratic elections in their new book, *Democracy for Realists: Why Elections Do Not Produce Responsive Government.* Achen and Bartels argue that the "familiar ideal of thoughtful citizens steering the ship of state from the voting booth is fundamentally misguided." They claim, "In the conventional view, democracy begins with the voters. Ordinary people have preferences about what their government should do. They choose leaders who will do those things, or they enact their preferences directly in referendums. In either case, what the majority wants becomes government policy—a highly attractive prospect."

Achen and Bartels dismiss this "folk theory of democracy" to argue that the more realistic view is that "citizens' perceptions of parties' policy stands and their own policy views are significantly colored by their party preferences. Even on purely factual questions with clear right answers, citizens are sometimes willing to believe the opposite if it makes them feel better about their partisanship and vote choices."

They conclude "that group and partisan loyalties, not policy preferences or ideologies, are fundamental in democratic politics."

The Barber-Pope study took advantage of Trump's exceptional propensity during the campaign to take multiple, often contradictory stands on issues. This allowed them to cite two opposing stands Trump had taken on a series of issues in order to test the willingness of Republican voters to follow Trump's position to the left or right.

The authors conducted a survey with YouGov of 1,300 voters broken into five subgroups, each of which was asked ten questions using a research design that employed "both 'conservative' and 'liberal' Trump cues."

For example:

1. "Do you support or oppose increasing the minimum wage to over $10 an hour?"
2. "Donald Trump has said that he supports this policy. How about you? Do you support or oppose increasing the minimum wage to over $10 an hour?"
3. "Donald Trump has said that he opposes this policy. How about you? Do you support or oppose increasing the minimum wage to over $10 an hour?"
4. "Congressional Republicans have said that they support this policy. How about you? Do you support or oppose increasing the minimum wage to over $10 an hour?"
5. "Congressional Republicans have said that they oppose this policy. How about you? Do you support or oppose increasing the minimum wage to over $10 an hour?"

The same variation was used on nine other contentious policy questions: increasing taxes on the wealthy, abortion, immigration, guns on school property, the Iran nuclear deal, universal health care, background checks for gun purchases, climate change, and funding Planned Parenthood. The survey also asked respondents how much they approved of Trump, how they would describe their own ideology on a five-point scale, and eight questions to rank their political knowledge.

Barber and Pope found that people who identified themselves as strong Republicans were among the most malleable voters. When told Trump had adopted a liberal stance, these voters moved decisively to the left; when told Trump had taken a conservative position, they moved sharply to the right, as figure 13.2 shows.

The same patterns emerged in the case of voters who strongly approve of Trump and among voters who describe themselves as "strong conservatives," as I mentioned earlier. This last point suggests that instead of calling themselves strong conservatives, these voters are more accurately described as strong partisans.

This, in turn, helps explain why most elected Republican officials accepted Trump's equivocal response to the white supremacist marchers in Charlottesville, Virginia, last month.

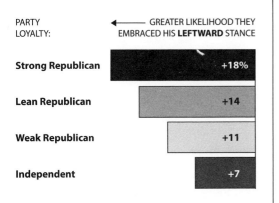

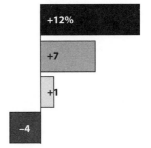

WHEN TRUMP TOOK A LIBERAL POSITION
Republicans who were informed of Trump's liberal positions were more likely to endorse his leftward stance than Republicans who were not informed of what Trump had said.

Trump's leftward sway was highest among die-hard Republicans.

WHEN HE TOOK A CONSERVATIVE POSITION
Likewise, Trump tugged Republicans' views rightward when he took conservative stances.

Again, he had more sway with die-hards.

PARTY LOYALTY: ◄────── GREATER LIKELIHOOD THEY EMBRACED HIS **LEFTWARD** STANCE

GREATER LIKELIHOOD THEY ──────► EMBRACED HIS **RIGHTWARD** STANCE

Party Loyalty	Leftward	Rightward
Strong Republican	+18%	+12%
Lean Republican	+14	+7
Weak Republican	+11	+1
Independent	+7	–4

Independents were, on average, immune to Trump's sway on conservative issues.

FIGURE 13.2. TUGGING REPUBLICANS LEFT AND RIGHT. President Trump has proved adept at getting Republicans to go along with his views, even if they clash with party dogma. Here's what happened in 2016 and the early months of his presidency, according to researchers.
Sources: Michael Barber and Jeremy C. Pope, Brigham Young University. From The New York Times. © 2017 The New York Times Company. All rights reserved. Used under license.

Nathaniel Persily, a professor of law and political science at Stanford, described his surprise at the docility of Republican officials in an email: "While I and others had written extensively about the partisan tribalism of both elites and the mass public, I guess I would have expected greater defections by Republicans in the wake of Charlottesville."

Persily went on to argue a related point: "To some extent, I think that each Republican realizes that the electoral and political costs of opposing the president may always exceed the benefits—no matter what the issue."

The extraordinary approval ratings Trump gets from his core voters further reinforce the unwillingness of Republican elected officials to defy him. Among Republicans who voted for Trump in the primaries, his approval rating in a *Wall Street Journal* / NBC News poll earlier this month stood at 98 percent. Among Republicans who did not vote for Trump in the primaries, his approval rating stood at 66 percent.

I asked both Barber and Pope of Brigham Young what their thoughts on American politics are now that Trump has been in office eight months.

Pope argued in an email that there has been too much emphasis on polarization and not enough on partisanship.

While elites—elected officials and party activists—are ideologically polarized, the best the general public "can manage is a kind of tribal partisanship that does not really reflect the content of the elite discussion," Pope wrote. "Citizens pick a team, but they don't naturally think like the team leadership does. And when Trump tells Republicans to think in a new way, lots of people happily adopt that new position because they were never that committed to the old ideas anyway. They're just committed to the label."

Republican leaders in the House and Senate, in Pope's view, are struggling to come to terms with a hard truth: that much of the Republican electorate "is not really interested in the conservative project as expressed by Paul Ryan or Mitch McConnell or the Freedom Caucus. They are hostile to immigrants and rather nationalist in outlook, but not consistently market-oriented or libertarian in their thinking the way that some Republican elites continue to be."

In a separate email, Barber wrote that the commonplace phrase "All politics is identity politics" is a good description "of the state of the Republican Party, and the Democratic Party to a degree."

He noted that a large corporate tax cut "isn't really an ideological priority for much of the rank and file" of the Republican Party, but "if it means that their side has 'won,' then they are in favor of it. More broadly, I think it shows us that teamsmanship is much more important than any particular policy agenda."

What can we take away from all of this?

First, Trump's base has given him considerable leeway and his strongest supporters are likely to back him when he violates Republican orthodoxy—as he did recently by agreeing to a debt ceiling strategy proposed by Democratic leaders over the objections of their Republican counterparts.

Second, the claims of ideological conservatives that a large segment of the electorate has turned to the right on policy issues is suspect at best.

Third, and most significant, if the Barber-Pope, Broockman-Daniels, and Achen-Bartels conclusions are right, American politics is less a competition of ideas and more a struggle between two teams.

In other words, insofar as elections have become primal struggles, and political competition has devolved into an atavistic spectacle, the prospect for a return to a politics of compromise and consensus approaches zero, no matter what temporary accommodations professional politicians make.

14

The Increasing Significance of the Decline of Men

At one end of the scale, men continue to dominate.

In 2016, 95.8 percent of *Fortune* 500 CEOs were male, and so were 348 of the *Forbes* 400. Of the 260 people on the *Forbes* list described as "self-made," 250 were men. Wealth—and the ability to generate more wealth—must still be considered a reliable proxy for power.

But at the other end of the scale, men of all races and ethnicities are dropping out of the workforce, abusing opioids, and falling behind women in both college attendance and graduation rates.

Since 2000, wage inequality has grown more among men than among women.

A study by the Dallas Federal Reserve published in 2014, "Middle-Skill Jobs Lost in U.S. Labor Market Polarization," found that "while women were hit much harder than men by the disappearance of middle-skill jobs, the majority of women managed to upgrade their skills and find better-paying jobs. By comparison, more than half of men who lost middle-skill jobs had to settle for lower-paying occupations."

This article first appeared in *The New York Times* on March 16, 2017. Copyright © 2017 by Thomas Edsall and The New York Times Company. All rights reserved.

From 1979 to 2007, 7 percent of men and 16 percent of women with middle-skill jobs lost their positions, according to the Dallas Fed study. Four percent of these men moved to low-skill work, and 3 percent moved to high-skill jobs. Almost all the women, 15 percent, moved into high-skill jobs, with only 1 percent moving to low-skill work.

Men whose childhood years were marked by family disruption seem to fare the worst.

In a 2016 paper, David Autor, an economist at MIT, and four coauthors measured academic and economic outcomes of brothers and sisters in Florida born in the decade between 1992 and 2002.

For boys and girls raised in two-parent households, there were only modest differences between the sexes in terms of success at school, and boys tended to earn more than their sisters in early adulthood.

Among children raised in single-parent households, however, boys performed significantly less well than their sisters in school, and their employment rate as young adults was lower. "Relative to their sisters," Autor and his collaborators wrote, "boys born to disadvantaged families"—with disadvantage measured here by mother's marital status and education—"have higher rates of disciplinary problems, lower achievement scores, and fewer high-school completions."

When the children in the study reached early adulthood, the same pattern emerged in employment: "Employment rates of young women are nearly invariant to family marital status, while the employment rates of young adult men from non-married families are eight to ten percentage points below those from married families at all income levels."

Autor and his coauthors conclude that family structure "is more consequential for the skills development and labor market outcomes of boys than girls."

The recent increase in dysfunctional behavior among non-college-educated white men correlates with the substantial increase in the rate of white nonmarital births, up from 22.2 percent in 1993 to 35.7 percent in 2014. In 1965, the white nonmarital birthrate was 3.4 percent.

At the same time, the divorce rate for college graduates has declined from 34.8 percent among those born between 1950 and 1955 to 29.9 percent among those born between 1957 and 1964. In contrast, the divorce rate for those without college degrees increased over the same period from 44.3 percent to 50.6 percent.

While marriages are breaking up more in the working class, an extensive study of divorce found that "infidelity, domestic violence, and substance abuse were the most often endorsed 'final straw' reasons" for the dissolution of marriages. These are all behaviors that men from disrupted families—who often have difficulty holding relationships together—frequently demonstrate.

For many men without college degrees, the scaffolding that underpinned their fathers' lives has been torn down. David Leege, an emeritus professor of political science at Notre Dame, wrote me by email, "The institutions they knew to process authoritatively the economic and social changes they faced in earlier times are gone or undermined—the union, the Catholic Church, the industrial bar with co-workers, the compliant wife—and what has replaced it, if anything, is an unvetted information technology that yields little truth or comfort, and nurtures anomie and anger."

David Geary, a professor of psychology at the University of Missouri, describes a vicious cycle that entraps men who either drop out of the workforce or take low-skill jobs with few prospects of improvement: "The long-term political implications of large numbers of unengaged and underemployed men are potentially very serious. Marriage typically reduces men's aggressiveness and rule breaking and focuses them on family and engagement with the community. However, if large numbers of them are not attractive as potential husbands, due to poor long-term economic prospects, then this 'civilizing' influence is lost to them. I don't know what the tipping point would be, but the potential for large-scale discontentment and destabilization increases as the proportion of these men increases."

David Buss, a professor of psychology at the University of Texas–Austin, elaborated on Geary's point in an email, stressing the lower proportion of men than women getting college degrees: "Women have strong mate preferences such that they do not want to mate or marry men who are less educated, less intelligent, and less success-ful than they are."

And this, Buss said, "creates a surplus of men" at the low end who are not going to get married.

Millions of these less well-educated men are not going to get the benefits of marriage: "Married men live longer, are less likely to become alcoholic, take drugs, commit suicide, etc."

In a phone interview a number of years ago, Richard Freeman, a Harvard economist, was prescient: "Men are really going to have to change their act or have big problems. I think of big guys from the cave days, guys who were good at lifting stuff and hunting and the things we got genetically selected out for. During the indus-trial revolution that wasn't so bad, but it's not going to be there anymore."

Asked to confirm his earlier views, Freeman wrote me that what he predicted "has occurred and continues, and perhaps is linked to the penchant for some male workers to be more favorable to right-wing populism than might have been the case."

David Deming, a professor of public policy at Harvard's Kennedy School, suggests that things are not as simple for men as "changing their act."

In a 2015 paper, "The Growing Importance of Social Skills in the Labor Market," Deming writes, "High-paying, difficult-to-automate jobs increasingly require social skills. Nearly all job growth since 1980 has been in occupations that are relatively social skill-intensive. Jobs that require high levels of analytical and math-ematical reasoning but low levels of social interaction have fared especially poorly."

What this means, according to Deming, is that "the economy-wide shift toward social skill-intensive occupations has occurred dis-proportionately among women rather than men. This is consistent with a large literature showing sex differences in social perceptive-ness and the ability to work with others."

Studies of gender differences, according to Deming, show that "females consistently score higher on tests of emotional and social intelligence. Sex differences in sociability and social perceptiveness have been shown to have biological origins, with differences appearing in infancy and higher levels of fetal testosterone associated with lower scores on tests of social intelligence."

In an email, Deming suggested two reasons that men may be reluctant to take jobs in the growing service sector. The first, he said, is that "if service sector and other 'pink collar' jobs were higher-paying and more secure (perhaps unionized), they would attract more men."

The second reason, in Deming's view, is that "many service sector jobs involve 'serving' people of higher social status. I think women are more willing to do this—for cultural or genetic reasons, who knows."

From another perspective altogether, Allan Schore, a professor of psychiatry and biobehavioral sciences at the UCLA School of Medicine, explores the slower development among boys "in right-brain attachment functions."

This "maturational delay" in brain function, Schore writes in an essay that was published earlier this year in the *Infant Mental Health Journal*, "All Our Sons: The Developmental Neurobiology and Neuroendocrinology of Boys at Risk," makes boys "more vulnerable over a longer period of time to stressors in the social environment and toxins in the physical environment that negatively impact right-brain development."

This vulnerability, in turn, makes boys more susceptible to "attention deficit hyperactivity disorder, and conduct disorders as well as the epigenetic mechanisms that can account for the recent widespread increase of these disorders in U.S. culture."

Schore argues that a major factor in rising dysfunction among boys and men in this country is the failure of the United States to provide longer periods of paid parental leave, with the result that many infants are placed in daycare when they are six weeks old.

Six weeks old, Schore writes, is "the exact time of the initiation of the postnatal testosterone surge found only in males." Schore notes that "research has documented that boys more so than girls raised in single-mother families show twice the rate of behavioral problems than do boys in two-parent families" and argues that a "mis-attuned insecure mother" can be "a source of considerable relational stress, especially when the immature male toddler is expressing high levels of dysregulated aggression or fear."

When a child is eighteen to twenty-four months old, fathers play a crucial role, Schore writes, pointing to "the male infant's attachment transactions with the father in the second year, when he is critically involved in not only androgen-controlled rough-and-tumble play but in facilitating the male (and female) toddler's aggression regulation. This same period (18–24 months) involves the initiation of a critical period of growth in the left hemisphere, and so the 'paternal attachment system' of father-son interactions would presumably forge an androgenic imprint in the toddler's evolving left-brain circuits, including the left dorsolateral prefrontal cortex, allowing for his regulation of the male toddler's testosterone-induced aggression ('terrible twos')."

What does all this suggest?

First, there are irreversible changes in the workplace, particularly the rise of jobs requiring social skills (even STEM jobs) that will continue to make it hard for men who lack those skills.

Second, male children suffer more from restricted or nonexistent parental leave policies and contemporary childcare arrangements, as well as from growing up in single-parent households.

It would be paradoxical if the right-wing takeover of the country on November 8 were to instigate significant policy initiatives to address this problem. Or perhaps not so paradoxical, given that males who are particularly conflicted about their disempowered status in American life—and who are the most loyal Donald Trump supporters—might be the ultimate beneficiaries of this kind of reform.

On September 13, 2016, in Aston, Pennsylvania, at the height of the presidential campaign, Trump, with his daughter Ivanka, who helped craft the policies as a self-described working mother, said that he would seek to make childcare expenses tax deductible for families earning less than $500,000 and called for establishing tax-free accounts to be used for childcare and child enrichment activities.

He also called for guaranteeing six weeks' maternity leave by extending unemployment insurance benefits to working mothers whose employers do not offer paid maternity leave.

"For many families in our country, childcare is now the single largest expense—even more than housing," Trump said, speaking from prepared remarks. "Our plan will bring relief to working and middle class families."

It has been a long-standing objective of right-wing regimes to push women back into traditional gender roles. Is that what's going on here? Or could it be something less pernicious and more important?

2018

The off-year congressional elections of 2018 constituted a decisive victory for the Democratic Party. Liberal discontent with the Trump administration produced a surge of support for Democrats challenging incumbent Republicans in the House, who lost forty-one seats, and control. The Senate, however, was a different story. Democrats picked up two seats but lost four, for a net loss of two.

Democratic success in taking back the House gave the party false hope that the 2020 election would be a landslide victory, a clear and explicit renunciation of Donald Trump. One reason that was not the case is that for decades, liberal economists had warned that globalization, offshoring, and roboticization were wreaking havoc on employment in the manufacturing sector, especially in the industrial Midwest—the states that had formed a blue wall, a base of support for Democratic presidential candidates. Democratic congressional majorities had done little to address the crisis facing these workers, and the result was Trump's election in 2016. The wounds, in part self-inflicted, to the Democratic Party became increasingly apparent, according to economists like MIT's David Autor and Daron Acemoglu, Harvard's Gordon Hanson, and Berkeley's David Card. The problems cited by these analysts festered and turned the 2020 contest into a much closer battle than expected.

15

Robots Can't Vote, but They Helped Elect Trump

When you look across America to see where jobs and wages have been lost to robotics, machine learning, artificial intelligence, and automation, it is the middle of the country that stands apart from the rest.

Figure 15.1, which was produced by Daron Acemoglu of MIT and Pascual Restrepo of Boston University, shows the size and scope of the region that has borne the brunt of postindustrial modernization.

It is not a coincidence that this map sheds light on President Donald Trump's Electoral College victory in 2016.

"My take is that grievances, both racial and against cosmopolitan, liberal elites, have played an important role," Acemoglu wrote me in an email. "But economic hardships, as they often do, made these fault lines more salient. Dormant grievances have become more alive."

Acemoglu argues that recent technological developments have helped drive voters to the right: "The swing to Republicans between

This article first appeared in *The New York Times* on January 11, 2018. Copyright © 2018 by Thomas Edsall and The New York Times Company. All rights reserved.

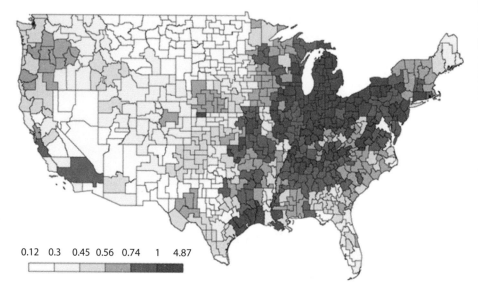

FIGURE 15.1. WHERE THE ROBOTS LIVE. Robots per one thousand workers. *Sources*: Daron Acemoglu, Massachusetts Institute of Technology, and Pascual Restrepo, Boston University. From The New York Times. © 2018 The New York Times Company. All rights reserved. Used under license.

2008 and 2016 is quite a bit stronger in commuting zones most affected by industrial robots. You don't see much of the impact of robots in prior presidential elections. So it's really a post 2008 phenomenon."

In their March 2017 paper, "Robots and Jobs: Evidence from US Labor Markets," Acemoglu and Restrepo found that the addition of "one more robot per thousand workers reduces the employment to population ratio by about 0.18–0.34 percentage points and wages by 0.25–0.5 percent."

Who are the workers forced to bear the costs of the increase in workplace robots?

According to Acemoglu and Restrepo, men take about twice as big a hit in terms of lost jobs as women do. Although both sexes suffer wage losses when robots replace people, the size of the drop in employment for women was about half that of men.

In terms of occupational sectors, the authors found that "the effects of robots concentrate in automobile manufacturing, electronics,

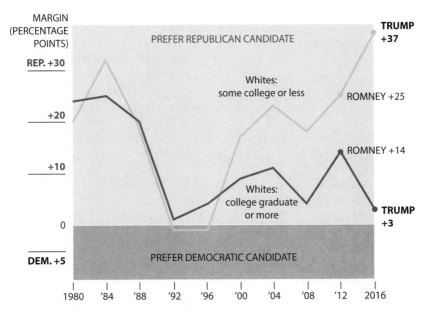

MARGIN
(PERCENTAGE
POINTS)

PREFER REPUBLICAN CANDIDATE

TRUMP
+37

REP. +30

Whites:
some college or less

ROMNEY +25

+20

ROMNEY +14

+10

Whites:
college graduate
or more

TRUMP
+3

0

DEM. +5

PREFER DEMOCRATIC CANDIDATE

1980   '84   '88   '92   '96   '00   '04   '08   '12   2016

FIGURE 15.2. HOW TRUMP CHANGED THE WHITE VOTE. Preferences of whites, by education level, in the last ten presidential elections. In 2016, less-educated whites sharply increased their support of the Republican candidate, while those with more education significantly reduced it.
Source: Pew Research Center. From The New York Times. © 2018 The New York Times Company. All rights reserved. Used under license.

metal products, chemicals, pharmaceuticals, plastic, food, glass and ceramics."

Workers without college degrees experience substantially larger wage and employment losses when exposed to competition from robots, while the same competition results in "a small and marginally significant negative effect on employment for workers with college, and no effect on employment and wages for workers with post-college degrees."

In political terms, the workers who experience the highest costs from industrial automation fit the crucial Trump voter demographic: white non-college-educated voters, disproportionately male, whose support for the Republican nominee surged from 2012 to 2016—as shown in figure 15.2, which is based on data from the Pew Research Center.

The figure shows a major transformation of the Republican presidential electorate. Among whites with college degrees, support for Trump fell by 11 percentage points compared with support for Mitt Romney; among whites without degrees, Trump's support rose by 12 points when compared with Romney's.

The increase in workplace robots was not alone in driving voters to the right. Communities where industries lost ground to imports from China followed a similar pattern.

In a September 2017 paper, "Importing Political Polarization? The Electoral Consequences of Rising Trade Exposure," David Autor, who is also an economist at MIT, and three of his colleagues dug further into the demographics of those suffering the economic costs of trade with China.

Autor and his coauthors found that "trade exposure catalyzed strong movements towards conservative Republicans between 2002 and 2010 in counties with majority non-Hispanic white populations."

The gains made by hard-right Republicans came at the expense of moderate Republican and Democratic incumbents.

Even more significant, Autor determined that though, generally speaking, trade shocks did not "favor conservative politicians," shocks "that disproportionately affect white males" did.

The authors provide more detail, explaining that the "rightward shift is driven by trade shocks to industries that have traditionally employed white men in relatively large numbers, and is largely unrelated to shocks to other industries."

Autor and his coauthors cite research showing that "voters choose to supply fewer public goods when a significant fraction of tax revenues collected from one ethnic group is used to provide public goods shared with other ethnic groups" and that "voters in an in-group object to their tax contributions being used to support individuals in out-groups."

That translates to the following: white voters, especially white men, oppose paying taxes for programs that primarily provide services to others. In practice, the authors suggest, trade shocks "catalyze anti-redistributionist sentiment (seen in the election of conservative Republicans) in majority white non-Hispanic locations where taxpayers may perceive themselves as transfer-payment donors."

This white male effect was critical to the link connecting, as Autor and his coauthors write, "economic adversity to in-group/out-group identification, as motivated by group-based resource competition or opportunistic use of political extremism."

Their analysis resonates, they suggest, "with the themes of recent literature on the political economy of right-wing populism, in which economic shocks to dominant population groups engender a political response that sharpens group identities and enhances support for conservative politicians. This pattern is evident in our finding that the impact of trade shocks on political polarization appears largely attributable to increases in foreign competition facing manufacturing industries that are intensive in the employment of non-Hispanic white males."

Acemoglu, Autor, and their colleagues provide a synthesis between the economic and the sociocultural explanations of the rise of the populist Right. In doing so, they provide a corrective to the recent tendency in segments of the liberal media to downplay economic factors and to focus instead on racial resentment and cultural dislocation as the primary forces motivating Trump voters.

I myself have written that "Republican voters have a strong sense of white identity, they harbor high levels of racial resentment and they sometimes exhibit authoritarian leanings."

The point here is that the two generalized explanatory realms—the one focused on race and the other on economic shock—overlap. It is not either-or but both that gave us President Trump.

Still, explanations tend to become monocausal.

Take, for example, the December 15, 2017, headline at the Vox website: "The Past Year of Research Has Made It Very Clear: Trump Won Because of Racial Resentment." According to German Lopez, the article's author, "employment and income were not significantly related to that sense of white vulnerability." What was? "Racial resentment."

A May 9, 2017, story in the *Atlantic* asserted that "fear of societal change, not economic pressure, motivated votes for the president among non-salaried workers without college degrees."

Those stories were by no means alone. *Salon*: "Liberals Were Right: Racism Played a Larger Role in Trump's Win than Income and Authoritarianism"; the *Nation*: "Economic Anxiety Didn't Make People Vote Trump, Racism Did."

The debate over the role of economic hardship among whites in building support for Trump began while the campaign was in full swing.

Nate Silver, founder and editor of the FiveThirtyEight website, wrote "The Mythology of Trump's 'Working Class' Support" in the midst of the primary fight for the Republican nomination.

"Compared with most Americans, Trump's voters are better off. The median household income of a Trump voter so far in the primaries is about $72,000," Silver pointed out, "well above the national median household income of about $56,000."

Silver's argument is accurate insofar as it goes, but it does not go far enough.

In the primaries, Trump's voters were more affluent than the general electorate. But among Republican primary voters, the core of Trump's support was among those with the lowest level of education and, in most cases, the lowest income levels.

Take a look at the exit polls from the March 1 Virginia primary. Trump beat his closest competitor, Senator Marco Rubio, among those without college degrees, 43 percent to 25 percent, while Rubio beat Trump among those with degrees, 37 percent to 27 percent. Trump beat Rubio 39 percent to 25 percent among voters making less than $100,000, but Rubio beat Trump 40 percent to 27 percent among those making more than $100,000. The same pattern was repeated over and over again in primaries across the country.

Trump's strongest support in the primaries and in the general election came disproportionately from the least well-educated whites—those who, as Acemoglu and Autor argue, are most vulnerable to the economic dislocation resulting from automation, the rise of a robot workforce, global trade, and outsourcing.

In an email, Autor describes how the two explanatory models dovetail. He starts with a question: "Do you think non-college, non-urban whites would feel so dislocated if their job prospects were strong and their wages rising?"

He then goes on to point out that "all of these observations—authoritarianism, racism, cultural dislocation—have relevance. The only claim that's irrelevant because it's already been disproved is that economic factors were unimportant to Trump's victory."

16

Trump's Tool Kit Does Not Include the Constitution

Since before President Donald Trump was elected—and with greater frequency afterward—historians, political scientists, and journalists have wondered how autocratic our democracy might become.

Here is some evidence of how the public sees it. Bright Line Watch, a consortium of political scientists formed after the 2016 election, just released a survey of two thousand voters that shows that public faith in twenty-seven key democratic principles—ranging from the independence of the judiciary to constitutional limits on executive power—has declined across the board.

Four political scientists—Gretchen Helmke of the University of Rochester, Brendan Nyhan and John Carey of Dartmouth, and Susan Stokes of Yale—report that from September 2017 to January 2018, voters' assessments of the ability of the courts, Congress, and the Constitution to "effectively check executive power dropped by 7–8 percentage points." In the same period, "confidence that the elected branches respect judicial independence fell by 17 percentage points."

This article first appeared in *The New York Times* on February 8, 2018. Copyright © 2018 by Thomas Edsall and The New York Times Company. All rights reserved.

The results also reveal "substantial declines (greater than 10 percentage points) in the belief that the government does not interfere with the press, protects free speech rights, that opinions on policy are heard and that candidates disclose information."

Helmke and her colleagues warn that these trends constitute a threat to democracy: "If scholars are right that erosion proceeds on a piecemeal basis, and that the first steps often entail targeting democracy's 'referees,' then our results regarding declines in judicial independence and support for a free press are especially disturbing."

The release of the Bright Line survey comes at a moment when Trump has once again defied traditional norms and constraints concerning the treatment of political opponents.

On Monday, he charged that Democratic members of the House and Senate were treasonous in their failure to applaud him during his State of the Union address. In a speech in Blue Ash, Ohio, Trump described how he saw it: "You're up there, you've got half the room going totally crazy, wild—they loved everything, they want to do something great for our country. And you have the other side, even on positive news—really positive news, like that—they were like death and un-American. Un-American. Somebody said, 'treasonous.' I mean, yeah, I guess, why not? Can we call that treason? Why not?"

One day later, Trump declared, "If we don't change the legislation, get rid of these loopholes where killers come into our country and continue to kill, if we don't change it, let's have a shutdown. We'll do a shutdown, and it's worth it for our country."

The decline of public faith in America's democratic institutions can be seen in figure 16.1, which shows Bright Line's findings.

Those polled were asked to rate whether the United States fully meets, mostly meets, partly meets, or does not meet more than two dozen principles of democracy. The bars in the figure capture the drop in the percentage of people who agree that the United States fully or mostly lives up to democratic standards.

The authors of the analysis of the survey conclude that the "overall picture is sobering," citing public agreement "that the

-1.6 Equal voting rights
-1.7 Patriotism not questioned
-2.5 Contributions don't determine policy
-2.6 Campaign funds transparent
-2.8 Voter participation is high
-4.3 Protest tolerated
-4.6 No political violence
-5.3 Fraud-free elections
-5.7 No private gains from office
-5.8 Equal political/legal rights
-6.6 Districts not biased
-6.6 All political parties allowed
-7.1 Constitution limits executive authority
-7.2 Legislature can limit executive
-7.3 Compromise sought
-7.4 No foreign influence
-7.8 Sanctions for misconduct
-8.0 Judiciary can limit executive power
-8.1 Investigations are free from politics
-8.1 Common understanding of facts
-8.3 Gov't agencies don't punish opponents
-9.7 Votes have equal impact
-10.3 Access to information about candidates
-10.3 Citizen opinions heard on policy
-12.9 Free speech protected
-16.2 No interference with press
-16.7 Politicians respect judicial independence

Substantial declines: more than 10 points

FIGURE 16.1. DEGRADED CONFIDENCE IN AMERICAN POLITICS. Decline, from September to January, in public ratings of twenty-seven aspects of democracy. Figures in percentage points.
Source: Bright Line Watch. From The New York Times. © 2018 The New York Times Company. All rights reserved. Used under license.

performance of U.S. democracy has declined" during Trump's tenure in office.

The degradation of politics, in the view of Kathleen Dolan, a political scientist at the University of Wisconsin–Milwaukee, has complex roots.

"The damage being done is twofold," Dolan wrote by email. "The president's strategy is doing permanent damage to the view of law enforcement agencies, at least among the segment of the population that takes what he says as truth."

This is only part of "the more general problem we are having today with the success Trump and others have had in creating the view that there is no objective truth," Dolan argued. "The manipulation of the truth by the president and other Republicans continues to degrade public discussion of issues."

While polarization has created a political universe composed of two truths, one Democratic, the other Republican, Trump has driven, and profited from, this duality.

"Am I concerned that Trump's attacks on the Department of Justice, the F.B.I. and the ongoing investigations into collusion may undermine fundamental institutions and norms including the rule of law?" Shanto Iyengar, a political scientist at Stanford, wrote me by email. "For sure."

Iyengar posed the following hypothetical: "Let's assume that Mueller uncovers evidence of collusion and close associates of the Prez are implicated. Republicans are likely to deny the validity of the charges on the grounds that the investigators are biased and Republicans in Congress, as they've repeatedly demonstrated, will stick by Trump since the base is with him. Trump, of course, will continue with the 'hoax' narrative, and his surrogates in the media will be only too happy to back him up. At that point, we will have a very real threat to the rule of law."

Trump's attacks on the FBI are a case study in his polarization strategy. Since its founding in 1908, the FBI has had substantial popular support, especially among Republicans. Historical poll data is revealing. A 1949 Gallup poll asked, "What is your opinion of the F.B.I.?" Forty-one percent said, "Very high, excellent, it does a wonderful job," and 53 percent said, "Good, approve of it," for a total of 94 percent. Three percent voiced "mild disapproval," and the responses of 1 percent were "derogatory."

More recently, an NBC News / *Wall Street Journal* poll tracked partisan views of the FBI from December 2014 to January 2018. Over that three-year period, the percentage of Democrats voicing "a great deal or quite a bit of confidence" in the agency rose from 34 percent to 53 percent.

Republican confidence moved in the opposite direction, from 46 percent to 31 percent.

Just this month, a February 1–2 Survey Monkey poll sponsored by Axios found that favorable views of the FBI among Republicans—

putatively members of the law-and-order party—had fallen to 38 percent, while a plurality, 47 percent, disapproved. Among all voters, 49 percent approved of the FBI and 28 percent disapproved; Democrats were favorable by 64 percent to 14 percent.

Alex Theodoridis, a political scientist at the University of California–Merced, wrote me, "Polarization by party identity is so powerful at the moment that most voters see the world through thick red and blue lenses. Almost everything is politicized. And, in almost every study I have run, I find that Republicans are more intense partisans than Democrats on average. We've seen partisanship color Republican evaluations of the FBI (negatively) and Russia and Putin (positively)."

Theodoridis argued that the damage to "any given institution is not likely to last beyond its usefulness in a specific political context." But, he warned, "the more pernicious problem is the very phenomenon of universal politicization. If everything, even the most esteemed institutions and norms, is subjected to the power of partisan motivated reasoning, then there really cease to be esteemed institutions and norms."

Moving from politicization to politics, how likely are these trends to play out in the midterm elections?

"A Democratic turnaround in 2018 is far from assured," Robert Y. Shapiro, a political scientist at Columbia, emailed me. "If the economy stays strong and swing voters see benefits to the economy and themselves from tax cuts, the Republicans may well hold on to the House and, more easily, the Senate."

The recent volatility of the stock market poses dangers to Trump and the Republican Party generally. Still, Trump's ratings, always unfavorable, have improved in recent weeks.

In a setback for Democrats, the generic House vote in opinion surveys—"Are you likely to vote for a Democrat or Republican for the House?"—has fallen from a 12.9-point Democratic advantage as recently as December 30 to a 6-point Democratic advantage on February 7. A rough rule of thumb is that Democrats will need at least a 10-point advantage on the generic vote to have a shot at retaking the House.

In a report published just before Trump's State of the Union address last week, Gallup reported significant improvements during Trump's first year in office on voters' outlook on the economy, the nation's military preparedness, its policies to control crime, and the danger posed by terrorism.

Perhaps more significant, Gallup found that the percentage of adults saying "now is a good time to find a quality job" rose from 42 percent in 2016 to 58 percent in 2017, the highest it has been over the seventeen years that Gallup has asked the question.

And the most recent Quinnipiac Poll conducted February 2–5 should make Democratic strategists nervous. Trump has a negative 40–55 percent approval rating, but it's "his best overall score in seven months." Seventy percent of voters described the economy as excellent or good, the highest since 2001, and by a margin of 48 percent to 41 percent they credit Trump more than President Barack Obama.

Howard Rosenthal, a political scientist at New York University, brought the discussion down to less abstract levels by noting in an email that in politics, "what matters in the economy is real disposable income over the 6–12 months before an election."

If Rosenthal is right, then the future of democracy in America during the Trump administration depends as much or more on unemployment, take-home pay, the Dow Jones industrial average, tax rates, and the gross domestic product as on principled support for the rule of law.

In all likelihood, as the investigation by the special counsel, Robert Mueller, continues to pursue lines of inquiry reaching deep into the White House, Trump will have plenty of opportunities in the near future to push the envelope on the rule of law.

Stephen Ansolabehere, a political scientist at Harvard, described in an email the unique political position Trump has staked out. "His approval is almost 20 points lower than approval of most of his policy initiatives," Ansolabehere noted. "Presidential approval and the economy are the two big contextual predictors of congressional elections in the midterms. And those are pushing in opposite directions."

Looking forward toward the midterm elections, Ansolabehere is not optimistic about Democratic prospects to win back control of the House: "I see the Democrats poised right now to make net gains of about 10 to 14 seats. They need 25 or so depending on vacancies."

That could all change, he added: "A sag in the economy over the summer or really bad news for Trump could tip twenty or so races that are leaning GOP right now."

A colleague of Ansolabehere's in the Harvard government department, Jon Rogowski, suggested that Trump may pay a price for his highly controversial behavior. He wrote me that in research conducted with Andrew Reeves at Washington University in Saint Louis, "consistently, we find that Americans oppose the concentration of authority in the presidency; in fact, we find that Democrats and Republicans exhibit far greater agreement in their opposition to unilateral powers than they exhibit in their evaluations of the sitting president. This opposition, we find, is driven by their beliefs in constitutional principles. Further, we find that the public penalizes presidents for circumventing the constitutional order to take matters into their own hands."

In other words, Rogowski wrote, "our research suggests that how presidents wield power matters, and the public does not view presidents fondly for violating accepted constitutional arrangements. Democrats, therefore, have an opportunity to mobilize public support against President Trump by emphasizing the president's violations of constitutional norms."

At the same time, Rogowski added,

Sometimes the other institutions push back. For instance, Franklin Roosevelt's seeking of a third (and then a fourth) term is among the most important norm violations in American political history. He hadn't been dead for two years before both chambers of Congress proposed the 22nd amendment to limit presidents to two terms. After Lincoln's use of emergency powers to flex presidential power in ways not previously seen, Congress fought back against his successor, Andrew Johnson. More of his vetoes were overridden (15) than for any other president and Congress limited presidential influence over executive branch employment by passing the Tenure of Office Act (1867).

The Rogowski and Reeves thesis faces a certain test. Trump won the Republican nomination and the presidency by conducting a campaign directly challenging the notion that the electorate will punish a politician for "violating accepted constitutional arrangements."

He has not wavered from this course throughout the first year of his presidency, and, barring unforeseen events, it will guide him into the 2020 election.

If Republicans retain control of both branches of Congress in 2018—even if by just one vote in the House and a 50–50 split (with Vice President Mike Pence the tiebreaker) in the Senate—Trump will claim vindication. His assault on the pillars of democracy will continue unabated, with increasingly insidious effect.

17

Trump against the Liberal Tide

Democratic voters, especially young, white liberals, have been moving sharply in a progressive direction, not only on issues of race but across the board—on the economy, on immigration, and on the environment.

Zach Goldberg, a doctoral candidate in political science at Georgia State University, has been tracking ideological trends among liberal, moderate, and conservative whites, using survey data collected by American National Election Studies.

Figure 17.1 measures support for higher immigration levels from 1992 to 2016. White moderates and conservatives, including Republicans and independents, showed relatively little change over those twenty-four years. Among white liberals, though, support for increased immigration grew from a low of 4 percent in 1996 to 38 percent in 2016.

Goldberg broke down the data by age groups and found that the driving force was young, white liberals aged eighteen to twenty-four. In an email, Goldberg wrote, "To sum up, both social media and the progressive direction of the Obama years helped lay the groundwork for the progressive/multicultural normative context

This article first appeared in *The New York Times* on May 31, 2018. Copyright © 2018 by Thomas Edsall and The New York Times Company. All rights reserved.

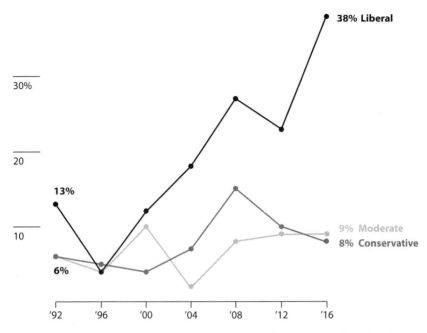

FIGURE 17.1. WARMING TO IMMIGRANTS. Support for increasing immigration among whites, by ideology.
Source: Zach Goldberg, Georgia State University. From The New York Times.
© 2018 The New York Times Company. All rights reserved. Used under license.

that Trump would later enter and threaten to smash. For liberals, Trump and his supporters were perceived as white supremacists who aspired to 'make America white again.'"

In other words, he continued, "in an era where 'whiteness' has become increasingly associated with moral injustice (past and present), liberals are determined to distinguish themselves as 'inclusive' and 'unlike the deplorable white majority.'"

In further support of his argument, Goldberg produced figure 17.2 from ANES surveys.

In our email exchange, Goldberg argued that Trump's election produced what he calls "moral panic" among liberals: "Liberal progressives perceive Trump as a threat to the increasingly egalitarian/multicultural moral order. They fear that he will undo or turn back the clock on many of the gains they've made over the past few decades. America under Obama was trending in the progressive direction—

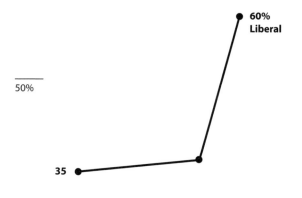

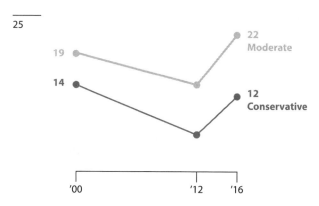

FIGURE 17.2. THE MAJORITY REFLECTS. Percentage of whites, by ideology, who feel that whites have "too much influence."
Source: Zach Goldberg, Georgia State University. From The New York Times. © 2018 The New York Times Company. All rights reserved. Used under license.

towards a proverbial 'end of history' or egalitarian multicultural utopia. Trump then emerges and is perceived as not only 'crashing the party,' but also as threatening to return it to its 'whites only'/ exclusivist format."

The Pew Research Center has documented some of the most striking shifts in a liberal direction among Democratic voters. For an October 2017 report, Pew asked respondents to choose between two statements: first, "Immigrants strengthen the country because of their hard work and talents," and second, "Immigrants burden the country by taking jobs, housing and health care."

The percentage of self-identified Democrats and Democratic leaners who agreed that immigrants strengthened the country grew from 48 percent in 2010 to 84 percent in 2017. Conversely, the share of Democrats describing immigrants as a burden fell from 60 percent in 1994 to 12 percent in 2017.

"Many pro-immigrant positions are at an all-time high (among Democrats) in public opinion," Nick Gourevitch, a Democratic pollster, told me by email, "especially questions around immigration strengthening society and the positive impact of immigration."

"Taking that position is now a signal that you are not with Trump and you are not with white nationalist elements of the Republican Party," Gourevitch added. "If you are strongly anti-Trump now, you are almost, by definition, pro-immigrant, pro-racial justice."

Immigration in essence is an issue that hinges on race. White conservatives vote on race. As Michael Tesler, a political scientist at the University of California at Irvine, put it in the *Washington Post* in November 2016, "Racial attitudes became strongly connected to whether whites identified as Democratic or Republican during Barack Obama's presidency. That, by itself, meant that racial attitudes would matter a great deal in 2016—even above the powerful impact of partisanship itself. There is now a stronger partisan divide than ever between racially sympathetic and racially resentful whites. Indeed, the divide is so large it exceeds what was true in 2008 and 2012—when there was an actual African-American candidate on the ballot."

Republican turnout swamped Democrats in 2016: as my colleague David Leonhardt wrote last year, if liberals voted at the same rate as conservatives, Hillary Clinton would be president.

A June 2017 report issued by the bipartisan Democracy Fund's Voter Study Group found that a subset of all voters that the organization calls "American preservationists" gave Trump 20 percent of his total vote. It was these voters who composed "the core Trump constituency that propelled him to victory in the early Republican primaries." American preservationists, the study group found, "take the most restrictionist approach to immigration—staunchly opposing not just illegal but legal immigration as well."

In testing racial attitudes, Pew asked voters to choose between two statements: "Blacks who can't get ahead in this country are mostly responsible for their condition," and "Racial discrimination is the main reason why many black people can't get ahead these days." The percentage of Democrats citing discrimination grew from 28 percent in 2010 to 50 percent in 2016 to 64 percent in 2017.

A similar pattern, although less extreme, can be seen in responses to questions on environmental issues. For example, from 2006 to 2014, the percentage of Democrats who believed that there is "solid evidence that the average temperature on earth is getting warmer" fluctuated from the mid- to high 70s. In 2017, it shot up to 92 percent.

Celinda Lake, a Democratic pollster, sees the trends among Democratic voters as a clear plus, with little downside: "There has been a tremendous shift in the public to progressive positions and awareness—on marijuana, on marriage equality, on calling out racism, on #MeToo, on support for comprehensive sex education and women's reproductive health issues. Democrats are both leading the way and catching up. Millennials are the future and they are totally in support of these positions."

Jonathan Cowan, president of Third Way, a centrist Democratic think tank, is more ambivalent.

On the plus side, he wrote in an email, "this shorter-term trend clearly comports with the multi-decade trend in which both the country at large and the Democratic Party itself have become increasingly more open-minded, pluralistic and progressive on a range of social issues, including racial justice, immigration and women's rights."

Cowan then shifted to what he called "the rest of the story": "Not all of the country is moving at the same pace. Donald Trump won a national election playing a brand of racial politics not seen in this country since George Wallace. So while Democrats fight for progress and justice on racial issues, we cannot be dismissive or scornful of voters who do not share precisely the same views or beliefs, but who nonetheless want an alternative to the hard-core misogyny, nativism and racism of Trump."

Third Way analyzed all 435 House districts in anticipation of the 2018 election and reached the conclusion that the key fights will be in districts that require appeals to swing voters to win.

The study found that 168 districts are virtually certain to elect Democrats, who currently hold 165 of these seats. On average, these districts are 44 percent white and 56 percent minority.

Conversely, there are 195 districts almost certain to elect Republicans. They are 75 percent white and 25 percent minority. Republicans hold 193 of them, and, based on past voting records, Democrats face long odds making gains in these deep-red districts.

In the middle, there are 72 so-called purple districts that are key to control of the House. They are, on average, 70 percent white and 30 percent nonwhite. Democrats currently hold just over a third of these seats, 27, and must make major gains to reach a House majority. The whites in these disproportionately suburban, relatively high-income districts stand out in that they are far better educated than the national average, suffer less poverty, and register lower unemployment rates.

Lee Drutman, a senior fellow at liberal-leaning New America, contends that the hostility of Democratic elites to Trump is driving the leftward shift among Democratic voters.

"Opinion leadership among Democratic elites has become much more 'woke' over the past several years," Drutman said by email. "Democratic politicians and journalists have spent more time talking about social justice issues and championing the causes of historically disadvantaged groups, and there's a basic cue-following that happens. What it means to be a Democrat is shifting, and voters are updating their views to fit with that."

At the same time, Drutman noted, many conservative whites have left the Democratic Party, effectively increasing "the percentages of self-identified Democrats taking more liberal stands on cultural issues."

Perhaps most important, "Democrats are defining themselves in opposition to Trump, and to stand in opposition to Trump is to take liberal stands on social and cultural issues."

Animosity to Trump is one of many factors driving liberal positioning among Democrats. Matt Grossmann, a political scientist at Michigan State, pointed to some of these in an email: "It's hard to sort out the roles of Black Lives Matter, police violence, Trump statements, Democratic comments on Trump, social desirability pressures for educated liberals, increasing education among Democrats, campus movements, #MeToo, etc."

Grossmann added, "The general explanation is that, as a result of all of that, political elites, including the presidential candidates, and the media are talking more about these views, with Democrats publicly taking liberal positions and Trump-era Republicans taking the opposite views."

Cowan argues that rapid advances in digital communications have played a crucial role in the liberalization of Democratic voters: "There are a series of Great American Awakenings sweeping the country in the early part of the 21st century, and each of these awakenings are being radically accelerated by the ubiquity and advent of digital technology and the stories and movements it enables people to tell and build, e.g. the outrageous mistreatment of African Americans at Starbucks now caught on cellphone video or dash cams, the rise of the #MeToo Movement and the ability of social media platforms to empower, amplify and sustain the stories of Dreamers."

From a strategic vantage point, there is no question that the United States—and the world for that matter—is moving in the same direction as the Democratic Party. Still, a question remains: Is the Democratic Party too far ahead of the electorate, in danger of being swamped by reaction?

Public Opinion Strategies, a Republican firm that conducts polling for NBC and the *Wall Street Journal*, provided data in an email suggesting that the Democratic Party is at the leading edge on the issue of immigration.

In a series of surveys for NBC/*WSJ*, Public Opinion Strategies asked voters to make a choice similar to the one posed earlier by Pew:

A. "Immigration adds to our character and strengthens the United States because it brings diversity, new workers, and new creative talent to this country."
B. "Immigration detracts from our character and weakens the United States because it puts too many burdens on government services, causes language barriers, and creates housing problems."

The percentage of all voters choosing A has grown steadily from 41 percent in 2005 to 47 percent in 2010 to 54 percent in 2013 to 64 percent in 2017. Democrats have led the charge, going from 42 percent in 2005 to 81 percent in 2017, but equally significant are the shifts that Public Opinion Strategies found among Republican constituencies.

In 2010, a majority, 54 percent, of white Southerners agreed that immigration weakens the country; by 2017, a majority, 53 percent, said immigration strengthens the country. Similarly, 59 percent of women without college degrees said immigration hurts the country; by 2017, 53 percent said immigration helps the nation.

Immigration is one of a package of issues that fall under the broad category of liberalization—something Steven Pinker, a professor of psychology at Harvard, calls emancipation.

The worldwide trends on emancipation have been moving decisively in a liberal direction, as shown in figure 17.3, developed from Pinker's new book, *Enlightenment Now: The Case for Reason, Science, Humanism, and Progress.*

Over the course of the years covered by the figure, from the 1960s to 2010, America's two major parties have taken opposing sides in a large-scale social struggle over emancipation: the Democrats on the front lines fighting against conservative resistance, a rear-guard Republican action that is determined to maintain the status quo or

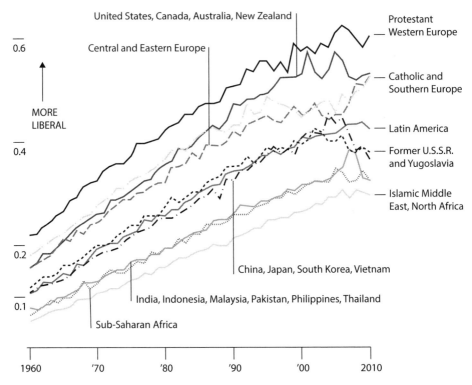

FIGURE 17.3. THE GLOBAL MARCH OF LIBERALIZATION. Christian Welzel, a German political scientist, has devised an index to measure commitment to liberal values—gender equality, freedom of personal choice, political rights and other issues. Every region of the world has become markedly more liberal since 1960, although there has been some backsliding. Analysis through 2010. The index ranges from 0 to 1, the latter being the most liberal possible.
Sources: Christian Welzel, Leuphana University; Steven Pinker, Harvard University. From The New York Times. © 2018 The New York Times Company. All rights reserved. Used under license.

roll it back. The advantage has rotated from one party to the other over the past several decades.

The Republicans are back in power now. Trump's fervent millions stand loyally behind him. The president is pushing ever more aggressively to bring the emancipation project to a halt. But his foothold is insecure—and he is rowing against the current.

18

The Class Struggle according to Donald Trump

According to Alan Krueger and Eric Posner, in their tough minded— and much-needed— "Proposal for Protecting Low-Income Workers from Monopsony and Collusion," the ideal labor market is one in which "workers can move freely to seek the most desirable opportunities for which they are qualified."

If only.

As Adam Cobb, a professor of management at the Wharton School at the University of Pennsylvania, put it in an email conversation, "Life doesn't operate so cleanly and the fact that a worker's wealth and well-being is much more dependent upon her employer than the employer is on a given worker tilts things in the employer's favor."

The trend in recent years has been an inexorable shift of bargaining power to employers at the expense of employees.

The Supreme Court is expected to rule soon in the case of *Janus v. American Federation of State, County, and Municipal Employees, Council 31*, which challenges the right of public-employee unions in

This article first appeared in *The New York Times* on June 7, 2018. Copyright © 2018 by Thomas Edsall and The New York Times Company. All rights reserved.

twenty-two states to collect dues from nonmembers who benefit from a union agreement that covers the cost of collective bargaining and contract compliance.

If the court rules against organized labor as expected, it will inflict punishing financial hardship on the affected unions and will threaten the viability of many locals.

Worker power has already suffered death by a thousand cuts, some political, others judicial and regulatory; some at the hands of a changing domestic workplace, others stemming from relentless global forces.

Corporate America recognized these trends early on and capitalized on them ruthlessly. Labor organizations were ill equipped to do so and have been on the defensive for the past four decades.

Two trends demonstrate the decline of labor and the ascent of business. Since 1979, after-tax corporate profits as a share of gross domestic product have grown by 22.8 percent, while the share of nonfarm business-sector income going to labor has dropped by 10.3 percent.

In response to my query, Martha McCluskey, a professor of law at the University at Buffalo, emailed, "The decline in worker bargaining power in the United States is the cumulative effect of numerous small and large changes over recent decades reaching into almost every area of law and policy. This combines with a decline in the enforcement of existing laws that could protect workers' bargaining power—laws protecting unions, laws against wage theft, nondiscrimination laws, and more."

The "small and large changes over recent decades" to which McCluskey refers increase the clout of corporate management and reduce the power of workers over wages, benefits, and job security.

Among these changes is the requirement that employees sign what are known as "noncompete" and "no-raid" agreements, both of which restrict workers' ability to extract pay hikes by threatening to take similar jobs at competing companies.

"Non-competes are sometimes used to protect trade secrets, which can promote innovation," according to a 2016 report by the Treasury Department, but "less than half of workers who have non-competes also report possessing trade secrets." The report went on to question the use of noncompete agreements, especially for low-wage workers: "When entry-level workers at fast food restaurants are asked to sign two-year non-competes, it becomes less plausible that trade secrets are always the primary motivation for such agreements."

The Treasury report estimated that thirty million American workers have signed noncompete agreements.

Krueger, an economist at Princeton and the former chairman of the Council of Economic Advisers, wrote in an essay last year, "The Rigged Labor Market," "New practices have emerged to facilitate employer collusion, such as noncompete clauses and no-raid pacts, but the basic insights are the same—employers often implicitly, and sometimes explicitly, act to prevent the forces of competition from enabling workers to earn what a competitive market would dictate."

In a paper published last month, "Noncompetes in the U.S. Labor Force," Evan Starr of the University of Maryland, J. J. Prescott of the University of Michigan, and Norman Bishara of the University of Michigan found that "nearly 1 in 5 labor force participants were bound by noncompetes in 2014, and nearly 40 percent had signed at least one noncompete in the past."

These included what the authors decried as "sweeping non-competes signed by temporarily employed Amazon packers and minimum-wage sandwich makers."

Just as companies have weakened employee power through agreements like these, they have capitalized on the increased use of mandatory arbitration of employment disputes to limit their obligations to workers.

Sachin S. Pandya, a law professor at the University of Connecticut, wrote me that in its recent decision *Epic Systems Corp. v. Lewis*, the Supreme Court effectively "fueled employer use of mandatory arbitration clauses to cover individual employment disputes, including allegations of workplace discrimination and sexual harassment."

By preventing covered workers from joining forces to take legal action over workplace issues, the decision undercuts employees' leverage and empowers employers to "require their employees to waive their right to class actions," wrote Jeffrey Hirsch, a professor at the University of North Carolina School of Law, on the *Workplace Prof Blog*. Hirsch cited the dissent written by Justice Ruth Bader Ginsburg: "If these untoward consequences stemmed from legislative choices, I would be obliged to accede to them. But the edict that employees with wage and hours claims may seek relief only one-by-one does not come from Congress. It is the result of take-it-or-leave-it labor contracts harking back to the type called 'yellow dog,' and of the readiness of this Court to enforce those unbargained-for agreements. The Federal Arbitration Act demands no such suppression of the right of workers to take concerted action for their 'mutual aid or protection.'"

In much the same way that mandatory arbitration works, corporate outsourcing of jobs in combination with the general spread of precarious employment—in the creative economy, for example, as well as in the digital or gig economy (at Lyft and Uber, for example)—steadily undermines the security and status of workers.

These developments may be masked for a while when unemployment declines, but not forever.

By exchanging direct employment for contract work or outsourcing, David Weil, dean of the Heller School for Social Policy and Management at Brandeis, writes in his book *The Fissured Workplace: Why Work Became So Bad for So Many and What Can Be Done to Improve It*, major corporations succeed in "substantially reducing costs and dispatching the many responsibilities connected to being the employer of record."

This shift, in turn, "creates downward pressures on wages and benefits, murkiness about who bears responsibility for work conditions, [and] increased likelihood that basic labor standards will be violated."

Krueger and Lawrence Katz, an economist at Harvard, document a sharp increase in outsourcing of all kinds in their paper "The Rise and Nature of Alternative Work Arrangements in the United States, 1995–2015": "The percentage of workers engaged in alternative work arrangements—defined as temporary help agency workers, on-call workers, contract workers, and independent contractors or freelancers—rose from 10.7 percent in February 2005 to 15.8 percent in late 2015."

That's roughly twenty-four million workers.

In addition, Katz and Krueger found that "workers in alternative work arrangements earn considerably less per week than do regular employees with similar characteristics and in similar occupations," that "workers in alternative work arrangements work fewer hours per week," and that a "larger share of alternative workers are involuntary part-time workers compared with employees in traditional jobs."

Perhaps more significant, Katz and Krueger found, "A striking implication of these estimates is that 94 percent of the net employment growth in the U.S. economy from 2005 to 2015 appears to have occurred in alternative work arrangements."

The growing emphasis on "shareholder value" has provided additional justification for all of these antiworker developments.

Peter Cappelli, a professor of management at Wharton, wrote me that "the shareholder value movement starting in the late 1980s and now institutionalized through industry analysts" was crucially important in the devaluation of employees: "Accounting in business is mainly about costs. Finance people hate fixed costs because of the challenges they raise to share price valuation when there is uncertainty, and the biggest fixed costs are labor. Simply moving the same labor costs from employees to outside staffing companies moves it from one part of the accounting ledger to another and makes analysts happier."

This mentality, in turn, encourages "the use of temps and contractors" to fill high-wage jobs because "that way the employer doesn't have to raise wages for all their employees."

Hirsch, of the University of North Carolina, explained that the automobile industry provides the classic example of these trends: "When that industry was dominated by the Big Three in Detroit, union organizing was relatively easy. The UAW could organize all of the competitors by controlling most of the relatively generally homogeneous, geographically tight work force."

Once "automakers in other countries, and now the South, made more inroads, the UAW's task became far more difficult," Hirsch argued, because "companies could outsource work to areas with cheaper labor and less of a union presence. This both weakened the union and ramped up competitive pressure on the companies that were unionized. The result was fewer unions. This has obviously played out in many other industries."

Hirsch's point is supported by the Bureau of Labor Statistics. In 2017, 6.5 percent of the private-sector workforce was unionized, down from 35 percent in 1955; 34.4 percent of public-sector workers were unionized.

In addition, Hirsch pointed out, "many union jobs are simply no longer in the U.S. Entire industries (e.g., textiles) were essentially moved offshore."

The result is a "death spiral effect," according to Hirsch: "As membership declines unions are able to exert less influence. Moreover, as fewer employees have experience with unions or know others who have, it becomes harder to organize."

The contemporary weakness of organized labor and the threatened status of employees have roots in the breakdown in the 1970s of the postwar capital-labor accord—what A. H. Raskin, the legendary labor reporter for the *Times*, called a "live-and-let-live relationship" that held sway for thirty years.

The end of the labor-management détente—and the emergence of a merciless assault by business and the Republican Party on workers' pay, security, and bargaining strength—has been especially cruel to workers without college degrees.

In their book *The Second Machine Age*, Erik Brynjolfsson and Andrew McAfee, both economists at MIT, don't hold out much hope for this broad class of workers: "Rapid and accelerating digitization is likely to bring economic rather than environmental disruption, stemming from the fact that as computers get more powerful, companies have less need for some kinds of workers. Technological progress is going to leave behind some people, perhaps even a lot of people, as it races ahead."

For those with special skills or the right education, they write, "there's never been a better time." For those "with only 'ordinary' skills and abilities to offer," however, "there's never been a worse time to be a worker."

A colleague of Brynjolfsson and McAfee, David Autor, offers a more optimistic take in a 2015 paper: "In many cases, machines both substitute for and complement human labor. Focusing only on what is lost misses a central economic mechanism by which automation affects the demand for labor: raising the value of the tasks that workers uniquely supply."

At a more concrete level, Krueger and Posner, in their Brookings paper, offer a series of well-thought-out legal and regulatory reforms aimed at improving the bargaining power of workers.

First, they would alter antitrust enforcement to require consideration of the likely effect of mergers on concentration in the labor market, in order to prevent "too high a risk of wage suppression."

Second, Krueger and Posner would support legislation making noncompete agreements "uniformly unenforceable and banned if they govern a worker who earns less than the median wage in her state."

In the case of "no-raid" agreements between companies that bar participating businesses from making job offers to employees of competitors, Krueger and Posner would ban such arrangements altogether: "We propose a per se rule against no-poaching agreements regardless of whether they are used outside or within franchises. In other words, no-poaching agreements would be considered illegal regardless of the circumstances of their use."

The reality, of course, is that the Krueger-Posner proposals have no chance with President Trump in the White House and Republicans in control of both houses of Congress.

Trump's appointees to the National Labor Relations Board have clearly signaled their plans to kill pro-worker regulations adopted during the Obama administration. So, too, apparently, has the Supreme Court.

For the time being, at least, the problems of the least skilled workers in the labor market will fester.

In the 2016 election, Trump profited from the conviction of rural and working-class voters that they were on a downward trajectory. If anything, Trump appears to be gambling that letting those voters' lives continue to languish will work to his advantage in 2020.

Trump's trade policies show signs of backfiring, and his proposals do nothing to address the long-term phenomenon that may prove to be most destructive to low-skill employment: automation, particularly roboticization.

Trump campaigned as the ally of the white working class, but any notion that he would take its side as it faces off against employers is a gross misjudgment.

His administration has turned the executive branch, the federal courts, and the regulatory agencies into the sworn enemy of workers, organized and unorganized. Trump is indisputably indifferent to the plight of anyone in the bottom half of the income distribution: look at his appointments, look at his record in office, look back at his business career, and look at the man himself.

19

How Much Can Democrats Count on Suburban Liberals?

Just how dependable is suburban liberalism?

In affluent, largely white Massachusetts communities like Wellesley, Southborough, and Dedham, Hillary Clinton crushed Donald Trump by margins ranging from 23 to 50 percentage points.

These and other townships surrounding Boston epitomize the gains the Democratic Party has made nationwide in liberal, well-educated suburbs.

Ryan Enos, a political scientist at Harvard, published a book last year, *The Space between Us*, suggesting that the ideological commitment of liberals in these and other, similar communities may waver, or fail entirely, when their white homogeneity is threatened.

Not only is the upscale wing of the Democratic Party an unreliable ally of the Left on economic issues—as I have noted in this column before and as Lily Geismer and Matthew D. Lassiter eloquently pointed out in the *Times* last week—but Enos demonstrates that the liberal resolve of affluent Democrats can disintegrate when racially or ethnically charged issues like neighborhood integration are at stake.

This article first appeared in *The New York Times* on June 14, 2018. Copyright © 2018 by Thomas Edsall and The New York Times Company. All rights reserved.

Six years ago, Enos looked at nine townships southwest of Boston that were "overwhelmingly racially and politically liberal." As such, these communities were a "test of the power of demographic change because these were people who, we might think, would be unlikely to change their attitudes in the face of immigration."

Enos and his colleagues conducted an experiment, which is described in detail in a 2014 paper, "Causal Effect of Intergroup Contact on Exclusionary Attitudes," published by the National Academy of Sciences. The results are thought-provoking.

Enos described the experiment as "a randomized controlled trial testing the causal effects of repeated intergroup contact, in which Spanish-speaking confederates were randomly assigned to be inserted, for a period of days, into the daily routines of unknowing Anglo-whites living in homogeneous communities in the United States, thus simulating the conditions of demographic change."

To achieve this goal, during the summer of 2012, Enos dispatched "a small number of Spanish-speaking confederates to commuter train stations in homogeneously Anglo communities every day, at the same time, for two weeks."

The stations were on two Massachusetts Bay Transportation Authority commuter rail lines into Boston—one starting in Worcester, the other in Forge Park—at nine stations in upscale, mostly white towns.

Enos reported that the Anglo commuters he studied had an average income of $143,365, and 88 percent had college degrees, compared with 30.4 percent nationally that year. The median household income for the country at large was $51,371 in 2012, according to the census.

The study had a complicated design, and I invite readers who are so inclined to ascertain the details for themselves. Here is Enos's description of his experiment:

Under the assumption that people with similar characteristics tend to ride the train at the same time, I selected pairs [of trains] that were close together in time so that the treatment units [train platforms onto which Spanish-speaking confederates had been inserted] within each station would have similar passengers. Within a matched pair of train times at each station, one was randomly assigned to treatment and one to control, resulting in 18 matched pairs of train times. This design means that we should expect subjects in the treatment and control conditions to be, in expectation, identical.

Enos continues, "Subjects were exposed to the same Spanish-speaking persons in a location near their homes for an extended period, as would be the situation if immigrants had moved into their neighborhood and used the public transportation."

The Spanish-speaking confederates reported to Enos that "persons noticed and displayed some unease with them: for example reporting that 'Because we are chatting in Spanish, they look at us. I don't think it is common to hear people speaking in Spanish on this route.' After the experiment, the confederates reported that other passengers were generally friendly to them but also reported that they felt people noticed them for 'not being like them and being Latino.'"

Members of the treatment groups and control groups were surveyed before and after the two weeklong experiments in an effort to identify the effect of exposure to Spanish-speaking people. In both surveys, respondents were asked three questions about immigration along with other, more general questions:

1. Do you think the number of immigrants from Mexico who are permitted to come to the United States to live should be increased, left the same, or decreased?
2. Would you favor allowing persons that have immigrated to the United States illegally to remain in the country if they are employed and have no criminal history?
3. Some people favor a state law declaring English as the official language. Some other people oppose such a law. Would you favor such a law?

How did the respondents' answers change? "Treated subjects were far more likely to advocate a reduction in immigration from

Mexico and were far less likely to indicate that illegal immigrants should be allowed to remain in this country."

The experiment, Enos wrote, "demonstrated that exclusionary attitudes can be stimulated by even very minor, noninvasive demographic change: in this case, the introduction of only two persons."

In his 2017 book, reflecting on the results of his experiment, Enos is more direct: "The good liberal people catching trains in the Boston suburbs became exclusionary." Exposure to "two young Spanish speakers for just a few minutes, or less, for just three days had driven them toward anti-immigration policies associated with their political opponents."

Enos examined national precinct- and county-level voting results in recent elections to see what effect a Black president, Barack Obama, had on whites living in segregated areas as opposed to those living in unsegregated areas.

In the 2008 election, Enos found that with a Black Democratic nominee, "white voters in the most-segregated counties were between five and six percentage points less likely to vote for Obama than white voters in the least-segregated counties."

That pattern had not emerged in the previous four presidential elections when the Democratic nominee was white.

"Every time a white Democrat had run going back to 1992—segregation had had no such effect on the vote," Enos wrote. "In 2008, this was a massive effect of segregation: the gap between the most and least-segregated counties was almost equivalent to the gap between men and women."

Enos then looked at results from 124,034 precincts, almost every precinct in the United States. Again, "a white voter in the least-segregated metropolitan area was 10 percentage points more likely to vote for Obama than a white voter in the most-segregated area."

These voting patterns, according to Enos, reflect what might be called a self-reinforcing cycle of prejudice.

In the mid- to late twentieth century, Enos writes, "whites—spurred by forces including their own racism—abandoned the inner cities." But, he goes on, that "is not where the story ends. Attitudes do not remain static." In practice, the very fact of being segregated creates an environment in which hostile views "become even more negative and their political consequences even more severe."

In other words, "prejudice may have helped cause segregation, but then the segregation helped cause even more prejudice."

Looking beyond the borders of the United States, Enos argues that as much as support for diversity is integral to modern democracy, diversity can make governing more difficult:

> The negative effects of diversity may be responsible for some of the profound differences between places such as Denmark and Zambia or Singapore and India. Noting that these four countries are all democracies, we see the consequences of voters—normally separated by geographic, social, and psychological space— coming together to govern and having to make decisions and allocate resources. It appears that when people are faced with these decisions in a diverse democracy, rather than a homogeneous one, they often choose not to do the things that "make democracy work," failing to bridge the space between groups by cooperating to share resources and provide for the common welfare.

This tendency, according to Enos, demonstrates "why diversity is such a vexing problem."

Liberal democracies endorse diversity, Enos writes—"indeed, it is often considered one of our strengths and liberal individuals usually favor diversity as a matter of ideology and public policy. We often support diversity out of a genuine ideological commitment and because we rightly perceive that diversity can improve the performance of many organizations, such as universities and businesses."

But, he continues, "looking across the world and even across states and cities within the United States, most of us would rather not live with some of the social, economic, and political consequences of diversity." This is what Enos calls "the liberal dilemma."

Enos cites Gordon Allport, formerly a professor of psychology at Harvard, who described "contact theory" in his 1954 book, *The*

Nature of Prejudice. Under the right circumstances, Allport argued, interracial contact could reduce hostility. Those circumstances, Enos notes, include "economic equality and social integration."

In practice, Enos points out, "Allport's conditions for prejudice reduction are seldom fulfilled. One of these conditions was that interpersonal contact would reduce prejudice when members of each group were of equal social standing."

In reality, "not only does equality between groups not exist, but true interpersonal contact across groups seldom takes place, even when groups are proximate. Two groups can live in the same area without having meaningful interpersonal contact."

It almost goes without saying that the patterns Enos describes have been crucial to President Trump's political success.

Trump's "most dramatic gains," Enos observes—"that is, where a greater percentage of voters voted Republican than had done so in 2012—were in the places where the Latino population had grown most quickly."

Not all of Enos's findings are bleak. Group hostility, he writes, grows as the size of the immigrant population grows until it reaches a certain point and then begins to recede: "The relationship between the proportion of an out-group in an area and group-based bias is curvilinear: it becomes greater as the out-group proportion increases until reaching a tipping point and then starting to decrease. This means that when a group makes up a large portion of a place— for concreteness, say 40 percent—each additional person above 40 percent actually decreases group-based bias."

For those seeking to unravel what happened in the 2016 election, *The Space between Us* is one of the most consequential of recent political books, a list that also includes two I have written about before: Lilliana Mason's *Uncivil Agreement: How Politics Became Our Identity* and the forthcoming *Identity Crisis: The 2016 Presidential Campaign and the Battle for the Meaning of America*, by John Sides, Michael Tesler, and Lynn Vavreck.

I asked a number of political scientists for their views on the questions raised by Enos's book, including Tesler, a professor at the University of California, Irvine.

Tesler emailed, "Ryan's book is brilliant and his findings dovetail with my belief that we're in for a tough road ahead as the country diversifies, at least in the short term."

The 2016 election, in which Trump's rhetoric resonated with voters living in communities undergoing high rates of change, "was a perfect recipe" for the expression of anti-immigrant sentiments at the ballot box, Tesler said.

That does not "have to always be the case," Tesler continued, noting a paragraph at the conclusion of the book he wrote with Sides and Vavreck: "Public opinion contains reservoirs of sentiment that can serve to unify or to divide. Take immigration. Places that experience rapid growth in the population of Latino immigrants do not necessarily become more anti-immigrant."

"But the polarizing rhetoric of politicians 'politicizes' the places where Americans live," Sides, Tesler, and Vavreck observe, "and people who live in places with a recent influx of immigrants then become more concerned about immigration. This unfolded in 2016: white Democrats voted for Trump in the highest numbers where the Latino population had grown the most."

In other words, it takes a politician like Trump to light the match.

"What gave us the 2016 election, then, was not changes among voters," Sides, Tesler, and Vavreck write. "It was changes in the candidates. Only four years earlier, issues like race and immigration were not as central either to the candidates or to voters. That changed in 2016 because of what the candidates chose to do and say—and then after the election because of what Trump has chosen to do and say as president."

A 2010 study, conducted before Trump appeared on the political scene, reinforced the key role of politicians in fanning the flames. Daniel Hopkins, a political scientist at the University of Pennsylvania, found in "Politicized Places: Explaining Where and When Immigrants Provoke Local Opposition," "When faced with a sudden, destabilizing change in local demographics, and when salient national rhetoric politicizes that demographic change, people's views turn anti-immigrant. In other conditions, local demographics might go largely unnoticed, or else might remain depoliticized."

Enos himself was ambivalent in response to my question, "What does your book say about the prospects for an integrated society, particularly a residentially integrated America?" He wrote back, "Like many things, it depends on whether you want to take the optimistic or pessimistic view. The optimistic view is that many, if not most, groups that are once segregated visible minorities seem to be integrated over time, almost as if there is something natural about this process."

However, Enos continued, "the pessimistic view, which is a cold shot of reality, is that some groups have never residentially integrated in the U.S. and elsewhere. The most obvious example is African-Americans. We are still living with pernicious outcomes of the segregation of blacks."

The big question facing America, in Enos's view, "is whether other groups, especially Latinos, might follow a similar path as blacks and never be residentially integrated with Anglos or whether they will look more like previous immigrant groups."

On this score, Enos is not optimistic: "Current trends in residential patterns may make this problem worse. As our cities sprawl and more of us move to suburbs (which are still growing faster than central cities), our chances for contact are reduced and our ability to form enclaves is heightened."

It is, he added, "difficult to see how these forces can be reined in."

In fact, the predictable "decrease in group based bias" notwithstanding, the force that may prove most challenging to rein in is Trump and the legion of Republican candidates who have seen how effective anti-immigration rhetoric and policy has been in turning Democrats into Republicans.

In politics, once a new strategy or tactic has proved a winner, no matter how reprehensible, it's next to impossible to return to the past.

20

Why Don't We Always Vote in Our Own Self-Interest?

One question that has troubled Democrats for decades is freshly relevant in the Donald Trump–Mitch McConnell era: Why do so many voters support elected officials who are determined to cut programs that those same voters rely on?

Take Kentucky, which has a median household income that ranks forty-fifth out of the fifty states.

Over the past half century, residents of Kentucky have become steadily more reliant on the federal government. In the 1970s, federal programs provided slightly under 10 percent of personal income for Kentucky residents; by 2015, money from programs ranging from welfare and Medicaid to Social Security and Medicare more than doubled to 23 percent as a share of Kentuckians' personal income.

Twenty years ago, there was only one county (out of 120) in which residents counted on the federal government for at least 40 percent of their personal income. By 2014, twenty-eight counties were at 40 percent or higher.

This article first appeared in *The New York Times* on July 19, 2018. Copyright © 2018 by Thomas Edsall and The New York Times Company. All rights reserved.

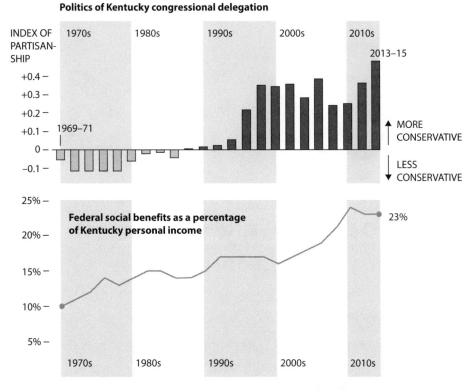

Politics of Kentucky congressional delegation

FIGURE 20.1. WHY DID SOCIAL BENEFITS AND CONSERVATISM RISE IN TANDEM? In Kentucky, use of federal social benefits rose as the state's politics became much more conservative from 1969 to 2015. Benefits include payments from Social Security, the Supplemental Nutrition Assistance Program (SNAP), unemployment insurance, and more than forty other federal programs.
Source: Analysis by Suzanne Mettler, Cornell University. From The New York Times. © 2018 The New York Times Company. All rights reserved. Used under license.

But as their claims on federal dollars rose, the state's voters became increasingly conservative. In the 1990s, they began to elect hard-right, antigovernment politicians determined to cut the programs their constituents were coming to lean on.

Suzanne Mettler, a professor of government at Cornell, describes these developments—which can be found in states across the South, the Mountain West, and the Midwest—in her new book, *The Government-Citizen Disconnect*.

Figure 20.1, based on Mettler's data, documents the steady rise in government dependency among Kentucky voters as their representatives in Congress moved to the right.

In her book, Mettler gives the example of the Republican congressman Andy Barr, who represents the Sixth District, which includes Wolfe County, where "52 percent of income—approximately $12,000 per resident—flows from federal social policies."

In the adjoining Fourth District, Representative Thomas Massie, also a Republican, "resides in Lewis County, in which 43 percent of income comes from federal government transfers." Massie, Mettler notes, "stridently opposes social welfare spending, having been among the group of Republicans who forced the end of the long tradition of bipartisan cooperation on the farm bill in 2013 because they opposed its inclusion of the food stamp program."

So what's going on with Kentucky voters?

Kentucky stands out in that it is exceptionally white, at 84.6 percent, compared with 60.7 percent nationally; it has a low median household income, $44,811 compared with $55,332 in all states; a higher poverty rate, 18.5 percent compared with 12.7 percent nationally; and fewer college graduates, 22.7 percent compared with 30.3 percent nationwide.

There is, however, one thread that runs through all the explanations of the shift to the right in Kentucky and elsewhere.

Race, the economists Alberto F. Alesina and Paola Giuliano write, "is an extremely important determinant of preferences for redistribution. When the poor are disproportionately concentrated in a racial minority, the majority, ceteris paribus, prefer less redistribution."

Alesina and Giuliano reach this conclusion based on the "unpleasant but nevertheless widely observed fact that individuals are more generous toward others who are similar to them racially, ethnically, linguistically."

Leonie Huddy, a political scientist at the State University of New York–Stony Brook, made a related point in an email: "It's important to stress the role of negative racial and ethnic attitudes in this process. Those who hold Latinos and African-Americans in low esteem also believe that federal funds flow disproportionally to members of these groups. This belief that the federal government is more willing to help blacks and Latinos than whites fuels the white threat and resentment that boosted support for Donald Trump in 2016."

In their 2004 book, *Fighting Poverty in the U.S. and Europe: A World of Difference*, Alesina and Edward L. Glaeser, an economist at Harvard, found a pronounced pattern in this country: states "with more African-Americans are less generous to the poor."

This pattern continues today. The states with the lowest ceiling on maximum grants in the Temporary Assistance to Needy Families program (which replaced traditional welfare in 1996) are in the region with the highest percentages of African Americans, the South, and are overwhelmingly represented at the state and federal levels by conservative Republicans. Figure 20.2 illustrates this pattern.

How does race intersect with other factors contributing to the opposition toward redistributive policies found not only in Kentucky but in many regions of the country?

Let's start with a concept known as "last place aversion." In a paper by that name, Ilyana Kuziemko, an economist at Princeton; Taly Reich, a professor of marketing at Yale; and Ryan W. Buell and Michael I. Norton, both at Harvard Business School, describe the phenomenon in which relatively low-income individuals "oppose redistribution because they fear it might differentially help a 'last-place' group to whom they can currently feel superior." Those thus positioned "exhibit a particular aversion to being in last place, such that a potential drop in rank creates the greatest disutility for those already near the bottom of the distribution."

Among the findings of this group of researchers: people "making just above the minimum wage are the most likely to oppose its increase."

Applying last-place aversion theory to means-tested federal programs for the poor reveals that the group most likely to voice opposition is made up of relatively poor whites right above the cutoff level to qualify for such programs.

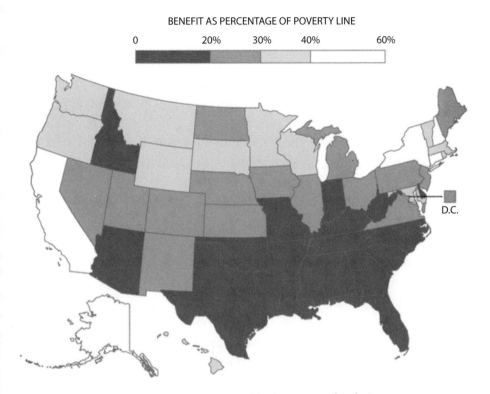

FIGURE 20.2. THE UNGENEROUS SOUTH. Maximum grant levels, in percentage of the poverty line, for poor recipients of the Temporary Assistance for Needy Families program. Even the most generous states leave a family of three at no more than 60 percent of the poverty line.
Source: Center on Budget and Policy Priorities. From The New York Times.
© 2018 The New York Times Company. All rights reserved. Used under license.

Take the case of Medicaid. Nationally, Blacks and Hispanics together make up a plurality of recipients, at 46 percent (21 percent African American and 25 percent Hispanic); whites make up 40 percent.

Even more important than "last place aversion," though, is the issue of what we might call deservingness: white Americans, more than citizens of other nations, distinguish between those they view as the deserving and the undeserving poor, and they are much more willing to support aid for those they see as deserving: themselves.

"Americans believe that the poor are lazy; Europeans believe the poor are unfortunate," report Alesina and Glaeser.

Lars Lefgren, a professor of economics at Brigham Young University and the lead author of "The Other 1%: Class Leavening, Contamination and Voting for Redistribution," emailed me about his research, "Individuals are more willing to vote for redistribution when they perceive the recipients as being deserving. By this I mean that the recipients are willing to work hard but were experiencing bad luck that left them in need of assistance."

This distinction often translates into a differentiation between poor whites and poor minorities.

"Depictions of immigrants or minorities in discussions or media who seem to be gaming the system may lead to beliefs that recipients of government programs are undeserving of assistance," Lefgren pointed out, adding that "there is a developed literature examining the role of racism in the political economy of redistribution. If voters perceive that the primary beneficiaries of redistribution are from a group that they view negatively, they may be unwilling to support redistribution programs."

In 2016, Michael Tesler, a political scientist at the University of California, Irvine, reported on the results of a survey that asked one half of those polled whether they agreed with the statement, "Over the past few years, blacks have gotten less than they deserve." The other half of poll respondents were asked a nearly identical question, substituting "average Americans" for Blacks, so it read, "Over the past few years, average Americans have gotten less than they deserve."

Among white respondents, the differences in the responses were striking: more than half, 58 percent, said average Americans got less than they deserved; 28 percent, however, said that African Americans do not get what they deserve.

The difference, Tesler wrote, grows out of a "double standard in deservingness." He described the double standard as follows: "Different portraits have their origins in what social psychologists call 'ultimate attribution error.' This error means that when whites struggle, their troubles are generally attributed to situational forces (e.g., outsourcing); but when nonwhites struggle, their plight is more often attributed to dispositional traits (i.e., poor work ethic). Consequently, whites are considered 'more deserving' than blacks."

Last May, Mick Mulvaney, Trump's director of the Office of Management and Budget, addressed his view of the division between the deserving and undeserving poor in a column published by the *Post and Courier* in Charleston, South Carolina: "For years, we've focused on how we can help Americans receive taxpayer-funded assistance. Under President Trump's leadership, we're now looking at how we can respect both those who require assistance and the taxpayers who fund that support. For the first time in a long time, we're putting taxpayers first. Taking money from someone without an intention to pay it back is not debt. It is theft. This budget makes it clear that we will reverse this larceny."

The top priority in Trump's budget, according to Mulvaney, whom I have cited before, is not the legitimate needs of the poor, but rather

> the folks who work hard and pay taxes. This budget is for you. It is your government's—your new government's—way of thanking those of you who are working two jobs, saving for your kids' education, or working to buy a home or start your own business. We cannot express our gratitude and respect enough for what you do to make your families, your communities, and this nation work. Americans are the hardest working people who have ever lived. We worked hard to build this country together and will work hard to restore this country together.

In exploring the issue of race and deservingness, a key question comes up: Why would race play such a pivotal role in the growing conservatism of a state like Kentucky, which is, as I mentioned earlier, overwhelmingly white?

Two reasons.

As I reported in an earlier column, a key factor distinguishing counties that moved in a decisively Republican direction in 2016 was not the absolute number of African Americans or immigrants, but the rate at which minority populations were growing.

In 2000, Kentucky was 90.08 percent white and 8.8 percent Black and Hispanic; in 2017, the state remained decisively white, but Blacks and Hispanics made up 12.1 percent of the population. This seemingly modest 3.3-point rise amounted to a significant 37.5 percent increase, making the issue more politically salient than it might have otherwise been.

The Trump administration is now moving forward with a proposal to allow all states to impose work requirements on three means-tested programs that provide crucial benefits to the poor everywhere: Medicaid, SNAP (food stamps), and subsidized housing.

Earlier this month, Trump's Council of Economic Advisers issued a report, *Expanding Work Requirements in Non-cash Welfare Programs*, that declared, "Non-disabled working-age adults made up the majority of adult recipients on Medicaid (61 percent), the Supplemental Nutrition Assistance Program (SNAP) (67 percent), and rental housing assistance programs (59 percent) as of December 2013."

Existing safety-net programs have "contributed to a dramatic reduction in poverty," according to the report, but at the expense of "a decline in self-sufficiency among non-disabled working-age adults."

Liberal groups are fighting these requirements. The Center on Budget and Policy Priorities contends, for example, that the imposition of work requirements on Medicaid beneficiaries "will cause many low-income adults to lose health coverage, including people who are working or are unable to work due to mental illness, opioid or other substance use disorders, or serious chronic physical conditions, but who cannot overcome various bureaucratic hurdles to document that they either meet work requirements or qualify for an exemption from them."

These concerns, and many others raised by the budget center and other groups, document the unintended consequences of blanket work requirements. But in the contemporary world of politics, a Democrat running in most competitive congressional and Senate races in the country would face a tough sell making the case against the imposition of work requirements.

The broader reality is that the civil rights revolution of the 1960s unleashed both progress and a backlash that continues to resonate in American politics five decades later. This backlash is in many ways more insidious than the blatant discrimination of the past and potentially more dangerous. It is an object of constant political anxiety for the Left and continuous, concerted, calculated manipulation by the Right, made more overt by the president of the United States, who has dispensed with the dog whistle and picked up a bullhorn.

21

The Democrats' Left Turn Is Not an Illusion

Over the past eighteen years, the Democratic electorate has moved steadily to the left, as liberals have displaced moderates. Self-identified liberals of all races and ethnicities now command a majority in the party, raising the possibility that views once confined mainly to the party elite have spread into the rank and file.

From 2001 to 2018, the share of Democratic voters who describe themselves as liberal has grown from 30 percent to 50 percent, according to data provided by Lydia Saad, a senior editor at the Gallup Poll.

The percentage of Democrats who say they are moderate has fallen from 44 percent to 35 percent; the percentage of self-identified conservative Democrats has gone from 25 percent to 13 percent.

Well-educated whites, especially white women, are pushing the party decisively leftward. According to Gallup, the share of white Democrats calling themselves liberal on social issues has grown since 2001 from 39 percent to 61 percent. Because of this growth, white liberals are now roughly 40 percent of all Democratic voters.

This article first appeared in *The New York Times* on October 18, 2018. Copyright © 2018 by Thomas Edsall and The New York Times Company. All rights reserved.

While a substantial percentage of Democratic minorities identify as liberals, those percentages have not been growing at anywhere near the rate that they have for white Democrats, so Blacks and Hispanics have not contributed significantly to the rising percentage of self-identified Democratic liberals. Over the past seventeen years, for example, the percentage of Black Democrats who identify themselves as liberals grew by a modest 3 percentage points, according to both Gallup and the Pew Research Center.

In fact, white liberals are well to the left of the Black electorate on some racial issues.

Take the issue of discrimination as a factor holding back African American advancement. White liberals are to the left of Black Democrats, placing a much stronger emphasis than African Americans on the role of discrimination and much less emphasis on the importance of individual effort.

Among white liberals, according to Pew survey data collected in 2017, 79.2 percent agreed that "racial discrimination is the main reason why many black people can't get ahead these days" (figure 21.1). In contrast, 18.8 percent agreed that "blacks who can't get ahead in this country are mostly responsible for their own condition," a 60.4-point difference, according to a detailed analysis of the Pew data provided to the *Times* by Zach Goldberg, a doctoral candidate in political science at Georgia State University.

Among Blacks, 59.9 percent identified discrimination as the main deterrent to upward mobility for African Americans, and 32.0 percent said Blacks were responsible for their condition—in other words, Blacks are more conservative than white liberals on this issue.

The dominant role of well-educated, relatively upscale white Democrats in moving the party to the left reflects the declining role of the working class in shaping the party's ideology.

Politically speaking, there are clear pluses and minuses to this trend.

On the positive side for Democrats, more educated whites are expected to play a key role in the party's efforts to retake control of the House, especially in suburban districts. Women, in particular,

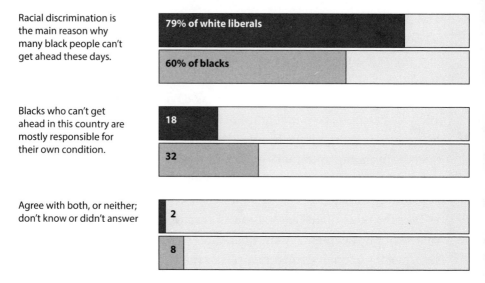

Racial discrimination is the main reason why many black people can't get ahead these days.

79% of white liberals

60% of blacks

Blacks who can't get ahead in this country are mostly responsible for their own condition.

18

32

Agree with both, or neither; don't know or didn't answer

2

8

FIGURE 21.1. TO THE LEFT OF BLACK AMERICANS. White liberals view questions of racial inequality more uniformly than Black liberals do. A survey asked: Which statement comes closer to your own views even if neither is exactly right?
Source: Pew Summer 2017 Political Landscape Survey. White liberal figures do not add up to 100 percent because of rounding. From The New York Times. © 2018 The New York Times Company. All rights reserved. Used under license.

have shifted by the millions toward favoring Democratic congressional candidates.

In 2014, women voted for Democratic congressional candidates, according to exit polls, by a 4-point margin; the October 2, 2018, Quinnipiac poll shows women supporting Democratic candidates by 18 points. Women this year are also the most active constituency driving Democratic mobilization.

On the negative side, conservatives are already seeking to capitalize on the ideological shift. President Donald Trump has taken to portraying his critics as "an angry left-wing mob." This headline in the right-leaning *Investor's Business Daily* nicely catches the spirit of this effort: "It's Official: Democrats Are the Extremists Today."

According to Gallup, the leftward shift among Democrats is more pronounced on social issues involving race, gender, and sexual identity than it is on economic matters.

In a detailed analysis, Gallup found that the lion's share of the increase in support for socially liberal positions "has occurred among non-Hispanic whites. Whereas just 39 percent of white Democrats said they were liberal on social issues back in 2001–2005, that has risen to 61 percent since 2015–2017. By contrast, blacks' views have hardly changed: 34 percent in the 2001–2005 period vs. 37 percent in 2015–2017."

In addition, according to Gallup, social liberalism grew substantially more among Democratic women than it did among men and more among college-educated Democrats than among those without degrees.

Separately, in a September 2017 analysis of polling trends, the Pew Research Center found that from 2000 to 2017 the percentage of white Democrats identifying themselves as liberal grew by 27 points, from 28 percent to 55 percent.

Black Democrats' self-described ideology was very different, according to Pew: 28 percent said they were liberals, 40 percent identified themselves as moderates, and 30 percent as conservatives.

A widely circulated report issued earlier this month provides further detail on the liberal wing of the Democratic Party. The study, *Hidden Tribes: A Study of America's Polarized Landscape*, was produced by a group called More in Common, which says it seeks "to build communities and societies that are stronger, more united and more resilient to the increasing threats of polarization and social division."

The report identified the most liberal constituency as "progressive activists," a constituency that is expected to make up a quarter of Democratic voters this year, according to Stephen Hawkins, research director at More in Common.

These voters stand apart with "the highest levels of education and socioeconomic status" of all the groups studied. They are "highly sensitive to issues of fairness and equity in society, particularly with regards to race, gender and other minority group identities." In addition, a third of progressive activists view political correctness as having gone too far, compared with 80 percent of the population as a whole.

There are a number of other areas where progressive activists differ from the average American, according to the More in Common study. Progressive activists are "more than twice as likely to say that they never pray" (50 percent to 19 percent), "almost three times more likely to be 'ashamed to be an American'" (69 percent to 24 percent), 11 percentage points more likely to be white (80 percent to 69 percent), and "twice as likely to have completed college" (59 percent to 29 percent).

Goldberg, the doctoral candidate at Georgia State University, has documented the changing character of the Democratic electorate in a working paper, "The 2016 Election and the Left's Lurch Left."

Using American National Election Studies data, Goldberg found that among white liberal women, the share identifying themselves as "feminist" rose from 45 percent in 1992 to 83 percent in 2016. For white liberal men, the percentage saying they were feminists grew from 34 percent to 59 percent.

Goldberg's analysis shows a surge of racial liberalism among white Democrats. In 2016, "racial sympathy among white liberals soared to the highest levels ever recorded by the American National Election Studies. Likewise, the proportion of those who believe that whites have 'too much' political influence and that racial discrimination is the foremost impediment to black mobility also crested in 2016."

White liberal racial sympathy was, in turn, by far the strongest among the most affluent white liberals, as figure 21.2 illustrates.

In case you are wondering how racial empathy is measured, ANES uses the responses to four statements to make its determination: "Over the past few years, blacks have gotten less than they deserve"; "Irish, Italian, Jewish and many other minorities overcame prejudice and worked their way up. Blacks should do the same without any special favors"; "It's really a matter of some people not trying hard enough; if blacks would only try harder, they could be just as well off as whites"; "Generations of slavery and discrimination have created conditions that make it difficult for blacks to work their way out of the lower class."

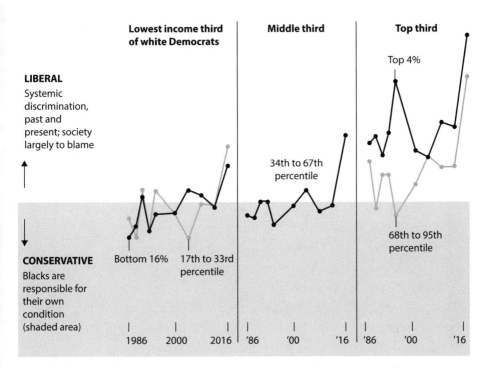

FIGURE 21.2. RACIAL SYMPATHIES OF WHITE DEMOCRATS. In the last 30 years, white Democrats have trended toward liberal explanations of discrimination against black Americans. The wealthier the Democrats are, generally, the more liberal their views.
Source: Analysis of American National Election Studies data by Zach Goldberg, Georgia State University. From The New York Times. © 2018 The New York Times Company. All rights reserved. Used under license.

The shift of white liberals on racial empathy, Goldberg wrote, is part of a larger movement to the left among white Democratic activists: "Importantly, these drastic attitudinal changes coincide with surges in white liberal support for progressive policy positions, including higher immigration levels, affirmative action and government assistance to African Americans."

According to Goldberg, 2016 marked the first year on record that "white liberals rated ethnic and racial minorities more positively than they did other whites."

The same pattern emerges on a host of specific issues. Take the case of immigration: 40 percent of Democrats and 50 percent of liberals surveyed by ANES supported increasing the level of legal immigration, which Goldberg reported to be "the highest proportion on record."

While white liberals make up roughly 40 percent of the Democratic electorate, this faction includes a disproportionate share of the party's activists and exerts a powerful influence on the party's agenda, including the party platform. These voters also turn out at much higher levels than their numbers would suggest in primaries and caucuses.

One question is whether the recent heightened emphasis that white liberal Democrats place on social issues—as opposed to economic issues—contributed to the 2016 decline in minority voting and possibly to the long-term decline of Democratic support from the white working class.

In an email, Yascha Mounk, a lecturer in government at Harvard, wrote, "One of the dangers for the Democratic Party—and the left-leaning parts of the establishment more broadly—is that they confound their actual audience with a small but highly visible group of activists."

Mounk argues that "a majority of Americans is horrified by hate speech; disgusted by the Trump administration's attacks on immigrants; and committed to the fight against sexual harassment. But a majority of Americans also feels that 'call-out culture' often attacks people for innocent mistakes and that some attempts to remedy racism actually serve to divide the country further along racial lines."

Strategically, Mounk contends, "if Democrats couch their fight against the evident injustices that still persist in our country in universal language that has deep roots in the American tradition, they have a good chance of winning elections—and making a real difference for the most vulnerable members of our society. If, on the contrary, they become captured in language games that are only understood by the most political and best educated progressive activists, they are likely to alienate a lot of potential supporters—including a large number of women and people of color."

In many respects, the issue of immigration embodies the Democrats' problem.

According to Pew, Democrats share with much of the general public a positive view of immigrants. Sixty-five percent of all Americans agree that immigrants strengthen the country, compared with 84 percent of Democrats and 42 percent of Republicans.

While the immigration data suggests that Democrats should not have a significant problem with the broad issue of immigration on Election Day, the numbers mask a more subtle reality. Men and women opposed to immigration are much more likely to vote Republican on the issue than supporters are to base a vote for a Democratic candidate on a pro-immigration position.

That is one of the reasons that even after the backlash on Trump's child separation policies, Republicans have continued to emphasize anti-immigration policies. Republicans are "painting Democrats as the ones pursuing an extreme immigration agenda that would fill the country with 'sanctuary cities' where violent criminals roam free," my colleague Julie Hirschfeld Davis wrote in the *Times* on October 14. "Democrats have found that in politically competitive states, particularly ones that Mr. Trump carried in 2016, the attacks can easily turn crucial voting blocs against Democrats."

The ongoing mobilizing force of the immigration issue raises a question for Democrats that never disappears completely: How far can the party push an agenda of social liberalism while keeping the support of at least 50 percent of the voters, plus one?

Lee Drutman, a senior fellow in the political reform program at New America, wrote me by email, "The danger for Democrats is that the electorate overall is probably still a little right-of-center on social issues, and older voters who vote at consistently higher rates are decidedly conservative on social issues. To the extent that these issues define elections, especially Senate elections (where conservative rural voters matter more), Democrats are at a disadvantage."

The party's strengthened social liberalism may help Democrats mobilize more left-leaning Gen Y and Gen Z voters (those between the ages of eighteen and twenty-eight), Drutman pointed out, which would be crucial. But Drutman added a cautionary note for liberal enthusiasts: "Democrats have consistently been disappointed by hopes of mobilizing younger voters, particularly in midterms."

And here's another cautionary note: the very nature of political polarization suggests that even as liberals pull sharply to the left, conservatives are pulling sharply to the right, and it is unclear who will win the tug of war.

22

In Our "Winner-Take-Most" Economy, the Wealth Is Not Spreading

Even as corporate America has unleashed insatiable consumer demand for innovative low-cost goods and technology, it has driven economic trends that continue to increase inequality, stall wage growth, and strengthen the power of business.

The fact that in the face of this onslaught Republicans now control the White House, both branches of Congress, both legislative branches in thirty-two states, and the Supreme Court is a testament to the continuing electoral liabilities of the Democratic Party and the vulnerable spots of the liberal agenda.

Nearly half the country's voters support a president who embraces upwardly redistributive policies that many of them do not benefit from.

Why? Because on race, religion, abortion, LGBTQ rights, and immigration, President Donald Trump—unlike previous Republican presidents—has given his voters exactly what they want.

This article first appeared in *The New York Times* on July 26, 2018. Copyright © 2018 by Thomas Edsall and The New York Times Company. All rights reserved.

This is patently true in the case of immigration. As the *Washington Post* reported in June, "The Trump administration has ramped up arrests of illegal immigrants, slashed refugee programs, criminalized unauthorized border crossings," and secured a ban on travelers from six majority-Muslim nations.

But recent scholarly research shows how the interests of those on top of the economic pyramid are gaining strength.

"Industries are increasingly characterized by a 'winner take most' feature where a small number of firms gain a very large share of the market," David Autor, an economist at MIT, and four coauthors write in "The Fall of the Labor Share and the Rise of Superstar Firms."

They go on: "Markets have changed such that firms with superior quality, lower costs, or greater innovation reap disproportionate rewards relative to prior eras. Since these superstar firms have higher profit levels, they also tend to have a lower share of labor in sales and value-added. As superstar firms gain market share across a wide range of sectors, the aggregate share of labor falls."

According to Autor and his colleagues, the decline in the size of the pie going to labor—known among economists as "labor share"—coincides with the rise of superstar firms and increasingly with the use of outsourcing to "temporary help agencies and independent contractors and freelancers for a wider range of activities previously done in-house, including janitorial work, food services, logistics and clerical work."

The outcome of these developments, Autor writes, is the "fissuring of the workplace," which "can directly reduce the labor share by saving on the wage premia typically paid by large high-wage employers to ordinary workers and by reducing the bargaining power of both in-house and outsourced workers in occupations subject to outsourcing threats and increased labor market competition."

Together, these workplace trends account "for a significant portion of the increase in U.S. wage inequality since 1980."

The steady erosion of workers' bargaining power described by Autor is one part of a much broader phenomenon encompassing both the private and public sectors.

Policy-making, judicial decisions, and structural changes in the economy have functioned in concert to weaken the clout of voters, consumers, workers, and minorities—with considerable support and little or no objection from a key part of the electorate.

The Supreme Court has played a well-documented role in this process, especially in decisions on campaign finance and business law that have empowered corporations and the super-rich.

"The Court has given the green light to restrictive voter identification laws, without requiring states to prove that such laws prevent any appreciable amount of voter fraud or promote public confidence in the fairness of the electoral process," Richard Hasen, a law professor at the University of California, Irvine, wrote in an email in response to my inquiry. "It refused to rein in partisan gerrymandering. The court's decisions also limit the power of unions, as in June's Janus decision, and the Court's love of arbitration and dislike of class actions have made it much harder for employees and consumers to achieve any kind of effective redress when faced with illegal behavior by employers and businesses."

A team of four economists at the Brookings Institution's Hamilton Project—Jay Shambaugh, Ryan Nunn, Audrey Breitwieser, and Patrick Liu—captured many of these trends in a paper they published in June, "The State of Competition and Dynamism: Facts about Concentration, Start-Ups, and Related Policies."

The authors document increasing market concentration: "From 1997 to 2012 the average revenues of the top four firms in a given industry rose from 24 percent to 33 percent of total industry revenues."

Over the same period, investment returns for nonfinancial firms in the 90th percentile "grew 160 percent" while firms "in the 25th percentile grew only 2 percent."

What economists' technical language can mask is that this amounts to a lot of pain for a lot of people.

The downstream consequences of concentration for employees are substantial, Shambaugh and colleagues write: "Concentration in product markets can be mirrored by its labor market equivalent—monopsony—that exists when employers face limited competition

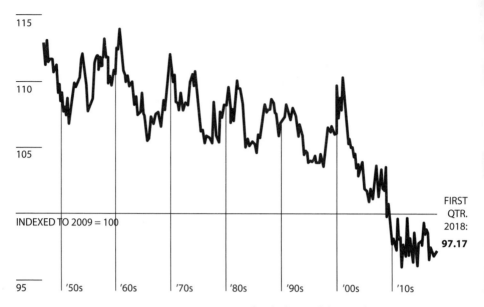

FIRST
QTR.
2018:
97.17

FIGURE 22.1. LESS FOR THE WORKERS. Labor's share of the nonfarm business
sector; seasonally adjusted.
Source: Federal Reserve Bank of St. Louis. From The New York Times. © 2018
The New York Times Company. All rights reserved. Used under license.

for workers." Firms dominating concentrated labor markets "face
relatively inelastic labor supply" (i.e., job choices are limited), which,
in turn, allows employers to "reduce wages without losing all (or
even a large fraction) of their workforces."

Reduced competition between corporations contributed to a wide
range of adverse consequences, according to Shambaugh and his colleagues: "Measured productivity growth has slowed, investment by
firms (relative to their profits) is lower than in the past, job mobility
across firms has declined, and labor's share of income has fallen."

Among economists, one of the most discussed developments is
the precipitous decline in the percentage of total economic output
flowing to labor, as shown in figure 22.1.

In a 2016 paper, "Declining Labor and Capital Shares," Simcha
Barkai, a professor of finance at the London School of Business, found
that the decline in labor share produced a big winner, the profit share,
which rose from 2 percent of gross domestic product in 1984 to

16 percent in 2014. Barkai writes, "To offer a sense of magnitude, the combined shares of labor and capital decline 13.9 percentage points, which amounts to $1.2 trillion in 2014. Estimated profits in 2014 were approximately 15.7 percent, which is equal to $1.35 trillion or $17,000 for each of the approximately 80 million employees in the corporate nonfinancial sector."

In other words, shareholders and business owners amassed profits amounting to $1.35 trillion, or $17,000 per employee, as a result of the increase in profit share.

Barkai contends that market concentration is a major factor in the decline of labor share: "Results show that the decline in the labor share is strongly associated with an increase in concentration."

Luigi Zingales, professor of entrepreneurship and finance at the University of Chicago, wrote that the sharp increase in profits reflects Warren Buffett's investment dictum: "I look for economic castles protected by unbreachable 'moats'"—profits have risen "because firms became better at creating product differentiation and erecting barriers to entry."

What does all this mean? I asked Daron Acemoglu, a professor of economics at MIT, and he emailed me back,

> Both the decline in the labor share and stagnating median wages are a consequence of the fact that three things are happening:
>
> 1. Production is becoming more capital intensive (automation is part of it).
> 2. Some jobs are being offshored, so no more employment and wages in these jobs in the US, but companies doing the offshoring are still performing less labor-intensive parts of production and getting profits.
> 3. A general increase in profits.

Acemoglu notes that the third point should be considered separately because "without any change in production techniques and organization of production, the labor share may decline and wages may stagnate because firms that have greater market power (think

Apple, think Google, think Microsoft) make a lot more (a lot a lot a lot more) profits."

Autor pointed out that the shift in the share of gross domestic product (GDP) from labor to profits "affects inequality in that payments to capital and profits are much more unequally distributed than payment to wages. So if a larger fraction of G.D.P. is being paid to owners of capital and to claimants on profits (shareholders, owners of privately held corporations) and less in wages and salaries, this implies a rise in income inequality between typical households— which live on wage/salary income—and wealthier households that often have these other assets and instruments."

This bleak tale does not end here, as new pieces of evidence accumulate.

Dominique Guellec and Caroline Paunov, senior economists at the Organization for Economic Cooperation and Development, argued in a 2017 paper, "Digital Innovation and the Distribution of Income," that without government intervention, increased inequality is virtually inevitable: "The growing importance of digital innovation— new products and processes based on software code and data—has increased market rents, which benefit disproportionately the top income groups. In line with Schumpeter's vision, digital innovation gives rise to 'winner-take-all' market structures, characterized by higher market power and risk than was the case in the previous economy of tangible products."

Increased profits, in turn, "accrue mainly to investors and top managers and less to the average workers, hence increasing income inequality."

Looking at inequality from a different angle, Annette Alstadsæter, Niels Johannesen, and Gabriel Zucman, professors of economics at the Norwegian University of Life Sciences, the University of Copenhagen, and Berkeley, respectively, found in their paper "Who Owns the Wealth in Tax Havens?" that wealth inequality worldwide has been substantially underestimated because so much of it is put into overseas tax havens.

How much money are we talking about? "The equivalent of 10 percent of world GDP is held in tax havens globally, but this average masks a great deal of heterogeneity—from a few percent of

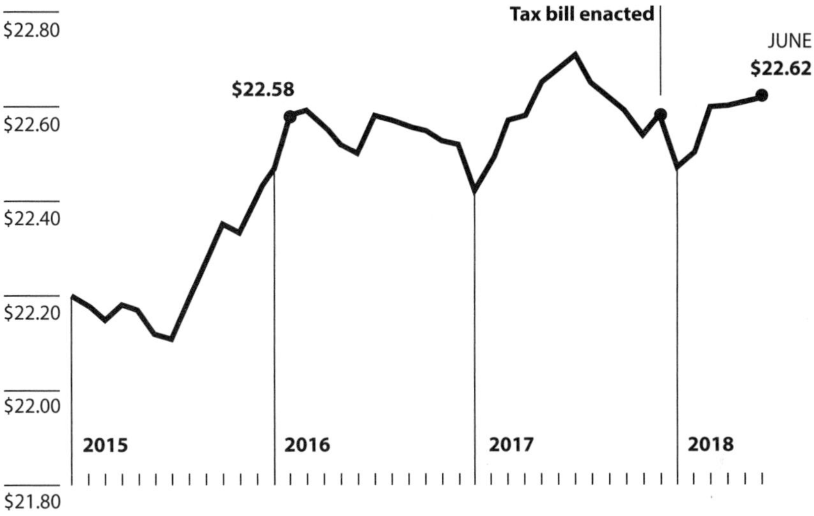

FIGURE 22.2. THE BROKEN PROMISE OF WAGE GROWTH. Real wages have stagnated for more than two years.
Source: Jared Bernstein, Center on Budget and Policy Priorities. Figures adjusted to June 2018 dollars. From The New York Times. © 2022 The New York Times Company. All rights reserved. Used under license.

GDP in Scandinavia, to about 15 percent in Continental Europe, and 60 percent in Gulf countries and some Latin American economies."

In the United States, the top 0.01 percent holds 9.9 percent of the nation's total wealth excluding deposits in tax havens. When wealth in tax havens is included, the share held by the top 0.01 percent rises to 11.2 percent.

While an increase from 9.9 percent to 11.2 percent amounts to a 1.3 percentage point increase, in real dollars that translates to $1.06 trillion, or roughly $40 million for every adult in the top 0.01 percent.

A continued failure of wages to advance (figure 22.2), despite job growth, while corporate profits shoot up to record levels would give Democrats a significant counterargument to legitimate Republican claims of overall economic improvement.

Wage stagnation or growth will play a crucial role in answering the key political question, Which party will win control of the House in 2018? Democrats are generally favored, but they do not have a lock by any means.

Larry Sabato, a political scientist at the University of Virginia and a political prognosticator, recently suggested the possibility of a modest Democratic tilt—and even then was extremely cautious: "Democrats are now a little better than 50–50 to win the House. This is the first time this cycle we've gone beyond 50–50 odds on a House turnover."

That is, there is just shy of a 50 percent chance that the nation will remain under full Republican control after November 6.

Throwing a wrench into these calculations—amid increasing ambiguity about the precision of political projections—is recent research suggesting that more sophisticated techniques in predicting election outcomes actually drive down turnout.

In a paper published in February, "Projecting Confidence: How the Probabilistic Horse Race Confuses and Demobilizes the Public," Sean Westwood, Solomon Messing, and Yphtach Lelkes of Dartmouth, Pew, and the University of Pennsylvania, respectively, write, "Horse race coverage in American elections has shifted focus from late-breaking poll numbers to sophisticated meta-analytic forecasts that often emphasize candidates' probability of victory."

These improvements, in turn, "lower uncertainty about an election's outcome, which lowers turnout under the model."

The effect, then, is that "when one candidate is ahead, win probabilities convey substantially more confidence that she will win compared to vote share estimates. Even more importantly, we show that these impressions of probabilistic forecasts cause people not to vote in a behavioral game that simulates elections. In the context of the existing literature, the magnitude of these findings suggests that probabilistic horse race coverage can confuse and demobilize the public."

If Westwood, Messing, and Lelkes are right, the question for 2018 will be which demographic and generational groups will see their turnout climb or drop the most.

Since 2016, Trump has successfully angered millions of voters, especially women, who have been mobilizing in support of Democratic House and Senate candidacies. Vilified and insulted members of racial and ethnic minorities are seething. At the same time, millions of others—a majority of them men—have been infuriated by economic and cultural developments they feel have devastated neighborhoods, local environments, and workplaces so that they can no longer recognize them.

How many Americans will yield to apathy, and how many will believe with conviction that each vote matters?

2019

The year 2019 saw a widening of the ideological, cultural, and economic gap between red and blue America. Two differing sets of values and belief systems governed the competing regions of the country. In the aftermath of the 2008 Great Recession, blue America had prospered, experiencing steady growth, while red America stagnated. These contrasting economic trends exacerbated longstanding differences over race, religion, and values, spurred by Donald Trump's determination to mobilize his supporters by demonizing the Left and, in part, by the overreaching policy demands of the liberal wing of the Democratic Party.

The election of Alexandria Ocasio-Cortez in New York, Ilhan Omar in Minnesota, Ayanna Pressley in Massachusetts, and Rashida Tlaib in Michigan—"the Squad"—marked the escalation of intense internal division within the Democratic Party, pitting a centrist wing against a more radical left wing hostile to police and to capitalism. The stage was set to turn the 2020 election into, first, a battle for control of the Democratic Party and then a monumental struggle between Right and Left.

23

The Deepening "Racialization" of American Politics

In 1992, before Bill Clinton became "our first black president," before Newt Gingrich's "Republican revolution," before the advent of Barack Obama, I wrote a book about how race had come to dominate American politics.

I argued that the enactment of the Civil Rights Act of 1964 "set in motion a realignment of the two parties. As whites began to feel the costs of the civil rights revolution—affirmative action, busing, urban violence—Republicans recognized the potential of race to catalytically interact with the broader rights revolution and the anti-tax movement to drive working and middle class voters out of the Democratic Party."

I also wrote about the political power of racial resentment: "Race gave new strength to themes that in the past had been secondary—themes always present in American politics, but which previously lacked, in themselves, mobilizing power. Race was central, Richard Nixon and key Republican strategists began to recognize, to the fundamental conservative strategy of establishing a new, noneconomic

This article first appeared in *The New York Times* on February 27, 2019. Copyright © 2019 by Thomas Edsall and The New York Times Company. All rights reserved.

polarization of the electorate, a polarization isolating a liberal, activist, culturally permissive, rights-oriented and pro-black Democratic Party against those unwilling to pay the financial and social costs of this reconfigured social order."

The situation hasn't changed much.

Heading into the 2020 election, President Donald Trump is prepared for the second time in a row to run a racist campaign. He continues, for example, to denigrate, in virulent terms, immigrants from Mexico and Central America.

At the same time, Democrats are doubling down on a racially liberal political agenda, becoming more outspoken and more confrontational in their defense of diversity and multiculturalism. Two of the party's top-tier candidates for president, Senator Cory Booker and Senator Kamala Harris, are African American; one, Julián Castro, is Latino; and all of the current Democratic contenders unabashedly promote the rights of racial and ethnic minorities.

The continuing Democratic quandary is how to maximize essential minority turnout and at the same time retain—or recruit—sufficient numbers of white working-class voters to secure victory on Election Day.

My *Times* colleagues Jonathan Martin and Alexander Burns reported on February 25 that Democratic operatives are debating whether the party should spend "time, money and psychic energy tailoring their message to a heavily white, rural and blue-collar part of the country" or focus instead on areas where "their coalition is increasingly made up of racial minorities and suburbanites."

The dispute, according to Martin and Burns, "is not merely a tactical one—it goes to the heart of how Democrats envision themselves becoming a majority party. The question is whether that is accomplished through a focus on kitchen-table topics like health care and jobs, aimed at winning moderates and disaffected Trump voters, or by unapologetically elevating matters of race and identity, such as immigration, to mobilize young people and minorities with new fervor."

Poll data suggests that Trump is driving Democratic liberals further left and conservative Republicans further right on a key test of racial attitudes.

Michael Tesler, a political scientist at the University of California, Irvine, and the author of the 2016 book *Post-racial or Most-Racial?*, writes in "Racial Attitudes and American Politics," a chapter in a forthcoming book, "Democratic and Republican voters do not simply disagree about what the government should do on racially charged issues like immigration and affirmative action, they now inhabit increasingly separate realities about race in America."

The growing alignment between racial attitudes and public opinion, Tesler continues, "has polarized the electorate and helped make American politics increasingly vitriolic."

Racial attitudes have, in turn, become indelibly linked to partisan identification, and "party identification influences just about everything in contemporary American society," Tesler writes. "Partisanship is not only the most important determinant of our vote choices and policy preferences, but it shapes countless other beliefs and behaviors. Party identification has even been linked to who we find attractive and who we decide to marry, how we perceive objective conditions like the unemployment rate and federal budget deficit, which neighborhoods we want to live in, and the type of TV shows and cars we like."

Because of this, Tesler argues, "the racialization of party identification is by itself the racialization of American politics and society."

Ryan Enos, a Harvard political scientist, notes that "the pull of racial attitudes seems to be moving both directions—so that racial conservatives are being drawn into the GOP and racial liberals are being drawn into the Democratic Party."

Political ideology, Enos continued in an email, "is a broad orientation that is influenced by basic psychological traits and these traits orient a person toward a particular worldview that can be ideologically conservative or liberal and also causes one to be more or less ethnocentric."

The growing linkage between ideological and ethnocentric views has, in turn, contributed to a striking development in congressional elections.

Stephen M. Utych, a political scientist at Boise State University, conducted a detailed analysis—"Man Bites Blue Dog: Are Moderates

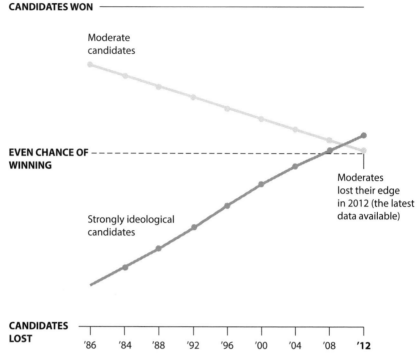

CANDIDATES WON

Moderate
candidates

EVEN CHANCE OF
WINNING

Moderates
lost their edge
in 2012 (the latest
data available)

Strongly ideological
candidates

CANDIDATES
LOST

'86   '84   '88   '92   '96   '00   '04   '08   '12

FIGURE 23.1. RUNNING FOR CONGRESS? STEP AWAY FROM THE CENTER.
Moderate candidates for U.S. House seats used to have a big edge over those
who were much more ideological (either toward the left or the right). In 2012,
the ideologues were more successful, and moderates' odds of winning fell to
about 50–50.
Source: Analysis of Database on Ideology, Money in Politics and Elections
(Adam Bonica, Stanford University) by Stephen Utych, Boise State University.
From The New York Times. © 2019 The New York Times Company. All rights
reserved. Used under license.

Really More Electable than Ideologues?"—of winners and losers in
House races from 1980 to 2012.

Utych found that a core premise of both political operatives and
political scientists—that "moderate candidates should be more electable in a general election than ideologically extreme candidates"—is
no longer true.

In fact, in 2012, ideologically extreme candidates became more
electable than moderates, as figure 23.1 shows.

In 1980, at the start of the period Utych studied, "moderates were quite likely to win—very extreme candidates were less than 20 percent likely to win election in 1980, while ideologically moderate candidates were nearly 80 percent likely to win."

By 2008, however, Ultych observes, "ideologically extreme candidates and moderates became indistinguishable in their likelihood of winning an election, with predicted probabilities of winning hovering around 50 percent for both."

In an email, Utych pointed out that racial views are extremely significant in the trends he describes: "The importance of racial attitudes, and how intertwined with politics they've become, can go a long way to explaining polarization."

Tesler and many other academics use a set of polling questions to determine the intensity of what they call "racial resentment." Whites who score high in racial resentment have consistently voted in higher percentages for Republican presidential candidates.

"From 1988 to 2012 average white resentment scores were very stable, but in 2016 something quite notable happened," Tesler explained by email. Referring to data from the American National Election Studies, Tesler pointed out that "white resentment was significantly lower in 2016 than had ever been recorded in the ANES. It's not just the ANES or resentment, either. Across several surveys and attitudes, the country has grown significantly more liberal on several questions related to race, immigration, Islam and gender since Trump's campaign."

The shift to the left was not, however, across the board. It was driven by one group: Democrats and voters who lean toward the Democratic Party.

"This growing tolerance is largely confined to Democrats and Democratic leaning Independents," Tesler wrote, adding that "Democrats have grown more tolerant as a backlash against Trumpism. It also means that while the country is growing more tolerant, they're also more polarized over race and ethnicity."

Figure 23.2, based on data provided by Tesler, demonstrates the growing partisan division over race, in this case showing levels of

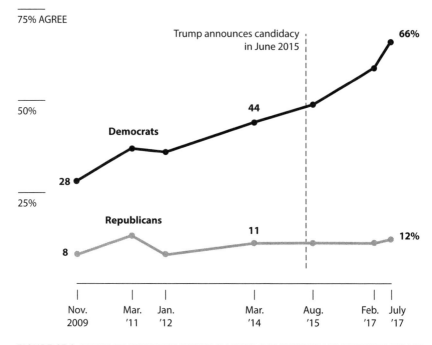

FIGURE 23.2. DEMOCRATS RECOGNIZE RACIAL DISCRIMINATION MORE THAN
THEY USED TO. A Pew survey found that a majority of Democrats, after the
election of President Trump, agreed with this statement: "Racial discrimination is
the main reason why many black people can't get ahead these days." Republican
views scarcely budged.
Sources: Pew Research Center; "Identity Crisis: The 2016 Presidential Campaign
and the Battle for the Meaning of America Hardcover," by John Sides, Michael
Tesler, and Lynn Vavreck. From The New York Times. © 2019 The New York
Times Company. All rights reserved. Used under license.

agreement with the statement, "Racial discrimination is the main
reason why many black people can't get ahead these days."

From 2008 through 2016, very few Republicans agree, and their
disagreement remains constant. Democratic agreement, in contrast,
shot up, from just over a quarter to well over half.

Tesler argues that racially resentful voters turned against Obama in
higher percentages than in past elections when the Democratic nominee was white, but Obama made up for his losses with higher turnout
and stronger margins of victory among Blacks and white liberals.
Tesler calls this phenomenon "two sides of racialization": "Obama

performed particularly poorly among racially resentful whites, but garnered more votes from African Americans and white racial liberals than a similarly situated white Democratic candidate."

Instead of costing him votes, Tesler continued, the "large effects of racial attitudes in Obama's election, therefore, did not so much hurt him electorally as they polarized voter preferences based on their feelings about African-Americans."

In 2016, even though both presidential candidates were white, race played an even larger role than it did in the two Obama elections.

That year, Tesler wrote, "the American public saw a much wider gulf between Clinton and Trump's positions on issues like immigration and federal aid to African Americans than they had perceived between prior Democratic and Republican presidential candidates."

That, in turn, set the stage for "attitudes about race and ethnicity to matter more in 2016 than they had in modern times. Across several different racial attitude measures in a number of different surveys, views about race and ethnicity were more strongly related to vote choice in 2016 than they were in Obama's elections."

On February 19, Gallup reported that the liberal faction of the Democratic Party is growing: "Increased liberal identification has been particularly pronounced among non-Hispanic white Democrats, rising 20 percentage points from an average 34 percent in the early 2000s to 54 percent in the latest period. By contrast, Gallup trends show a nine-point rise in the percent liberal among Hispanic Democrats, from 29 percent to 38 percent, and an eight-point increase among black Democrats, from 25 percent to 33 percent."

Lydia Saad, a senior editor at Gallup, provided additional survey data showing a marked leftward trend among white Democrats during and after the election of President Trump. The percentage of white Democrats who describe themselves as "socially liberal" grew from 39 percent in 2001–6 to 50 percent in 2007–12 and to 63 percent in 2013–18, according to Gallup. This 24-point increase outpaced Black Democrats, who went from 33 percent to 41 percent, and Hispanic Democrats, who went from 28 percent to 36 percent. (Of course, the percentage of white voters who identify as Democrats is much lower than it is for African American or Hispanic voters.)

The Gallup data showed similar leftward shifts among white Democrats on taxing the rich, abortion, gay rights, and a wide range of other issues.

Not only has the Trump presidency pushed Democrats in a progressive direction, Trump himself has played a crucial role in maintaining Democratic unity, according to Gallup: "The Democrats' grand unifier stands outside the party. Despite differing ideologies and opposing views on some issues, on average last year, 82 percent of conservative Democrats, 91 percent of moderate Democrats and 96 percent of liberal Democrats disapproved of the job President Donald Trump was doing as president."

As they prepare for the general election, Democrats battling for the nomination (and their strategists) will struggle to understand how and where their increasingly strong commitment to racial and cultural liberalism conflicts with the views of the general electorate.

This week, for example, the Pew Research Center released a study showing that 73 percent of Americans oppose racial and ethnic affirmative action policies in college admissions. Pew reported that 7 percent of those surveyed said race should be a major factor, while 19 percent said it should be a minor factor.

Similarly, Democratic strategists will be evaluating the issue of reparations, which three major candidates—Kamala Harris, Elizabeth Warren, and Julián Castro—have endorsed so far, in various forms.

In 2015, CNN and the Kaiser Family Foundation polled Americans' view of reparations and found that while African Americans were in favor (52 percent to 42 percent), Hispanics (at 57 percent to 37 percent) and whites (89 percent to 8 percent) were firmly against.

In "The Distorting Effects of Racial Animus on Proximity Voting in the 2016 Elections," Carlos Algara and Isaac Hale, political scientists at the University of California at Davis, show how powerful race has become in mobilizing support for Republicans: "Not only did Trump's frequent invocations of race in the 2016 campaign prime voters with high levels of racial animus to evaluate the presidential contest in racial terms," they write, but the increased salience of race in the 2016 campaign "percolated to relatively low-information congressional contests as well."

The result, Algara and Hale show, is that voters liberal on issues other than race defect "to Republican candidates up and down the ticket when they harbor racial animus." Racial animosity, they write, hurts both Black and white Democratic candidates: "Racial animus (at least when salient) harms Democratic candidates across the board."

I began this column with a pair of quotes from my 1992 book, *Chain Reaction*. Here is another pair:

> As the civil rights movement became national, as it became clearly associated with the Democratic Party, and as it began to impinge on local neighborhoods and schools, it served to crack the Democratic loyalties of key white voters. Crucial numbers of voters—in the white, urban and suburban neighborhoods of the North, and across the South—were, in addition, deeply angered and distressed by aspects of the rights revolution. It had been among the white working and lower-middle classes that many of the social changes stemming from the introduction of new rights—civil rights for minorities, reproductive and workplace rights for women, constitutional protections for the criminally accused, immigration opportunities for those from developing countries, free-speech rights to pornographers, and the surfacing of highly visible homosexual communities—have been most deeply resisted.

And from the book's conclusion: "At stake is the American experiment itself, endangered by a rising tide of political cynicism and alienation, and basic uncertainties as to whether or not we are capable of transmitting a sense of inclusion and shared citizenship across an immense and diverse population—whether or not we can uphold our traditional commitment to the possibilities of justice and equality expressed in our founding documents and embedded in our most valued democratic institutions."

The question stands out even more starkly now than it did twenty-seven years ago, with a president we could not then have imagined, who is willing, even eager, to play with fire.

24

No One Should Take Black Voters for Granted

The African American electorate has been undergoing a quiet, long-term transformation, moving from the left toward the center on several social and cultural issues, while remaining decisively liberal, even radical, on economic issues, according to a series of studies by prominent African American scholars.

"There has been a shift in the attitudes of black masses about the extent to which systematic discrimination and prejudice are the primary reasons blacks continue to lag behind whites," Candis Watts Smith, a political scientist at Penn State, wrote in a paper published in the *Journal of Black Studies* in 2014, "Shifting from Structural to Individual Attributions of Black Disadvantage: Age, Period and Cohort Effects on Black Explanations of Racial Disparities."

Smith argues that older Black Americans with deeply ingrained memories of the civil rights struggles of the 1960s and 1970s have been joined by a younger generation, with the result that "African Americans' attention has increasingly shifted from structural reasons of black disadvantage (e.g., systematic discrimination in the job or

This article first appeared in *The New York Times* on September 11, 2019. Copyright © 2019 by Thomas Edsall and The New York Times Company. All rights reserved.

housing markets) to individual-based explanations (e.g., lack of individual motivation; oppositional attitudes to school and learning) of these disparities, especially in the post–civil rights era."

In her book *What's Going On? Political Incorporation and the Transformation of Black Public Opinion*, Katherine Tate, a political scientist at Brown, wrote that starting in the 1980s, "public opinion revealed a distinctive shift toward political moderation. The black opinion shift, I argue, is based on the transformation of African-American politics, away from radical challenges to the political status quo toward inclusive, bipartisan electoral politics."

Contemporary polling provides evidence of moderation among Black Democrats compared with the views of white Democrats. The poll data suggests a reversal of traditional roles. More conservative and more centrist Democratic whites were once the tempering force within party ranks. Now, on some of the most controversial issues currently under debate, African Americans—who make up an estimated 25 percent of Democratic primary voters—have emerged as a force for more moderate stands as white Democrats have moved sharply left.

Public Opinion Research, one of two firms that conduct surveys for the *Wall Street Journal* and NBC News, provided the *Times* with data describing the views of white and Black Democratic primary voters.

According to *WSJ*/NBC polling, the percentage of white voters describing themselves as very liberal or liberal is roughly twice as large as the percentage of Black voters who do so. Conversely, the percentage of African Americans describing themselves as moderate or conservative is almost twice as large as the percentage of white Democratic primary voters who describe themselves that way.

In the case of abortion, the *WSJ*/NBC surveys show that 97 percent of white primary voters agree that the procedure should be "totally legal," compared with two-thirds of Black primary voters. A vanishingly small number of white Democratic primary voters—3 percent—said abortion should be illegal, compared with a third of Black Democrats.

A CBS News poll of Democrats in states holding early primaries that was conducted between August 28 and September 4 reinforced these findings.

While less committed to many of the broad social and cultural issues important to white liberals, Black Democrats remain more committed than their white counterparts to progressive stands on economic issues of the type that characterized the New Deal coalition of the last century that also established the Great Society programs of the 1960s like Medicare and Medicaid.

Asked to rate the importance to them of jobs and wages, 84 percent of Black Democrats said both are "very important," 20 points more than the 64 percent of white Democrats who said so.

Black Democrats showed more caution than their white counterparts when it came to their views of several major changes in public policy that Democratic presidential candidates have proposed.

Asked by CBS, "Would you favor or oppose the U.S. creating a national, government-administered 'Medicare for All' program, available to all individuals?" 59 percent of white Democrats said they support it, compared with 47 percent of Black Democrats.

CBS posed a broad question testing whether Democratic primary voters want a moderate or more radical approach: Should the message in 2020 be that the party and its candidates will try "to return the country to the way it was before Donald Trump took office" or "to advance a more progressive agenda than the country had under Barack Obama"?

On this question, white Democrats preferred to advance a more progressive agenda 64 percent to 36 percent, while Black Democrats leaned toward a return to a pre-Trump era, 52 percent to 48 percent.

An earlier but more detailed CBS survey of Democratic primary voters (with forty-one questions as opposed to twenty-nine), conducted in March, found similar splits between white and Black Democrats.

Asked to rank how important it was to hear candidates' views on "protecting immigrants and their families," 59 percent of white Democrats said that they "must hear" them, compared with 47 percent of Black Democrats.

Asked if they "must hear" from candidates about their policies on creating jobs, 39 percent of whites agreed, compared with 68 percent of African Americans. Conversely, 76 percent of white Democrats and 48 percent of Black Democrats said they must hear candidates' proposals to combat climate change.

One of the largest divisions was over whether they must hear candidates' proposals to lower taxes: 25 percent for whites, 55 percent for African Americans. Another big gap was on the question of keeping the country safe: 41 percent of white Democrats said it was "extremely important," while a much higher percentage of Black Democrats, 69 percent, ranked it that high.

Tasha Philpot, a political scientist at the University of Texas, emailed in response to my inquiry, "In my own work, I've found a growing number of self-identified black conservatives over the last 5 decades."

She stressed, however, that among African Americans of all ideological leanings, "levels of group consciousness remain high as does Democratic Party identification." African Americans, she argued, "hold two beliefs simultaneously—the belief that blacks should take responsibility for their own success but also that there still are systemic barriers to doing so."

In her 2017 book *Conservative but Not Republican: The Paradox of Party Identification and Ideology among African Americans*, Philpot reports that "when group consciousness is high, blacks regardless of ideology will identify with the Democratic Party," adding that "blacks use a different set of criteria when placed on the liberal-conservative continuum than" whites do.

The result? "Black conservatives behave more like black liberals than they do white conservatives," according to Philpot. "In 2012, for instance, 96 percent of black liberals and 78 percent of black conservatives identified with the Democratic Party."

Philpot's book cites exit-poll data from 2004 (her overall point remains relevant) showing strong support among Blacks and whites in a number of red states for referendums that sought to ban same-sex marriage, but with quite different voting patterns.

In Georgia, for example, 75 percent of whites and 78 percent of Blacks voted to prohibit same-sex marriage, but 88 percent of whites in Georgia voted for George W. Bush, compared with 15 percent of Blacks. In Michigan, there was a 1-point difference between white and Black support for the ban, 58 percent and 57 percent, but a 59-point difference between white and Black support for Bush, 71 percent to 12 percent.

Philpot's most provocative and significant argument is that Blacks and whites define conservatism in substantially different ways, a subject my colleague Jamelle Bouie wrote about in his newsletter last week.

For African Americans, as opposed to whites, identifying as a conservative does not mean holding laissez-faire or free market economic views, according to Philpot. She points out that the crucial role of an activist government in ending slavery and outlawing discrimination mutes advocacy of minimal government among African Americans.

The same pattern holds for support of the military: it significantly increases conservative self-identification among whites but not among African Americans.

Instead, the three key dimensions contributing to Black self-identification as conservative are religiosity, opposition to social welfare, and, to a lesser extent, moral conservatism on social and cultural issues. All three had "a statistically significant effect on blacks' ideological self-identification," Philpot wrote.

The minority of Blacks who were conservative on social welfare, Philpot wrote, "were against government handouts, and were particularly skeptical about the United States' welfare state."

According to Philpot, in surveys asking for descriptions of what it is to be morally conservative or liberal, "whites were nearly three times as likely as blacks to describe the moral dimension in terms of religious leaders, organizations or denominations. Blacks, on the other hand, were more likely to describe this dimension in terms of knowing the difference between right and wrong, traditional values, and the expected behaviors that accompany each side of the moral divide."

Alongside an increase in the number of self-identified Black conservatives, Lawrence Bobo, a professor of sociology at Harvard, noted a parallel development in an email: "There has been a decline among blacks since the 1990s in the perception that discrimination is a cause of racial economic disparities and a rise in the percentage of blacks faulting cultural shortcomings for these disparities."

Bobo said there were multiple potential explanations for the shift, but he remains convinced that "the evidence to explain the trend is less clear than the trend itself." According to Bobo, these factors include "changes among somewhat younger African-Americans"; the likelihood that "blacks receive fewer leadership signals calling for understanding group inequality in structural, discrimination based terms"; and the possibility that "blacks may be encountering less, or at least more subtle and inconsistent discrimination than in years past."

Still, Bobo added, "African-Americans remain far more likely than whites to see racial discrimination operating in most domains of life and as a general source of racial inequality."

In a paper presented at the 2018 annual meeting of the American Political Science Association, "Disentangling Race and Individualism," Ashley Jardina, a political scientist at Duke University and the author of *White Identity Politics*, and LaFleur Stephens-Dougan, an expert on racial attitudes in the Political Science Department at Princeton, argue that past research has created a false dichotomy in seeking an "explanation for inequality" "such that if one endorses societal and institutional factors such as slavery and discrimination as an explanation for inequality, then one cannot also believe in the value of hard work and self-reliance."

In contrast to that approach, Jardina and Stephens-Dougan write, "we treat individualism as a multidimensional concept, such that one can believe in hard work, self-reliance, and the existence of an open opportunity structure, while also endorsing the role of societal and institutional factors such as racism and discrimination, as explanations for the persistence of racial inequality in the United States."

For many Americans, the two authors continue, and "especially for African-Americans, these beliefs exist in tandem," which, in turn, "helps to explain why blacks appear individualistic on some measures, but egalitarian on other measures in some surveys."

In recent years, there has been far less attention paid to the complexities of African American ideology and partisanship than to the changing voting patterns of whites.

The result has been an unchallenged belief among white liberals that as they continue their sharply leftward movement of recent years, they will be able to rely on Black Democrats for continuing political support. But before Democrats get to the general election, they have to negotiate their way through the primaries, which pose their own set of risks.

Another colleague, David Leonhardt, noted in his Monday column, "Democrats, Stop Helping Trump," that many of the Democratic contestants have failed to recognize the liabilities of some of the policies they have been pushing: "The mistake that Democratic candidates have made is thinking that just because they should activate their progressive id on some issues, they should do so on all issues."

Leonhardt cited two specific concerns.

First, decriminalizing border crossings, despite the finding in an NPR/*PBS NewsHour*/Marist Poll that "67 percent of registered voters called decriminalization 'a bad idea.'"

Second, "a proposal to eliminate private health insurance and require people to have Medicare," a plan to which, Leonhardt pointed out, "most Americans say no thanks."

Black Democrats, as the surveys cited earlier show, are much more skeptical of these two policies. If the party and its nominee adopt these particular policies, Black voters are not going to shift en masse to Trump, but their wariness could signal that there is a risk of lower turnout—not only among African American voters but among the less ideological members of the Democratic coalition.

The reality is that without exceptionally high African American turnout, the Democratic Party is unlikely to win any presidential election. From 2012 to 2016, African American turnout fell 7 percentage points, plummeting from 66.6 percent to 59.6 percent according to the census, a fatal blow to Hillary Clinton's bid.

At the same time, the contemporary multiracial, multiethnic Democratic Party needs more than vigorous Black mobilization; it also needs high turnout from constituencies with conflicting agendas—radical and progressive millennials, the "creative class," suburban women, Latinos, Asian Americans, Muslims, and those working- and middle-class whites who still count themselves Democrats.

The danger for the Democratic Party is that each time it ramps up one sector of its coalition, it risks depressing turnout in another.

Democrats require every device, every tool, every stratagem— and even that may not be enough, as Trump and his Republican Party whip up fear and demonize gays, lesbians, feminists, immigrants from Latin America and the Middle East, and people of color generally.

To deal with all this, Democrats will need an overarching message broad enough to bring together their entire coalition in a political uprising against Trump's presidency at the same time that it will need to rely on the tools of narrowcasting: hyperpersonalization of campaign messages, segmented appeals to dedicated niches, slipping voters into discrete "bubbles." They will need a firm grasp of America's disparate, conflicted, and warring center-left alliance. Without an ingenious campaign, even widespread hatred of Trump will not be sufficient to dislodge him from the White House.

25

Red and Blue Voters Live in Different Economies

In the aftermath of the 2016 presidential election, scholars, journalists, and ordinary citizens battled over whether economic anxiety or racial and cultural animus were crucial to the outcome.

Soon a consensus formed, however, among most—though not all—political analysts, in support of the view that attitudes about race, immigration, sexism, and authoritarianism had more of an effect on Trump voters than the experience of economic hardship.

Matt Grossmann, a political scientist at Michigan State, summarized this argument in a May 2018 essay, "Racial Attitudes and Political Correctness in the 2016 Presidential Election." Grossmann wrote that he had "reviewed nearly every academic article containing the name 'Donald Trump'" and concluded, "The dominant findings are clear: attitudes about race, gender and cultural change played outsized roles in the 2016 Republican primaries and general election, with economic circumstances playing a limited role."

But economic decline was—and is—a compelling factor in generating conservative hostility to social and cultural liberalism.

This article first appeared in *The New York Times* on September 25, 2019. Copyright © 2019 by Thomas Edsall and The New York Times Company. All rights reserved.

Let's start with a paper Brookings released on September 19, "America Has Two Economies—and They're Diverging Fast," by Mark Muro, a senior fellow, and Jacob Whiton, a research analyst, which lays the groundwork for a more detailed analysis of concerns that help drive voters' support for Trump.

Muro and Whiton compare a broad range of economic indicators that reflect conditions in all 435 House districts at two different junctures: in 2008 and after the midterm elections, in 2018. Over that period, the number of Republican-held districts grew from 179 to 200 and the number of Democratic-held districts fell from 256 to 235.

Muro and Whiton report that not only have red and blue America experienced "two different economies, but those economies are diverging fast. In fact, radical change is transforming the two parties' economies in real time."

Figure 25.1 demonstrates the divergence between red and blue America.

The average Democratic district's gross domestic product grew from $35.7 billion in 2008 to $48.5 billion in 2018, an inflation-adjusted average increase of 35.9 percent. In Republican districts, GDP fell from an average of $33.3 billion to $32.6 billion over the same decade, a 2.1 percent decline.

The same partisan split—gains for Democrats, losses for Republicans—took place in median household incomes. In Democratic districts, household income rose from an average of $54,000 to $61,000, a 13 percent increase. In Republican districts, household income fell from $55,000 to $53,000, a 3.6 percent decline.

Similar trends are reflected in education and productivity patterns.

The share of adults with college degrees grew from 28.4 percent to 35.6 percent in Democratic districts; from 26.6 percent to 27.8 percent in Republican districts. In Democratic districts, productivity per worker grew from $118,000 to $139,000; in Republican districts from $109,000 to $110,000.

The most important finding in the Muro-Whiton analysis is that even though Democrats in 2018 held fewer seats, 235, than they did

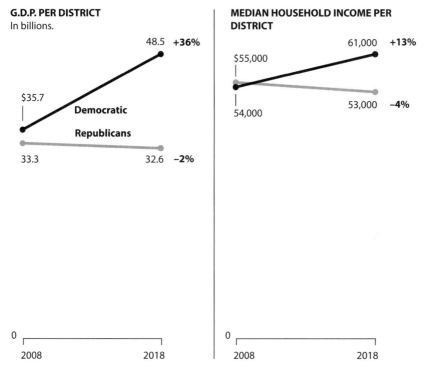

G.D.P. PER DISTRICT
In billions.

48.5 **+36%**

$35.7

Democratic

Republicans

33.3   32.6 **−2%**

0

2008   2018

MEDIAN HOUSEHOLD INCOME PER DISTRICT

61,000 **+13%**

$55,000

54,000   53,000 **−4%**

0

2008   2018

FIGURE 25.1. WHILE BLUE DISTRICTS RISE, THE RED STAGNATE. How economic output and income for Democratic and Republican House districts diverged over the last decade.
Source: Brookings; figures adjusted for inflation. From The New York Times.
© 2019 The New York Times Company. All rights reserved. Used under license.

a decade earlier, 256, the share of the nation's total gross national product created in Democratic districts grew from 60.6 percent to 63.6 percent.

"This increase is absolutely striking," Muro wrote in an email. Democrats are winning in the "very powerful, dense, and prosperous economic areas that increasingly dominate the American economy." In other words, Muro said, "Democrats control the places that are most central to American economic power and prosperity."

In their paper, Muro and Whiton write, "To be sure, racial and cultural resentment have been the prime factors of the Trump backlash, but it's also clear that the two parties speak for and to dramatically different segments of the American economy."

A growing body of work demonstrates that scarcity, economic stagnation, and relative decline are powerful factors driving intensified conservatism on issues of race, culture, and immigration.

I asked Ronald Inglehart, a political scientist at the University of Michigan who has written extensively about the rise of authoritarian right-wing movements worldwide, to comment on the Muro-Whiton paper.

Inglehart made the case that a "combination of economic insecurity and cultural insecurity has contributed to the Trump vote."

He went on, "For most of the twentieth century, working class voters in developed countries mainly supported left-oriented parties, while middle class and upper class voters supported right-oriented economically-conservative parties."

In the post–World War II period, however, Inglehart noted, "generations emerged with a postmaterialist outlook, bringing declining emphasis on economic redistribution and growing emphasis on noneconomic issues." It was "this, plus large immigration flows from low-income countries with different cultures and religions," Inglehart wrote, that "stimulated a reaction in which much of the working class moved to the right, in defense of traditional values."

Most critical, in Inglehart's view, is that treating economic and social issues separately creates a false dichotomy: "The interaction between insecurity caused by rapid cultural change and economic insecurity drives the xenophobic reaction that brought Trump to power and is fueling similar reactions in other high-income countries. And the rise of the knowledge society is driving this polarization even farther."

In a June 2009 study published in the *Journal of Experimental Social Psychology*, "Threat Causes Liberals to Think like Conservatives," Paul Nail, a professor of psychology at the University of Central Arkansas, and four colleagues found that "liberals became more conservative following experimentally induced threats. In fact, the threats consistently caused liberals to become as conservative as conservatives chronically were."

In one test, for example, half of the participants were prompted to think about the threat of death by asking them to describe in writing "the feelings that the thought of your own death arouses in you" and answer the question, "What do you think will happen physically as you die and once you are dead?" The other half was asked to write about the bland experience of watching television.

The authors found that the threat of death caused those who previously demonstrated a "liberal openness" to experience a shift "toward conservative closure." Similar shifts from left to right occurred under different variations of the threat scenario.

Nail and his coauthors wrote that "political conservatism has psychological properties that make it particularly appealing when vulnerability is dispositionally or situationally salient," before adding, "We conclude that significant threats always induce a tendency toward conservative social cognition."

Four other psychologists—Jaime L. Napier at New York University–Abu Dhabi, Julie Huang at Stony Brook, Andrew J. Vonasch at the University of Canterbury, and John A. Bargh at Yale—addressed this question from the opposite direction: What happens to conservatives when the sense of threat or insecurity is decreased?

In their March 2018 paper, "Superheroes for Change: Physical Safety Promotes Socially (but Not Economically) Progressive Attitudes among Conservatives," the four authors conducted a series of experiments including one in which they induced "feelings of physical safety by having participants imagine that they are endowed with a superpower that rendered them invulnerable to physical harm."

The superpower manipulation "had no effect on Democrats' level of social conservatism," they wrote, but Republicans "reported being significantly less socially conservative in the physical invulnerability condition."

Napier and her three colleagues used the same superpower manipulation in a second experiment designed to measure liberal and conservative resistance to social change based on responses to two prompts: "I would be reluctant to make any large-scale changes to the social order" and "I have a preference for maintaining stability in society, even if there seems to be problems with the current system."

Those surveyed, Napier reports, were made to "feel significantly safer when they imagine having physical invulnerability." While liberals remained consistent in their support of change, conservatives shifted in a liberal direction. Among conservatives, "resistance to change was significantly lower in the invulnerability condition," she and her colleagues wrote.

The authors conclude, "Decades ago, Roosevelt noted that fear can paralyze social change; here, we offer empirical support for his observation by showing that ameliorating fear can facilitate social change. Just as threat can turn liberals into conservatives, safety can turn conservatives into liberals—at least while those feelings of threat or safety last."

There are some logical inferences that can be drawn from all of this.

Why does Trump spend so much time and energy keeping people off kilter? He has no interest in increasing the sense of security of his base. To do so would only make these voters more receptive to Democratic appeals.

The relative material deprivation of many Republican voters that continued into the first two years of the Trump administration reinforces their sustained dedication to Trump, even as the regions of the country where they disproportionately live fall further behind.

Conversely, the exceptional success in 2018 of Democratic House candidates in well-to-do, highly educated, formerly Republican districts suggests that Democrats gain from prosperity, affirming the Inglehart thesis that liberal values thrive under conditions of economic security.

As the 2020 election approaches, we can expect Trump not to be deterred by the prospect of impeachment. He will embrace it. He has proved repeatedly—compulsively, really, both in business and in politics—that he is willing to gamble on his ability to profit from a climate of chaos and threat, to rely on an ever-present sense of crisis to fortify and expand his base.

What we don't know, and don't want to find out, is how much damage he is prepared to inflict.

26

How Can Democrats Keep Themselves from Overreaching?

During my political lifetime, there have been four moments when the continuing viability of the Republican Party has been cast in doubt: the 1964 landslide defeat of Barry Goldwater, Watergate, the 1992 defeat of George H. W. Bush, and the 2008 loss by John McCain.

In each case, Democratic ascendancy proved fleeting, and conservative Republican forces struck back with devastating impact.

This is not, I should add, a problem exclusive to the Democratic Party.

On November 3, 2004, the day after that year's presidential election, the chairman of the National Republican Congressional Committee declared that his party had built a "hundred-year majority" in the House. It lasted two years.

There are some strategists—most prominently Stan Greenberg, a Democratic pollster and the author of a new book, *RIP GOP: How the New America Is Dooming the Republicans*—who argue that the 2020 election will produce a resilient Democratic majority coalition

This article first appeared in *The New York Times* on October 9, 2019. Copyright © 2019 by Thomas Edsall and The New York Times Company. All rights reserved.

made up of what Greenberg has called the Rising American Electorate, which will usher in "a New America that is ever more racially and culturally diverse, younger, millennial, more secular, and unmarried, with fewer traditional families and male breadwinners, more immigrant and foreign born."

This New America, Greenberg continues, "is ever more racially blended and multinational, more secular and religiously pluralistic. The New America embraces the country's immigrant and foreign character. It now includes the college-educated and suburban women who want respect and equality in a multicultural America."

According to Greenberg, this coalition will drive the country "toward a new progressive era in which Democrats are hegemonic."

There are, however, a number of flashing yellow lights Democrats may want to consider before proclaiming victory.

For one thing, many of the factors that helped Trump get elected in the first place have not disappeared. Take a survey conducted in October 2018, nearly two years after Trump's victory, "Hidden Tribes: A Study of America's Polarized Landscape." The survey found that among all voters, 80 percent agreed that "political correctness is a problem in our country," including 79 percent of those under twenty-four, 82 percent of Asian Americans, and 87 percent of Hispanics—core constituencies of "the New America" Greenberg sees as ascendant.

Most significantly, there was a small but highly influential constituency that stood out because a strong majority of its members either look favorably on political correctness or are neutral. Among these voters, defined by the architects of the poll as "progressive activists," opposition to political correctness fell to 30 percent.

The role progressive activists play in setting the Democratic agenda provided Trump with an ideal target, helping him portray the Democratic Party as dominated by a doctrinaire elite. In the *Atlantic*, Yascha Mounk, a senior fellow at the Johns Hopkins Stavros Niarchos Foundation Agora Institute, characterized these progressive activists as "much more likely to be rich, highly educated—and white. They are nearly twice as likely as the average to make more than $100,000 a year. They are nearly three times as likely to have a postgraduate degree. And while 12 percent of the overall sample in the study is African-American, only 3 percent of progressive activists are."

Trump's efforts to demonize liberal elites resonated in part because of the ascendance of a powerful, upscale, well-educated wing of the Democratic Party that dates back at least to the takeover of the party by antiwar activists and liberal reformers in the aftermath of the 1968 election. Even now, it is shaping the outcome of House contests.

In 2008, according to a 2019 Brookings study (which I have cited before), Democrats represented eighteen of the thirty congressional districts with the highest median household income, and Republicans twelve. Ten years later, in 2018, Democrats held twenty-six of the thirty most affluent districts, and Republicans four.

At the other end of the scale, in 2008 Democrats represented a majority of the thirty poorest districts, twenty-two to eight. After the 2018 election, the poorest districts were evenly split between the two parties.

Greenberg, of course, understands this perfectly well. He pointedly notes in *RIP GOP* that "Democratic leaders contributed mightily to the alienation of voters that produced successive disruptive elections that put the Republicans in power" and argues that "the Democrats will not run in 2020 calling out to every aggrieved group in its potential winning coalition, as Hillary Clinton did so disastrously in 2016."

While well-to-do Democrats became increasingly preoccupied with moving the party in a progressive direction on social and cultural issues, many low- and moderate-income voters living in less densely settled regions of the country had different concerns.

Anusar Farooqui, a doctoral candidate in history at Columbia, writes for *Policy Tensor*. He argues that the inability of the Obama administration to ameliorate the devastating consequences of the 2008 economic meltdown in much of rural and small-town America contributed to the 2016 swing to Trump in working- and middle-class districts that had voted for Obama:

> The strong correlations between education, population decline, and deaths of despair on the one hand, and the electoral swing to Trump on the other, is clear. There has been a breakdown in elite-mass relations.
>
> Vast portions of the country are in serious trouble. A lot of faith was invested in Obama in 2008 in the shadow of the financial crises. That faith was already shattered in 2012, despite the false dawn of Obama's victory.

Trump, Farooqui continues, "was no surprise. An enterprising political analyst could have looked at the pattern already evident in 2012 and predicted further instability."

Isabel Sawhill, a senior fellow at Brookings, has been thinking along similar lines. She wrote me, "Democrats did not do enough when they were in power to tackle the rise in inequality, inadequate education and health care, stagnant wages, and declining communities that would, in time, create a frustrated electorate—all too ready to elect a Donald Trump in 2016."

Sawhill focuses on economic liberalism with little or no reference to the social and cultural issues that have often proved most problematic for Democrats.

"My conclusion," Sawhill wrote: "Democrats must first win the White House and the Congress and then begin to address the deep-seated problems that have been neglected for far too long. Trump's current problems make that possible, just as Watergate made Carter's election possible, but it would be a mistake to move too far left and lose the chance to begin the reform process."

If they are victorious, will Democrats overreach either on the nexus of social and cultural issues or on economic issues? Will they raise taxes on the middle classes to pay the costs, say, of Medicare for all? Or will they take Sawhill's advice and focus on more easily achievable progressive economic policy aimed at building financial security and an improved standard of living for those in the bottom four-fifths of the income distribution?

There are no obvious answers here, despite the flame throwing on both sides of the left-versus-left-of-center debate. There is a credible argument, as Ryan Enos, a professor of government at Harvard, contends, that the public is prepared to support a turn to the left: "The question is whether the mass public had already begun moving to the left before Trump and I think there is reason to believe this is the case."

Trump "may be the last gasp of a dying policy regime of Reagan conservatism that started to end with the election of Obama," according to Enos. If that's true, "then Democrats will have much more freedom to enact liberal policy reform because the policy mood of the median voter has already moved left and would have done so even without the extra push provided by Trump."

Along similar lines, Gary Jacobson, professor emeritus of political science at the University of California–San Diego, wrote in reply to my inquiry, "The Republican coalition is on the defensive, threatened by demographic changes, and the overall trend of public opinion is in a more liberal direction, certainly on social issues but probably on environmental and economic issues as well."

Jacobson sees little or no prospect for a renewal of "a strong rightward shift in aggregate opinions on national issues more generally. Support for gay marriage, etc., is here to stay, and demands for action on climate change will only grow because the consequences of inaction are becoming increasingly obvious and prospectively dire."

Let's shift from academics back to political practitioners for a moment. Paul Begala, a Democratic strategist, succinctly described the danger of Democratic overreach: "I am deeply concerned about Democratic presidential candidates getting too far over their ski tips."

Democrats, in Begala's view, "should do all they can to reduce their losses among high-school-educated, rural and exurban voters, but with Dems solidifying their hold on the rising American electorate (people of color, younger voters and unmarried women), adding college-educated whites would make the Democrats dominant."

In this political climate, Begala continued, the best thing a Democratic presidential candidate can do is "tell voters that Trump has proposed hundreds of billions of dollars in cuts to Medicaid, Medicare, and Social Security. I did not hear one candidate raise that in the last Democratic debate, but it is the issue most likely to defeat Trump."

Fred Wertheimer, the founder and president of the campaign finance reform advocacy group Democracy 21 and an adviser to the House Democratic leadership on impeachment, notes that if Democrats win the presidency, they will no longer have "uniform opposition to Trump as their organizing principle." In those circumstances, "they will need a president with a program to avoid constant policy arguments," he said, adding, "I doubt they will overreach with a left agenda."

Matt Grossmann, a professor of political science at Michigan State, pointed out that "the last two Democratic presidents have had large agendas and attempted to move policy substantially leftward across issue areas, resulting in public opinion moving in a conservative direction in response and contributing to historic midterm losses in 1994 and 2010."

The next Democratic president, he continued, "will face pressure to make large-scale changes in health care and the environment and to address numerous issues of importance to the party's myriad constituencies." But no matter what a prospective Democratic administration does, it "will likely generate a conservative backlash either way."

In one of the more interesting essays on the danger of Democratic overreach, "Left-Wing Policies Aren't Risky for Democrats. Unpopular Ones Are," Eric Levitz, a senior writer for *New York Magazine*, made the case that "there is no tight correlation between a policy's ideological extremity—as judged by its distance from status quo policy or the dictates of political theory—and its electoral viability. Many 'far left' ideas are broadly popular (e.g., installing workers' representatives on corporate boards, soaking the rich, giving federal jobs to all the unemployed), while some 'centrist' ones are politically toxic ('entitlement reform,' the individual mandate for health insurance)."

Within this context, Levitz writes, there are "some aspects of progressive ideology that put the left in perpetual tension with majoritarian intuitions. The left exists to oppose arbitrary hierarchy and champion those who are oppressed and exploited by the status quo social order."

What this constant tension suggests, in Levitz's view, is "that the left can't presume its moral truths are self-evident to the 99 percent it claims to champion, or the 50-plus percent of voters whose support it aims to win."

Instead, he writes,

> if progressives wish to maximize their near-term power, then their electoral strategy must account for majoritarian sentiment. Which is to say, it must be formulated around unsentimental answers to questions like: Where are voters with us, and where are they against us? What is the probability of changing the public's mind on [unpopular policy x] within the duration of a single election cycle (i.e., how widespread and consistent over time is the public's opposition to our stance)? How salient is [unpopular policy x] with swing constituencies? Is there a way to mitigate the electoral detriment of [unpopular policy x] without abandoning our commitment to advancing that goal?

Levitz describes the strategies it might take for the Democrats to stay in power, if they win full control of the government, a counterpoint to the often-repeated contention that demographics will inevitably put Democrats in power.

In that context, Marc Hetherington, a political scientist at the University of North Carolina, wrote, "For about 20 years, Democratic strategists have been arguing that demographic change will soon provide Democrats a durable advantage. They failed to foresee the force of the white backlash against these demographic trends."

Trump, Hetherington continued, "might well be the last Republican who can win a national election by exploiting race the way he has. But political parties are sophisticated organizations that can and do make strategic adjustments when they need to."

I came back to Stan Greenberg with a few questions. He remains firm in his conviction that "these are different times." First of all, he says, the Republican Party is shrinking. Trump has driven "McCain conservatives and socially liberal moderates" out, Greenberg said, leaving "a shattered party that will have trouble mounting opposition to the new president and agenda."

On the left, Greenberg argues, there is "the unity of liberals and moderate Democrats on issues. Democracy Corps released a memo which showed that an extraordinary number of moderates wanted to tax the rich, for government to play a big role in health care, and address the big gender and race gaps."

Greenberg also asked rhetorically, "Do you really think the Democratic nominee is going to be running on Medicare for All and do you really think that will be the dominant health care filter when the president is running on abolishing protections for pre-existing conditions and failed to rein in prescription drug costs?"

In conclusion, he put the situation this way: "Look at the change in the country in the proportion who believe there is an unfinished agenda for women and African Americans. A sizable majority believe that—and particularly true for all Democrats and millennials."

Recent history has shown regular swings back and forth from left to right. Both Democrats and Republicans have repeatedly demonstrated a capacity to self-destruct, but also to reinvent themselves. If Democrats are lucky enough to sweep the elections in 2020, they will face an enormous challenge: maintaining internal cohesion while retaining sustained public support.

This challenge has proved insurmountable in the past, and it may well continue to feel that way—until it is, once again, surmounted.

27

Is Politics a War of Ideas or of Us against Them?

Is the deepening animosity between Democrats and Republicans based on genuine differences over policy and ideology, or is it a form of tribal warfare rooted in an atavistic us-versus-them mentality?

Is American political conflict relatively content-free—emotionally motivated electoral competition—or is it primarily a war of ideas, a matter of feuding visions both of what America is and of what it should become?

Jonathan Rauch, a senior fellow at Brookings, recently put the issue this way in an essay at the *National Affairs* website: "Here we reach an interesting, if somewhat surreal, question. What if, to some significant extent, the increase in partisanship is not really about anything?"

This debate has both strategic and substantive consequences. If Left and Right are split mainly because of differences over policy, the chances of achieving compromise and overcoming gridlock are higher than if the two sides believe that their values, their freedom,

This article first appeared in *The New York Times* on November 6, 2019. Copyright © 2019 by Thomas Edsall and The New York Times Company. All rights reserved.

their right to express themselves, their very identity, are all at stake. It's easier to bend on principle than to give up a piece of yourself.

The 2020 presidential contest has taken on the attributes, in the words of Michael Anton, a senior fellow at the Claremont Institute, of a "Flight 93 Election," an election with potentially devastating consequence for the loser.

If the opposition wins, Anton wrote about the 2016 election—in a view that holds even more true for the 2020 contest—the assault on one's own values and principles will be worse than any "of us have yet imagined in our darkest moments. Nor is even that the worst. It will be coupled with a level of vindictive persecution against resistance and dissent hitherto unseen in the supposedly liberal West." Anton was writing from the Right, but the same apocalyptic fear of the consequences of defeat applies to the Left.

The dispute over the nature and origins of partisanship is a major issue within contemporary academic political science, with enormous practical consequences.

"This is probably one of the most debated questions among people who study American political behavior," Steven Webster, a political scientist at the Washington University in Saint Louis, told me.

Lilliana Mason, a political scientist at the University of Maryland, is a leading scholar of the us-versus-them school, which has come to be known as "affective partisanship." She sets out her argument in *Uncivil Agreement: How Politics Became Our Identity*.

"Group victory is a powerful prize," Mason writes, "and American partisans have increasingly seen that as more important than the practical matter of governing a nation."

She goes on: "American partisans today are prone to stereotyping, prejudice, and emotional volatility. Rather than simply disagreeing over policy outcomes, we are increasingly blind to our commonalities, seeing each other only as two teams fighting for a trophy."

Shanto Iyengar, a political scientist at Stanford and a pioneer in the study of affective partisanship, put it this way in response to my email: "There is a growing body of work showing that policy preferences are driven more by partisans' eagerness to support their party rather than considered analysis of the pros and cons of opposing positions on any given issue."

Iyengar cited a paper by James N. Druckman, Erik Peterson, and Rune Slothuus, political scientists at Northwestern, Texas A&M, and Aarhus Universities, respectively, "How Elite Partisan Polarization Affects Public Opinion Formation," that found "stark evidence that polarized environments fundamentally change how citizens make decisions. Specifically, polarization intensifies the impact of party endorsements on opinions, decreases the impact of substantive information and, perhaps ironically, stimulates greater confidence in those—less substantively grounded—opinions."

Instead of voters making reasoned policy choices, "party endorsements carry the day," the authors note, adding that "elite polarization fundamentally changes the manner in which citizens make decisions."

I asked Druckman by email about the basis for partisanship, and he replied, "The evidence is clear that, over the past twenty years, partisan emotions have splintered such that people feel more attached to their party and more animus toward the other party. A likely effect is that when partisan elites are also separated, policy substance becomes less relevant. So yes, I think it is clear emotions have increased and this has the potential to undermine substance."

Alan Abramowitz, a political scientist at Emory, is a leader of the opposing camp. Instead of partisanship propelling ideological and policy decisions, Abramowitz argues that "policy and ideological differences are the primary drivers of polarization. Democratic and Republican voters today hold far more distinctive views across a wide range of issues than they did in the past. And it is among those Democrats and Republicans who hold views typical for their party, that is liberal Democrats and conservative Republicans, that dislike of the opposing party is strongest."

Webster, writing with Abramowitz, argued in a 2017 paper, "The Ideological Foundations of Affective Polarization in the U.S.," that ideology plays the central role in partisanship. Citing American National Election Studies data, Webster and Abramowitz contend that "opinions on social welfare issues have become increasingly consistent and divided along party lines and social welfare ideology is now strongly related to feelings about the opposing party and its leaders." In addition, Webster and Abramowitz tell us, survey experiments demonstrate "that ideological distance strongly influences feelings toward opposing party candidates and the party as a whole."

In an email, Peterson cited further evidence supporting the importance of policy and ideological conviction. "There is a substantial component of partisanship that reflects sincerely held issue opinions," Peterson wrote, pointing out that "when I've asked partisans to evaluate hypothetical co-partisan politicians who do not toe the party line on highly salient issues (e.g., Obamacare repeal, assault weapon bans), they are substantially less supportive of candidates who they disagree with on these core issues."

In other words, partisans' beliefs trumped their loyalty to party. Similarly, Peterson wrote, "on salient issues (e.g., abortion, the appropriate threshold for the minimum wage), partisans are also more than willing to disapprove of policy proposals that come from a co-partisan when they disagree with the content of the policy."

These patterns, Peterson stressed, "are not something that would be expected if partisanship swamped all other considerations."

At the same time, however, there is intriguing evidence pointing to the malleability of voters' views on key issues in response to partisan pressure—evidence, in other words, that voters are willing to change their stance in order to conform to the views of fellow partisans.

In a March 2019 study, "White People's Racial Attitudes Are Changing to Match Partisanship," Andrew Engelhardt, a political scientist at Brown, explored changing views among whites from 2016 to 2018, based on surveys conducted by the American National Election Studies. Tracking a measure of white views of Black Americans, he found that there has been

a profound shift in whites' evaluations of black Americans in just a two-year period. The modal white Democrat moves from placing at the scale's midpoint in 2016 to locating at the scale's minimum (least racially resentful) in 2018. For Republicans, the modal respondent still places at the scale's maximum (most resentful), but the percentage of white Republicans here increases from 14 percent to 21 percent. While these shifts may seem small given the scale, I show below they represent a rather substantial change on a measure that has otherwise evolved quite slowly since the 1980s.

On a separate American National Election Studies thermometer measure of group favorability, where 0 is very unfavorable and 100 is very favorable, Engelhardt reported that "in 2018 Democrats rated black people at a 77, up 7 points from 2016. But they rated whites at a 70, a 2 point decrease. Republicans' feelings about black people improved slightly (64 vs. 69) in these two years but this was far outpaced by increased warmth toward white people (74 vs. 81). While Republicans consistently feel more positively about white people than black people, white Democrats' attitudes look quite different. White Democrats now feel more warmly toward black people than white people."

Engelhardt's findings lend support to the views of Alexander Theodoridis, a political scientist at the University of California–Merced, who contended in an email,

> For most people, party identity appears to be far more central and salient than particular issue positions. We see increasing evidence of people adjusting their issue positions or priorities to fit their party allegiance, more than the reverse. We are very good at rationalizing away cognitive dissonance. More important than this chicken-or-egg question is the reality that ideology and party have become very highly sorted today. Liberal and Conservative are now tantamount to Democrat and Republican, respectively. That was not always the case. Furthermore, all sorts of descriptive and dispositional features (ranging from religion and race to personality type and worldview) are also more correlated with political party than they were in the past. All this heightens the us-versus-them nature of modern hyperpolarization.

This debate is sometimes framed in either-or terms, but the argument is less a matter of direct conflict and more a matter of emphasis and nuance.

Yphtach Lelkes, a professor of political communication at the University of Pennsylvania, wrote me that "ideology and partisanship are very hard, and likely impossible, to disentangle," but, he argued, the larger pattern appears to be that "while both seem to be occurring, ideology driving partisanship only seems to be occurring among those that are most aware of politics, while partisanship driving ideology seems to be happening among everyone."

Similarly, Leonie Huddy, a political scientist at the State University of New York at Stony Brook, wrote me that the debate "is more complicated than simple tribalism versus consistent ideology."

There is "clear evidence of partisan tribalism," Huddy observed, "especially when it comes to a potential win or loss on matters such as impeachment, presidential elections, and policy issues central to electoral victory or defeat," but at the same time, "Democrats and Republicans have become increasingly divided on social, moral, and group-linked issues and are less likely to follow the party on these matters." She pointed out that the tribal loyalty of many Republican voters would be pushed beyond the breaking point if the party abandoned its opposition to abortion, just as it is "difficult to imagine feminist women continuing to support the Democratic Party if it abandoned its pro-choice position on abortion."

While both sides in the debate over "affective" versus "ideological" partisanship marshal reams of survey data in support of their positions—often data from the same surveys—one thing both sides are in full agreement on is that partisan hostility has reached new heights. This is reflected in two recent papers, one by Abramowitz and Webster, "Negative Partisanship: Why Americans Dislike Parties but Behave like Rabid Partisans," and one by Nathan Kalmoe, a political scientist at Louisiana State, and Lilliana Mason, "Lethal Mass Partisanship."

Negative partisanship—based on animosity toward the opposition party, not love of your own—turns out to be one of the crucial factors in the outcome of recent elections, and it will almost certainly be a key factor going into the next election.

An astute Democratic strategist, who did not have authorization to speak on the record, sent me calculations from the 2016 and 2018 elections showing that the overwhelming majority of voters hold the opposition party in contempt. They are immovable, in his opinion, and impossible to convert: "We're seeing anti-party sorting—an increasing number of voters are rejecting at least one of the parties, and they are doing so more strenuously," he said by email. There are, he continued, more voters who "have a very negative opinion of just one party (87 percent) than identify with one of the parties (67 percent). So, negative partisanship explains the behavior of many more voters."

In addition, "negative partisans vote more consistently against the opposite party than partisans vote for their party."

The remaining "persuadables"—an estimated 13 percent of voters, with little or no partisan commitment—will play a central role in determining the outcome in 2020.

My source cited polling data from a "consortium of Democratic groups" showing that in 2016 the small fraction of the electorate made up of persuadables voted for Trump 41 percent to 36 percent, but in 2018 they voted for Democratic House candidates 57 percent to 41 percent. At the moment, he said, polling shows that these swing voters currently prefer a generic Democrat to Trump 54 percent to 28 percent, with 19 percent undecided.

I asked the strategist how he expects this volatile group to make up its collective mind in 2020. His answer should not provide comfort to anti-Trump partisans: "Your question is among the most urgent ones facing Democratic strategists. There won't be a single answer— that group is not a monolith, and who the Democratic nominee is will make a difference. That said, we're not there yet. Unfortunately, too many Democratic strategists with the most money to spend are still using content development practices that don't match what we know about those voters."

At the moment, he said, "no one—including political commentators—has evidence-based answers to your question of what will move this group (or any other definition of 'swing' voters)."

In other words, in an unpredictable world of intensifying partisanship and rancor, Democratic strategists—and Republican strategists too—are pretty much flying blind.

2020

The year 2020 was the one in which Donald Trump could not let go. He lost the presidential election but contested the results in explicit attacks on the rules of American democracy. Although Trump lost, after multiple failed suits and maneuvers, the election itself did not resolve the partisan struggle. Republicans gained House seats and controlled fifty Senate seats. It's fair to say that had Trump not mishandled the COVID-19 pandemic, he would have been reelected with Republican majorities in both the House and Senate. Thus, the Democratic victories of 2020 are by no means reassuring and have, instead, a hollow ring.

The 2020 election revealed the ongoing class schism between the political parties. Democrats continued to make gains among white college-educated voters, while Black and Hispanic working-class voters, especially men, shifted slightly—but, from the Democratic vantage point, ominously—toward the GOP.

Trump's refusal to concede had no basis in fact, but reflected the continuing failure of both parties to establish a governing majority—either anything approaching the Democratic New Deal or the conservative majority of 1968–92. While the country entered the third decade of the twentieth century, the American commitment to democracy came under constant attack—from within.

28

Trump Has His Sights Set on Black Voters

The Trump campaign is investing more money and resources in an attempt to attract African American voters than any Republican presidential campaign in recent memory.

The drive includes highly visible television advertising, such as an $11 million Super Bowl commercial, along with ad purchases in local Black newspapers and on radio stations; "Black Voices for Trump"; storefronts in key battleground states; and a sustained social media campaign directed at Black voters whose consumer, religious, and demographic profiles suggest potential support, including on such issues as immigration, abortion, gender roles, and gay rights.

For Trump, the effort became all the more crucial as the Super Tuesday primaries demonstrated Joe Biden's strong appeal to Black voters. Exit polls showed Biden winning 57 percent of the votes cast by African Americans on Tuesday, 40 points higher than his closest competitor, Bernie Sanders, at 17 percent.

Adrianne Shropshire, executive director of the pro-Democratic BlackPAC and the affiliated nonpartisan Black Progressive Action

This article first appeared in *The New York Times* on March 4, 2020. Copyright © 2020 by Thomas Edsall and The New York Times Company. All rights reserved.

Coalition, wrote in an email that Trump has already communicated with a large segment of the African American electorate, although she disputes the effectiveness of Trump's bid to win Black support: "We've had a significant number of black voters tell us that they have gotten Trump ads on their social media platforms. That tracks with our recent poll where nearly 30 percent of those surveyed said that they had been contacted by the campaign."

Many Democrats and their liberal allies downplay the president's efforts, arguing that not only is Black support for the Democratic Party rock solid but animosity to Trump among minority voters has reached record highs. Democratic politicians and strategists who act on these assumptions do so at their own risk.

Robert Jones, founder and CEO of the Public Religion Research Institute, wrote in an email that "just ahead of the 2016 election, only 5 percent of African Americans said they thought Trump 'understands the problems of people like them,' and 75 percent of African-Americans said they did not know a single person among their friends and family who was supporting Trump; moreover, Trump's favorability in PRRI polling in 2016 was 7 percent among African Americans."

PRRI's most recent series of weekly surveys, conducted from late March through December 2019 with a total of forty thousand interviews, show that Trump's positive numbers among African Americans, although still low, have more than doubled. Jones pointed out by email that Trump's favorability rating among Black voters overall increased from 7 percent in 2016 to 18 percent in 2019, with a large gender gap; Trump's favorability rating among Black men in 2019 was 23 percent and 14 percent among Black women.

Despite this shift, Jones argues that he sees little evidence "that the Trump campaign should expect significant defections among African-American voters in 2020," noting,

> Nearly 8 in 10 (77 percent) of African Americans continue to hold an unfavorable view of the president, including a majority (56 percent) who hold a VERY unfavorable view. Our fall 2019 American Values Survey showed his job approval among

African Americans was 15 percent approve, 86 percent disapprove; and among those who disapproved of his job performance, about 8 in 10 (79 percent) say there is virtually nothing Trump could do to win their approval. Perhaps most notably, more than three quarters (77 percent) of African Americans report that they believe that President Trump has encouraged white supremacist groups.

Jones agreed that "the absolute numbers are up a bit" and argued that "the gender gap, and particularly the 23 percent support for Trump among African American men, is something Democrats would want to keep a discerning eye on, but at this point I would not classify it as an issue about which Democrats should sound an alarm. In my opinion, the issue of turnout and enthusiasm among AAs is a much larger concern than losing voters to the other side of the ledger."

Looking back to 2016, there is data that suggests—although it certainly does not prove—that Trump's efforts to demonize Hillary Clinton among African American voters helped to suppress Black turnout.

That year, Trump ran ads in battleground states and on Facebook quoting Clinton's 1996 reference to minorities in organized gangs as "superpredators": "They are not just gangs of kids anymore. They are often the kinds of kids that are called superpredators—no conscience, no empathy. We can talk about why they ended up that way, but first, we have to bring them to heel."

Trump's superpredator ads were designed as much to suppress Black turnout as they were to actually persuade African American voters to cast ballots for Trump. One of the more effective ways to suppress turnout is to cross-pressure voters, to make them more ambivalent and less likely to go to the trouble of actually voting.

At a postelection Pennsylvania rally in December 2016, Trump acknowledged the crucial role turnout suppression played in his victory: "We did great with the African-American community. I talk about crime, I talk about lack of education, I talk about no jobs. And I'd say, what the hell do you have to lose? Right? It's true. And they're smart and they picked up on it like you wouldn't believe. And you know what else? They didn't come out to vote for Hillary. They didn't come out. And that was a big—so thank you to the African-American community."

There is no question that Black turnout suffered in 2016. Take a look at voting in Detroit, a city that is 78.6 percent Black.

In 2012, Barack Obama won the city with 281,743 votes to Mitt Romney's 6,019. Four years later, Hillary Clinton won Detroit, 234,871 to Trump's 7,682. Trump modestly improved on Romney by 1,663 voters, but Clinton saw a 46,872-vote drop from 2012.

While Clinton would not be expected to match Obama in an overwhelmingly Black city, consider the pattern in Ohio's Cuyahoga County, which encompasses Cleveland. Unlike Detroit, where digital election records go back to 2008, Cuyahoga records go back to 2000, making it possible to compare the vote for Hillary with another losing white Democratic presidential candidate, John Kerry.

Here is how many votes Democratic candidates received in the presidential elections from 2004 to 2016: Kerry in 2004, 448,503; Obama in 2008, 458,422; Obama in 2012, 447,254; and Clinton in 2016, 398,276. In other words, compared with the three previous elections, the Democratic vote in Cuyahoga County fell in 2016 by roughly 50,000.

There is another, even earlier, warning signal for Democrats concerning Trump's courtship of Black voters: the 2004 Bush campaign.

That year, Bush operatives realized they needed to win every possible vote in battleground states, including winning over socially conservative Black voters. To do that, they sent Black voters who subscribe to conservative Christian magazines and attend socially conservative churches a barrage of messages, through direct mail, contending that Democrats were intent on legalizing same-sex marriage.

It is hard to gauge from poll data how effective these messages were, but in the key battleground state of Ohio, Bush's margin among Black voters rose from 9 percent in 2000 to 16 percent in 2004; in Florida, by 6 points, 7 percent to 13 percent; in Pennsylvania by 9 points, from 7 percent to 16 percent; and in Illinois, by 3 points, from 7 percent to 10 percent.

None of this data proves that Trump will make significant inroads among Black voters this year, but the record suggests that Democrats should be prepared for a tougher fight than expected, both in turning out African American voters and in winning by strong enough margins to give their nominee crucial backing.

Shropshire, the executive director of BlackPAC, argues that "Trump's disapproval numbers are extremely high among black voters across the board." She added, "Black voters are triggered by Trump, and messaging and imagery about him or his campaign has a negative impact."

Nonetheless, Shropshire cautioned, "eight months of continuous advertising, coupled with the opening of field offices in black communities, could have the intended effect of peeling off enough voters to improve his standing by a couple of points, while raising enough doubt about the Democratic nominee that other voters simply stay home, à la 2016."

The prospect of such a setback, Shropshire noted, shifts the burden back onto Democratic donors and allied organizations to mount a full-court press on those "who voted 3rd party or did not vote in 2016," in order to avoid a repeat of the election results that year.

Ismail K. White and Chryl N. Laird, political scientists at Duke and University of Maryland, respectively, and the authors of a new book, *Steadfast Democrats: How Social Forces Shape Black Political Behavior*, argue that Trump's efforts to win Black support will be futile. In a February *Atlantic* essay, they write, "Political solidarity has been a crucial political asset of black Americans during a long struggle against racial injustice, and a few symbolic gestures or policy initiatives won't win significant black support for Republicans."

They make an intriguing—and eminently reasonable—case for the strategy Republicans should adopt if they are in fact serious about winning over African American voters: "If Republicans want black votes, their strategy should be simple: End racial segregation—which not only leads to societal inequities that most African Americans strongly deplore, but also reinforces the social structures and conventions by which black adults encourage one another to vote Democratic."

Continued segregation, they write, plays a crucial role in maintaining Black loyalty to the Democratic Party: "Racial segregation—the very phenomenon that created a need for African-American political unity—also allows the group to censure defectors. Because of spatial segregation, many African Americans have social relationships almost exclusively with other black people. As a result, these black individuals then find themselves compelled to either accept the dominant political beliefs of the racial group or risk loss of status within these largely black social networks."

Vincent L. Hutchings, a political scientist at the University of Michigan, noted that the Trump campaign "recognizes that no Democratic presidential candidate can win the White House without near unanimous support from blacks, coupled with relatively high turnout." As a result, "the real issue is whether he can peel off enough to make a difference, or if he can diminish support for the Democratic nominee."

While there are "some things that the Trump administration can tout to potentially appeal to a critical slice of black voters, e.g., criminal justice reforms, low unemployment, etc.," Hutchings argued these issues will not "make much of a dent." Group loyalties, both partisan and racial, "are far more important. And, these group loyalties—particularly in a general election campaign—are likely to encourage considerable, and enthusiastic, opposition to the Trump campaign."

Pearl K. Dowe, professor of political science and African American studies at Emory University, shares Hutchings's doubts.

"Trump's outreach is not about picking up a significant number of African-American voters but to message to black voters that Trump may not be as bad as they believe," Dowe wrote by email.

The Trump campaign could succeed in influencing "a few black voters who might decide to stay home if they feel there isn't a real option that could positively impact their lives." But, Dowe argued, "the strong disdain black voters have for Trump" will produce a "higher turnout rate for African-American voters and an overwhelming support for the Democratic candidate regardless of who it is."

Sekou Franklin, a political scientist at Middle Tennessee State University, is optimistic about Democratic prospects with Black voters, but he added some significant caveats in his email: "Blacks believe that this is a do or die election with high stakes, and many see Trump as a threat to their long-term livelihood. This message will be reinforced by black leaders, civil rights groups, and opinion makers—and these social pressures matter in terms of consolidating the black vote."

However, Franklin noted, if "Trump were to make inroads among black voters—and this is a big IF—it will be among black men versus black women. Black men voted for Trump at a higher rate than black women in 2016, and black women are the most committed Democratic Party voters."

In addition, Franklin cautioned, "if a civil war breaks out inside the Democratic Party between Bernie Sanders's supporters and another candidate," the conflict "could cause chaos such that young blacks could choose to stay home and not vote on Election Day, which would give Trump an advantage."

Franklin predicted a replay of 2016 in the event that Joe Biden is the Democratic nominee, with the Trump campaign stressing Biden's vote for the 1994 crime bill. Both Franklin and Dowe agreed this line of attack was effective against Clinton in 2016, and both argued that it received strong reinforcement via Russian interference.

In 2016, "Trump's ads and Facebook posts were effective, but they were augmented by an even more effective foreign intervention according to the U.S. Senate Intelligence Committee report," Franklin wrote. The Senate Intelligence Committee found that Russia engaged in a massive disinformation campaign, Franklin noted, and "it was extraordinarily important in misleading blacks in order to convince them that there was no difference between Clinton and Trump."

The Senate Intelligence Committee "found that no single group of Americans was targeted" by Russian operatives associated with the Saint Petersburg–based Internet Research Agency "more than African-Americans. By far, race and related issues were the preferred target of the information warfare campaign designed to divide the country in 2016."

Gary Jacobson, a political scientist at the University of California–San Diego, argued in an email that Trump "will have an uphill battle" actually winning over Black voters, and the focus of Trump's effort will "be more on discouraging blacks from voting at all (by trashing whichever Democrat gets the nomination) than on persuading them to show up and vote for Trump."

Not only are African Americans' assessments of Trump "over-whelmingly negative," Jacobson writes, but "most blacks think he's a racist, and the proportion expressing that opinion has if anything risen over time." Jacobson cited a series of Quinnipiac surveys that asked Black voters whether Trump is a racist. In February 2018, "74 percent of blacks said yes, 14 percent said no. In July 2018, it was 79 percent yes, 19 percent no. In July 2019, it was 80 percent yes, 11 percent no. In a Washington Post/IPSOS poll taken this January, it was 83 percent yes, 13 percent no. There is no sign that Trump has made any progress in persuading the large majority of blacks that he is not a racist."

John McWhorter, a professor of English and comparative literature at Columbia University, examined Trump's prospects for winning Black votes from an entirely different vantage point. In an email, McWhorter wrote, "Trump's racism is less important to probably most black people than it is to the minority of black people in academia/the media/collegetownish circles. Beyond the contingent we today can roughly delineate as 'Twitter people,' the idea that someone is immediately disqualified from moral worth by harboring any degree of bigotry is an abstraction. As such, there is a kind of black person—mostly male, I suspect—who connects with Trump's Alpha Male routine, which has a lot in common with the rapper persona. It is, therefore, not remotely surprising that Kanye West likes him."

Despite this, McWhorter continued, "I do know this: if Biden is the nominee, no. Most voters, of whatever color, vote on the basis of certain gut instincts. Biden appeals to black people partly because of a certain vernacular glint in his eye and partly now because of his connection with Obama. Wielding that will 'trump' all but about seven black voters' affection for Trump's 'swagger.'"

In the case of Sanders, McWhorter wrote, it's "hard to say. Most black people are not leftists," and "my gut tells me" that "most of those unmoved by Sanders would simply stay home rather than go out and cast a vote for Trump."

One problem facing Democrats and liberals is an overemphasis on what pollsters call the headline or top-line figures in polling reports, which unquestionably show deep hostility to the Trump administration, and inadequate attention to some less prominent details.

A survey of 804 registered African American voters conducted last month for BlackPAC by Cornell Belcher's firm, Brilliant Corners Research & Strategies, produced this bullet list of findings:

- 76 percent of Black voters disapprove of Donald Trump's job performance, with 65 percent saying they strongly disapprove.
- 77 percent agree that Trump is a racist with 66 percent saying they strongly agree.
- 75 percent disapprove of congressional Republicans with 59 percent strongly disapproving. Also, the majority of Black voters (61 percent) think the Republican Party is also racist.

Further on in the report on the poll, there are some numbers that are less comforting for Democrats. Nearly one out of five, 18 percent, either strongly (13 percent) or somewhat (5 percent) approve of Trump's job performance.

Even more disconcerting to Democrats: according to the Belcher poll, their party "is underperforming in the generic ballot" among African Americans. Of those interviewed, 70 percent said they plan to vote for the Democratic nominee, 12 percent said they plan to vote for Trump, and another 12 percent said they will vote for a third-party candidate. Six percent said they were undecided. In comparison, Belcher noted, "Obama got 93 percent in 2012." Clinton received 91 percent of the Black vote in 2016.

In other words—despite Trump's record in office; his describing some white supremacists in Charlottesville as "very fine people"; his referring to Haiti and African nations as "shithole countries"; and his calling Elijah Cummings's majority-Black Seventh Congressional District "a disgusting, rat and rodent infested mess"—the numbers in the BlackPAC survey warn that the loyalty of a quarter of Black voters to the Democratic Party may be waning.

Assuming that the 2020 election is close, any increase in defections, or a repeat of the relatively low Black turnout of 2016, could seriously endanger Democratic prospects. Clearly the Trump campaign understands this, but it remains uncertain whether the Democratic Party does.

29

How Far Might Trump Go?

On election night and the days that follow, the country may be in for a roller-coaster ride, with ups and downs that raise and dash expectations, provoking anger and frustration.

Here is a scenario, sketched out by Edward B. Foley, a professor of constitutional law at Ohio State, in his 2019 paper "Preparing for a Disputed Presidential Election: An Exercise in Election Risk Assessment and Management."

Foley presents a hypothetical widely discussed by election experts— with an outcome that hangs on the willingness of Republican-controlled legislatures to support Trump in the event that he loses the popular vote and refuses to commit to a peaceful transfer of power, as he has frequently threatened.

"The president might attempt to defy even a landslide in the popular vote in battleground states," Foley writes. "The risk of a seriously disputed election depends in part on the preliminary returns available on election night, as well as the willingness of gerrymandered state legislatures to consider repudiating the popular vote, and the degree to which there develop genuine problems to fight over in court, or the ability to generate perceived problems

This article first appeared in *The New York Times* on October 28, 2020. Copyright © 2020 by Thomas Edsall and The New York Times Company. All rights reserved.

that would give state legislatures cover for taking matters into their own hands."

Foley outlined a set of possible worst-case developments that could lead to not only bitter legislative and court fights but also protests by whichever side emerges as the loser: "This time it is all eyes on Pennsylvania, as whoever wins the Keystone State will win an Electoral College majority. Trump is ahead in the state by 20,000 votes, and he is tweeting 'The race is over. Another four years to keep Making America Great Again.'"

In Foley's speculative account, the Associated Press and the networks do not call the election on November 3, fully aware that there are still thousands of votes to be counted. The next morning, in this version of reality, "new numbers show Trump's lead starting to slip. Trump holds a press conference, however, to announce 'I've won re-election. The results last night showed that I won' and warns that 'I'm not going to let machine politicians in Philadelphia steal my re-election victory from me—or from my voters!'"

The vote counting, in this scenario, continues as Trump's lead slowly evaporates.

Foley, imagining what comes next, continues, "Trump insists, by tweet and microphone, 'THIS THEFT WILL NOT STAND!!!' 'WE ARE TAKING BACK OUR VICTORY.'"

If events were in fact to unfold this way, and if Trump were to get the backing of the Pennsylvania State Senate and House, both currently controlled by Republicans, the stage could indeed be set for what Foley and other legal experts have described as a battle with few precedents.

Barton Gellman, in a long essay in the *Atlantic*, "The Election That Could Break America," makes extensive use of Foley's conjecture. "Trump's crusade against voting by mail is a strategically sound expression of his plan for the Interregnum," the period from Election Day until the inauguration of January 20. Trump, Gellman continues, "is preparing the ground for post–election night plans to contest the results. It is the strategy of a man who expects to be outvoted and means to hobble the count."

Lawrence Tabas, the Pennsylvania Republican Party chairman, told Gellman that he has discussed the possibility of the legislature rejecting some or all mailed-in ballots and subsequently choosing a slate of pro-Trump electors to cast the state's twenty Electoral College votes for the incumbent. "I just don't think this is the right time for me to be discussing those strategies and approaches," Tabas told Gellman, but direct appointment of electors "is one of the options. It is one of the available legal options set forth in the Constitution."

If two sets of electors were sent to Washington, the US House and Senate would determine whether to accept electors from Pennsylvania chosen by the Republican legislature, or electors certified by Pennsylvania's Democratic governor, Tom Wolf.

Working in the same vein as Foley, Larry Diamond, a political scientist and senior fellow at Stanford's Hoover Institution, described by email what he called "by far the most dangerous scenario": "Trump is leading when the in-person votes are counted on election night. If you just stopped counting at midnight on election night, Trump would be the winner, even though many millions of mail-in ballots in key swing states are still to be counted."

When the "blue wave comes in," Diamond continues, "and gives Biden a victory in states with more than 270 electoral votes, Trump cries foul and demands that the Republican legislators in states like Pennsylvania, maybe Florida, give him their electoral votes, even though he didn't win according to the vote count."

In a September 8 *Atlantic* essay, Diamond and Foley, writing together, warn of the possibility that "Jan. 20 could arrive with Vice President Pence, in his role as Senate president, insisting that President Trump has been re-elected to a second term—while at the same time, Speaker Pelosi insists that there is no president-elect, because the process remains deadlocked, and hence she will assume the role of acting president until the counting of electoral votes from the states resumes with the disputed state resolved."

Richard Hasen, a professor of law and political science at the University of California, Irvine, emailed his version of a worst-case situation: "If it turns out to be really close and it comes down to Pennsylvania, God help the United States of America."

Hasen warns that Pennsylvania is expected to be one of the last states to complete the tabulation of votes, and, in that case, Pennsylvania's twenty Electoral College votes could determine the winner. If that is the case, Hasen says, "it will be trench warfare over ballots and a president seeking to cast major doubt over the legitimacy of the election even without evidence of major problems. It would be much worse than Bush v. Gore because of Trump's rhetoric, because we are more polarized and many see this election in existential terms, and because internal and external forces can use social media to spread disinformation and fan the flames of hate."

Barry Burden, a political scientist at the University of Wisconsin–Madison, shared Hasen's worries, outlining in an email what he views as "the most likely scenario": "President Trump falsely condemns the election as fraudulent and illegal. He will build on his allegations that millions of noncitizens voted illegally in 2016 to claim that millions of absentee ballots were submitted in duplicate or by foreign governments, neither of which will be true. He will intensify his rants against the supposed fraud as Biden's lead in the popular vote grows in the days following the election."

A flood of lawsuits "on postal delays, questions over the matching of voter signatures on absentee ballots, and lines at the polls" will likely "cause suspicious voters to think something is afoot," Burden wrote. "This suspicion along with the possibility of a longer vote count this year will make it even more tempting for Trump and other politicians to begin making false allegations on election night."

Richard Pildes, a law professor at New York University, pointed out in an email that policy makers who support extended vote-processing deadlines "face a trade-off. The longer the permitted time, the more ballots will be valid. But the longer that time, the longer it will take for the final result to be known."

In more normal elections, Pildes continued, "that would not pose any risk, but in our climate of existential politics, partisans all-too-prepared to believe (or charge) that elections are being manipulated, and a social-media environment poised to heap fuel onto the fire, the longer after Election Day any significant changes in vote totals takes place, the greater the risk that the side that loses will cry that the election has been stolen."

Going back to November 3, if Trump fears he is headed for defeat, the critical period during which he would have to throw the first of many monkey wrenches into the process could be the late hours after polls close and through the early hours of the fourth—at the height of what election experts call "the red mirage"—the period of time in which those votes cast in person, who are disproportionately Republican, outnumber those not-yet-counted votes cast by mail or at off-site ballot boxes, disproportionately Democratic—a period of time known as "the blue shift."

If, as many of these experts anticipate, a "red mirage" emerges as the polls shut on Election Day, Trump could, at that moment, have the opportunity to declare victory and set in motion the workings of the federal government, especially the Department of Justice under Attorney General William Barr.

Nathaniel Persily, a law professor at Stanford, described this period to *Politico* magazine as "the fog of war in the 24 hours after the polls close," when "there's going to be a competition to explain what's taking place by the candidates, the news media, perhaps even foreign actors."

Barr has in fact already begun setting the stage to challenge the results, to foster distrust of the outcome, and to dispute votes cast by mail.

Last month, Barr told CNN that mailed-in balloting "is very open to fraud and coercion. It's reckless and dangerous, and people are playing with fire."

At a news conference in Phoenix on September 10, Barr sowed further confusion, contending that many "ballots are mailed out profligately" and many are misdirected "because of inaccuracy of voting lists. There are going to be ballots floating around."

Any drive to seriously contest the election would have to be conducted during what Gellman described as the interregnum, the seventy-nine days between the November 3 election and January 20, Inauguration Day.

During this period, there are four key dates: December 14, when the electors meet in each state to cast their ballots; January 3, when the new House and Senate are sworn in; January 6, when the two branches meet to certify the vote of the Electoral College; and January 20, when the president is sworn in.

What follows is based on Foley's description in an email of how Trump could attempt to manipulate the outcome during the interregnum.

States with Republican legislatures and Democratic governors—like Pennsylvania, Michigan, or Wisconsin—could end up submitting two slates of electors to Congress, one chosen by the Republican legislatures that reject enough mailed-in ballots to give Trump the win, the other by the Democratic governors of these states, who would certify slates backing Biden.

Insofar as such challenges could end up before the Supreme Court, Trump would have the advantage of a six-member conservative majority—with the swearing in this week of Amy Coney Barrett—a majority that could survive the possible defection of Chief Justice John G. Roberts Jr.

I asked Persily about Barrett's role in future litigation.

"This is both the most important question and the one most impossible to answer," Persily replied, adding that "the Republicans clearly think their chances with her on the court are better than without her."

If any of this comes to pass, Barrett's role in election litigation could quickly become apparent in the way the Supreme Court approaches a renewed attempt by the Republican Party of Pennsylvania to overturn a state supreme court ruling. The ruling requires election officials to count mail-in ballots postmarked on Election Day or before but received as late as November 6. These ballots would likely favor Democrats.

In an earlier four-to-four decision, with Roberts joining the three liberal justices, the court let the Pennsylvania Supreme Court ruling stand.

On October 23, the Pennsylvania state Republican Party asked the Supreme Court to take up the case again on its merits. If the court does so—back at full membership with Barrett potentially positioned to cast the tiebreaking vote—it raises the possibility that the outcome could once again be in the hands of the Supreme Court, just as it was in *Bush v. Gore* in 2000. The election would have to be close for this scenario to develop, but it is not impossible. (After this column was published, the Supreme Court decided not to review the case again before Election Day, but three justices signaled their willingness to look into it after Election Day.)

An eventuality along these lines would play out against a background of grassroots mobilization on both the right and left that heightens the prospect of civic disruption. If Trump were to take advantage of chaos on Election Day and in its aftermath to claim victory, there is the near-certain prospect of protests that would make this past summer's Black Lives Matter demonstrations look mild in comparison.

The radical Right is currently the greatest focus of a potential for disruption.

The Armed Conflict Location & Event Data Project, a liberal nonprofit group, issued a report earlier this month, *Standing By: Right-Wing Militia Groups and the US Election,* that "maps a subset of the most active right-wing militias," including the Three Percenters, the Oath Keepers, the Light Foot Militia, the Civilian Defense Force, and the "street movements that are highly active in brawls," including the Proud Boys and Patriot Prayer.

The Armed Conflict Location Group report warns, "Militia groups and other armed nonstate actors pose a serious threat to the safety and security of American voters. Throughout the summer and leading up to the general election, these groups have become more assertive, with activities ranging from intervening in protests to organizing kidnapping plots targeting elected officials."

The group's report noted that both the Department of Homeland Security and the Federal Bureau of Investigation "have specifically identified extreme far right-wing and racist movements as a primary risk factor heading into November, describing the election as a potential 'flash point' for reactionary violence."

At the same time, liberal groups have not been sitting on their hands.

A relatively moderate entity called Holdtheline has issued *A Guide to Defending Democracy* by Hardy Merriman, Ankur Asthana, Marium

Navid, and Kifah Shah, all active in leftist advocacy groups. The guide warns that "we are witnessing ongoing actions that destroy our democracy bit by bit."

The guide pointedly stresses nonviolence and describes two categories of protest, "acts of commission," including engaging in demonstrations, marches, or nonviolent blockades and "acts of omission," including "strikes of all kinds; deliberate work slowdowns; boycotts of all kinds; divestment; refusing to pay certain fees, bills, taxes, or other costs; or refusal to observe certain expected social norms or behaviors."

A second liberal group, Choosing Democracy, is preparing for nonviolent protest in the event of "an undemocratic power grab—a coup." The group asks supporters to take the following pledge:

> We will vote.
>
> We will refuse to accept election results until all the votes are counted.
>
> We will nonviolently take to the streets if a coup is attempted.
>
> If we need to, we will shut down this country to protect the integrity of the democratic process.

As the Black Lives Matter protests in Portland, Seattle, New York, and other cities demonstrated last summer, in large-scale protests it can be difficult to enforce a commitment to nonviolence.

Not only that, but the federal indictment of Ivan Harrison Hunter, a member of the Boogaloo Bois, on charges that he "discharged 13 rounds from an AK-47 style semiautomatic rifle into the Minneapolis Police Department's Third Precinct building" suggests that in the event of protests from the Left, right-wing groups will attempt to foster and encourage violence.

Police departments across the nation are gearing up to deal with violence on Election Day and in its aftermath.

"It's fair to say the police are preparing in ways they never would have had to for Election Day," Chuck Wexler, director of the Police Executive Research Forum, a Washington-based think tank, told *Time* magazine. Andrew Walsh, a deputy chief of the Las Vegas

Metropolitan Police Department, told the *Washington Post*, "I don't think we've seen anything like this in modern times."

All of this—the political and legal battles, the possibility of civic strife—raises the question: Why have politics and elections become such sources of volatility?

In an essay in the *Washington Post* on October 23, Foley sought to explain why an unprecedented Trump-Republican refusal to accept the outcome of the 2020 election is within the bounds of possibility: "The notion of a state's elected politicians acting to subvert the will of their own citizens should be unthinkable. But that's, in effect, what gerrymandering is. Elections are supposed to be held for the benefit of voters so that the public obtains the officeholders it wants. Gerrymandering is premised on the contrary approach: letting incumbent politicians manipulate the electoral system to defy the popular will for partisan advantage."

In state after state, the Republican Party has used gerrymandering to stay in power, winning majorities with fewer votes than cast for Democrats.

"Soon," Foley wrote, "the country may be forced to confront the question of whether this anti-democracy attitude has so taken hold that it could actually undo a presidential election."

A large part of the answer to Foley's question lies in what the Republican Party has become over the past two decades, as the once-ascendant conservative coalition has struggled to remain viable.

The reality is that in order to remain competitive, the party has been forced to adopt policies and strategies designed to restrict and constrain the majority electorate: voter suppression; gerrymandering; dependence on an Electoral College that favors small, rural states; and legislation designed to weaken and defund the labor movement.

In this context, it's not a surprise that Trump and his partisan allies would be guided by an "anti-democracy attitude" that "has so taken hold that it could actually undo a presidential election." What is more surprising is that it could succeed.

30

What Is Trump Playing At?

As newspapers and media across the country and around the world reported Joe Biden's victory and Donald Trump's defeat in last week's election, Trump himself—along with his Republican allies in Congress, including the entire Senate majority leadership and the Republican House minority leadership—remained defiant.

I queried a number of American historians and constitutional scholars to see how they explain what should be an inexplicable response to an election conducted in a modern democracy—an election in which Republican victories up and down the ballot are accepted unquestioningly, while votes for president-elect Biden on the same ballots are not.

Many of those I questioned see this discrepancy as stemming from Trump's individual personality and characterological deficiencies—what they call his narcissism and his sociopathy. Others offer a more starkly political interpretation: that the refusal to accept Biden's victory stems from the frustration of a Republican Party struggling to remain competitive in the face of an increasingly multicultural electorate. In the end, it appears to be a mixture of both.

This article first appeared in *The New York Times* on November 11, 2020. Copyright © 2020 by Thomas Edsall and The New York Times Company. All rights reserved.

Many observers believe that the current situation presents a particularly dangerous mix, one that poses a potentially grave danger to American democracy.

Jonathan Gienapp, a professor of history at Stanford and the author of *The Second Creation: Fixing the American Constitution in the Founding Era*, noted by email that there have been close, contested elections in the past, "but none of these earlier examples featured what we see now: a completely manufactured controversy based on no evidence whatsoever, purely to maintain power, and to overturn a legitimate election."

In this context, "Trump's refusal to concede and his congressional allies' refusal to object to what he is doing is indeed most dangerous. If it continues to be given oxygen, it's hard not to think that there could be lasting damage to the republic."

This, Gienapp concluded, "is what rot looks like."

James T. Kloppenberg, a professor of American history at Harvard, responded to my inquiry with a broad overview, worth quoting at length: "Trump's refusal to acknowledge defeat is unprecedented. Yet it is consistent with everything he's done throughout his life, so it should not surprise us. While political scientists often focus on institutions and political practices, democracy, where it exists, rests on deeper cultural predispositions that are harder to see. Unless a culture has internalized the norms of deliberation, pluralism, and above all reciprocity, there is no reason to concede to your worst enemy when he wins an election, nor is there any reason to acknowledge the legitimacy of opponents."

It is just these underpinnings of democracy that Trump threatens, especially now: "Norm-busting has been Trump's modus operandi from a very early age, so to expect him now to conform to democratic norms is unrealistic. Conceding defeat is a tradition consistent with the ethic of reciprocity: you admit defeat, move on, work with those you disagree with, and try to win the next election. Establishing those norms is the work of centuries, not decades. The colonies that became the United States had been at it since the 1630s. By 1787 those cultural pillars were already in place."

Trump's behavior, Kloppenberg argues, is the culmination of long-term developments within Republican ranks:

> Many conservatives considered the New Deal a repudiation of the laissez-faire dogmas they claimed were written into American life. They were wrong about that, as a generation of progressives had shown for decades before FDR's election. But from Goldwater and Reagan through Gingrich to the present, many Republicans have viewed deviations from what they consider the gospel of free-market capitalism as heresy. Of course there has never been anything remotely resembling a free market in the United States. State, local, and federal governments were involved in daily life from the nation's first days. But the fantasy of unrestrained capitalism has endured, as has the strategy of condemning as "un-American" anyone who dares suggest otherwise. Given Trump's four years of hate-mongering and his stubborn refusal to acknowledge reality, his behavior since the election is to be expected—and criticized as the direct challenge to democracy that it is.

Sean Wilentz, a professor of history at Princeton, was outspoken:

> It would be not simply a major departure but a deeply dangerous one were Trump to deny the legitimacy of Biden's election. It would be a brutal renunciation of American democracy. It would create not simply a fissure but a chasm in the nation's politics and government, telling his tens of millions of supporters as well as his congressional backers to reject Biden's presidency. It would be an act of disloyalty unsurpassed in American history except by the southern secession in 1860–61, the ultimate example of Americans refusing to respect the outcome of a presidential election.

In fact, Wilentz warned, "Trump would be trying to establish a center of power distinct from and antagonistic to the legitimately elected national government—not formally a separate government like the Confederacy but a virtual one, operating not just out in the country but inside the government, above all in Congress."

Wilentz envisaged "a counter-government, administered by tweets, propped up by Fox News or whatever alternative outlet Trump might construct for himself—a kind of Trumpian government in exile, run from Mar a Lago or maybe from wherever else Trump selects to reside in, in order to avoid prosecution by the State of New York."

Wilentz and others argue that Trump is gearing up to violate a principle of peaceful transition established shortly after the founding of the nation.

"You have to go back to the very odd and dangerous election of 1800 for anything remotely similar," Ned Foley, a constitutional scholar and professor of law at Ohio State, told me via email. "The Federalist Party considered various scenarios for depriving Thomas Jefferson of the presidency, including the possibility of a Federalist acting president if the House remained deadlocked over the tie."

John Adams "was not in on any of those Federalist machinations," Foley continued, but "it's worth focusing on just how dangerous it was that the Federalists were thinking of depriving Jefferson of his victory."

Both Virginia and Pennsylvania, Foley wrote, "called out their militia to make sure that Jefferson would get installed, and the Federalists would not 'steal' the election from Jefferson. There was a genuine risk of a civil war."

Nonetheless, Jefferson was inaugurated and in his March 4, 1801, address not only declared that "we are all Republicans, we are all Federalists," but told Americans of all political stripes to "bear in mind this sacred principle, that though the will of the majority is in all cases to prevail, that will to be rightful must be reasonable; that the minority possess their equal rights, which equal law must protect, and to violate would be oppression. Let us, then, fellow-citizens, unite with one heart and one mind."

"From my perspective," Foley wrote, "the lesson of 1800 is that we are never supposed to go through anything like that again. It's what started the tradition of the peaceful transition of presidential power from one party to another. It might have been a bit of a rocky start to that tradition, but it was successful."

Wilentz noted that after his defeat in the 1800 election, Adams "wrote bitterly that 'we have no Americans in America,' and that 'a group of foreign liars, encouraged by a few ambitious native gentlemen, have discomfited the education, the talents, the virtues, and the property of the country.' Adams was so disgusted that he refused to attend the inauguration of his successor, Thomas Jefferson."

Despite this bitterness, Wilentz explained, Adams—in contrast to Trump—"owned the reality that, as he wrote, 'we federalists' had been 'completely and totally routed and defeated.'"

Manisha Sinha, a professor of history at the University of Connecticut and the author of *The Counterrevolution of Slavery*, pointed out in an email that there was one time when there was a substantial rejection of the outcome of a presidential contest: "Indeed it happened in 1860 when most Deep South states refused to accept the election of Abraham Lincoln to the presidency on an antislavery platform and seceded from the Union."

While many of the scholars I questioned described Trump's actions as predictable, they were gravely concerned at the support Republican officeholders have displayed for Trump—or at the silence they have kept. So far, only five out of fifty-three Republican senators have publicly suggested that Trump take steps to open the transition process to Biden; none are in the leadership.

As my *Times* colleagues Nicholas Fandos and Emily Cochrane put it earlier this week, "Leading Republicans rallied on Monday around President Trump's refusal to concede the election, declining to challenge the false narrative that it was stolen from him or to recognize President-elect Joseph R. Biden Jr.'s victory."

Frank Wilkinson, a writer at Bloomberg and a friend of mine, provided the best explanation for Republican complicity in a July 15 column. His headline says it all: "Trump's Party Cannot Survive in a Multiracial Democracy."

In other words, Trump's refusal to concede, and the support he is getting from his fellow Republicans, is part and parcel of the sustained drive by the Right, especially since Barack Obama won a majority in 2008, to constrain and limit political participation by minorities by every available means: gerrymandering, voter suppression, restricting the time and place of balloting, setting new rules for voter identification, and so forth.

On this theory, allowing the November 3 vote to stand would, in the face of rising minority participation, endanger the ability of the Republican Party to compete in future national elections.

Richard Johnson, a lecturer in US politics and policy at Queen Mary University of London, wrote me in an email that the current situation in the United States has key parallels to the end of the Reconstruction period in the late nineteenth century.

That period, Johnson wrote, "provides many unfortunate examples of election losers refusing to accept defeat, as well as examples of constitutional chicanery and political violence to overturn U.S. election results."

In his book *The End of the Second Reconstruction*, Johnson described "the refusal of Democrats in Louisiana and North Carolina to accept local elections which saw Black Republicans in municipal offices. In these disputes—in Colfax, Louisiana and Wilmington, North Carolina—the election winners and their supporters were murdered and the local party infrastructure (e.g., printing houses of supportive newspapers, local party headquarters) were burnt to the ground."

On November 9, Senator Lindsey Graham of South Carolina, who had just survived a challenge by a Black Democrat, declared on Fox, "If Republicans—if we don't challenge and change the U.S. election system, there'll never be another Republican president elected again. President Trump should not concede."

Eric Foner, a professor of history at Columbia, was cautious in his assessment of the threat posed by Trump, but he voiced concern: "How dangerous this situation may be will become clearer soon. Legally speaking Biden is not officially the victor until mid-December when the electors cast their votes and the states certify them. If Trump plans to fight until then, however, it will certainly poison the political atmosphere for quite a while."

Foner pointed out that "there have not been very many defeated incumbent presidents. John Adams, John Quincy Adams, Martin Van Buren, Grover Cleveland, Benjamin Harrison, William Howard

Taft, Herbert Hoover, Gerald Ford, Jimmy Carter, George H.W. Bush. I don't believe any of them challenged the legitimacy of the result."

Over the short term. Greg Grandin, a professor of history at Yale, sees the Trump challenge petering out, but he argues that the challenge represents a long-term threat to American governance: "I think it is dangerous, less for what is going to happen in this moment—I imagine Trump will give up, in some form, and we will have a series of 'bent not broken op-eds.'"

Over time, however, "we see a pattern. First, in terms of ever more extremist right wing presidencies, there is an evolution: Nixon, Reagan, Bush, and now Trump. Each would have been unthinkable were it not for the precedent and policies of their predecessor. Second, I think Trump and Trumpism signal a weakening, or a collapse, of the two-party system's ability to absorb tensions and conflicts."

A few decades from now, Grandin wrote in his email, "Trump will be seen as significant, but really just a minor blip compared to the crisis that lay ahead."

Samuel Moyn, a Yale historian, discounted fears of a Trump-led insurgency for a different reason: that Trump is not up to playing the role of strongman.

"I think we will come to understand him as the weakest recent president," Moyn wrote by email, "and this 'unprecedented' situation in which he refuses to acknowledge election results is just more proof."

Moyn rejected the notion that "we are in a dangerous situation," because instead of a serious threat, "we have something more like a parody of a coup, one which moreover is something like a conclusive demonstration of the limits of Donald Trump's power all along."

James T. Campbell, a historian at Stanford, emailed, "No sitting president—no presidential candidate, with the partial exception of Jackson in 1824—has refused to accept the results of an election. I'm not surprised that Trump is threatening to do so, but refusing to accept the results of an election may be a bridge too far."

Still, Campbell has been surprised before.

The thing that most astonished me in the 2016 campaign was Trump saying, repeatedly and quite casually, that he would refuse to agree to accept the results of the election unless he won it and then doubling down by saying that his first act on taking office would be to jail Hillary Clinton.

The authoritarianism expressed in those statements was so naked that I simply couldn't believe that they weren't immediately and universally denounced by Democrats and Republicans alike. Turns out he wasn't kidding.

Campbell noted that "one of the most penetrating comments on Trump's character in 2016 came from none other than Ted Cruz, who described him as a sociopath, who wholeheartedly believed whatever he happened to be saying at the time."

It's quite likely, Campbell continued, "that Trump is not deliberately 'lying' in his recent statements, that he genuinely believes that evil forces are conspiring to steal an election that he actually won."

On that note, Cruz's remarks about Trump in May 2016, which appear in sharp contrast to his sycophancy now, capture the essence of our president—and why the combination of this man and this historic moment is so worrying:

This man is a pathological liar. He doesn't know the difference between truth and lies. He lies practically every word that comes out of his mouth. And in a pattern that I think is straight out of a psychology textbook, his response is to accuse everybody else of lying.

He accuses everybody on that debate stage of lying. And it's simply a mindless yell. Whatever he does, he accuses everyone else of doing. The man cannot tell the truth, but he combines it with being a narcissist. A narcissist at a level I don't think this country has ever seen.

Everything in Donald's world is about Donald. And he combines being a pathological liar, and I say pathological because I actually think Donald, if you hooked him up to a lie-detector test, he could say one thing in the morning, one thing at noon and one thing in the evening, all contradictory and he'll pass the lie detector test each time. Whatever lie he's telling, at that minute he believes it.

Cruz added, "Bullies don't come from strength, bullies come from weakness. Bullies come from a deep, yawning cavern of insecurity."

The fact that Trump does not care about the scope of the mayhem he creates—that he revels in anarchic conflagration—creates exceptional danger.

Philip Bobbitt, a professor of law at the University of Texas and at Columbia, is an expert in national security. He raised the question of what is called "continuity of government."

If Trump succeeds in preventing acceptance of Biden as president all the way to January 20, 2021, Bobbitt notes in an email, what is known as "continuity of government" becomes a problem. "Continuity of Government is an artifact of the nuclear age: what happens to the National Command Authority vested in the president—and to nuclear deterrence—if a surprise attack decapitates the US leadership? The problem resurfaced after 9/11 when it became known that the fourth plane seized by Al Qaeda was headed to the Capitol and would have struck during morning business in the House. The result could have rendered Congress helpless until new elections replaced enough House members to reconstitute a quorum; in the interim martial law would have prevailed."

These problems could be lethal in the chaos Trump is seeding.

A number of scenarios, Bobbitt noted, "by no means fanciful, could result in the constitutional drop-dead date of Jan. 20, leaving the country and many elements of government deeply divided as to who the rightful occupant of the presidency is."

In that event, Bobbitt asked, "What happens to the national command authority vested in the president?"

"There is a second, related problem," Bobbitt continued. "The continuity of government vulnerability spawned a number of emergency powers granted to the president, some highly classified. We could well face the use of these powers by the president based on his professed belief that the election was irredeemably flawed and that a 'coup' against him is underway."

While the focus now is on the period until December 14 because "Dec. 8 is the deadline for resolving election disputes and completing any state recounts and contests, and Dec. 14 is the day the electors meet in each state to vote and execute their ballots," Bobbitt warns that "the subsequent period from the 14th to Jan. 20 may be even more fraught and the worst outcome would be confusion on the 20th. What, for example, would be the response of the United States government if North Korea or Russia took some aggressive action in their respective theaters on the 20th?"

The unpredictable danger Trump and his henchmen are putting the nation in has no antecedent. Trump's irrationalism has become a contagion. As he presides over the destruction of reason, he exploits and electrifies his public. No one knows where this will lead. Delusion can become tragedy. It's happened before.

31

"The Far Left Is the Republicans' Finest Asset"

The Democratic Party is struggling with internal contradictions, as its mixed performance on Election Day makes clear.

Analysts and insiders are already talking—sometimes in apocalyptic terms—about how hard it will be for Joe Biden to hold together the coalition that elected him as the forty-sixth president. But it's important to remember that conflicts are inherent in a party that seeks to represent constituencies running the gamut from Alexandria Ocasio-Cortez's Fourteenth District in New York (50 percent Hispanic, 22 percent non-Hispanic white, 18 percent Asian, 8 percent Black) to seventh-generation Utahan Ben McAdams's Fourth District in Utah (74 percent white, 1 percent Black, 3 percent Asian, 17 percent Hispanic).

Jonathan Rodden, a political scientist at Stanford who has explored the structural difficulties facing Democrats in his book *Why Cities Lose*, wrote in an email that the concentration of liberals in urban communities creates a built-in conflict for the party: "The 'presidential wing' of the party," he said, referring to the wing

This article first appeared in *The New York Times* on November 18, 2020. Copyright © 2020 by Thomas Edsall and The New York Times Company. All rights reserved.

most concerned with winning the national election for the White House, "faces no incentives to worry about the geography of Congressional or state legislative districts at all." The ideal platform for winning presidential elections, Rodden continued, "might be one that hurts the party in pivotal Congressional races. This dynamic might be even more pronounced if the 'presidential wing' decides to pursue a strategy of mobilizing the urban base in order to win those pivotal states."

Race, Rodden added, "only enhances this effect. Given the urban concentration of African-Americans in Northern cities, the Democratic political strategy that maximizes the probability of winning the electoral votes of a pivotal state is probably more responsive to the policy priorities of African-American voters than the strategy that would maximize the probability of winning the mostly white pivotal exurban district in that state."

Julie Wronski, a political scientist at the University of Mississippi, put the problem this way: "The Democratic Party's intraparty schism is closely tied to the nationalization of Congressional elections. What works in local campaigns between urban, suburban and rural areas cannot be neatly packaged into a one-size-fits-all national message. You end up with this tension between what drives national media coverage and donations, and what actually works on the ground for a particular district's constituents. This is part and parcel of the breadth and heterogeneity of the Democratic Party's electoral coalition."

A Democratic operative with experience working on elections from the presidency on down to local contests emailed me his views on the complexities involved in developing Democratic strategies. He insisted on anonymity to protect his job. "I do think that defund the police and socialism hurt in Trump-leaning swing districts with more culturally conservative swing voters," he wrote, but, he continued, "it's not clear what one can do about it as you can't reject your own base. You do need progressive politicians to be a bit more 'OK' with centrists denouncing their own base. And you need centrist politicians being OK that the grass roots will have ideas that they don't like."

Achieving this delicate balance is no easy task. This strategist continued:

This all needs to be more of a "wink wink do what you need to do" arrangement, but it's not there right now—it's all too raw and divisive. So as someone involved in campaign strategy, that is frustrating. But to me, this is less of a campaign and message issue, and more of a political one—it's about organizing and aligning the various constituencies of our party to work together. If we can do that, then we can figure out how to solve the message puzzle. But if you don't do that, then this conflict will continue.

The strategist stressed his own ambivalence: "We need to extend the tent and extend the map further in some way—out of necessity. That's where I sympathize with the centrists. You also need a strong, passionate, determined base. That's where I sympathize with the progressives."

The Democratic Party, he noted, is inherently "hard to manage. From race, to culture, to socioeconomic status. All of these items— knowledge professions vs. working class, young vs. old, rural vs. suburban vs. urban—makes us far more complex to manage than the G.O.P."

The intraparty dispute burst out full force on November 5 during a three-hour House Democratic Caucus telephone meeting—a tape recording of which was put up on the *Washington Post* website.

Moderates angrily lashed out at liberals, accusing them of allowing divisive rhetoric such as "defund the police" and calls for socialism to go largely unchallenged. Those on the left pushed right back, accusing centrists of seeking to downgrade the demands of minorities, including those voiced at Black Lives Matter protests.

Abigail Spanberger, who represents the Seventh Congressional District in Virginia—which runs from the suburbs of Richmond through the exurban and rural counties in the center of the state— voiced her instantly famous critique of the liberal wing of her party during the phone call: "We have to be pretty clear about the fact that Tuesday—Nov. 3—from a congressional standpoint, was a failure," she told her Democratic colleagues. "The number one concern that people brought to me" during the campaign "was defunding the police."

Spanberger, who barely survived her bid for a second term—50.82 percent to 49.0 percent—was relentless: "We need to not ever use the words 'socialist' or 'socialism' ever again because while people think it doesn't matter, it does matter. And we lost good members because of that."

If House Democrats fail to address these liabilities, she continued, "we are going to get torn apart in 2022," Spanberger said, intensifying her comment with a word that can't appear here.

Representative Rashida Tlaib, whose Michigan district is among the poorest in the country, and who is a member of the Democratic Socialists of America—directly countered Spanberger and other moderates: "To be real, it sounds like you are saying stop pushing for what Black folks want."

Other Democrats who describe themselves as democratic socialists, including the former Democratic presidential candidate Bernie Sanders, have become a substantial Democratic constituency. In addition to Alexandria Ocasio-Cortez and Tlaib, there are multiple members of the Democratic Socialists of America in state legislatures and city councils. The number of DSA college chapters has more than tripled in the past five years.

In March 2020, Gallup found that "a slight majority of Americans, 51 percent, say they would not vote for an otherwise well-qualified person for president who is a socialist while 47 percent say they would." Some 65 percent of Democrats said they have a favorable view of socialism, compared to 9 percent of Republicans and 41 percent of independents.

The realities of maintaining a liberal, multiracial coalition are complex.

Tom Emmer, chairman of the National Republican Congressional Committee, told the *Wall Street Journal* that the attack on Democrats over defunding the police was effective "everywhere that it was used," adding, "You can't equivocate. You either support the men and women of law enforcement or you don't."

Marc Farinella—a frequent adviser to Democratic campaigns for Senate and governor and now the executive director of the University of Chicago's Center for Survey Methodology—voiced his concerns in an email: "The party is being pushed too far to the left, thereby jeopardizing Democratic candidates and incumbents in suburban districts. Many Democratic candidates are feeling compelled to give lip-service to—or at least not take issue with—unrealistic and out-of-the-mainstream policy proposals in order to avoid running afoul of the activist minority who dominate primaries and who could make the difference in general elections."

Race, according to Farinella, continues to be problematic terrain for Democrats: "This year, some major Democratic candidates forcefully pledged to 'build wealth for Black families.' Of course, we must do that. But, upon hearing this pledge, I bet many white middle-class families wondered if these candidates were calling for an expensive new social welfare program to help 'someone else,' and wondered why government isn't also helping their families build wealth since many non-Black families are struggling, too."

To remain competitive, Farinella argued, "Democrats have to focus more on policies that lift all boats and that give everyone—not just targeted groups—a chance for a better life. Fighting to ban exclusion for pre-existing conditions is a step in the right direction. So is protecting Medicare. The reason these policies work so well for Democrats is, at least in part, because they are not perceived as giving special treatment to one group over another."

Farinella stressed that he is "absolutely not suggesting that Democrats abandon their commitment to fight for disadvantaged or oppressed groups. But I am suggesting that being the champion of each struggling group individually is not a substitute for being the champion of the working class and middle class collectively."

Dane Strother, a Democratic consultant whose firm has represented candidates in states from New Hampshire to Montana, was more outspoken in his view: "Four years ago, Democrats' final messaging was 'which bathroom one could use.' This year it was Defund the Police. The far left is the Republicans' finest asset. A.O.C. and the squad are the 'cool kids' but their vision in no way represents half of America. And in a representative democracy 50 percent is paramount."

Bruce Cain, a political scientist at Stanford, agreed that "it is pretty clear that the Republican characterization of the Democratic Party as radically left leaning worked to mobilize support for Trump in 2020."

In an email, Cain argued that "Biden and the Democratic leadership will have a plausible case for reining in the far left," unless the party is successful in the two Georgia Senate runoffs. In that case, the Democrats would have control of both the White House and Congress, and pressure would increase for the enactment of liberal policies, according to Cain's analysis: "If the Democrats do flip the Georgia seats, it will make coalition management a little harder and raise tensions between factions, but even then, I do not think the votes in the Senate will be there due to defections from Joe Manchin and others representing purple states."

Bernard Grofman, a political scientist at the University of California, Irvine, shares Strother's assessment but is still more assertive in his belief that the Far Left has inflicted significant damage on Democratic candidates. He wrote by email, "'Defund the police' is the second stupidest campaign slogan any Democrat has uttered in the twenty first century. It is second in stupidity only to Hillary Clinton's 2016 comment that half of Trump's supporters belong in a 'basket of deplorables.'"

Moreover, Grofman continued, "the antifa 'take back the neighborhood' in Seattle, where a part of the city became a police no-go zone, with the initial complicity of Democratic office holders, hasn't helped either, especially after someone was killed within the zone. That allowed the Democrats to be seen as in favor of antifa, and, worse yet, to be portrayed as in favor of violence."

Even more damaging, in Grofman's view, "have been the scenes of rock throwing demonstrators and boarded up stores that Republicans have regularly used for campaign fodder and that were a long-running story on Fox News. Every rock thrown, every broken window, is one more Republican vote."

Darren Kew, a professor in the University of Massachusetts–Boston Department of Conflict Resolution, pointed out that the internal tensions within the Democratic Party are exacerbated by polarization between the parties: "Political culture is often that part of the system that is hardest to see—the values, norms, and patterns of behavior that govern our actions within the context of institutions— but it's the glue that holds it all together," Kew wrote by email, noting that "20–30 percent of Americans on either end of the political spectrum are getting their information from highly politicized sources and are therefore not agreeing on the basic facts of whether an event has even happened or not."

The Left has not remained silent in this debate. On November 10, four key progressive groups—New Deal Strategies, Justice Democrats, Sunrise Movement, and Data for Progress—released a seven-page report, *What Went Wrong for Congressional Democrats in 2020*.

The report observes that Democrats have in the past been wary of "the simple statement 'Black Lives Matter,'" of "being too closely associated with Colin Kaepernick and Black athletes kneeling during the national anthem."

In this context, the report suggests, "the latest choice for Democrats to locate our fear and blame is the slogan from many Black and young activists who marched the streets this summer: 'Defund The Police.' Conservative Democrats may change the terms and people we blame and fear year-by-year, but Democrats must take on the Republican Party's divide-and-conquer racism head-on and not demobilize our own base."

The Democratic base, the report contends, was crucial: "This election, the Black youth leading the Black Lives Matter movement have turned their power in the streets into votes and have helped secure Biden's victory in key cities."

The report turns its fire on the Democratic leadership: "Democratic leadership has failed over the years to make sustained investments in field organizing, forcing grass roots organizations to carry the bulk of organizing work in key battleground states on their own."

The Democratic leadership, according to *What Went Wrong*, also failed in other ways: "When Democratic leaders make unforced errors like showing off two subzero freezers full of ice cream on national television or cozy up with Wall Street executives and corporate lobbyists while Trump tells voters we are the party of the swamp, it is not surprising that we lose."

The report refers to House Speaker Nancy Pelosi's late-night TV appearance in which she showed off her subzero freezer, filled with upscale ice cream bars. The appearance became the subject of a Trump ad that declared, "Not everyone has a $24,000 stocked fridge. Pelosi snacks on ice cream while millions of Americans lose their paychecks, 'Let them eat ice cream'—Nancy Antoinette."

The report argues, furthermore, that "scapegoating progressives and Black activists for their demands and messaging is not the lesson to be learned here. It was their organizing efforts, energy and calls for change needed in their communities that drove up voter turnout."

The authors of *What Went Wrong* acknowledge that "there is no denying Republicans levied salient rhetorical attacks against Democrats," but argue that "these will continue to happen as they do every cycle. We cannot let Republican narratives drive our party away from Democrats' core base of support: young people, Black, Brown, working class, and social movements who are the present and future of the party."

Michael Podhorzer, senior adviser to Richard Trumka, president of the AFL-CIO, emailed to voice his across-the-board criticism of all those seeking to place blame for the Democrats' setbacks in down-ticket races: "It is far too early to make any kind of comprehensive judgment about the results of the election. But, distressingly, those who had axes before the election are grinding them with cherry picked data points that provide no credible causal evidence for their case."

While Podhorzer faulted all those making judgments, the focus of his critique appeared to be more on complaints from the center or moderate wing of the party: "They are asking us to believe that after four years of colossal disasters, with more than 200,000 dead from mismanaged Covid, with millions waiting without hope for needed relief to continuing mass unemployment, with more than $14 billion in spending, with massive disruptions to established norms and a President who made this a referendum on four more years of the same, what made the difference was this or that position advocated in the debate that neither Biden nor House Democrats endorsed."

Eitan Hersh, a political scientist at Tufts and the author of the book *Politics Is for Power*, is not persuaded of the good faith and ultimate commitment of the affluent Left. In addition to arguing that "moderate Democrats don't want their brand tied to progressive policy priorities," Hersh questioned the depth of conviction of the so-called progressive elite: "Many of the supporters who say they want big liberal policies at the national level don't really mean it. For example, well-to-do liberals in fancy suburbs who say they prioritize racial equality but do not want to actually level the playing field in educational opportunities between their districts and majority-minority districts."

He cited his own state, Massachusetts: "Here there's tons of liberal energy and money to support taking big progressive fights to Washington. Meanwhile, our schools are segregated, our transit system is broken, our housing is unaffordable, our police force is a mess of corruption and there's little pressure being put on the state legislature and governor to fix any of it."

What, Hersh asks, "to make of all this?" His answer: "The push for big progressive policy is something of a facade."

The political reality, however, is that the constituency Hersh criticizes so sharply has become a crucial part of the Democratic coalition, one that cannot be excised or dismissed without endangering future majorities.

Dani Rodrik, a Harvard economist, suggests that any reconciliation of the Democratic Party's internal conflicts requires an upheaval in contemporary liberal thinking. In "The Democrats' Four-Year Reprieve," an essay published November 9 on Project Syndicate, Rodrik argues that the central question is, "How did Donald Trump manage to retain the support of so many Americans—receiving an even larger number of votes than four years ago—despite his blatant lies, evident corruption, and disastrous handling of the pandemic?" It is clear, Rodrik continued, "that the election does not resolve the perennial debate about how the Democratic Party and other center-left parties should position themselves on cultural and economic issues to maximize their electoral appeal."

What is also apparent, in Rodrik's view, is that "political leaders on the left need to fashion both a less elitist identity and a more credible economic policy."

Parties on the left everywhere, he continued, "have increasingly become the parties of educated metropolitan elites. As their traditional working-class base has eroded, the influence of globalized professionals, the financial industry, and corporate interests has risen. The problem is not just that these elites often favor economic policies that leave middle and lower-middle classes and lagging regions behind. It is also that their cultural, social, and spatial isolation renders them incapable of understanding and empathizing with the worldviews of the less fortunate."

In an email, Rodrik wrote, "The first priority of the Democratic Party ought to be to have a sound program for economic transformation—one that promises to increase the supply of good jobs for all, including the lagging regions of the country."

Both strategically and substantively, Rodrik may be dead on, but his argument raises a set of questions that have no easy answers: the Democratic Party represents an enormous group of competing constituencies, running the gamut from trade unionists to feminists, from minorities to environmentalists, from secular Americans to LGBT advocates, a list that can be extended to multiple pages, with many people in the party answering to several of these descriptions, further complicating matters.

It is the very determination of each of these blocs to place a priority on its own agenda that casts doubt on the ability of the Democratic Party to unite in support of the kind of economic platform Rodrik describes, a step that would require the subordination of narrower interests in favor of the party's collective interest. Unfortunately, this demand for a willingness to sacrifice or compromise factional interests comes at a time when there has been a steady erosion of a national commitment to collective responsibility.

In a way, this is yet another tragic legacy of the Trump administration. Liberal advocacy groups have become more in-your-face, more intense, partly in reaction to the intransigence of the Trump regime, a development that is in turn irrevocably linked to the intensity of the conflicts across the country and within the Democratic Party itself.

32

America, We Have a Problem

The turbulence that followed the November 3 election has roiled American politics, demonstrating an ominous vulnerability in our political system.

Donald Trump used the forty-one-day window between the presidential election and the December 14 meeting of the Electoral College to hold the country in thrall based on his refusal to acknowledge Joe Biden's victory and his own defeat.

Most troubling to those who opposed Trump, and even to some who backed him, was the capitulation by Republicans in the House and Senate. It took six weeks from Election Day for Mitch McConnell, the Senate majority leader, to acknowledge on Tuesday that "the Electoral College has spoken. Today I want to congratulate President-elect Joe Biden."

Trump's refusal to abide by election law was widely viewed as conveying an implicit threat of force. Equally alarming, Trump, with no justification, focused his claims of voter fraud on cities with large African American populations in big urban counties, including Detroit in Wayne County, Milwaukee in Milwaukee County, Philadelphia in Philadelphia County, and Atlanta in Fulton County.

This article first appeared in *The New York Times* on December 16, 2020. Copyright © 2020 by Thomas Edsall and The New York Times Company. All rights reserved.

Bob Bauer, a senior legal adviser to the Biden campaign, told reporters that the Trump campaign's "targeting of the African-American community is not subtle. It is extraordinary," before adding, "It's quite remarkable how brazen it is."

Viewing recent events through a Trump prism may be too restrictive to capture the economic, social, and cultural turmoil that has grown more corrosive in recent years.

On October 30, a group of fifteen eminent scholars (several of whom I also got a chance to talk to) published an essay—"Political Sectarianism in America"—arguing that the antagonism between Left and Right has become so intense that words and phrases like "affective polarization" and "tribalism" were no longer sufficient to capture the level of partisan hostility.

"The severity of political conflict has grown increasingly divorced from the magnitude of policy disagreement," the authors write, requiring the development of "a superordinate construct, political sectarianism—the tendency to adopt a moralized identification with one political group and against another."

Political sectarianism, they argue, "consists of three core ingredients: othering—the tendency to view opposing partisans as essentially different or alien to oneself; aversion—the tendency to dislike and distrust opposing partisans; and moralization—the tendency to view opposing partisans as iniquitous. It is the confluence of these ingredients that makes sectarianism so corrosive in the political sphere."

There are multiple adverse outcomes that result from political sectarianism, according to the authors. It "incentivizes politicians to adopt antidemocratic tactics when pursuing electoral or political victories," since their supporters will justify such norm violation because "the consequences of having the vile opposition win the election are catastrophic."

Political sectarianism also legitimates "a willingness to inflict collateral damage in pursuit of political goals and to view copartisans who compromise as apostates. As political sectarianism has surged in recent years, so too has support for violent tactics."

In a parallel line of analysis, Jack Goldstone, a professor of public policy at George Mason University, and Peter Turchin, a professor of ecology and evolutionary biology at the University of Connecticut, contend that a combination of economic and demographic trends point to growing political upheaval. Events of the last six weeks have lent credibility to their research: On September 10, they published an essay, "Welcome to the 'Turbulent Twenties,'" making the case that the United States is "heading toward the highest level of vulner-ability to political crisis seen in this country in over a hundred years." There is, they wrote, "plenty of dangerous tinder piled up, and any spark could generate an inferno."

Goldstone and Turchin do not believe that doomsday is inevi-table. They cite previous examples of countries reversing downward trends, including the United States during the Great Depression: "To be sure, the path back to a strong, united and inclusive America will not be easy or short. But a clear pathway does exist, involving a shift of leadership, a focus on compromise and responding to the world as it is, rather than trying desperately to hang on to or restore a bygone era."

The Goldstone-Turchin argument is based on a measure called a "political stress indicator," developed by Goldstone in his 1991 book, *Revolution and Rebellion in the Early Modern World*. According to Goldstone, the measure "predicted the 1640s Puritan Revolution, the French Revolution of 1789, and the European Revolutions of 1830 and 1848."

Goldstone wrote that "popular mobilization is more likely when the population is experiencing declining material conditions, plus urbanization and youth; when social competition for elite positions become heightened, political polarization and factionalism will be more likely as groups struggle for power and positions; and when state expenses fall behind revenues, as states become less capable of meeting expected demands and thus less legitimate, as well as more likely to enter conflicts with elites over taxation. And I argued that only when all of these factors coincide does a state face rising risks of major upheavals."

Turchin, in a 2017 book, *Ages of Discord: A Structural-Demographic Analysis of American History*, graphed political stress in this country, showing that from 1970 to 2012 it shot up sharply, increasing fortyfold. In the eight years since then, stress has continued to surge, Goldstone wrote, "as income inequality, political polarization and state debt have all risen further."

While the United States is particularly vulnerable to violent upheaval, Turchin argues, a disaster "is not foreordained. On the contrary, we may be the first society that is capable of perceiving, if dimly, the deep structural forces pushing us to the brink."

In congressional testimony this year, Christopher Wray, the director of the FBI, warned of the dangers posed by white extremists. Take, for example, the largely unprintable postings on thedonaldwin—one of the more extreme right-wing pro-Trump websites—on December 11, the day the Supreme Court rejected nine to zero the Texas attorney general's attempt to invalidate Biden's victories in Michigan, Wisconsin, Pennsylvania, and Georgia. The pro-Trump participants used their anonymous internet pseudonyms to voice outrage that swiftly turned into extraordinary levels of frustration and rage at a Republican elite that they claimed had failed to protect their leader.

A poster whose name cannot be printed here declared, "I can't wait to taste your blood." MakeLiberalsCryAgain put the case bluntly: "It's INSANE. Many of these contested states have REPUBLICAN majorities in their legislatures. They had the power all along to stop this, and they haven't done blankety blank. They held hearings to give the appearance of caring, but in the end, they all cucked out like the spineless, traitorous cowards they are. It looks like the uniparty is reality. What's the point in voting when they're all the same?"

Even more explicit, dinosaurguy declared, "War it is," joined by AngliaMercia, "We kill now." Chipitin warned, "Never forget those justices were handpicked by McConnell and the Federalist Society. They told him they'll help him out picking the best—only to make sure they'll pick those that will betray him. Time to go to war with the Republican Party."

These views on the hard right are not isolated. At the pro-Trump rally in Washington on December 12, the day after the Supreme Court decision, the crowd chanted, "Destroy the GOP," at the urging of Nick Fuentes, a Far Right opponent of immigration.

Gary Jacobson, professor emeritus of political science at the University of California–San Diego, told me that the current upheaval on the right is "quite dangerous if the myth that the election was stolen from Trump persists at the current level among ordinary Republicans and is refuted by so few Republicans in Congress."

Sectarianism, Jacobson continued in an email, "feeds on itself; it is exacerbated by the ideologically fragmented media environment. It also reflects real differences in beliefs and values and conceptions of what American is, or should be, all about. Cleavages of race, region, education, religion, occupation, and community type now put people more consistently on one side or the other, feeding the culture wars and aggravating negative partisanship."

Compounding the problem, Jacobson argues, is the fact that "grievances on both sides have a real basis—e.g., the economic and social decay of small town and rural communities for Trump supporters, systematic racism besetting minorities who vote Democratic—but there is no simple symmetry. For example, whites who believe they suffer more discrimination or fewer opportunities than Black and other minorities are for one reason or another simply oblivious to reality."

Eli Finkel, a professor of psychology at Northwestern and the first author of the paper on political sectarianism I started with, contended in an email that "if we consider Trump's efforts in isolation, I am not especially concerned," because the failure of his attempts to overturn the election so far have "provided a crucial and unprecedented stress test of our electoral system."

If, however, "we consider the support for Trump's efforts from officials and the rank-and-file in the Republican Party, I am profoundly concerned," Finkel continued. "The foremost political story of the Trump era is not that a person like Trump could be so shamelessly self-dealing, but that Republicans have exhibited such fealty along the way, including a willingness to cripple the founding document they claim to view as sacrosanct."

Political sectarianism, Finkel concluded, "has now grown so severe that it functions as the most serious threat to our political system since the Civil War. And although scholars debate whether one party is guiltier than the other, antidemocratic trends are growing stronger on both sides. If we don't figure out a way to get this sectarianism under control, I fear for the future of our republic."

Some of those I contacted cite changes in mass media as critical to this increasing sectarianism.

Shanto Iyengar, a political scientist at Stanford and another of the paper's authors, emailed to say,

> I would single out the profound transformations in the American media system over the past 50 years. Basically, we've moved from an "information commons" in which Americans of all political stripes and walks of life encountered the same news coverage from well-regarded journalists and news organizations to a more fragmented, high choice environment featuring news providers who no longer subscribe to the norms and standards of fact-based journalism. The increased availability of news with a slant coupled with the strengthened motivation to encounter information that depicts opponents as deplorable has led to a complete breakdown in the consensus over facts.

Iyengar noted that research he and Erik Peterson, a political scientist at Texas A&M University, have conducted shows that "the partisan divide in factual beliefs is genuine, not merely partisans knowingly giving the incorrect answer to factual questions because they realize that to do so is 'toeing the party line.'"

In the case of views of COVID-19, he and Peterson found that even though "beliefs about appropriate health practices can have life or death consequences, misinformation over the pandemic is rampant among Republicans and does not dissipate when we offer financial incentives to answer correctly."

Cynthia Shih-Chia Wang, a professor of management and organization at Northwestern's Kellogg School of Management and also a coauthor of the paper, shares Iyengar's concern over the role of ideologically driven sources of information.

"Media is a big contributor to political sectarianism," Wang wrote by email, adding that research she and her colleagues have conducted shows that "consuming ideologically homogeneous media produced greater belief in conspiracy theories endorsed by that media."

In Wang's view, Trump's refusal to acknowledge his election loss is dangerous because of "the number of political elite—the 18 attorneys general and 128 members of the House—who are sowing seeds of doubt around the ethicality of the elections," with the result that "the system is being severely challenged by a president that refuses to concede, by an us-versus-them mentality that contributes to continued congressional gridlock as a pandemic rages, and especially by the doubt cast on the credibility of the American system."

For the moment, Wang wrote, "the system of government seems to be withstanding these unprecedented challenges—the fact that the conservative-leaning Supreme Court dismissed the challenge above should give us some optimism."

Peter Ditto, a professor of psychological science at the University of California, Irvine, and another coauthor, argued in an email that the most toxic element in contemporary politics "is moralization. Our political culture has devolved into what both sides see as an existential battle between good (us) versus evil (them), and in that environment almost any lie can be believed, almost any transgression excused, as long as it helps your side."

Politics, Ditto continued, "has metastasized into something akin to a religious battle—a war between two sects of the American civil religion, each with its own moral vision and each believing it must defend to the death the 'true' vision of the founders against heretics seeking to defile it."

The decision to coin the term *political sectarianism* "was our attempt to capture the moral fervor of our current political climate and the collateral damage it leaves in its wake."

Diana Mutz, a political scientist at the University of Pennsylvania, wrote that after every election since 1996, she has asked voters in a poll "about why they think the winner won." She found that in past years, those on the losing side have consistently claimed the winner was illegitimate for a variety of reasons: "He lied to people in his advertising; he had more money to spend because he represented corporate interests; states changed their voting laws and let illegal people vote; the Russians intervened; they suppressed turnout; the press was biased against him; He was wrongly blamed for . . . ; some people voted twice; etc."

"What's new this year," Mutz continued, "is taking these sour grapes feelings to court."

Steven Pinker, a professor of psychology at Harvard, provided a complex answer to my inquiries.

"Humans can believe things for two reasons: because they have grounds for thinking they're true, or to affirm a myth that unites and emboldens the tribe," Pinker wrote. "Any fair-weather friend can say that rocks fall down, but only a blood brother would be willing to say that rocks fall up. But usually, reality imposes limits on how far we can push our myths. What's extraordinary about the present moment is how far most Republicans have gone in endorsing beliefs that are disconnected from reality and serve only to bind the sect and excommunicate the unfaithful."

The key but unanswerable question, Pinker continued, "is how strongly reality will push back once Trump's power and pulpit are diminished. There undoubtedly will be Lost Cause warriors and post-1945-Japan-style cave fighters, and it would be nice to think they will eventually be marginalized by their own preposterousness. But myths can persist within a closed network when belief in them is enforced by punishment, so a denialist G.O.P. faction could survive for a while."

Trump is doing everything he can to perpetuate the myth and has repeatedly demonstrated his ability to avoid marginalization. Goldstone and Turchin argue that Trump is a symptom, not a cause, of the breakdown of the system. One question that will be answered over time is whether Trump will continue to be uniquely gifted in putting a match to the gasoline. Or has the political, cultural, and economic mix become so combustible that any spark can set it off, regardless of which party or person is in office?

2021

The aftermath of the 2020 election provides no indication of a more consensus-driven America. The year 2021 began with the January 6 insurrection, a violent attempt to wrest control of the US Capitol and to prevent congressional recognition of Joe Biden's victory. The culture wars intensified as the battleground featured critical race theory, "cancel culture," and "wokism." The 2021 elections in Virginia, in New Jersey, and across the nation revealed a highly vulnerable Democratic Party. Rather than unifying the nation, the ongoing COVID-19 crisis further polarized it.

The basic question, Has the United States passed a tipping point? became a legitimate issue in 2021–22, and most signs pointed toward worsening divisions. The columns in this concluding section are pessimistic. The Republican Party has become a renegade institution, and the Democratic Party struggles to remain competitive. This is not America's finest hour.

33

"The Capitol Insurrection Was as Christian Nationalist as It Gets"

It's impossible to understand the January 6 assault on the Capitol without addressing the movement that has come to be known as Christian nationalism.

Andrew L. Whitehead and Samuel L. Perry, professors of sociology at Indiana University–Purdue University Indianapolis and the University of Oklahoma, respectively, describe Christian nationalism in their book *Taking America Back for God*: "It includes assumptions of nativism, white supremacy, patriarchy and heteronormativity, along with divine sanction for authoritarian control and militarism. It is as ethnic and political as it is religious. Understood in this light, Christian nationalism contends that America has been and should always be distinctively 'Christian' from top to bottom—in its self-identity, interpretations of its own history, sacred symbols, cherished values and public policies—and it aims to keep it this way."

In her recent book, *The Power Worshippers: Inside the Dangerous Rise of Religious Nationalism*, Katherine Stewart, a frequent contributor to these pages, does not mince words: "It is a political

This article first appeared in *The New York Times* on January 28, 2021. Copyright © 2021 by Thomas Edsall and The New York Times Company. All rights reserved.

movement, and its ultimate goal is power. It does not seek to add another voice to America's pluralistic democracy, but to replace our foundational democratic principles and institutions with a state grounded on a particular version of Christianity, answering to what some adherents call a 'biblical worldview' that also happens to serve the interests of its plutocratic funders and allied political leaders."

This, Stewart writes, "is not a 'culture war.' It is a political war over the future of democracy."

While much of the focus of coverage of the attack on the halls of the House and Senate was on the violence, the religious dimension went largely unnoted (although my colleagues Elizabeth Dias and Ruth Graham made the connection).

I asked Perry about the role of the religious Right, and he replied by email, "The Capitol insurrection was as Christian nationalist as it gets."

Perry elaborated: "Obviously the best evidence would be the use of sacred symbols during the insurrection such as the cross, Christian flag, Jesus saves sign, etc. But also the language of the prayers offered by the insurrectionists both outside and within the Capitol indicates the views of white Americans who obviously thought Jesus not only wanted them to violently storm the Capitol in order to take it back from the socialists, globalists, etc., but also believed God empowered their efforts, giving them victory."

Together, Perry continued, the evidence "reflects a mind-set that clearly merges national power and divine authority, believing God demands American leadership be wrested from godless usurpers and entrusted to true patriots who must be willing to shed blood (their own and others') for God and country. Christian nationalism favors authoritarian control and what I call 'good-guy violence' for the sake of maintaining a certain social order."

The conservative evangelical pastor Greg Locke, the founder of the Global Vision Bible Church in Mount Juliet, Tennessee, epitomizes the mind-set Perry describes. In his September 2020 book, *This Means War*, Locke writes, "We are one election away from losing everything we hold dear." The battle, Locke continued, is "against everything evil and wicked in the world." It is "a rallying of the troops of God's holy army. This is our day. This is our time. This means something for the Kingdom. As a matter of fact, THIS MEANS WAR."

On January 5, Locke tweeted, "May the fire of the Holy Spirit fall upon Washington DC today and tomorrow. May the Lamb of God be exalted. Let God arise and His enemies be brought low."

Along similar lines, Tony Perkins, president of the Family Research Council and a leading figure among conservative evangelicals, was asked in a 2018 Politico interview, "What happened to turning the other cheek?"

"You know, you only have two cheeks," Perkins replied. "Look, Christianity is not all about being a welcome mat which people can just stomp their feet on."

Robert Jones, the founder and CEO of the Public Religion Research Institute (PRRI), a nonprofit organization that conducts research on religion and politics, argues in his book *White Too Long: The Legacy of White Supremacy in American Christianity* that Christianity in America has a long history of serving as a cloak for a racist political agenda.

"The norms of white supremacy have become deeply and broadly integrated into white Christian identity, operating far below the level of consciousness," Jones writes. "The story of just how intractably white supremacy has become embedded in the DNA of American Christianity—is also personal."

On January 7, the mainstream Baptist News published comments from twenty-one Baptist leaders, including Steve Harmon, professor of theology at Gardner-Webb University School of Divinity: "Minister friends, we must confront directly the baseless conspiracy theories and allegations that our own church members are embracing and passing along. They are not just wrongheaded ideas; they have consequences, and to tie these falsehoods to the salvation of Jesus is nothing less than blasphemy."

Charles Kimball, a professor of religious studies at the University of Oklahoma–Norman, shares some of Jones's concerns. In his 2002 book, *When Religion Becomes Evil*, Kimball wrote, "History clearly shows that religion has often been linked directly to the worst examples of human behavior. It is somewhat trite, but nevertheless sadly true, to say that more wars have been waged, more people killed and these days more evil perpetuated in the name of religion than by any other institutional force in human history."

In an email, Gerardo Marti, a professor of sociology at Davidson College, described a fundamental strategic shift among many on the religious right toward a more embattled, militantly conservative approach: "Today's evangelical conservatives have given up on spiritual revival as a means of change. Even in the recent past, conversion—a change of heart and mind that is the fruit of repentance and spiritual regeneration—was thought to be the means by which America would become a morally upright nation: change enough individuals, and the change on a personal level would result in broad change on a collective level."

Marti contends that "the accumulated frustrations of not being able to ease their sense of religious decline, their continued legal struggles against abortion and gay marriage, and the overwhelming shifts in popular culture promoting much less religiously restrictive understandings of personal identity have prompted politically active religious actors to take a far more pragmatic stance."

As a result, Marti continues, revivalism has largely "been abandoned as a solution to changing society. Their goal is no longer to persuade the public of their religious and moral convictions; rather, their goal has become to authoritatively enforce behavioral guidelines through elected and nonelected officials who will shape policies and interpret laws such that they cannot be so easily altered or dismissed through the vagaries of popular elections. It is not piety but policy that matters most. The real triumph is when evangelical convictions become encoded into law."

I asked Philip Gorski, a professor of sociology at Yale and the author of the book *American Covenant: A History of Civil Religion from the Puritans to the Present*, if supporters of Christian nationalism were a dominant force in the January 6 assault on Congress. He replied, "Many observers commented on the jarring mixture of Christian, nationalist and racist symbolism amongst the insurrectionists: there were Christian crosses and Jesus Saves banners,

Trump flags and American flags, fascist insignia and a 'Camp Auschwitz' hoodie. Some saw apples and oranges. But it was really a fruit cocktail: White Christian Nationalism."

Gorski described the Christian nationalist movement as a loose confederation of people and institutions that share "a certain narrative about American history. In rough outline: America was founded as a Christian nation; the Founding Fathers were evangelical Christians; the Nation's laws and founding documents were indirectly based on 'biblical' principles, or even directly inspired by God, Himself. America's power and prosperity are due to its piety and obedience."

The narrative is propagated through a network of channels, Gorski wrote: "The history curricula used by many Christian home-schoolers are organized around a Christian nationalist perspective. Christian Nationalist activists also seek to influence the history curricula used in public schools."

In addition, Gorski said, "Some evangelical pastors have made national reputations by preaching Christian Nationalism. Robert Jeffress of Dallas' First Baptist Church is a well-known example. In recent years, some Christian Nationalist pastors have formed a network of so-called 'Patriot Churches' as well."

It should be noted that Jeffress went out of his way on the afternoon of January 6 to dissociate himself from the attack on the Capitol.

In a discussion of religion published at the Immanent Frame—a forum of the Social Science Research Council—Gorski drew a sharp distinction between Christian nationalism and traditional religious doctrine: "Christian nationalists use a language of blood and apocalypse. They talk about blood conquest, blood sacrifice, and blood belonging, and also about cosmic battles between good and evil. The blood talk comes from the Old Testament, the apocalyptic talk from the Book of Revelation."

In contrast, according to Gorski, the American version of civil religion "draws on the social justice tradition of the Hebrew prophets, on the one hand, and, on the other, the civic republican tradition that runs from Aristotle through Machiavelli to the American

Founders. One of the distinctive things about this tradition in America is that it sees Christianity and democracy as potentially complementary, rather than inherently opposed."

Paul D. Miller, a professor of international affairs at Georgetown University's School of Foreign Service, reasons along parallel lines: "Christian nationalism is the pursuit of tribal power, not the common good; it is identity politics for right-wing (mostly white) Christians; it is the attempt to 'own and operate the American brand,' as someone else wrote; it is an attitude of entitlement among Christians that we have a presumptive right to define what America is. I oppose identity politics of all kinds, including the identity politics of my tribe."

Christian nationalism reveals what Benjamin Lynerd, a professor of political science at Christopher Newport University and the author of *Republican Theology: The Civil Religion of American Evangelicals*, calls "the tragedy of evangelical politics, a tragedy that the unrestrained loyalty to President Trump lays bare, but which stretches well beyond this moment in American history," when "political theology serves merely as cover for the more pragmatic agenda of social empowerment."

There is a difference, Lynerd writes, "between searching out the implications of the Christian gospel for politics and leveraging this gospel to advance the social position of American Christians. When evangelicals disguise the latter in the robes of the former, not only do they engage in dishonesty, but they also give fuel to the cynical view that there really is no difference—that the theological is nothing more than a cloak for the political."

Jones, the founder of PRRI, made a related point in an email: "While many media outlets focused on decoding the myriad white supremacist signs and symbols, they too easily screened out the other most prominent displays: the numerous crosses, Bibles, and signs and flags with Christian symbols, such as the Jesus 2020 flag that was modeled on the Trump campaign flag."

Those religious symbols, Jones continued, "reveal an unsettling reality that has been with us throughout our history: The power of White supremacy in America has always been its ability to flourish within and be baptized by white Christianity."

Many of those I contacted for this column described Whitehead and Perry's book, *Taking America Back for God*, as the most authoritative study of Christian nationalism.

The two authors calculate that roughly 20 percent of adult Americans qualify, in Perry's words, as "true believers in Christian nationalism." They estimate that 36 percent of Republican voters qualify as Christian nationalists. In 2016, the turnout rate among these voters was an exceptionally high 87 percent. Whitehead wrote that "about 70 percent of those we identify as Christian nationalists are white."

A small percentage of African Americans qualify as Christian nationalists, but Perry pointed out that "it's obvious Black and White Americans are thinking of something completely different when they think about the nation's 'Christian heritage.'"

To ask white Americans about restoring America's Christian character, Perry continued, "is essentially to ask them how much they want to take the country back to the days when they (white, native-born, conservatives) were in power. To ask Black Americans about America's Christian past is more likely to evoke thoughts of what we've traditionally thought of as 'civil religion,' our sacred obligation to being a 'just' nation, characterized by fairness, equality, and liberty."

Samuel P. Perry, a professor of communications at Baylor—and no relation to Samuel L. Perry—argued on January 15 in an essay, "The Capitol Siege Recalls Past Acts of Christian Nationalist Violence," that the confrontations with federal law enforcement officials at Ruby Ridge, Idaho, in 1992 involving white supremacists and Waco, Texas, in 1993 involving an extremist Christian sect together marked a key turning point in uniting white militias with the hardcore Christian Right: "Christian fundamentalists and white supremacist militia groups both figured themselves as targeted by the government in the aftermath of the standoffs at Ruby Ridge and Waco. As scholar of religion Ann Burlein argues, 'Both the Christian right and right-wing white supremacist groups aspire to overcome a culture they perceive as hostile to the white middle class, families, and heterosexuality.'"

In an email, Samuel P. Perry followed up on this thought: "The insurrection or assault on the Capitol involved unlikely coalitions of people in one way. You do not necessarily think of religious evangelicals and fundamentalists being in line with Three Percenters or Proud Boys," but, he continued, the "narrative of chosenness and superiority made for a broader group of support. I would not attribute Jan. 6 to Christian Nationalism alone, but I would not underestimate the involvement of the contingent of Christian Nationalists and the way the rhetoric of Christian Nationalism became a standard trope for Trump."

The emergence of Christian nationalism has in fact prompted the mobilization, in 2019, of a new group, Christians against Christian Nationalism. The organization has lined up prominent religious leaders to serve as "endorsers," including Rev. Dr. Paul Baxley of the Cooperative Baptist Fellowship; Sister Simone Campbell, the executive director of NETWORK; and Tony Campolo, founder and leader of the Evangelical Association for the Promotion of Education.

More than sixteen thousand ministers, pastors, and parishioners have signed a statement that reads in part, "As Christians, our faith teaches us everyone is created in God's image and commands us to love one another. As Americans, we value our system of government and the good that can be accomplished in our constitutional democracy."

In contrast, "Christian nationalism seeks to merge Christian and American identities, distorting both the Christian faith and America's constitutional democracy. Christian nationalism demands Christianity be privileged by the State and implies that to be a good American, one must be Christian. It often overlaps with and provides cover for white supremacy and racial subjugation. We reject this damaging political ideology and invite our Christian brothers and sisters to join us in opposing this threat to our faith and to our nation."

There is evidence, Robert Jones argues, that even though both Christian nationalists and, more broadly, white evangelicals are in decline as a share of the electorate, the two constituencies may become more, not less, assertive. Jones noted that his data suggests that the more a group believes it is under siege from the larger culture, the more activated it becomes.

Some of the clearest evidence of this phenomenon lies in the continually rising level of Election Day turnout among white evangelicals, even as they decline as a share of the electorate.

Jones wrote, "The trend among white evangelical Protestants—declining numbers in the general population but stability in the proportion of voters in the exit polls—is basically what we found over the last decade. Compared to 2008, white evangelical Protestants have declined from 21 percent of the population to 15 percent of the population. But the 'white born again or evangelical' category has remained stable over this period at approximately one quarter (25 percent) of all voters."

Even more worrisome, in Jones's view: "It's also worth noting that even AFTER the insurrection at the U.S. Capitol, PRRI's final favorability poll showed white evangelical Protestants' favorability toward Trump remained at 62 percent—double the level of Trump's favorability rating among the public (31 percent)."

Unsurprisingly, the assertiveness of white evangelicals, and especially of Christian nationalists, is activating their adversaries in the traditional moderate religious mainstream. The rise of the Christian Right is also feeding a tide of secularization that steadily thins the ranks of the religiously observant.

David Campbell, a political scientist at Notre Dame, further elaborates on Jones's argument, writing in a June 2020 article, "The Perils of Politicized Religion," that "it is not just that the United States is becoming a more secular nation. It is that Americans' secularization is, at least in part, a backlash to the employment of religion for partisan ends. The widely held perception that religion is partisan has contributed to the turn away from religious affiliation."

In other words, as members of the Christian Right have become angrier and more adversarial, some to the point of violence, their decline from dominant to marginal status has bred a provocative resentment that is serving to spur the very secularization process that so infuriates them. If the evidence of the Capitol attack and its aftermath is any guide, this vicious circle does not bode well for the future.

34

White Riot

There is no question that out-and-out racism and a longing to return to the days of white supremacy were high on the list of motivations of the pro–Donald Trump mob that ransacked the Capitol on January 6.

That should not end the discussion about why it happened, though. There are other questions we need to ask that do not (and could never) justify the violence and mayhem but seek instead to help us gain further insight into the lethal force that attacked Congress a week ago and is poised to strike again.

It may sound trivial at first, in light of what happened, but how important is the frustration among what pollsters call noncollege white men at not being able to compete with those higher up on the socioeconomic ladder because of educational disadvantage? How critical is declining value in marriage—or mating—markets? Does any of that really matter?

How toxic is the combination of pessimism and anger that stems from a deterioration in standing and authority? What might engender existential despair, this sense of irretrievable loss? How hard is it for any group, whether it is racial, political, or ethnic, to come to

This article first appeared in *The New York Times* on January 13, 2021. Copyright © 2021 by Thomas Edsall and The New York Times Company. All rights reserved.

terms with losing power and status? What encourages desperate behavior and a willingness to believe a pack of lies?

I posed these questions to a wide range of experts. This column explores their replies.

Bart Bonikowski, a professor of sociology at New York University, was forthright:

> Ethnonationalist Trump supporters want to return to a past when white men saw themselves as the core of America and minorities and women "knew their place." Because doing so requires the upending of the social order, many are prepared to pursue extreme measures, including racial violence and insurrection. What makes their actions all the more dangerous is a self-righteous belief— reinforced by the president, the Republican Party, and right-wing conspiracy peddlers—that they are on the correct side of history as the true defenders of democracy, even as their actions undermine its core institutions and threaten its stability.

There is evidence that many non-college-educated white Americans who have been undergoing what psychiatrists call "involuntary subordination" or "involuntary defeat" both resent and mourn their loss of centrality and what they perceive as their growing invisibility.

Andrew Cherlin, a sociologist at Johns Hopkins University, wrote by email, "They fear a loss of attention. A loss of validation. These are people who have always had racial privilege but have never had much else. Many feel passed over, ignored. Trump listened to them and spoke their language when few other politicians did. He felt their pain and was diabolical enough to encourage their tendency to racialize that pain. They fear becoming faceless again if a Democrat, or even a conventional Republican, were to take office."

Cherlin pointed to the assertion of a sixty-seven-year-old retired landscaper from North Carolina who joined the Trump loyalists on January 6 on the steps of the Capitol: "We are here. See us! Notice us! Pay attention!"

White supremacy and frank racism are prime motivators, and they combined with other elements to fuel the insurrection: a groundswell of anger directed specifically at elites and an addictive lust for revenge against those they see as the agents of their disempowerment.

It is this admixture of factors that makes the insurgency that wrested control of the House and Senate so dangerous—and it is likely to spark new forms of violence in the future. Each of the forces at work has helped drive millions of white voters to the right: working in tandem, they collectively provide the tinder for the destructive behavior we saw last week in the chambers of the US Congress.

"It is very, very difficult for individuals and groups to come to terms with losing status and power," Cameron Anderson, a professor at Berkeley's Haas School of Business, wrote by email. While most acute among those possessing high status and power, Anderson said, "people in general are sensitive to status threats and to any potential losses of social standing, and they respond to those threats with stress, anxiety, anger, and sometimes even violence."

Dacher Keltner, a professor of psychology at Berkeley, agrees in large part with Anderson, describing the fury and disappointment contributing to the takeover of Congress as concentrated among whites who see their position in the social order on a downward path. In an email, Keltner wrote, "The population of U.S. Citizens who've lost the most power in the past 40 years, who aren't competing well to get into college or get high paying jobs, whose marital prospects have dimmed, and who are outraged, are those I believe were most likely to be in on the attack."

When pressed to give up power, he added, "these types of individuals will resort to violence, and to refashioning history to suggest they did not lose."

In a September 2020 paper, "Theories of Power: Perceived Strategies for Gaining and Maintaining Power," Keltner and Leanne ten Brinke, a professor of psychology at the University of British Columbia, argue that "lower class individuals experience greater vigilance to threat, relative to high status individuals, leading them to perceive greater hostility in their environment."

This increased vigilance, Brinke and Keltner continue, creates "a bias such that relatively low socio-economic status individuals perceive the powerful as dominant and threatening—endorsing a coercive theory of power. Indeed, there is evidence that individuals of lower social class are more cynical than those occupying higher classes, and that this cynicism is directed toward out-group members—that is, those that occupy higher classes."

In other words, resentment toward successful white elites is in play here, as evidenced by the attack on Congress, an overwhelmingly white seat of power.

Before Trump, many of those who became his supporters suffered from what Carol Graham, a senior fellow at Brookings, describes as pervasive "unhappiness, stress and lack of hope" without a narrative to legitimize their condition: "When the jobs went away, families fell apart. There was no narrative other than the classic American dream that everyone who works hard can get ahead, and the implicit correlate was that those who fall behind and are on welfare are losers, lazy, and often minorities."

In a December 2020 Brookings paper, Graham and Sergio Pinto, a doctoral student at the University of Maryland, wrote that "despair—and the associated mortality trends—is concentrated among the less-than-college educated and is much higher among whites than minorities. The trends are also geographically dispersed, with populations in racially and economically diverse urban and coastal places more optimistic and with lower premature mortality."

What, however, could prompt a mob—including not only members of the Proud Boys and the Boogaloo Bois but also many seemingly ordinary Americans drawn to Trump—to break into the Capitol?

One possible answer: a mutated form of moral certitude based on the belief that one's decline in social and economic status is the result of unfair, if not corrupt, decisions by others, especially by so-called elites.

In "The Social and Political Implications of Moral Conviction," Linda J. Skitka and G. Scott Morgan, psychology professors at the University of Illinois–Chicago and Drew University, respectively, wrote that "although moral conviction motivates any number of normatively positive behaviors (e.g., voting, political engagement), moral conviction appears to also have a potential dark side."

Skitka and Morgan argued that "the terrorist attacks on 9/11, the Weatherman bombings in protest of the Vietnam War, ethnic cleansing in Bosnia, or the assassination of abortion providers, may be motivated by different ideological beliefs but nonetheless share a common theme: The people who did these things appear to be motivated by strong moral conviction. Although some argue that engaging in behaviors like these requires moral disengagement, we find instead that they require maximum moral engagement and justification."

Alan Page Fiske, a professor of anthropology at UCLA, and Tage Shakti Rai, a research associate at the MIT Sloan School of Management, make a parallel argument in their book *Virtuous Violence*, in which they write that violence is "considered to be the essence of evil. It is the prototype of immorality. But an examination of violent acts and practices across cultures and throughout history shows just the opposite. When people hurt or kill someone, they usually do it because they feel they ought to: they feel that it is morally right or even obligatory to be violent."

"Most violence," Fiske and Rai contend, "is morally motivated."

A key factor working in concert to aggravate the anomie and disgruntlement in many members of Trump's white working-class base is their inability to obtain a college education, a limitation that blocks access to higher-paying jobs and lowers their supposed "value" in marriage markets.

In their paper "Trends in Educational Assortative Marriage from 1940 to 2003," Christine R. Schwartz and Robert D. Mare, professors of sociology at the University of Wisconsin and UCLA, respectively, wrote that the "most striking" data in their research "is the decline in odds that those with very low levels of education marry up."

In the bottom ranks of educational achievement, they continued, trends in inequality are "consistent with the decline in the odds of marriage between high school dropouts and those with more education since the 1970s, a period over which the real wages of men in this education group declined."

Christopher Federico, a professor of political science and psychology at the University of Minnesota, described the key roles of education and employment opportunity in the right-wing mobilization of less educated white men: "A major development since the end of the 'Great Compression' of the 30 years or so after World War II, when there was less inequality and relatively greater job security, at least for white male workers, is that the differential rate of return on education and training is now much higher."

In this new world, Federico argues, "promises of broad-based economic security" were replaced by a job market where "you can have dignity, but it must be earned through market or entrepreneurial success (as the Reagan/Thatcher center-right would have it) or the meritocratic attainment of professional status (as the center-left would have it). But obviously, these are not avenues available to all, simply because society has only so many positions for captains of industry and educated professionals."

The result, Federico notes, is that "group consciousness is likely to emerge on the basis of education and training," and when "those with less education see themselves as being culturally very different from an educated stratum of the population that is more socially liberal and cosmopolitan, then the sense of group conflict is deepened."

None of these forces diminishes the key role of racial animosity and racism. Instead, they intensify racial resentment.

Jennifer Richeson, a professor of psychology at Yale, wrote by email that there is "very consistent and compelling evidence to suggest [that] some of what we have witnessed this past week is a reflection of the angst, anger, and refusal to accept an 'America' in which White (Christian) Americans are losing dominance, be it political, material, and/or cultural. And, I use the term dominance here, because it is not simply a loss of status. It is a loss of power. A more racially, ethnically, religiously diverse US that is also a democracy requires White Americans to acquiesce to the interests and concerns of racial/ethnic and religious minorities."

Trump, Richeson continued, "leaned into the underlying White nationalist sentiments that had been on the fringe in his campaign for the presidency and made his campaign about re-centering White-ness as what it actually means to be American and, by implication, delegitimizing claims for greater racial equity, be it in policing or any other important domain of American life."

Michael Kraus, a professor at the Yale School of Management, argued in an email that "racism is the key construct here in understanding why this sort of violence is possible. The other explanations would be the pathways through which racism creates these conditions. An individual experiences their standing in society as relative and comparative, so sometimes the gains of other groups feel like losses to Whites. Whites in the last 60 years have seen minoritized folks gain more political power, economic and educational opportunity. Even though these gains are grossly exaggerated, Whites experience them as a loss in group status."

Emily G. Jacobs, a professor of psychological and brain sciences at the University of California–Santa Barbara, argued that all the rights revolutions—civil rights, women's rights, gay rights—have been key to the emergence of the contemporary right wing:

> As the voices of women, people of color, and other traditionally marginalized communities grow louder the frame of reference from which we tell the story of America is expanding. The white male story is not irrelevant but it's insufficient, and when you have a group of people that are accustomed to the spotlight see the camera lens pan away, it's a threat to their sense of self. It's not surprising that QAnon support started to soar in the weeks after B.L.M. QAnon offers a way for white evangelicals to place blame on (fictional) bad people instead of a broken system. It's an organization that validates the source of Q-Anoners['] insecurity—irrelevance—and in its place offers a steady source of self-righteousness and acceptance.

Jane Yunhee Junn, a professor of political science at the University of Southern California, was outspoken in her view: "People of color in political office, women controlling their fertility, L.G.B.T.Q. people getting married, using their bathrooms, and having children go against the state of nature defined by white heteropatriarchy. This is a domain in which men and white men in particular stand at the apex of power, holding their 'rightful position' over women, nonwhites, perhaps non-Christians (in the U.S.), and of course, in their view, sexual deviants such as gay people."

Herbert P. Kitschelt, a professor of political science at Duke, wrote in an email that "compared to other advanced countries caught up in the transition to knowledge society, the United States appears to be in a much more vulnerable position to a strong right-wing populist challenge."

Kitschelt's listing of some of the reasons for American vulnerability to right-wing forces illuminates current events.

First, Kitschelt noted, "the difference between economic winners and losers, captured by income inequality, poverty, and illiteracy rates within the dominant white ethnicity, is much greater than in most other Western countries, and there is no dense welfare state safety net to buffer the fall of people into unemployment and poverty."

Another key factor, Kitschelt pointed out, is that "the decline of male status in the family is more sharply articulated than in Europe, hastened in the U.S. by economic inequality (men fall further under changing economic circumstances) and religiosity (leading to pockets of greater male resistance to the redefinition of gender roles)."

Unlike most European countries, Kitschelt wrote, "the United States had a civil war over slavery in the 19th century and a continuous history of structural racism and white oligarchical rule until the 1960s, and in many aspects until the present. Europe lacks this legacy."

On top of that, in the United States, "many lines of conflict mutually reinforce each other rather than crosscut: Less educated whites tend to be more Evangelical and more racist, and they live in geographical spaces with less economic momentum."

The coming days will determine how far this goes, but for the moment the nation faces, for all intents and purposes, the makings of a civil insurgency. What makes this insurgency unusual in American history is that it is based on Trump's false claim that he, not Joe Biden, won the presidency, that the election was stolen by malefactors in both parties, and that majorities in both branches of Congress no longer represent the true will of the people.

At the same time, hostility to Trump on the left can make it easy to overlook the shortcomings, such as they are, of the center-left political coalition in this country—and I think it is important that liberals, among whom I count myself, keep this in mind.

Bernard Grofman, a political scientist at the University of California, Irvine, put it this way in an email: "We would not have Trump as president if the Democrats had remained the party of the working class. The decline of labor unions proceeded at the same rate when Democrats were president as when Republicans were president; the same is, I believe, true of loss of manufacturing jobs as plants moved overseas."

President Barack Obama, Grofman wrote, "responded to the housing crisis with bailouts of the lenders and interlinked financial institutions, not of the folks losing their homes. And the stagnation of wages and income for the middle and bottom of the income distribution continued under Obama. And the various Covid aid packages, while they include payments to the unemployed, are also helping big businesses more than the small businesses that have been and will be permanently going out of business due to the lockdowns (and they include various forms of pork)."

The result, according to Grofman, was that "white less well-educated voters didn't desert the Democratic Party, the Democratic Party deserted them."

At the same time, though, and here I will quote Grofman at length,

more religious and less well-educated whites see Donald Trump as one of their own despite his being so obviously a child of privilege. He defends America as a Christian nation. He defends English as our national language. He is unashamed in stating that the loyalty of any government should be to its own citizens—both in terms of how we should deal with noncitizens here and how our foreign policy should be based on the doctrine of "America First."

He speaks in a language that ordinary people can understand. He makes fun of the elites who look down on his supporters as a "basket of deplorables" and who think it is a good idea to

defund the police who protect them and to prioritize snail dart-
ers over jobs. He appoints judges and justices who are true conservatives. He believes more in gun rights than in gay rights. He
rejects political correctness and the language-police and woke
ideology as un-American. And he promises to reclaim the jobs
that previous presidents (of both parties) allowed to be shipped
abroad. In sum, he offers a relatively coherent set of beliefs and
policies that are attractive to many voters and which he has
been better at seeing implemented than any previous Republican president. What Trump supporters who rioted in D.C. share
are the beliefs that Trump is their hero, regardless of his flaws,
and that defeating Democrats is a holy war to be waged by any
means necessary.

In the end, Grofman said, "trying to explain the violence on the
Hill by only talking about what the demonstrators believe is to miss
the point. They are guilty, but they wouldn't be there were it not for
the Republican politicians and the Republican attorneys general,
and most of all the president, who cynically exaggerate and lie and
create fake conspiracy theories and demonize the opposition. It is the
enablers of the mob who truly deserve the blame and the shame."

35

Democracy Is Weakening Right in Front of Us

A decade ago, the consensus was that the digital revolution would give effective voice to millions of previously unheard citizens. Now, in the aftermath of the Trump presidency, the consensus has shifted to anxiety that online behemoths like Twitter, Google, YouTube, Instagram, and Facebook have created a crisis of knowledge—confounding what is true and what is untrue—that is eroding the foundations of democracy.

These worries have intensified in response to the violence of January 6, and the widespread acceptance among Republican voters of the conspicuously false claim that Democrats stole the election.

Nathaniel Persily, a law professor at Stanford, summarized the dilemma in his 2019 report, *The Internet's Challenge to Democracy: Framing the Problem and Assessing Reforms*, pointing out that in a matter of just a few years, "the widely shared utopian vision of the internet's impact on governance has turned decidedly pessimistic. The original promise of digital technologies was unapologetically democratic: empowering the voiceless, breaking down borders to

This article first appeared in *The New York Times* on February 17, 2021. Copyright © 2021 by Thomas Edsall and The New York Times Company. All rights reserved.

build cross-national communities, and eliminating elite referees who restricted political discourse."

Since then, Persily continued, "that promise has been replaced by concern that the most democratic features of the internet are, in fact, endangering democracy itself. Democracies pay a price for internet freedom, under this view, in the form of disinformation, hate speech, incitement, and foreign interference in elections."

Writing separately in an email, Persily argued that "Twitter and Facebook allowed Trump both to get around legacy intermediaries and to manipulate them by setting their agenda. They also provided environments (such as Facebook groups) that have proven conducive to radicalization and mobilization."

Margaret Roberts, a political scientist at the University of California–San Diego, puts it differently. "The difficult part about social media is that the freedom of information online can be weaponized to undermine democracy."

Social media, Roberts wrote by email, "isn't inherently pro or anti-democratic, but it gives voice and the power to organize to those who are typically excluded by more mainstream media. In some cases, these voices can be liberalizing, in others illiberal."

The debate over the political impact of the internet and social media raises the question, Do the putatively neutral instruments of social media function for both good and evil, or are they inherently divisive?

Lisa Argyle, a political scientist at Brigham Young University, stressed additional aspects of the question in an email: "When talking about social media and politics," she writes, "it is really important to think about who is engaged in the conversation and who is not."

There are, she points out, "demonstrated race, class, age, and other demographic divides in who uses different platforms, so heavy reliance on social media for democratic ends has the potential to exacerbate existing inequalities."

In addition, Argyle notes, "within each platform there are a set of people who are highly politically interested, who discuss politics often, and who are most likely to have extreme opinions. Therefore, when people use social media as a proxy for political opinions writ large, they are likely to overestimate that amount of conflict and polarization that exist in the offline world."

Yochai Benkler, a law professor at Harvard, contends in an email that "it's a mistake to conceive of technology as an external force with a known definitive effect on social relations."

"Radio," Benkler argues, "was as available for F.D.R.'s fireside chats as it was for Hitler's propaganda. Ten years ago the internet in general, and Facebook in particular, was widely perceived as a liberation. Now it's blamed for the collapse of liberal democracy."

Digital media has distinctive characteristics that "can work both to improve participation and democratic governance and to undermine it," Benkler adds.

"It was citizens' video journalism capturing the evidence and broadcasting it on social media, coupled with the mass protests," he notes, "that changed the public conversation about police shootings of Black Americans. And it was also social media that enabled the organization and mobilization of Unite the Right in Charlottesville."

Ultimately, according to Benkler, "the epistemic crisis we experience in the United States today is elite-driven (Trump, other GOP leadership) and led by broadcast media—cable TV (Fox), radio (Limbaugh, Hannity), and major newspapers or large commercial websites (NY Post, Breitbart), coupled with some very bad reporting in the mainstream press."

Along parallel lines, Yannis Theocharis, a professor of digital governance at the Technical University of Munich, makes the point that "social media need to be seen as an incredibly potent medium in the toolset of both those who wish to strengthen democratic governance and those who wish to undermine it. They are used just as effectively and extensively as mobilizing tools by organized hate groups and those wishing to marginalize and silence others or challenge core democratic values, as they are used by activists and social movements aiming to strengthen citizens' political voice, increase the quality of democratic representation, or protest racial injustice."

There is an ongoing argument about whether the promotion of divisiveness and polarization is built into the marketing structure of social media.

Jack Balkin, a law professor at Yale, writes in an email, "Some of the most troubling features of social media come from business models based on surveillance and monetization of personal data. Social media will not improve as long as their current surveillance-based business models give them the wrong incentives."

Trump, in Balkin's view, "showed how to use social media for demagogic ends to harm democracy."

But, he added, "Trump's success built on decades of polarization strategies that relied on predigital media—talk radio and cable. Without talk radio and Fox News, Trump would have been a far less effective demagogue."

Do social media drive polarization? Balkin's answer: "The larger and more profound causes of polarization in the United States are not social media, which really become pervasive only around 2008 to 2010, but rather decades of deliberate attempts to polarize politics to gain political power. Once social media became pervasive in the last decade, however, they have amplified existing trends."

Robert Frank, professor emeritus of economics at Cornell, is a leading proponent of the argument that the current business model of Facebook and other social media is a significant contributor to political and social dysfunction.

Writing in these pages, Frank argued on February 14 that the economic incentives of "companies in digital markets differ . . . sharply from those of other businesses."

Digital aggregators like Facebook, he continued, "make money not by charging for access to content but by displaying it with finely targeted ads based on the specific types of things people have already chosen to view. If the conscious intent were to undermine social and political stability, this business model could hardly be a more effective weapon."

Frank notes that the algorithms digital companies use to "choose individual-specific content are crafted to maximize the time people spend on a platform. As the developers concede, Facebook's algorithms are addictive by design and exploit negative emotional triggers. Platform addiction drives earnings, and hate speech, lies and conspiracy theories reliably boost addiction."

The profit motive in digital media, Frank contends, drives policies that result in "the spread of misinformation, hate speech and conspiracy theories."

Eric B. Schnurer, president of Public Works, a policy consulting firm, is similarly critical of the digital business model, writing in an email, "The social media companies discovered that there were limited means for making money off social media, settling on an advertising-based model that required increasing and retaining 'eyeballs,' which quickly led to the realization that the best way to do so is to exploit nonrational behavior and create strong reactions rather than reasoned discourse."

Digital firms, in Schnurer's analysis, "have now metastasized into this model where their customers are their raw material, which they mine, at no expense, and sell to others for further exploitation; it is a wholly extractive and exploitive business model, whatever high-minded rhetoric the companies want to spread over it about creating 'sharing' and 'community.'"

There were early warnings of the dangers posed by new digital technologies.

Shoshana Zuboff, professor emeritus at Harvard Business School, pursued a line of inquiry as far back as 1981 with "The Psychological and Organizational Implications of Computer-Mediated Work" that led to the broad conclusions she drew in her 2016 paper, "Big Other: Surveillance Capitalism and the Prospects of an Information Civilization": "'Big data' is above all the foundational component in a deeply intentional and highly consequential new logic of accumulation that I call surveillance capitalism. This new form of information capitalism aims to predict and modify human behavior as a means to produce revenue and market control. Surveillance capitalism has gradually constituted itself during the last decade, embodying a new social relations and politics that have not yet been well delineated or theorized."

From a different vantage point, Christopher Bail, a professor of sociology at Duke and director of the university's Polarization Lab, writes in his forthcoming book *Breaking the Social Media Prism* that a key constituency is made up of those who "feel marginalized, lonely, or disempowered in their off-line lives."

Social media, Bail writes in his book, "offer such social outcasts another path. Even if the fame extremists generate has little significance beyond small groups of other outcasts, the research my colleagues and I conducted suggests that social media give extremists a sense of purpose, community, and—most importantly—self-worth."

The social media prism, Bail writes, "fuels status-seeking extremists, mutes moderates who think there is little to be gained by discussing politics on social media, and leaves most of us with profound misgivings about those on the other side, and even about the scope of polarization itself."

One of the striking findings of the research conducted at Bail's Polarization Lab is that contrary to expectations, increased exposure to the views of your ideological opponents does not result in more open-mindedness.

Bail emailed me to point out that "we surveyed 1,220 Republicans and Democrats" and "offered half of them financial compensation to follow bots we created that exposed them to messages from opinion leaders from the opposing political party for one month. When we resurveyed them at the end of the study, neither Democrats nor Republicans became more moderate. To the contrary, Republicans became substantially more conservative and Democrats became slightly more liberal."

Bail also offered an analysis of this phenomenon: "The reason I think taking people out of their echo chambers made them more polarized—not less—is because it exposes them to extremists from the other side who threaten their sense of status."

In his book Bail puts it this way: "People do not carefully review new information about politics when they are exposed to opposing views on social media and adapt their views accordingly." Instead, he observes, "they experience stepping outside their echo chamber as an attack upon their identity."

Nathaniel Persily makes a parallel—and important—point: "No one doubts that the internet provides 'safe spaces' for individuals to find common cause for antisocial activity otherwise deterred in the offline world. Of course, the ability of individuals to find communities of like-minded believers unconstrained by geography is one of the great benefits of the internet. Nevertheless, the darkest corners of the internet provide self-reinforcing havens for hate, terrorist recruitment, and propagation of conspiracy theories."

In his email, Persily listed some of those havens: "For sizable groups of people, the internet affords environments, such as Facebook groups, Subreddits, Parler, or chat rooms on 4chan and 8kun, where they can make common cause with people they would not find in their neighborhood or in face-to-face forums. In other words, there are shadowy places on the internet where conspiracy-communities, like QAnon, or hate groups can thrive."

Joshua Tucker, a political scientist at New York University, pointed out by email that "prior to social media, if you were the only one in your county who might support extremist views regarding the overthrow of the United States government, organizing with other like-minded but geographically dispersed compatriots would be a costly activity."

The arrival of social media, he argues, "drastically reduces these costs and allows such individuals to more easily find each other to organize and collaborate."

In addition, according to Tucker, "the tools developed by authoritarian regimes to influence their own online conversations—online trolls and bots—can also be used by small numbers of extremists in democratic societies to amplify their presence online, making their positions appear to be more popular than they might be, in what has the potential to become a self-fulfilling prophecy."

Tucker, like a number of other scholars of social media, stresses that "prior to the internet, news was in the domain of professional journalists and there were powerful gatekeepers in the form of editors and publishers. While this may have also prevented more progressive messages from entering mainstream media, it undoubtedly also blocked extreme anti-democratic voices as well, in addition to enforcing a certain level of quality in news reporting."

The internet, according to Tucker, "lowered the barrier to publishing news dramatically, but social media accelerated this process by making it possible to consume news without even taking the step of seeking out the publisher of that news by going to their home page. In addition, social media exacerbated the premium placed on news that delivered 'clicks,' highlighting the appeal of certain types of news—including blatantly false news."

Bryan Ford, a professor of computer and communication sciences at the Swiss Federal Institute of Technology in Lausanne, has become a technopessimist. "While I think technology has tremendous potential to strengthen democratic governance, in balance I think most of the major recent technological advances have unfortunately weakened it."

The reason? "The factors include (a) social media contributing to social echo chambers that more readily become detached from objective reality or truth; (b) the related global infatuation with big data and deep learning leading us to concentrate ever more decision-making power into opaque and democratically-unaccountable algorithms run by profit-motivated and democratically-unaccountable technology companies; (c) society's increasingly-ubiquitous use of manipulable and undemocratic online reputation metrics such as likes, follower counts, reviews, etc., as fundamentally-flawed proxies for democratic measures of reputation, public support for positions or opinions, truth or plausibility."

If the pessimists are right, what can be done to reverse the antidemocratic forces that find expression on the internet and its offspring, social media?

There is no consensus on this question except that effective reform will be difficult in this country for a variety of reasons, including First Amendment restrictions on regulating speech and political and ideological opposition to government-mandated changes to private-sector business models.

Persily points out that not only has election interference "become 'professionalized,' it has also become, like other arenas of internet activity, vulnerable to gang-like actions. The statelessness and disorganization of online associational life enables international coalitions of hackers, troublemakers, anarchists, and criminals to find solidarity in wreaking havoc against the establishment."

Asked what the long-range prospects are, Persily said there was no definitive answer. He worries "that the lack of trust in the democratic process, that festered over the last four years and exploded on Jan. 6, will have a severe and long-lasting impact."

For one thing, purveyors of misinformation and disinformation have become increasingly sophisticated.

Bryan Ford writes about advances in artificial intelligence: "The fashionable strategy in the tech sector—namely using more data, deeper deep learning, etc., to distinguish between real and fake news or real and fake accounts, is fundamentally misguided because it neglects to recognize the fact that all the bad guys have access to state-of-the-art machine learning too."

Ford continues, "Given any machine learning classification algorithm intended to make an important distinction, it's generally possible to train an 'adversarial' machine-learning algorithm that essentially figures out how to trick the first one systematically."

In other words, while designing systems to detect fraudulent postings "only gets harder and harder," Ford writes, it gets "easier and easier for machines, and botnet operators to train algorithms to create progressively-more-convincing fake news and fake user profiles that before long will appear 'more believable' to both machines and humans than real news or real user profiles."

Perhaps more significant, would-be reformers face an increasingly powerful array of digital firms that are certain to oppose any regulation that interferes with their exceptional profit margins.

The Bureau of Economic Affairs estimated that from 2006 to 2016, the digital economy grew at an average annual rate of 5.6 percent, more than three times the 1.5 percent average annual rate of growth for the overall US economy. By 2017, the bureau estimated, the digital economy accounted for 6.9 percent of the US gross domestic product, or $1.35 trillion.

And despite all the chatter, there is no significant public pressure to alter the practices of the digital industry. Insofar as these companies have transformed American politics, for a majority of the population it has been a slow, almost invisible process that has provoked little or no outcry. In a sense, this chain of events has resulted in the climate in which Donald Trump's extraordinary false claims elicited no protest in half the country. Quite the opposite, in fact.

As long as truth can be disguised—and as citizens lose the ability to distinguish truth from falsehood—democracy will continue to weaken, ultimately becoming something altogether different from what we are accustomed to. And all of this is happening while most of us continue to be unaware of the transformation that has taken place during our lifetime, functionally oblivious to the "epistemic crisis," both as a contributor to the problem and as an accelerant.

36

Why Trump Still Has Millions of Americans in His Grip

Beginning in the mid-1960s, the priorities of the Democratic Party began to shift away from white working- and middle-class voters—many of them socially conservative, Christian, and religiously observant—to a set of emerging constituencies seeking rights and privileges previously reserved for white men: African Americans, women's rights activists, and proponents of ethnic diversity, sexual freedom, and expressive individualism.

By the 1970s, many white Americans—who had taken their own centrality for granted—felt that they were being shouldered aside, left to face alone the brunt of the long process of deindustrialization: a cluster of adverse economic trends including the decline in manufacturing employment, the erosion of wages by foreign competition, and the implosion of trade unionism.

These voters became the shock troops of the Reagan Revolution; they now dominate Donald Trump's Republican Party.

This article first appeared in *The New York Times* on May 5, 2021. Copyright © 2021 by Thomas Edsall and The New York Times Company. All rights reserved.

Liberal onlookers exploring the rise of right-wing populism accuse their adversaries of racism and sexism. There is plenty of truth to this view, but it's not the whole story.

In "The Bitter Heartland," an essay in *American Purpose*, William Galston, a veteran of the Clinton White House and a senior fellow at Brookings, captures the forces at work in the lives of many of Trump's most loyal backers: "Resentment is one of the most powerful forces in human life. Unleashing it is like splitting the atom; it creates enormous energy, which can lead to more honest discussions and long-delayed redress of grievances. It can also undermine personal relationships—and political regimes. Because its destructive potential is so great, it must be faced."

Recent decades, Galston continues, "have witnessed the growth of a potent new locus of right-wing resentment at the intersection of race, culture, class, and geography"—difficult for "those outside its orbit to understand."

They—"social conservatives and white Christians"—have what Galston calls a "bill of particulars" against political and cultural liberalism. I am going to quote from it at length because Galston's rendering of this bill of particulars is on target.

- "They have a sense of displacement in a country they once dominated. Immigrants, minorities, non-Christians, even atheists have taken center stage, forcing them to the margins of American life."
- "They believe we have a powerful desire for moral coercion. We tell them how to behave—and, worse, how to think. When they complain, we accuse them of racism and xenophobia. How, they ask, did standing up for the traditional family become racism? When did transgender bathrooms become a civil right?"
- "They believe we hold them in contempt."
- "Finally, they think we are hypocrites. We claim to support free speech—until someone says something we don't like. We claim to oppose violence—unless it serves a cause we

approve of. We claim to defend the Constitution—except for the Second Amendment. We support tolerance, inclusion, and social justice—except for people like them."

Galston has grasped a genuine phenomenon. But white men are not the only victims of deindustrialization. We are now entering upon an era in which vast swaths of the population are potentially vulnerable to the threat—or promise—of a Fourth Industrial Revolution.

This revolution is driven by unprecedented levels of technological innovation as artificial intelligence joins forces with automation and takes aim not only at employment in what remains of the nation's manufacturing heartland but also increasingly at the white-collar managerial and professional occupational structure.

Daron Acemoglu, an economist at MIT, described in an email the most likely trends as companies increasingly adopt AI technologies. "A.I. is in its infancy. It can be used for many things, some of them very complementary to humans. But right now it is going more and more in the direction of displacing humans, like a classic automation technology. Put differently, the current business model of leading tech companies is pushing A.I. in a predominantly automation direction."

As a result, Acemoglu continued, "we are at a tipping point, and we are likely to see much more of the same types of disruptions we have seen over the last decades."

In an essay published in *Boston Review* last month, Acemoglu looked at the issue over a longer period. Initially, in the first four decades after World War II, advances in automation complemented labor, expanding the job market and improving productivity.

But, he continued, "a very different technological tableau began in the 1980s—a lot more automation and a lot less of everything else." In the process, "automation acted as the handmaiden of inequality."

Automation has pushed the job market in two opposing directions. Trends can be adverse for those (of all races and ethnicities) without higher education, but trends can also be positive for those with more education: "New technologies primarily automated the more routine tasks in clerical occupations and on factory floors. This

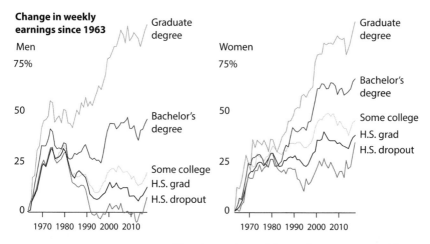

FIGURE 36.1. FALLING BEHIND. The change in weekly earnings among working-age adults since 1963. Those with more education are climbing ever higher, while those with less education—especially men—are falling further behind. *Source*: David Autor, Massachusetts Institute of Technology, "Work of the Past, Work of the Future." From The New York Times. © 2021 The New York Times Company. All rights reserved. Used under license.

meant the demand and wages of workers specializing in blue-collar jobs and some clerical functions declined. Meanwhile professionals in managerial, engineering, finance, consulting, and design occupations flourished—both because they were essential to the success of new technologies and because they benefited from the automation of tasks that complemented their own work. As automation gathered pace, wage gaps between the top and the bottom of the income distribution magnified."

Technological advancement has been one of the key factors in the growth of inequality based on levels of educational attainment, as figure 36.1 shows.

Acemoglu warns, "If artificial intelligence technology continues to develop along its current path, it is likely to create social upheaval for at least two reasons. For one, A.I. will affect the future of jobs. Our current trajectory automates work to an excessive degree while refusing to invest in human productivity; further advances will displace workers and fail to create new opportunities. For another, A.I. may undermine democracy and individual freedoms."

Mark Muro, a senior fellow at Brookings, contends that it is essential to look at the specific types of technological innovation when determining impact on the job market.

"Two things are happing at once, when you look at traditional 'automation' on the one hand and 'artificial intelligence' on the other," Muro wrote in an email. "The more widespread, established technologies usually branded 'automation' very much do tend to disrupt repetitive, lower-skill jobs, including in factories, especially in regions that have been wrestling with deindustrialization and shifts into low-pay service employment."

In contrast, Muro continued, "artificial intelligence really is a very different set of technologies than those we label as 'automation,' and it will for a while mostly affect college educated workers." But, and it's a big but, "there is a greater chance that such white collar workers, with their B.A.s, will be better equipped to coexist with A.I. or even benefit from it than will non-B.A. workers impacted by other forms of automation. And yet, there's no doubt A.I. will now be introducing new levels of anxiety into the professional class."

In a November 2019 paper, "What Jobs Are Affected by A.I.? Better-Paid, Better-Educated Workers Face the Most Exposure," Muro and two colleagues found that exposure to AI is significantly higher for jobs held by men, by people with college degrees or higher, by people in the middle and upper pay ranks, and by whites and Asian Americans generally.

In contrast, in a March 2019 paper, "Automation Perpetuates the Red-Blue Divide," Muro and his colleagues found that automation, as opposed to AI, hurts those who hold jobs that do not require college degrees the most, and that exposure to automation correlates with support for Trump: "The strong association of 2016 Electoral College outcomes and state automation exposure very much suggests that the spread of workplace automation and associated worker anxiety about the future may have played some role in the Trump backlash and Republican appeals."

More specifically, Muro and his colleagues found, "Heartland states like Indiana and Kentucky, with heavy manufacturing histories and low educational attainment, contain not only the nation's highest employment-weighted automation risks, but also registered some of the widest Trump victory margins. By contrast, all but one of the states with the least exposure to automation, and possessing the highest levels of educational attainment, voted for Hillary Clinton."

How do the risks of automation, foreign-trade-induced job loss, and other adverse consequences of technological change influence politics?

In his 2020 paper "Why Does Globalization Fuel Populism? Economics, Culture and the Rise of Right-Wing Populism," Dani Rodrik, an economist at Harvard's Kennedy School, explored what he called four political channels "through which globalization can stimulate populism."

The four channels are the following:

1) "a direct effect from economic dislocation to demands for anti-elite, redistributive policies"
2) "through amplification of cultural and identity divisions"
3) "through political candidates adopting more populist platforms in response to economic shocks"
4) "through adoption of platforms that deliberately inflame cultural and identity tensions"

In order to get a better sense of what underpinned Trump's populist appeal, Rodrik focused on a specific bloc of voters—those who switched from supporting Barack Obama in 2012 to Trump in 2016: "Switchers to Trump are different both from Trump voters and from other Obama voters in identifiable respects related to social identity and views on the economy in particular. They differ from regular Trump voters in that they exhibit greater economic insecurity, do not associate themselves with an upper social class and they look favorably on financial regulation. They differ from others who voted for Obama in 2012 in that they exhibit greater racial hostility, more economic insecurity and more negative attitudes toward trade agreements and immigration."

In an email, Rodrik wrote, "Automation hits the electorate the same way that deindustrialization and globalization have done, hollowing out the middle classes and enlarging the potential vote base of right-wing populists—especially if corrective policies are not in place. And the overall impact of automation and new technologies is likely to be much larger and more sustained, compared to the China shock. This is something to watch."

In their December 2017 paper, "Artificial Intelligence, Worker-Replacing Technological Progress and Income Distribution," the economists Anton Korinek, of the University of Virginia, and Joseph E. Stiglitz, of Columbia, describe the potential of artificial intelligence to create a high-tech dystopian future.

Korinek and Stiglitz argue that without radical reform of tax and redistribution politics, a "Malthusian destiny" of widespread technological unemployment and poverty may ensue.

Humans, they write, "are able to apply their intelligence across a wide range of domains. This capacity is termed general intelligence. If A.I. reaches and surpasses human levels of general intelligence, a set of radically different considerations apply." That moment, according to "the median estimate in the A.I. expert community[,] is around 2040 to 2050."

Once parity with the general intelligence of human beings is reached, they continue, "there is broad agreement that A.I. would soon after become super-intelligent, i.e., more intelligent than humans, since technological progress would likely accelerate."

Without extraordinary interventions, Korinek and Stiglitz foresee two scenarios, both of which could have disastrous consequences.

In the first, "man and machine will merge, i.e., . . . humans will 'enhance' themselves with ever more advanced technology so that their physical and mental capabilities are increasingly determined by the state of the art in technology and A.I. rather than by traditional human biology."

Unchecked, this "will lead to massive increases in human inequality," they write, because intelligence is not distributed equally among humans and "if intelligence becomes a matter of ability-to-pay, it is conceivable that the wealthiest (enhanced) humans will become orders of magnitude more productive—'more intelligent'—

than the unenhanced, leaving the majority of the population further and further behind."

In the second scenario, "artificially intelligent entities will develop separately from humans, with their own objectives and behavior, aided by the intelligent machines."

In that case, they write, "there are two types of entities, unenhanced humans and A.I. entities, which are in a Malthusian race and differ—potentially starkly—in how they are affected by technological progress."

In this hypothetical race, "A.I. entities are becoming more and more efficient in the production of output compared to humans," the authors write, because "human technology to convert consumption goods such as food and housing into future humans has experienced relatively little technological change." By contrast, "the reproduction technology of A.I. entities—to convert A.I. consumption goods such as energy, silicon, aluminum into future A.I.—is subject to exponential progress."

In their conclusion, Korinek and Stiglitz write, "The proliferation of A.I. and other forms of worker-replacing technological change can be unambiguously positive in a 1st-best economy in which individuals are fully insured against any adverse effects of innovation, or if it is coupled with the right form of redistribution. In the absence of such intervention, worker-replacing technological change may not only lead to workers getting a diminishing fraction of national income, but may actually make them worse off in absolute terms."

There is no dearth of grim prediction. In "The Impact of Automation on Employment: Just the Usual Structural Change?," Ben Vermeulen of the University of Hohenheim in Germany, writing with three colleagues, puts it this way: "There is literature arguing that the pace at which employment is destroyed by the introduction of productivity-enhancing technology may exceed the pace at which mankind is able to find new uses for those becoming unemployed."

If fully enacted, could Joe Biden's $6 trillion-plus package of stimulus, infrastructure, and social expenditure represent a preliminary step toward providing the social insurance and redistribution necessary to protect American workers from the threat of technological innovation? Can spending on this scale curb the resentment or heal the anguish over wrenching dislocations of race, culture, and class?

37

Is Wokeness "Kryptonite for Democrats"?

As Republicans well know, Democrats are divided on a host of volatile racial, cultural, and sexual issues.

Take a look at the polls.

In 2019, the Democracy Fund Voter Study Group commissioned a survey asking for agreement or disagreement with the statement, "There are only two genders, male and female."

In the full sample, a decisive majority, 59 percent, agreed, including 43 percent who "strongly agreed," 32 percent who disagreed, and 9 percent who said they weren't sure. Among Republicans, it was no contest: 78 percent agreed and 16 percent disagreed. Independents mirrored the whole sample.

Democrats were split: a plurality, 48 percent, disagreed, and 44 percent agreed.

The survey itself arguably embodied what critics might call "transphobic framing"—transgender issues are among the most polarizing in contemporary politics, and much contemporary cultural conflict in fact stems from framing disputes.

This article first appeared in *The New York Times* on May 26, 2021. Copyright © 2021 by Thomas Edsall and The New York Times Company. All rights reserved.

An August–September 2017 Pew Research survey asked respondents to choose between two statements: "Whether a person is a man or a woman is determined at birth," and "Whether a person is a man or a woman can be different from the sex at birth."

A 54 percent majority of all those surveyed said sex "is determined at birth," and 44 percent said it "can be different from the sex at birth." Republican voters and those who lean Republican chose "at birth" 80 percent to 19 percent. Democratic voters and those who lean Democratic said sex can be different from the sex at birth 64 percent to 34 percent.

Or take the public's view of the "defund the police" movement that gained momentum after the murder of George Floyd a year ago.

A March 1–2 *USA Today*/Ipsos poll found that voters were opposed to defunding the police 58 percent to 18 percent, with the strongest opposition among whites (67 percent to 13 percent support, the rest undecided) and Republicans (84 percent to 4 percent), while a plurality of Democrats were opposed (at 39 percent to 34 percent), which was also true among African Americans (37 percent to 28 percent).

These surveys are complemented by others that measure the fear that our public dialogue is too constricted. A Harvard/Harris survey in February asked, "Do you think there is a growing cancel culture that is a threat to our freedom or not?" By 64 percent to 36 percent, a majority of voters said they thought there was. Republicans see a threat by 80 percent to 20 percent, independents by 64 percent to 34 percent, but Democrats were split, with a slight majority, 52 percent to 48 percent, saying they do not see a threat. This basic pattern is observable across a number of issues.

Although centrist Democrats make up a majority of the party in the polls I just cited, the fact that a substantial minority of Democrats takes the more extreme stance allows Republicans to portray the Democratic Party as very much in thrall to its more "radical" wing.

The past twelve months have seen a centrist countermobilization designed to strengthen a mainstream image of the Democratic Party and to block the power of the more radical Left to set policy. New groups and digital publications include *Persuasion*, Counterweight,

American Purpose, Foundation against Intolerance and Racism, and the Academic Freedom Alliance.

Nadine Strossen, professor emerita at New York Law School and former president of the American Civil Liberties Union, wrote by email that she considers herself "a 'bleeding-heart liberal' but even more important to me are the classic liberal values that are under siege from all sectors of the political spectrum, left to right, including: freedom of speech, thought and association; academic freedom; due process; and personal privacy."

Strossen cites "the proliferation of new organizations that seek to counter the illiberal trends in academia and beyond."

There are of course plenty of people who sharply defend the progressive wing of the Democratic coalition.

Elizabeth Rose, a law student, argued, for example, in "In Defense of Cancel Culture" last year that "for all the condemnations on cancel culture as an un-American speech suppressing monster, I would argue that cancel culture is incredibly American."

Cancel culture, she continued,

> is essentially a boycott. It's refusing to participate or support those that promote racist, homophobic, sexist, transphobic, or otherwise ignorant behavior. Protest is at the heart of this country and it shouldn't be limited in the name of making already powerful people feel safer to spew ideas that are not tolerable in today's society. Because exposure by millions is so easy now with social media, celebrities, rich, powerful, connected, and beautiful, can no longer get away with disrespecting human dignity. They are not being held to a higher standard for being a public figure, they are being held to the bare minimum.

In a *New Republic* essay in 2019, "The Strange Liberal Backlash to Woke Culture," Ryu Spaeth makes an interesting argument that aligns with Rose's: "The foot-stamping insistence on individual rights obliterates what should be a tension between those rights and the well-being of the community as a whole. This is all the more relevant at a time when the political implications of unbridled individualism, represented by capitalism's self-made man, have never been clearer."

In this contest, Spaeth continues, "there must be a way to express oneself while also ensuring that others aren't silenced, oppressed, and forgotten. There must be a way to protect the individual while addressing dire problems that can only be fixed collectively, from environmental collapse to systemic racism and sexism. To err on the side of solidarity, even against one's strongest emotions, is not to sacrifice our individual humanity. It is to accept what Elizabeth Bennet (in 'Pride and Prejudice') finally learned: that the truth will set you free."

Or take this defense of the call to "defund the police" by Rushi Shah, a graduate student in computer science at Princeton's Center for Information Technology Policy. Shah wrote an op-ed in the January 21 *Daily Princetonian*: "The police determine when to escalate a situation through violence based on their own discretion of what counts as a crime and who is culpable. The past year has shown how that discretion is racist to this day: rubber-bullet rifles for Black Lives Matters protesters and red carpets for white supremacists."

Given this reality, Shah continued, "we should conclude that the police must be defunded, because they overwhelmingly use their budget to harm people of color and to stoke white supremacist movements. With that conclusion in mind, and in the service of humanity, we as Princeton students, staff, professors, administrators, and trustees can contribute to the ongoing effort to defund the police. You may be wondering what exactly people mean when they say, 'defund the police.' Yes, we mean literally abolish the police."

In some respects, this movement is the counter to right-wing populism in that the two share "an ideology of popular resentment against the order imposed on society by a long-established, differentiated ruling class which is believed to have a monopoly of power, property, breeding and culture," in the words of Edward Shils, a sociologist at the University of Chicago who died in 1995.

Frances E. Lee, a political scientist at Princeton, argued in her 2019 article "Populism and the American Party System: Opportunities and Constraints" that "today's major U.S. parties may be more vulnerable to populist internal challenge than they were at earlier points, given (1) developments in communications technology, (2) the unpopularity of mainstream parties and party leaders, and (3) representation gaps created by an increasingly racialized party system."

Populism from the Left and Right, Lee continued, "is a moralistic discourse that turns on a Manichean dichotomy between a corrupt governing elite and a virtuous, homogeneous people. The emphasis on the homogeneity of the people makes populism fundamentally anti-pluralist. Populism's harsh rhetoric around the corrupt elite scorns the legitimacy of political opposition: no institutional procedures or constraints should stand in the way of the people's will. Populist conceptions of the general will thus typically envision 'majority rule without minority rights.'"

The conflict within the Democratic Party and among progressives gets played out on at least two levels.

At one level, it is a dispute over ground rules. Can a professor quote literature or historical documents that use taboo words? What rights should be granted to a person accused of sexual harassment? Are there issues or subjects that should not be explored in an academic setting?

On another level, though, it is a conflict over practical politics. Do specific policies governing speech and sexual behavior win or lose voter support? Are there policies that attract criticism from the opposition party that will stick? Are certain policies so controversial that they divert attention from the opposition's liabilities?

In an article in March, "Why Attacking 'Cancel Culture' and 'Woke' People Is Becoming the G.O.P.'s New Political Strategy," Perry Bacon Jr., formerly a senior writer at FiveThirtyEight and now a *Washington Post* columnist, described the ways that policies the Democratic Left argued for provided political opportunities to the Republican Party: "First and perhaps most important, focusing on cancel culture and woke people is a fairly easy strategy for the G.O.P. to execute, because in many ways it's just a repackaging of the party's long-standing backlash approach. For decades, Republicans have used somewhat vague terms ('dog whistles') to tap into and foment resentment against traditionally marginalized groups like Black Americans who are pushing for more rights and freedoms. This resentment is then used to woo voters (mostly white) wary of cultural, demographic and racial change."

Among the reasons Republicans will continue to adopt an "anti-woke posture," Bacon writes, is that it "gives conservative activists and Republican officials a way to excuse extreme behavior in the past and potentially rationalize such behavior in the future. Republicans are trying to recast the removal of Trump's accounts from Facebook and Twitter as a narrative of liberal tech companies silencing a prominent conservative, instead of those platforms punishing Trump for using them to 'incite violence and encourage overturning the election results.'"

Insofar as Republicans suppress Democratic votes, Bacon continued, "or try to overturn election results in future elections, as seems entirely possible, the party is likely to justify that behavior in part by suggesting the Democrats are just too extreme and woke to be allowed to control the government. The argument would be that Democrats would eliminate police departments and allow crime to surge if they have more power, so they must be stopped at all costs. Polls suggest a huge bloc of G.O.P. voters is already open to such apocalyptic rhetoric."

Bacon's views are widely shared among Democratic Party strategists, whether or not they will say so publicly. And Bacon is hardly alone.

In a piece in *New York Magazine*, "Is 'Anti-wokeness' the New Ideology of the Republican Party?," Ed Kilgore makes the case that for Republicans, "casting a really wide range of ideas and policies as too woke and anyone who is critical of them as being canceled by out-of-control liberals is becoming an important strategy and tool on the right—in fact, this cancel culture/woke discourse could become the organizing idea of the post-Trump-presidency Republican Party."

This approach is particularly attractive to conservative politicians and strategists, Kilgore continued, because "it allows them and their supporters to pose as innocent victims of persecution rather than as aggressive culture warriors seeking to defend their privileges and reverse social change."

Jonathan Haidt, a social psychologist at New York University, argued in an email that the policies the Democratic Party's left wing is pushing are an anchor weighing down the party's prospects: "Wokeness is kryptonite for the Democrats. Most people hate it, other than the progressive activists. If you just look at Americans' policy preferences, Dems should be winning big majorities. But we have strong negative partisanship, and when people are faced with a party that seems to want to defund the police and rename schools, rather than open them, all while crime is rising and kids' welfare is falling, the left flank of the party is just so easy for Republicans to run against."

In much gentler terms, Barack Obama has voiced analogous concerns. "This idea of purity and you're never compromised and you're always politically woke and all that stuff, you should get over that quickly," Obama famously declared in October 2019. "The world is messy. There are ambiguities. People who do really good stuff have flaws. People who you are fighting may love their kids and share certain things with you."

James Carville, the top strategist for Bill Clinton's 1992 presidential campaign, was succinct in his assessment. He recently told Sean Illing, a writer at Vox, "Wokeness is a problem and everyone knows it. It's hard to talk to anybody today—and I talk to lots of people in the Democratic Party—who doesn't say this. But they don't want to say it out loud."

"Why not?" Illing asked.

"Because they'll get clobbered."

Carville's answer provides insight into the question of why, if the left wing of the Democratic Party is backing many policies that are unacceptable to a majority of voters and if some of those policies appear to violate constitutional protections of free speech and the rights of the accused, there hasn't been more pushback in both politics and academia.

I asked Jonathan Rauch, a senior fellow at Brookings and the author of the new book *The Constitution of Knowledge: A Defense of Truth*, about the lack of pushback, and he suggested a series of factors:

- "The younger generation (wrongly) perceives free speech as hazardous to minority rights."
- "The purist side has had more passion, focus and organization than the pluralist side."
- "Universities are consumeristic these days and very image-conscious, and so they have trouble withstanding pressure from their 'customers,' e.g., activist students."
- "The use of social pressure to manipulate opinion is a powerful and sophisticated form of information warfare. Anyone can be dogpiled in minutes for any reason, or no reason."
- "Activists have figured out that they can have disproportionate influence by claiming to be physically endangered and psychologically traumatized by speech that offends them."

Randall Kennedy, a law professor at Harvard and the author of the forthcoming book *Say It Loud! On Race, Law, History and Culture*, cited in an email a similar set "of reasons for the deficient response to threats against freedom of thought, expression and learning emanating from the left."

His list: "'Woke' folk making wrongful demands march under the banner of 'EQUALITY' which is a powerful and attractive emblem, especially in this George Floyd/Covid-19 moment when the scandalous inequities of our society are so heartbreakingly evident. On the campuses, many of the most vocal woke folk are students whom teachers and administrators want to mollify, comfort and impress. Many teachers and administrators seek desperately to be liked by students."

At the same time, Kennedy continued, many of the people demanding the diminution of what he sees as essential freedoms have learned how to package their insistence in effective ways. They have learned, Kennedy wrote, to deploy skillfully the language of "hurt"—as in "I don't care what the speaker's intentions were, what the speaker said has hurt my feelings and ought therefore to be prohibited."

Because of this, Kennedy argued, "authorities, particularly those at educational institutions, need to become much more skeptical and tough-minded when encountering the language of 'hurt.' Otherwise, they will continue to offer incentives to those who deploy the specters of bigotry, privilege and trauma to further diminish vital academic, intellectual and aesthetic freedoms."

For a political party on the front line of change, the centrists-versus-insurgents conflicts that currently plague the Democratic Party are inherent to a party that has chosen in general to take the liberal side on the racial and cultural issues that now play such a large role in politics. The questions of going too fast or too slow, of getting ahead of the voters, of responsibly engaging the obligations of leadership, are inescapable.

Diane Halpern, professor emerita of psychology at Claremont McKenna College and no stranger to politicized controversy as a result of her work on differences in learning skills, wrote in an email, "All social movements are a series of actions and reactions. For example, we can all agree that charges of sexual assault should be fair to all parties involved. But how does 'fairness' get operationalized? The swing from policies that seem to favor the person being accused, then the reverse, then back again, and so on is mirrored in many other topics where people disagree. Action in one direction is followed by reaction in the other direction."

The difficulty, Halpern continued, "is to get people to find what they can agree upon and continue from that point. For example, most people will agree that they want humane treatment of migrants who are fleeing almost certain death in their home country, and we can agree that the United States cannot admit everyone who wants to live here. If conversations began with a shared set of goals, there will still be strong disagreements, but the tone will reduce some of the hostility both sides feel toward each other."

In theory, Halpern is eminently reasonable. But the real question today is how amenable to reconciliation our politics actually are, given that there is profound conflict not only between the two parties but embedded within them.

38

Is Education No Longer the "Great Equalizer"?

There is an ongoing debate over what kinds of investment in human capital—roughly the knowledge, skills, habits, abilities, experience, intelligence, training, judgment, creativity, and wisdom possessed by an individual—contribute most to productivity and life satisfaction.

Is education no longer "a great equalizer of the conditions of men," as Horace Mann declared in 1848, but instead a great divider? Can the Biden administration's efforts to distribute cash benefits to the working class and the poor produce sustained improvements in the lives of those on the bottom tiers of income and wealth—or would a substantial investment in children's training and enrichment programs at a very early age produce more consistent and permanent results?

Take the case of education. On this score—if the assumption is "the more education, the better"—the United States looks pretty good.

From 1976 to 2016 the white high school completion rate rose from 86.4 percent to 94.5 percent, the Black completion rate from

This article first appeared in *The New York Times* on June 23, 2021. Copyright © 2021 by Thomas Edsall and The New York Times Company. All rights reserved.

73.5 percent to 92.2 percent, and the Hispanic completion rate rose from 60.3 percent to 89.1 percent. The graduation rate of whites entering four-year colleges from 1996 to 2012 rose from 33.7 percent to 43.7 percent, for African Americans it rose from 19.5 percent to 23.8 percent, and for Hispanics it rose from 22.8 percent to 34.1 percent.

But these very gains appear to have also contributed to the widening disparity in income between those with different levels of academic attainment, in part because of the very different rates of income growth for men and women with high school degrees, college degrees, and graduate or professional degrees.

Education lifts all boats, but not by equal amounts.

David Autor, an economist at MIT, together with the Harvard economists Claudia Goldin and Lawrence Katz, tackled this issue in a paper last year, "Extending the Race between Education and Technology," asking, "How much of the overall rise in wage inequality since 1980 can be attributed to the large increase in educational wage differentials?"

Their answer: "Returns to a year of K–12 schooling show little change since 1980. But returns to a year of college rose by 6.5 log points, from 0.076 in 1980 to 0.126 in 2000 to 0.141 in 2017. The returns to a year of post-college (graduate and professional) rose by a whopping 10.9 log points, from 0.067 in 1980 to 0.131 in 2000 and to 0.176 in 2017."

I asked Autor to translate that data into language understandable to the layperson, and he wrote back,

There has been almost no increase in the increment to individual earnings for each year of schooling between K and 12 since 1980. It was roughly 6 percentage points per year in 1980, and it still is. The earnings increment for a B.A. has risen from 30.4 percent in 1980 to 50.4 percent in 2000 to 56.4 percent in 2017. The gain to a four-year graduate degree (a Ph.D., for example, but an M.D., J.D., or perhaps even an M.B.A.) relative to high school was approximately 57 percent in 1980, rising to 127 percent in 2017.

These differences result in large part because ever-greater levels of skill—critical thinking, problem-solving, originality, strategizing—are needed in a knowledge-based society.

"The idea of a race between education and technology goes back to the Nobel Laureate Jan Tinbergen, who posited that technological change is continually raising skill requirements while education's job is to supply those rising skill levels," Autor wrote in explaining the gains for those with higher levels of income. "If technology 'gets ahead' of education, the skill premium will tend to rise."

But something more homely may also be relevant. Several researchers argue that parenting style contributes to where a child ends up in life.

As the skill premium and the economic cost of failing to ascend the education ladder rise in tandem, scholars find that adults are adopting differing parental styles—a crucial form of investment in the human capital of their children—and these differing styles appear to be further entrenching inequality.

Such key factors as the level of inequality, the degree to which higher education is rewarded, and the strength of the welfare state are shaping parental strategies in raising children.

In their paper "The Economics of Parenting," three economists, Matthias Doepke at Northwestern, Giuseppe Sorrenti at the University of Zurich, and Fabrizio Zilibotti at Yale, describe three basic forms of child-rearing:

The permissive parenting style is the scenario where the parent lets the child have her way and refrains from interfering in the choices. The authoritarian style is one where the parent imposes her will through coercion. In the model above, coercion is captured through the notion of restricting the choice set. An authoritarian parent chooses a small set that leaves little or no leeway to the child. The third parenting style, authoritative parenting, is also one where the parent aims to affect the child's choice. However, rather than using coercion, an authoritative parent uses persuasion: she shapes the child's preferences through investments in the first period of life. For example, such a parent may preach the virtues of patience or the dangers of risk during when the child is little, so that the child ends up with more adult-like preferences when the child's own decisions matter during adolescence.

There is an "interaction between economic conditions and parenting styles," Doepke and his colleagues write, resulting in the following patterns: "Consider, first, a low inequality society, where the gap between the top and the bottom is small. In such a society, there is limited incentive for children to put effort into education. Parents are also less concerned about children's effort, and thus there is little scope for disagreement between parents and children. Therefore, most parents adopt a permissive parenting style, namely, they keep young children happy and foster their sense of independence so that they can discover what they are good at in their adult life."

The authors cite the Scandinavian countries as key examples of this approach.

Authoritarian parenting, in turn, is most common in less developed, traditional societies where there is little social mobility and children have the same jobs as their parents: "Parents have little incentive to be permissive in order to let children discover what they are good at. Nor do they need to spend effort in socializing children into adultlike values (i.e., to be authoritative) since they can achieve the same result by simply monitoring them."

Finally, they continue, consider "a high-inequality society": "There, the disagreement between parents and children is more salient, because parents would like to see their children work hard in school and choose professions with a high return to human capital. In this society, a larger share of parents will be authoritative, and fewer will be permissive."

This model, the authors write, fits the United States and China.

There are some clear downsides to this approach: "Because of the comparative advantage of rich and educated parents in authoritative parenting, there will be a stronger socioeconomic sorting into parenting styles. Since an authoritative parenting style is conducive to more economic success, this sorting will hamper social mobility."

Sorrenti elaborated in an email: "In neighborhoods with higher inequality and with less affluent families, parents tend to be, on average, more authoritarian. Our models and additional analyses show that parents tend to be more authoritarian in response to a social environment perceived as more risky or less inspiring for children. On the other hand, the authoritative parenting styles, aimed at molding child preferences, is a typical parenting style gaining more and more consensus in the U.S., also in more affluent families."

What do these analyses suggest for policies designed to raise those on the lowest tiers of income and educational attainment? Doepke, Sorrenti, and Zilibotti agree that major investments in training, socialization, and preparation for schooling of very young (four and under) poor children along the lines of proposals by Nobel Laureate James Heckman, an economist at the University of Chicago, and Roland Fryer, a Harvard economist, can prove effective.

In an October 2020 paper, Fryer and three colleagues described

a novel early childhood intervention in which disadvantaged 3–4-year-old children were randomized to receive a new preschool and parent education program focused on cognitive and noncognitive skills or to a control group that did not receive preschool education. In addition to a typical academic year program, we also evaluated a shortened summer version of the program in which children were treated immediately prior to the start of kindergarten. Both programs, including the shortened version, significantly improved cognitive test scores by about one quarter of a standard deviation relative to the control group at the end of the year.

Heckman, in turn, recently wrote on his website, "A critical time to shape productivity is from birth to age five, when the brain develops rapidly to build the foundation of cognitive and character skills necessary for success in school, health, career and life. Early childhood education fosters cognitive skills along with attentiveness, motivation, self-control and sociability—the character skills that turn knowledge into know-how and people into productive citizens."

Doepke agreed: "In the U.S., the big achievement gaps across lines of race or social class open up very early, before kindergarten, rather than during college. So for reducing overall human capital inequality, building high quality early childcare and preschool would be the first place to start."

Zilibotti, in turn, wrote in an email, "We view our work as complementary to Heckman's work. First, one of the tenets of his analysis is that preferences and attitudes are 'malleable,' especially so at an early age. This is against the view that people's success or failure is largely determined by genes. A fundamental part of these early age investments is parental investment. Our work adds the dimension of 'how?' to the traditional perspective of 'how much?' That said, what we call 'authoritative parenting style' is relative to Heckman's emphasis on noncognitive skills."

The expansion of the Heckman $13,500-per-child test pilot program to a universal national program received strong support in an economic analysis of its costs and benefits by Diego Daruich, an economist at the University of Southern California. He argues in his 2019 paper "The Macroeconomic Consequences of Early Childhood Development Policies" that such an enormous government expenditure would produce substantial gains in social welfare, "an income inequality reduction of 7 percent and an increase in intergenerational mobility of 34 percent."

As the debate over the effectiveness of education in reducing class and racial income differences continues, the Moving to Opportunity project stresses how children under the age of thirteen benefit when they and their families move out of neighborhoods of high poverty concentration into more middle-class communities.

In a widely discussed 2015 paper, "The Effects of Exposure to Better Neighborhoods on Children," three Harvard economists, Raj Chetty, Nathaniel Hendren, and Katz, wrote,

> Moving to a lower-poverty neighborhood significantly improves college attendance rates and earnings for children who were young (below age 13) when their families moved. These children also live in better neighborhoods themselves as adults and are less likely

to become single parents. The treatment effects are substantial: children whose families take up an experimental voucher to move to a lower-poverty area when they are less than 13 years old have an annual income that is $3,477 (31 percent) higher on average relative to a mean of $11,270 in the control group in their mid-twenties.

There is a long and daunting history of enduring gaps in scholastic achievement correlated with socioeconomic status in the United States that should temper optimism.

In a February 2020 paper—"Long-Run Trends in the U.S. SES-Achievement Gap"—Eric A. Hanushek of the Hoover Institution at Stanford, Paul E. Peterson of Harvard's Kennedy School, Laura M. Talpey of Stanford's Institute for Economic Policy Research, and Ludger Woessmann of the University of Munich report that over nearly fifty years, "the SES-achievement gap between the top and bottom SES quartiles (75–25 SES gap) has remained essentially flat at roughly 0.9 standard deviations, a gap roughly equivalent to a difference of three years of learning between the average student in the top and bottom quartiles of the distribution."

The virtually unchanging SES-achievement gap, the authors continue, "is confirmed in analyses of the achievement gap by subsidized lunch eligibility and in separate estimations by ethnicity that consider changes in the ethnic composition."

Their conclusion: "The bottom line of our analysis is simply that—despite all the policy efforts—the gap in achievement between children from high- and low-SES backgrounds has not changed. If the goal is to reduce the dependence of students' achievement on the socio-economic status of their families, re-evaluating the design and focus of existing policy programs seems appropriate. As long as cognitive skills remain critical for the income and economic well-being of U.S. citizens, the unwavering achievement gaps across the SES spectrum do not bode well for future improvements in intergenerational mobility."

The pessimistic implications of this paper have not deterred those devoted to seeking ways to break embedded patterns of inequality and stagnant mobility.

In a November 2019 essay, "We Have the Tools to Reverse the Rise in Inequality," Olivier Blanchard of the Peterson Institute for International Economics and Dani Rodrik, an economist at Harvard, cited the ready availability of a host of policies with strong support among many economists, political scientists, and Democrats: "Many areas have low-hanging fruit: expansion of EITC [Earned Income Tax Credit]-type programs, increased public funding of both pre-K and tertiary education; redirection of subsidies to employment-friendly innovation, greater overall progressivity in taxation, and policies to help workers reorganize in the face of new production modes."

Adoption of policies calling for aggressive government inter-vention raises a crucial question, Autor acknowledged in his email: "whether such interventions would kill the golden goose of U.S. innovation and entrepreneurship." Autor's answer: "At this point, I'd say the graver threat is from inaction rather than action. If the citizens of a democracy think that 'progress' simply means more inequality and stratification, and rising economic insecurity stemming from technology and globalization, they're eventually going to 'cancel' that plan and demand something else—though those demands may not ultimately lead somewhere constructive (e.g., closing U.S. bor-ders, slapping tariffs on numerous friendly trading partners, and starving the government of tax revenue needed to invest in citizens was never going to lead anywhere good)."

A promising approach to the augmentation of human capital lies in the exploration of noncognitive skills—perseverance, punctuality, self-restraint, politeness, thoroughness, postponement of gratifica-tion, grit—all of which are increasingly valuable in a service-based economy. Noncognitive skills have proved to be teachable, especially among very young children.

Shelly Lundberg, an economics professor at the University of California–Santa Barbara, cites a range of projects and studies, including the Perry Preschool Project, an intensive program for three-to-four-year-old low-income children "that had long-term impacts on test scores, adult crime and male income." The potential gains from raising noncognitive skills are wide-ranging, she writes in a chapter of the December 2018 book *Education, Skills, and Technical Change: Implications for Future US GDP Growth*: "Noncognitive skills such as attention and self-control can increase the productivity of educational investments. Disruptive behavior and crime impose negative externalities in schools and communities that increased levels of some noncognitive skills could ameliorate."

But, she cautions, "the state of our knowledge about the production of and returns to noncognitive skills is rather rudimentary. We lack a conceptual framework that would enable us to consistently define multidimensional noncognitive skills, and our reliance on observed or reported behavior as measures of skill make it impossible to reliably compare skills across groups that face different environments."

Education, training in cognitive and noncognitive skills, nutrition, health care, and parenting are all among the building blocks of human capital, and evidence suggests that continuing investments that combat economic hardship among whites and minorities—and that help defuse debilitating conflicts over values, culture, and race—stand the best chance of reversing the disarray and inequality that plague our political system and our social order.

39

Trump's Cult of Animosity Shows No Sign of Letting Up

In 2016, Donald Trump recruited voters with the highest levels of animosity toward African Americans, assembling a "schadenfreude" electorate—voters who take pleasure in making the opposition suffer—that continues to dominate the Republican Party, even in the aftermath of the Trump presidency.

With all his histrionics and theatrics, Trump brought the dark side of American politics to the fore: the alienated, the distrustful, voters willing to sacrifice democracy for a return to white hegemony. The segregationist segment of the electorate has been a permanent fixture of American politics, shifting between the two major parties.

For more than two decades, scholars and analysts have written about the growing partisan antipathy and polarization that have turned America into two warring camps, politically speaking.

Lilliana Mason, a political scientist at Johns Hopkins, makes the case via Twitter that Trump has "served as a lightning rod for lots of regular people who hold white Christian supremacist beliefs." The solidification of their control over the Republican Party "makes it

This article first appeared in *The New York Times* on July 7, 2021. Copyright © 2021 by Thomas Edsall and The New York Times Company. All rights reserved.

seem like a partisan issue. But this faction has been around longer than our current partisan divide." In fact, "they are not loyal to a party—they are loyal to white Christian domination."

Trump's success in transforming the party has radically changed the path to the Republican presidential nomination: the traditional elitist route through state and national party leaders, the Washington lobbying and interest group community, and top fund-raisers across the country no longer ensures success and may, instead, prove a liability.

For those seeking to emulate Trump—Ted Cruz, Josh Hawley, and Ron DeSantis, for example—the basic question is whether Trump's trajectory is replicable or whether there are unexplored avenues to victory at the 2024 Republican National Convention.

When Trump got into the 2016 primary race, "he did not have a clear coalition, nor did he have the things candidates normally have when running for president: political experience, governing experience, or a track record supporting party issues and ideologies," Joseph Uscinski, a political scientist at the University of Miami, wrote in an email. Lacking these traditional credentials, Trump sought out "the underserved market within the Republican electorate by giving those voters what they might have wanted, but weren't getting from the other mainstream selections."

The objectives of the Trump wing of the Republican Party stand out in other respects, especially in the strength of its hostility to key Democratic minority constituencies.

Julie Wronski, a political scientist at the University of Mississippi—a coauthor, with Mason and John Kane of New York University, of a just-published paper, "Activating Animus: The Uniquely Social Roots of Trump Support"—put it this way in reply to my emailed query: "The Trump coalition is motivated by animosity toward Blacks, Hispanics, Muslims and L.G.B.T. This animosity has no bearing on support for any of the other G.O.P. elites or the party itself. Warmth toward whites and Christians equally predict support for Trump, other G.O.P. elites, and the party itself. The only area where Trump support is different than other G.O.P. support is in regards to harnessing this out-group animus."

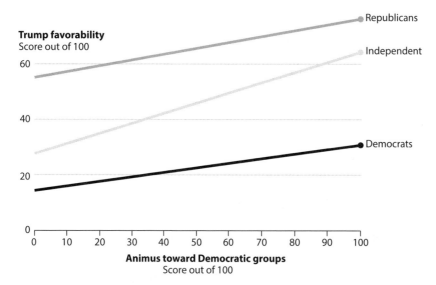

FIGURE 39.1. TRUMP SUPPORT RISES WITH ANIMUS. A study found that animus toward marginalized, Democratic-linked groups was a good predictor of future support for Trump, regardless of party.
Note: Groups include African Americans, Hispanics, Muslims, and LGBTQ. Favorability from 2018. Animus from 2011.
Source: Lilliana Mason, Julie Wronski, and John V. Kane, "Activating Animus: The Uniquely Social Roots of Trump Support." From The New York Times. © 2021 The New York Times Company. All rights reserved. Used under license.

For as long as Trump remains the standard-bearer of the Republican Party, Wronski continued, "this animosity coalition will define the party."

Animosity toward these four Democratic-aligned minority groups is not limited to Republican voters. Mason, Wronski, and Kane created an "animus to Democrat groups" scale, ranked from 0 at the least hostile to 1.0 at the most. Kane wrote me that "approximately 18 percent of Democrats have scores above the midpoint of the scale (which would mean negative feelings/animus). For Independents, this percentage grows to 33 percent. For Republicans, it jumps substantially to 45 percent."

Figure 39.1 demonstrates Kane's point.

The three authors go on: "Animosity toward Democratic-linked groups predicts Trump support, rather remarkably, across the political spectrum. Further, given the decisive role that Independents can play in elections, these results suggest that reservoirs of animosity are not necessarily specific to a particular party, and may therefore be tapped by any political elite."

Before Trump took center stage in 2015, Republican leaders were determined to "stymie Democratic policy initiatives, resist compromise, and make it clear that Republicans desire to score political victories and win back power from Democrats," Kane wrote in his email, but "establishment Republicans generally did not openly demonize, much less dehumanize, Democratic politicians at the national level."

Trump, Kane continued, "wantonly disregarded this norm, and now Trump's base may come to expect future Republican elites to be willing to do the same. If this practice eventually comes to be seen as a 'winning strategy' for Republican politicians as a whole, it could bring us into a new era of polarization wherein Republican cooperation with the 'Demon Rats' is seen not just as undesirable, but thoroughly unconscionable."

Most significantly, in Mason's view, is that "there is a faction in American politics that has moved from party to party, can be recruited from either party, and responds especially well to hatred of marginalized groups. They're not just Republicans or Democrats, they're a third faction that targets parties."

Bipartisanship, Mason continued in a lengthy Twitter thread, "is not the answer to the problem. We need to confront this particular faction of Americans who have been uniquely visible and anti-democratic since before the Civil War (when they were Democrats)."

In their paper, Mason, Wronski, and Kane conclude,

This research reveals a wellspring of animus against marginalized groups in the United States that can be harnessed and activated for political gain. Trump's unique ability to do so is not the only cause for normative concern. Instead, we should take note that these attitudes exist across both parties and among nonpartisans. Though they may remain relatively latent when leaders and parties draw attention elsewhere, the right leader can activate these attitudes and fold them into voters' political judgments. Should America wish to become a fully multiracial democracy, it will need to reconcile with these hostile attitudes themselves.

Adam Enders, a political scientist at the University of Louisville, and Uscinski, in their June 2021 paper "On Modeling the Social-Psychological Foundations of Support for Donald Trump," describe a "Trump voter profile": "an amalgamation of attitudes about, for example, racial groups, immigrants and political correctness—that rivals partisanship and ideology as predictors of Trump support and is negatively related to support for mainstream Republican candidates."

In an email, Enders described this profile as fitting those attracted to Trump's

> relatively explicit appeal to xenophobia, racial prejudice, authoritarianism, sexism, conspiracy thinking, in combination with his outsider status that gives him credibility as the anti-establishment candidate. The Trump voter profile is a constellation of social-psychological attitudes—about various racial groups, women, immigrants, and conspiracy theories—that uniquely predict support for Donald Trump.

Uscinski and Enders are the lead authors of a forthcoming paper, "American Politics in Two Dimensions: Partisan and Ideological Identities versus Anti-establishment Orientations," in which they argue that "our current conceptualization of mass opinion is missing something. Specifically, we theorize that an underappreciated, albeit ever-present, dimension of opinion explains many of the problematic attitudes and behaviors gripping contemporary politics. This dimension, which we label 'anti-establishment,' rather than explaining one's attitudes about and behaviors toward the opposing political coalition, captures one's orientation toward the established political order irrespective of partisanship and ideology."

In the case of Trump and other antidemocratic leaders around the world, Uscinski and Enders contend that "anti-establishment sentiments are an important ingredient of support for populist leaders, conspiratorial beliefs, and political violence. And, while we contend that this dimension is orthogonal to the left-right dimension of opinion along which partisan and ideological concerns are oriented, we also theorize that it can be activated by strategic partisan politicians. As such, phenomena which are oftentimes interpreted as expressions of 'far-right' or 'far-left' orientations may not be born of left-right views at all, but rather of the assimilation of anti-establishment sentiments into mainstream politics by elites."

Antiestablishment voters, Uscinski and Enders write, "are more likely to believe that the 'one percent' controls the economy for their own good, believe that a 'deep state' is embedded within the government and believe that the mainstream media is 'deliberately' misleading us." Such voters "are more prevalent among younger people, those with lower incomes, those with less formal education, and among racial and ethnic minority groups. In other words, it is groups who have historically occupied a tenuous position in the American socio-economic structure."

The most intensely partisan voters—very strong Democrats and very strong Republicans—are the least antiestablishment, according to Uscinski and Enders:

> Those on the extremes of partisan and ideological identity exhibit lower levels of most of these psychological predispositions. In other words, extreme partisans and ideologues are more likely to express civil attitudes and agreeable personality characteristics than less extreme partisans and ideologues; this contradicts growing concerns over the relationship between left-right extremism and antisocial attitudes and behaviors. We suspect this finding is due to strong partisans and ideologues being wedded to, and entrenched within, the established political order. Their organized, relatively constrained orientation toward the political landscape is built on the objects of establishment politics: the parties, party elites and familiar ideological objects.

That, in turn, leads Uscinski and Enders to another contrarian conclusion: "We find that an additional 'anti-establishment' dimension of opinion can, at least partially, account for the acceptance of political violence, distrust in government, belief in conspiracy theories, and support for 'outsider' candidates. Although it is intuitive to attribute contemporary political dysfunction to left-right extremism and partisan tribalism, we argue that many elements of this dysfunction stem from the activation of anti-establishment orientations."

One politician whose appeal was similar to Trump's, as many have noted, was George Wallace, the segregationist governor of Alabama, who ran for president four times in the 1960s and 1970s, openly using anti-Black rhetoric.

Omar Wasow, a political scientist at Berkeley, cites Wallace in an email: "There has always been a sizable bloc of American voters eager to support candidates articulating explicit appeals to out-group antipathy. Segregationist George Wallace, for example, won approximately 13.5 percent of the national three-way presidential vote in 1968."

Republican candidates before Trump used so-called dog-whistle themes designed to capitalize on white racial fears, Wasow pointed out, in such a way that they "could appeal to those animated by racial threat while also holding together a larger, winning coalition. That Trump was able to campaign like Wallace yet build a winning state-level coalition in 2016 like Nixon is remarkable but not obviously repeatable on a national scale, even by Trump himself (as evidenced in 2020). Regionally, however, Trump's style of overt ethnonationalist rhetoric will likely have enough support to remain highly viable for congressional and state-level candidates."

In their July 3 paper, "Partisan Schadenfreude and the Demand for Candidate Cruelty," Steven W. Webster, Adam N. Glynn, and Matthew P. Motta, political scientists at Indiana University, Emory, and Oklahoma State, respectively, explore "the prevalence of partisan schadenfreude—that is, taking 'joy in the suffering' of partisan others."

In it, they argue that a "sizable portion of the American mass public engages in partisan schadenfreude and these attitudes are most commonly expressed by the most ideologically extreme Americans."

In addition, Webster, Glynn, and Motta write, these voters create a "demand for candidate cruelty" since these voters are "more likely than not to vote for candidates who promise to pass policies that 'disproportionately harm' supporters of the opposing political party."

In response to my emailed inquiries, Webster answered, "Schadenfreude is a bipartisan attitude. In our study, the schadenfreude measure ranges from 0–6. For Republicans, the mean score on this measure is 2.81; for Democrats, it is 2.67. Notably, there is a considerable amount of variation in how much partisans express schadenfreude: some express very little schadenfreude, while others exhibit an extraordinary amount. Those who identify as a 'strong Democrat' or a 'strong Republican' tend to express greater levels of schadenfreude than those who do not strongly identify with their party."

The kind of pain voters would like to see inflicted on their adversaries varies by ideology, partisanship, and issue. Webster argues that "among those who accept the scientific consensus that climate change is occurring and is not attributable to natural causes, over one-third agreed that climate change deniers 'get what they deserve when disasters like hurricanes make landfall where they live.'"

Democrats and Republicans express two very different forms of schadenfreude over the COVID-19 pandemic, and Trump often capitalized on this. Trump's supporters, Webster wrote, "thrived off his willingness to upset the 'right' people, which is certainly an aspect of schadenfreude. In many ways, Trump's supporters were (and are) motivated by their frustrations over a society that appears to be moving away from one that they desire. So, this makes Trump's willingness to go 'against the grain,' so to speak, an attractive feature."

Webster went on: "Democrats experience schadenfreude when individuals do not follow CDC health guidelines and get sick from the coronavirus. In a similar manner, Republicans tend to express schadenfreude when people lose their job due to businesses following government regulations on the economy during the pandemic."

Along parallel lines, Christopher Sebastian Parker, a political scientist at the University of Washington, wrote me, "Trump stoked anger. Anger is typically a reaction to perceived injustice and threat. Action to correct the perceived injustice, and to neutralize the threat, is the general behavioral response. Trump's 'surprise' victory in 2016 is, at least in part, a response on the part of the reactionary right to recover from the 'injustice' of having a Black president, and to neutralize the threat associated with perceived social change."

Trump appealed to voters, Parker continued, who "wanted 'their' country back, so they mobilized in an effort to make that happen." These kinds of appeals can work in both directions.

"In some of my own research," Parker wrote, "I showed that when we primed Black people with material that depicted Trump as a threat to Black people, they were far more likely to report their intention to mobilize in the 2020 election than those who didn't have this prime. In short, explicit appeals are the order of the day."

From one vantage point, there is a legitimate argument that Trump has not really changed the Republican Party.

In an article in Vox in August 2020, "Trump Was Supposed to Change the G.O.P. But the G.O.P. Changed Him," Jane Coaston, now the host of the *Times*'s podcast *The Argument*, wrote, "The Trumpification of the Republican Party was not the remaking of the Republican Party into a populist outfit. Instead, it was the reshaping of Trump into a mainline Republican, one who values the 'beautiful boaters' over working-class voters whose politics were more heterodox than any observer realized back in 2016. The desire for populism Trump observed was real, but he didn't believe in it. As one conservative pundit told me, while Trump exploited a vacuum in conservative thought, 'what's so sad is that he never fulfilled or developed it.'"

More recently, my *Times* colleague Alexander Burns wrote on July 4 about "the frustrating reality of political competition these days: The president—any president—might be able to chip away at voters' skepticism of his party or their cynicism about Washington, but he cannot engineer a broad realignment in the public mood."

The electorate, Burns noted, "is not entirely frozen, but each little shift in one party's favor seems offset by another small one in the opposite direction. Mr. Trump improved his performance with women and Hispanic voters compared with the 2016 election, while Mr. Biden expanded his party's support among moderate constituencies like male voters and military veterans."

All true. But at the same time Trump has mobilized and consolidated a cohort that now exercises control over the Republican Party, a renegade segment of the electorate, perhaps as large as one-third of all voters, that disdains democratic principles, welcomes authoritarian techniques to crush racial and cultural liberalism, seeks to wrest away the election machinery, and suffers from the mass delusion that Trump won last November.

Regardless of whether Trump runs again, he has left an enormous footprint—a black mark—on American politics, which will stain elections for years to come.

40

How Strong Is America's Multiracial Democracy?

The issue cutting across every aspect of American politics today is whether—and how—the nation can survive as a multiracial democracy.

One key question is what the political impact has been of the decades-long quest to integrate America's schools.

A study published last year, "The Long-Run Effects of School Racial Diversity on Political Identity," examined how "the end of race-based busing in Charlotte-Mecklenburg schools, an event that led to large changes in school racial composition," affected the partisanship of students as adults.

The authors, Stephen Billings, of the University of Colorado; Eric Chyn, of Dartmouth; and Kareem Haggag, of UCLA's Anderson School of Management, found that "a 10-percentage point increase in the share of minorities in a student's assigned school decreased their likelihood of registering as a Republican by 8.8 percent." The drop was "entirely driven by white students (a 12 percent decrease)."

This article first appeared in *The New York Times* on September 1, 2021. Copyright © 2021 by Thomas Edsall and The New York Times Company. All rights reserved.

"What mechanisms can explain our results?" the authors asked.

Their answer: "Intergroup contact is a key potential channel. Several theoretical frameworks provide predictions for how exposure to more minority peers may shape party affiliation. For white students, we focus on the 'contact hypothesis,' which posits that meaningful contact with out-group members can reduce prejudice toward them. This theory suggests that exposure to minority peers should reduce the likelihood of registering as a Republican by weakening 'racially conservative' attitudes that have been linked to support for the Republican Party."

In support of their argument, the authors cite two additional papers, "The Impact of College Diversity on Behavior toward Minorities," by Scott E. Carrell, Mark Hoekstra, and James E. West, economists at the University of California–Davis, Texas A&M, and Baylor, respectively, which found "that white students who are randomly assigned a Black roommate in their freshman year are more likely to choose a Black roommate in subsequent years," and "Building Social Cohesion between Christians and Muslims through Soccer in Post-ISIS Iraq," by Salma Mousa, a political scientist at Yale, which found "evidence of positive impacts of religious-based and caste-based intergroup contact through sports."

In major respects, the busing of public school students in Charlotte-Mecklenburg in North Carolina meets the requirements for productive interracial contact posited by Gordon Allport, a professor of psychology at Harvard, in his classic 1954 book *The Nature of Prejudice.*

Allport wrote that prejudice "may be reduced by equal status contact between majority and minority groups in the pursuit of common goals. The effect is greatly enhanced if this contact is sanctioned by institutional supports (i.e., by law, custom, or local atmosphere), and provided it is of a sort that leads to the perception of common interests and common humanity between members of the two groups."

The Charlotte-Mecklenburg integration program had widespread public support. *Education Week* reported that after the federal courts in 1971 ordered busing to achieve integration,

"Charlotte's political and business leaders moved to support the busing order. Antibusing school-board members were voted out and replaced with supporters of the order. Parents of children scheduled to be bused joined together to seek ways to smooth the logistical problems. No serious protest has erupted since then, and the Charlotte-Mecklenburg district is often cited as a successful example of mandatory busing."

In that respect, Charlotte-Mecklenburg stood out in a nation where cities like Boston and Detroit experienced divisive and often violent protest.

A 2018 study, "Past Place, Present Prejudice," explored some of the complexities of court-ordered racial integration. The authors, Seth Goldman, a professor of communications at the University of Massachusetts, and Daniel Hopkins, a political scientist at the University of Pennsylvania, report that "if a non-Hispanic white person grew up in a county with no African Americans, we should expect that person's prejudice to be 2.3 points lower than an otherwise similar respondent growing up in a county that is 18 percent Black."

Goldman and Hopkins described their data as supporting the following conclusion: "Proximity during one's formative years increases racial prejudice years later."

Chyn, an author of the "School Racial Diversity" paper, and Goldman, an author of the "Past Place" paper, both stressed by email that they were comparing racial and political attitudes under different circumstances.

Goldman wrote,

I don't see any contradictions between the findings and those in my and Dan's paper. It is a common misperception that studies finding a relationship between living in more racially diverse places represented as larger geographic units such as counties and expressing higher levels of racial prejudice contradicts intergroup contact theory. On the contrary, this relationship is due to the lack of sustained interracial contact among most whites in racially diverse areas. The typical situation is one of proximity without contact: whereas merely being in proximity to members of different groups promotes threat responses, sustained contact helps to alleviate prejudice.

Chyn said, "At least one difference is that our work focuses on intergroup exposure within schools whereas Goldman and Hopkins study the influence of racial context at the broader county level. This distinction matters as it is often thought that sustained and cooperative contact is necessary to reduce prejudice between groups. Schools may be a particularly good setting where such beneficial contact can occur. Goldman and Hopkins's work may be picking up the effect of having geographic proximity to racial outgroups with no substantive interaction between children growing up in an area."

Brian T. Hamel, a political scientist at Louisiana State University, and Bryan Wilcox-Archuleta, a research scientist at Facebook, studied intergroup contact in a context more likely to intensify racial conflict. They reported in their paper "Black Workers in White Places: Daytime Racial Diversity and White Public Opinion" that "voting behavior in presidential and congressional elections, feelings of racial resentment and attitudes on affirmative action" of whites are more conservative in neighborhoods where the share of Black nonresident workers is significantly higher than in places with fewer Black nonresident workers.

"Whites respond to just the passing, irregular presence of Blacks who commute into their neighborhood for work," Hamel elaborated in an email. "The upshot is that Blacks do not have to even live in the same neighborhood as whites to get the kind of racial threat reactions that we see in other work."

David O. Sears, a political scientist at UCLA, contends in his 2014 paper "The American Color Line and Black Exceptionalism" that "people of African descent have an exceptional place in American political life because their history, described by the racial caste prototype of intergroup relations, has been unique among American ethnic minorities."

Sears adds that "the one-drop rule applied to blacks is considerably less permeable than is the color line applied to Latinos and

Asians, particularly in later generations further removed in time from immigration."

The history and experience of Black Americans, compared with other minorities, are unique, according to Sears: "Although Latinos and Asians have certainly faced discrimination and exclusion throughout U.S. history, the majority of contemporary U.S. residents who identify as Latino and Asian are not descendants of the generations who were subjected to second-class citizenship in the 19th or 20th centuries. Instead, most are true immigrants, often not yet citizens, and often do not speak English at home. In contrast, the vast majority of blacks living in the United States are native-born citizens, speak only English in all contexts, and are descendants of generations who were subjected to enslavement."

Sears cites data in support of his argument that African Americans have faced different historical contingencies in the story of American integration.

"In the 2010 census, the segregation of blacks from whites remained extremely high, with a dissimilarity index of 59," while the dissimilarity index (a measure of racial or ethnic segregation or isolation) was 48 for Latinos and 41 for Asian Americans.

Sears continued,

> Blacks (25 percent) were almost four times as likely as U.S.-born Latinos (7 percent) or Asians (5 percent) to show the highest level of aggrieved group consciousness.
>
> 55 percent of the blacks, as against 36 percent of the U.S.-born Latinos and 23 percent of the Asians, were at least moderately high in group consciousness.

In this regard, economic factors have been instrumental. In "The Color of Disparity: Racialized Income Inequality and Support for Liberal Economic Policies," Benjamin J. Newman and Bea-Sim Ooi, political scientists at the University of California–Riverside, and Tyler Thomas Reny, of Claremont Graduate University, compared support for liberal economic policies in ZIP codes where very few of the poor were Black with ZIP codes where a high proportion of the poor were Black.

"Exposure to local economic inequality is only systematically associated with increased support for liberal economic policies when the respective 'have-nots' are not Black," according to Newman, Ooi, and Reny.

A 2021 study, "The Activation of Prejudice and Presidential Voting," by Daniel Hopkins—a coauthor of "Past Place, Present Prejudice"—raises a related question: "Divisions between whites and Blacks have long influenced voting. Yet given America's growing Latino population, will whites' attitudes toward Blacks continue to predict their voting behavior? Might anti-Latino prejudice join or supplant them?"

Hopkins examined whites' responses to Donald Trump's 2016 campaign, which contained more overt anti-immigrant rhetoric than anti-Black themes. The result nonetheless: "Donald Trump's candidacy activated anti-Black but not anti-Latino prejudice," Hopkins writes.

Hopkins acknowledges that "people who expressed more restrictionist immigration attitudes in 2008 and 2012 were more likely to shift toward Trump," but he argues that it did not translate into increased bias against Hispanics because it reflected an even deeper-seated racism: "Although the 2016 campaign foregrounded issues related to Latino immigrants, our results demonstrate the enduring role of anti-Black prejudice in shaping whites' vote choices. Even accounting for their 2012 vote choice, partisanship and other demographics, whites' 2012 anti-Black prejudice proved a robust predictor of supporting G.O.P. nominee Donald Trump in 2016 while anti-Latino prejudice did not."

Hopkins speculates that Trump successfully activated anti-Black views because "generations of racialized political issues dividing Blacks and whites have produced developed psychological schema in many whites' minds, schema that are evoked even by rhetoric targeting other groups."

The long history of Black-white conflict has, Hopkins argues, "forged and reinforced durable connections in white Americans' minds between anti-Black prejudice and vote choice. It is those pathways that appear to have been activated by Trump, even in the presence of substantial rhetoric highlighting other groups alongside Blacks. Once formed, the grooves of public opinion run deep."

Against this generally troubling background, there are some noteworthy countervailing trends.

In an August 2021 paper, "Race and Income in U.S. Suburbs: Are Diverse Suburbs Disadvantaged?," Ankit Rastogi, a postdoctoral fellow at the University of Pennsylvania's Center for the Study of Ethnicity, Race, and Immigration, challenges "two assumptions: that people of color are concentrated largely in cities and that communities of color are disadvantaged."

Rastogi—using data from the 2019 American Community Survey—finds instead that, "by and large, racially diverse suburbs are middle class when comparing their median household income with the national value ($63,000). The most multiracial suburbs host populations with the highest median incomes (mean ~ $85,000). Black and Latinx median household incomes surpass the national value in these diverse suburbs."

By 2010, Rastogi points out, majorities of every major demographic group lived in suburbs: "51 percent of Black Americans, 62 percent of Asians, 59 percent of Latinx, and 78 percent of whites. Many people of color live in suburbs because they see them as desirable, resource-rich communities with good schools and other public goods."

In addition, Rastogi writes, "roughly 45 million people of color and 42 million white people lived in suburbs with diversity scores above 50 in 2019. On average, these people live in middle-class contexts, leading us to question stereotypes of race, place and disadvantage."

While Rastogi correctly points to some optimistic trends, David Sears presents a less positive view: "Blacks' contemporary situation reveals the force of their distinctive history. African Americans remain the least assimilated ethnic minority in America in the respects most governed by individual choice, such as intermarriage and residential, and therefore, school, integration. By the same criteria, Latinos and Asians are considerably more integrated into the broader society."

The key, Sears continues, "is America's nearly impermeable color line. Americans of all racial and ethnic groups alike think about and treat people of African descent as a particularly distinctive, exceptional group—not as just another 'people of color.'"

Sears does not, however, get the last word.

In a March 2021 report, *The Growing Diversity of Black America*, the Pew Research Center found some striking changes in recent decades.

From 2000 to 2019, the percentage of African Americans with at least a bachelor's degree rose from 15 percent to 23 percent, as the share with a master's degree or higher nearly doubled from 5 percent to 9 percent.

At the same time, the share of African Americans without a high school degree was cut by more than half over the same period, from 28 percent to 13 percent.

Median Black household income has grown only modestly in inflation-adjusted dollars, from $43,581 in 2000 to $44,000 in 2019, but there were improvements in the distribution of income, with the share earning more than $50,000 growing.

In 2000, 31 percent of Black households made $25,000 or less (in 2019 US dollar adjusted value); 25 percent made $25,000 to $49,999; 28 percent made $50,000 to less than $99,999; and 16 percent made $100,000 or more.

In 2019, 29 percent of Black households made less than $25,000; 25 percent earned $25,000 to $49,999; 17 percent made $50,000 to $74,999; 10 percent earned $75,000 to $99,999; and 18 percent earned more than $100,000.

Evidence of extraordinary Black progress has been underreported—indeed minimized—in recent years. That reality notwithstanding, there has been consistent and considerable achievement. Given the historical treatment of African Americans in school and in society, perhaps the most striking accomplishment has been in the rising levels of educational attainment. The economic gains have been more incremental. But neither set of gains can or should be ignored.

41

"It's Become Increasingly Hard for Them to Feel Good about Themselves"

Is there a whole class of men who no longer fit into the social order?

A decade ago, Marianne Bertrand and Jessica Pan, economists at the University of Chicago and the National University of Singapore, respectively, concluded in their paper "The Trouble with Boys: Social Influences and the Gender Gap in Disruptive Behavior,"

> Family structure is an important correlate of boys' behavioral deficit. Boys that are raised outside of a traditional family (with two biological parents present) fare especially poorly. For example, the gender gap in externalizing problems when the children are in fifth grade is nearly twice as large for children raised by single mothers compared to children raised in traditional families. By eighth grade, the gender gap in school suspension is close to 25 percentage points among children raised by single mothers, while only 10 percentage points among children in intact families.

This article first appeared in *The New York Times* on September 22, 2021. Copyright © 2021 by Thomas Edsall and The New York Times Company. All rights reserved.

Boys raised by teenage mothers also appear to be much more likely to act out.

Bertrand and Pan focus on the crucial role of noncognitive skills, on how "factors such as study habits, industriousness and perseverance matter as much as cognitive skills in explaining occupational achievement." Noncognitive skills, they write, "are not fixed but are in fact quite malleable, and can be shaped by early intervention programs."

The effects on boys of being raised in a single-parent household are particularly acute in the development of noncognitive skills, according to Bertrand and Pan: "Most striking are our findings regarding gender differences in the noncognitive returns to parental inputs. Across all family structures, we observe that boys' likelihood to act out is sharply reduced when faced with larger and better parental inputs. For girls, the relationship between parental inputs and behavioral outcomes appears to be much weaker. As these parental inputs are typically higher and of better quality in intact families, this largely contributes to why boys with single mothers are so much more disruptive and eventually face school suspension."

There are a number of research projects that illuminate the ongoing controversy on the subject of men and their role in contemporary America.

First, an excerpt from a 2016 paper by David Autor, an economist at MIT, and four colleagues: "In the United States in 2016, the female high school graduation rate exceeded the male rate by five percentage points, and the female college graduation rate exceeded the male rate by seven percentage points. What explains these gender gaps in educational attainment? Recent evidence indicates that boys and girls are differently affected by the quantity and quality of inputs received in childhood."

Second, part of a 2015 paper by Francesca Gino, Caroline Ashley Wilmuth, and Alison Wood Brooks, who were all at Harvard Business School at the time of writing: "We find that, compared to men, women have a higher number of life goals, place less importance on power-related goals, associate more negative outcomes (e.g., time constraints and trade-offs) with high-power positions, perceive power as less desirable, and are less likely to take advantage of opportunities for professional advancement."

Third, a passage from an article by Colleen Flaherty, a reporter at *Inside Higher Ed*: "The study suggests that men are overrepresented in elite Ph.D. programs, especially in those fields heavy on math skills, making for segregation by discipline and prestige."

And fourth, a quote from a 2013 paper, "Wayward Sons: The Emerging Gender Gap in Labor Markets and Education," by Autor and Melanie Wasserman, an economist at UCLA: "Although a significant minority of males continues to reach the highest echelons of achievement in education and labor markets, the median male is moving in the opposite direction. Over the last three decades, the labor market trajectory of males in the U.S. has turned downward along four dimensions: skills acquisition; employment rates; occupational stature; and real wage levels."

I sent these four references to Arlie Hochschild, a professor of sociology at Berkeley and the author of *Strangers in Their Own Land: Anger and Mourning on the American Right*, for her views. She emailed back, "Since the 1970s offshoring and automation have hit blue collar men especially hard. Oil, coal—automating, manufacturing, offshoring, and truck-driving about to go down. Non-B.A. males are in an especially vulnerable place. I saw it in Louisiana, and again where I'm interviewing in Appalachia. It's become increasingly hard for them to feel good about themselves."

In a 2018 essay in the *New York Review of Books*, "Male Trouble," Hochschild described the predicament of less well-educated men:

> Compared to women, a shrinking proportion of men are earning B.A.s, even though more jobs than ever require a college degree, including many entry-level positions that used to require only a high school diploma. Among men between twenty-five and thirty-four, 30 percent now have a B.A. or more, while 38 percent of women in that age range do. The cost of this disadvantage has only grown with time: of the new jobs created between the end of the recession and 2016, 73 percent went to candidates with a

B.A. or more. A shrinking proportion of men are even counted as part of the labor force; between 1970 and 2010, the percentage of adult men in a job or looking for work dropped from 80 to 70 while that of adult women rose from 43 to 58. Most of the men slipping out lack B.A.s.

While many of the men Hochschild writes about see a future of diminished, if not disappearing, prospects, men in elite professions continue to dominate the ranks of chief executives, top politicians, and the highest-paying professorships.

Frances E. Jensen, chair of the Department of Neurology at the University of Pennsylvania's Perelman School of Medicine, taking a different tack, argues that boys' brains mature more slowly than girls' brains do, a difference that is particularly striking in the adolescent years. In a 2017 interview with the School Superintendents Association, Jensen stressed the crucial role the still-maturing brain plays in the lives of teenagers: "Teens go through a period of increased emotional fluctuation and are like a Ferrari with weak brakes. The emotional center of the brain, the limbic system, which controls emotions, is fully connected, but the frontal lobe that sharpens critical thinking isn't well-connected. That means the part of the brain that makes them pause and say to themselves, 'Bad idea. Don't post that on Facebook because it might hurt my chances of getting a job in the future' or 'Don't jump in the lake, there may be a rock,' isn't mature."

The brain also becomes more efficient, Jensen said, "during a process called myelination. This is when a fatty substance called myelin grows slowly and wraps itself around miles of brain cells to better insulate them. Insulation makes the brain more efficient at sending and receiving signals. Myelination is a slow process that finishes in the mid-20s. Our brains have thousands of miles of networks and to insulate all of them with myelin takes over two and a half decades to finish."

Using MRI images, Jensen continued, "you can actually see the brain is laying down a layer of myelin over time when looked at year over year. You can measure those layers and see a dynamic process where the insulation is sharpening the rapidity of our signaling from one part of our brain to another."

And then she added a crucial point: "In adolescence, on average girls are more developed by about two to three years in terms of the peak of their synapses and in their connectivity processes."

A major 2015 study, "The Emergence of Sex Differences in Personality Traits in Early Adolescence: A Cross-Sectional, Cross-Cultural Study," on which Marleen De Bolle, then of Ghent University, was the lead author—with contributions from forty-eight additional scholars—described some of the consequences of differing rates of maturity and development: "Our findings demonstrate that adolescent girls consistently score higher than boys on personality traits that are found to facilitate academic achievement, at least within the current school climate. Stated differently, the current school environment or climate might be in general more attuned to feminine-typed personalities, which make it—in general—easier for girls to achieve better grades at school."

What are some of the other factors contributing to the differing academic performance of boys and girls?

In a 2019 paper, "Family Disadvantage and the Gender Gap in Behavioral and Educational Outcomes," Autor and Wasserman, along with David Figlio, Krzysztof Karbownik, and Jeffrey Roth, conclude that "family disadvantage disproportionately negatively affects the behavioral and academic outcomes of school-age boys relative to girls. The differential effect of family disadvantage on the outcomes of boys relative to girls is already evident by the time of kindergarten entry, is further manifested in behavioral and educational gaps in elementary and middle school performance, and crystallizes into sharp differences in high school graduations by age 18."

"Parental investments in boys versus girls," they write, "differ systematically according to family disadvantage. For example, parents in low-SES households, which are disproportionately female-headed, may spend relatively more time mentoring and interacting with daughters than sons."

In an email, Autor wrote that the downward trajectory of boys and men from single-parent homes should not mask the continuation of a very different trend at elite levels: "Even as one laments boys fall-ing behind, one should not for a moment think that all is well with women's status in higher education or the professions. In terms of major fields, fast-track careers, leadership positions, and prestigious branches of high-paid specialties, women are still not close to parity."

The consequences are depressing: "The stagnation of male edu-cational attainment bodes ill for the well-being of recent cohorts of U.S. males, particularly minorities and those from low-income households. Recent cohorts of males are likely to face diminished employment and earnings opportunities and other attendant mala-dies, including poorer health, higher probability of incarceration, and generally lower life satisfaction."

I am quoting at greater length than usual from Autor and Was-serman because they have done the most thorough job of bringing meticulously compiled and compelling evidence to bear on male dis-advantage. They warn that "a vicious cycle" may be emerging, "with the poor economic prospects of less-educated males creating differ-entially large disadvantages for their sons, thus potentially reinforcing the development of the gender gap in the next generation."

With the onset of "lower marriage rates of less-educated males, their children face comparatively low odds of living in econom-ically secure households with two parents present. Unsurprisingly, children born into such households also face poorer educational and earnings prospects over the long term. Even more concerning is that male children born into low-income, single-parent-headed households—which in the vast majority of cases are female-headed households—appear to fare particularly poorly on numerous social and educational outcomes."

There are other forces driving the vicious cycle, Autor and Was-serman write: "A growing body of evidence supports the hypothesis that the erosion of labor market opportunities for low-skill workers in general—and non-college males in particular—has catalyzed a fall in employment and earnings among less-educated males and a decline in the marriage rates of less-educated males and females. These devel-opments in turn diminish family stability, reduce household financial resources, and subtract from the stock of parental time and attention

that should play a critical role in fomenting the educational achievement and economic advancement of the next generation."

Why are boys falling further behind than their sisters? Autor and
Wasserman reply, "The absence of stable fathers from children's lives
has particularly significant adverse consequences for boys' psycho-
social development and educational achievement."

More specifically, "on a wide variety of self-control, acting-out,
and disciplinary measures (including eighth-grade suspension),
the gap between boys and girls is substantially greater for children
reared in single-mother-headed households than in households with
two biological parents."

Another reflection of this pattern, according to Autor and Was-
serman, "is the growing divergence in high school girls' and boys'
expectations of obtaining a four-year college degree." Among
cohorts of high school seniors interviewed between 1976 and 2006,
"a gap opens between boys' and girls' expectations for B.A. attainment starting in the early 1980s and cumulates thereafter." They add
that "growing up in a single-parent home appears to significantly
decrease the probability of college attendance for boys, yet has no
similar effect for girls."

It is not just fatherlessness, the two economists write. A key
factor is that single parents—disproportionately female—are "more
limited in the amount of time they can devote to childcare activities." If, then, "boys are more responsive to parental inputs (or the
absence thereof) than are girls, it is possible that the gender gradi-
ent in behavioral and academic development could be magnified
in single-parent households." They cite a study demonstrating that
single mothers "report feeling more emotionally distant from their
sons and engage in disciplinary action such as spanking more frequently with their sons. These disparities in parenting are largely
absent from dual-parent homes."

Adam Enders, a professor of political science at the University
of Louisville, sees the troubles of young white men in particular as
an outcome of their partisan resentments.

"My take is that lower-class white males likely have lower trust
in institutions of higher education over time. This bears out in the

aggregate," he wrote, citing a Pew Research Survey. "Part of the reason for this—at least among some conservative males—is the perception that colleges are tools for leftist indoctrination—a perception increasingly fueled by the right, including top Republican and conservative leaders. Indeed, there is a hefty split between Democrats and Republicans in their orientations toward the education system. Republicans became more negative than positive about education since around 2016."

Shelly Lundberg, a professor of economics at the University of California–Santa Barbara, does not dispute the data showing large gender differences in educational outcomes, but she has a different take on the underlying causes, focusing on "the concept of fragile or precarious masculinity, in which manhood (unlike womanhood) is seen as a social state that requires continual proof and validation."

In a 2020 article, "Educational Gender Gaps," Lundberg argues, "Social and cultural forces linked to gender identity are important drivers of educational goals and performance. A peer-driven search for masculine identity drives some boys toward risk-taking and noncompliance with school demands that hampers school achievement, relative to girls. Aspirations are linked to social identities—what you want and expect depends on who you think you are—and profound differences in the norms defining masculinity and femininity create a gender gap in educational trajectories."

Lundberg's position that different norms define masculinity and femininity, Enders's political take, and the argument of Autor and other scholars that boys suffer more than girls in dysfunctional homes are most likely more complementary than conflicting.

The bigger question is how the country should deal with the legions of left-behind men, often angry at the cataclysmic social changes, including family breakdown, that have obliterated much that was familiar. In 2020, white men voted for Donald Trump 61 percent to 38 percent. Many of these men have now become the frontline troops in a reactionary political movement that has launched an assault on democracy. What's next?

42

Democrats Can't Just Give the People What They Want

Over the twenty-year period from 1970 to 1990, white people, especially those without college degrees, defected en masse from the Democratic Party. In those years, the percentage of white working-class voters who identified with the Democratic Party fell to 40 percent from 60 percent, Lane Kenworthy, a sociologist at the University of California–San Diego, wrote in "The Democrats and Working-Class Whites."

Now, three decades later, the Democratic Party continues to struggle to maintain not just a biracial but a multiracial and multiethnic coalition—keeping in mind that Democrats have not won a majority of white voters in a presidential election since Lyndon Johnson's landslide victory in 1964.

There have been seven Democratic and seven Republican presidents since the end of World War II. Obstacles notwithstanding, the Democratic coalition has adapted from its former incarnation as an overwhelmingly white party with a powerful Southern segregationist wing to its current incarnation: roughly 59 percent white,

This article first appeared in *The New York Times* on October 13, 2021. Copyright © 2021 by Thomas Edsall and The New York Times Company. All rights reserved.

19 percent Black, 13 percent Hispanic, and 8 percent Asian American and other groups.

William Julius Wilson, a sociologist at Harvard, put the liberal case for the importance of such a political alliance eloquently in "Rising Inequality and the Case for Coalition Politics": "An organized national multiracial political constituency is needed for the development and implementation of policies that will help reverse the trends of the rising inequality and ease the burdens of ordinary families."

Joe Biden won with a multiracial coalition, but even in victory, there were signs of stress.

In their May 21 analysis, "What Happened in 2020," Yair Ghitza, chief scientist at Catalist, a liberal voter data analysis firm, and Jonathan Robinson, its director of research, found that Black support for the Democratic presidential nominee fell by 3 percentage points from 2016 to 2020, and Latino support fell by 8 points over the same period, from 71 percent to 63 percent.

At the same time, white people with college degrees continued their march into the Democratic Party: "The trends all point in the same direction, i.e., a substantial portion of this constituency moving solidly toward Democrats in the Trump era." Among these well-educated white voters, the percentage voting for the Democratic nominee rose from 46 percent in 2012 to 50 percent in 2016 to 54 percent in 2020. These gains were especially strong among women, according to Catalist: "White college-educated women in particular have shifted against Trump, moving from 50 percent Democratic support in 2012 to 58 percent in 2020."

In a separate June 2021 study, "Behind Biden's 2020 Victory," by Ruth Igielnik, Scott Keeter, and Hannah Hartig, Pew Research found that "even as Biden held on to a majority of Hispanic voters in 2020, Trump made gains among this group overall. There was a wide educational divide among Hispanic voters: Trump did substantially better with those without a college degree than college-educated Hispanic voters (41 percent vs. 30 percent)."

Biden, according to Pew, made significant gains both among all suburban voters and among white suburban voters: "In 2020,

Biden improved upon Clinton's vote share with suburban voters: 45 percent supported Clinton in 2016 vs. 54 percent for Biden in 2020. This shift was also seen among white voters: Trump narrowly won white suburban voters by 4 points in 2020 (51–47); he carried this group by 16 points in 2016 (54–38)."

Crucially, all of these shifts reflect the continuing realignment of the electorate by level of educational attainment or so-called learning skills, with one big difference: before 2020, education polarization was found almost exclusively among white voters; last year it began to emerge among Hispanics and African Americans.

Two Democratic strategists, Ruy Teixeira and John Halpin, both of whom publish their analyses at the Liberal Patriot website, have addressed this predicament.

On September 30 in "There Just Aren't Enough College-Educated Voters!," Teixeira wrote, "The perception that nonwhite working class voters are a lock for the Democrats is no longer tenable. In the 2020 election, working class nonwhites moved sharply toward Trump by 12 margin points, despite Democratic messaging that focused relentlessly on Trump's animus toward nonwhites. According to Pew, Trump actually got 41 percent of the Hispanic working class vote in 2016. Since 2012, running against Trump twice, Democrats have lost 18 points off of their margin among nonwhite working class voters."

In an effort to bring the argument down to earth, I asked Teixeira and Halpin three questions:

1. Should Democrats support and defend gender- and race-based affirmative action policies?
2. If asked in a debate, what should a Democrat say about Ibram X. Kendi's claim that "standardized tests have become the most effective racist weapon ever devised to objectively degrade Black and brown minds and legally exclude their bodies from prestigious schools"?
3. How should a Democrat respond to questions concerning intergenerational poverty, nonmarital births, and the issue of fatherlessness?

In an email, Teixeira addressed affirmative action:

Affirmative action in the sense of, say, racial preferences has always been unpopular and continues to be so. The latest evidence comes from the deep blue state of California which defeated an effort to reinstate race and gender preferences in public education, employment and contracting by an overwhelming 57–43 margin. As President Obama once put it: "We have to think about affirmative action and craft it in such a way where some of our children who are advantaged aren't getting more favorable treatment than a poor white kid who has struggled more." There has always been a strong case for class-based affirmative action which is perhaps worth revisiting rather than doubling down on race-based affirmative action.

Teixeira also weighed in on Kendi's arguments:

It is remarkable how willing liberal elites have been to countenance Kendi's extreme views which ascribe all racial disparities in American society to racism and a system of untrammeled white supremacy (and only that), insist that all policies/actions can only be racist or anti-racist in any context and advocate for a Department of Anti-Racism staffed by anti-racist "experts" who would have the power to nullify any and all local, state and federal legislation deemed not truly anti-racist (and therefore, by Kendi's logic, racist). These ideas are dubious empirically, massively simplistic and completely impractical in real world terms. And to observe they are politically toxic is an understatement.

The left, in Teixeira's view,

has paid a considerable price for abandoning universalism and for its increasingly strong linkage to Kendi-style views and militant identity politics in general. This has resulted in branding the party as focused on, or at least distracted by, issues of little relevance to most voters' lives. Worse, the focus has led many working-class voters to believe that, unless they subscribe to this emerging worldview and are willing to speak its language, they will be condemned as reactionary, intolerant, and racist by those who purport to represent their interests. To some extent these voters are right: They really are looked down upon by elements of the left—typically younger, well-educated, and metropolitan—who embrace identity politics and the intersectional approach.

In March, Halpin wrote an essay, "The Rise of the Neo-universalists," in which he argued that "there is an emerging pool of political leaders, thinkers and citizens without an ideological home. They come from the left, right, and center but all share a common aversion to the sectarian, identity-based politics that dominates modern political discourse and the partisan and media institutions that set the public agenda."

He calls this constituency "neo-universalists" and says that they are united by "a vision of American citizenship based on the core belief in the equal dignity and rights of all people." This means, he continued, "not treating people differently based on their gender or their skin color, or where they were born or what they believe. This means employing collective resources to help provide for the 'general welfare' of all people in terms of jobs, housing, education, and health care. This means giving people a chance and not assuming the worst of them."

How, then, would neo-universalism deal with gender- and race-based affirmative action policies?

"In terms of affirmative action, neo-universalism would agree with the original need and purpose of affirmative action following the legal dismantling of racial and gender discrimination," Halpin wrote in an email.

America needed a series of steps to overcome the legal and institutional hurdles to their advancement in education, the workplace, and wider life. Fifty years later, there has been tremendous progress on this front and we now face a situation where ongoing discrimination in favor of historically discriminated groups is hard to defend constitutionally and will likely hit a wall very soon. In order to continue ensuring that all people are integrated into society and life, neo-universalists would favor steps to offer additional assistance to people based on class- or place-based measures such as parental income or school profiles and disparities, in the case of education.

What did Halpin think about Kendi's views? "A belief in equal dignity and rights for all, as expressed in neo-universalism and traditional liberalism, rejects the race-focused theories of Kendi and others, and particularly the concept that present discrimination based on race is required to overcome past discrimination based on race. There is no constitutional defense of this approach since you clearly cannot deprive people of due process and rights based on their race."

In addition, theories like these, in Halpin's view, foster "sectarian racial divisions and encourage people to view one another solely through the lens of race and perceptions of who is oppressed and who is privileged." Liberals, he continued, "spent the bulk of the 20th century trying to get society not to view people this way, so these contemporary critical theories are a huge step backward in terms of building wider coalitions and solidarity across racial, gender, and ethnic lines."

On the problem of intergenerational poverty, Halpin argued,

Reducing and eradicating poverty is a critical focus for neo-universalists in the liberal tradition. Personal rights and freedom mean little if a person or family does not have a basic foundation of solid income and work, housing, education, and health care. Good jobs, safe neighborhoods, and stable two-parent families are proven to be critical components of building solid middle class life. Although the government cannot tell people how to organize their lives, and it must deal with the reality that not everyone lives or wants to live in a traditional family, the government can take steps to make family life more affordable and stable for everyone, particularly for those with children and low household income.

Although the issue of racial and cultural tension within the Democratic coalition has been the subject of debate for decades, the current focus among Democratic strategists is on the well-educated party elite.

David Shor, a Democratic data analyst, has emerged as a central figure on these matters. Shor's approach was described by my colleague Ezra Klein last week. First, leaders need to recognize that "the party has become too unrepresentative at its elite levels to continue being representative at the mass level," and then "Democrats should do a lot of polling to figure out which of their views are popular and which are not popular, and then they should talk about the popular stuff and shut up about the unpopular stuff."

How can Democrats defuse inevitable Republican attacks on contemporary liberalism's "unpopular stuff"—to use Klein's phrase—much of which involves issues related to race and immigration, along with the disputes raised by identity politics on the left?

Shor observes, "We've ended up in a situation where white liberals are more left wing than Black and Hispanic Democrats on pretty much every issue: taxes, health care, policing and even on racial issues or various measures of 'racial resentment.'" He adds, "So as white liberals increasingly define the party's image and messaging, that's going to turn off nonwhite conservative Democrats and push them against us."

The result?

"The joke is that the G.O.P. is really assembling the multiracial working-class coalition that the left has always dreamed of," Shor told Politico in an interview after the election in November.

On October 9, another of my colleagues, Jamelle Bouie, weighed in: "My problem is that I don't think Shor or his allies are being forthright about what it would actually take to stem the tide and reverse the trend. If anti-Black prejudice is as strong as this analysis implies, then it seems ludicrous to say that Democrats can solve their problem with a simple shift in rhetoric toward their most popular agenda items. The countermessage is easy enough to imagine—some version of 'Democrats are not actually going to help you, they are going to help them.'"

Bouie's larger point is this: "This debate needs clarity, and I want Shor and his allies to be much more forthright about the specific tactics they would use and what their strategy would look like in practice. To me, it seems as if they are talking around the issue rather than being upfront about the path they want to take."

Shor's critique of the contemporary Democratic Party and the disproportionate influence of its young, well-educated white liberal elite has provoked a network of countercritiques. For example, Ian Haney López, a law professor at Berkeley, recently posted "Shor Is Mainly Wrong about Racism (Which Is to Say, about Electoral Politics)" on Medium, an essay in which Haney López argues, "The core problem for the Democratic Party is not too many young, liberal activists. The fundamental challenge for Democrats is to develop a unified, effective response to the intense polarization around race intentionally driven by Trump and boosted by the interlocking elements of the right-wing propaganda machine."

Haney López agrees that

> Democratic messages alienate voters when they are predicated on a sense of identity that voters do not share. For instance, "defund the police" and "abolish ICE" are deeply connected to a story of the police and ICE as white supremacist institutions that oppress communities of color. In turn, this story depicts the country as locked into a historic conflict between white people and people of color. It thus asks white voters to see themselves as members of an oppressive group they must help to disempower; and it asks voters of color to see themselves as members of widely hated groups they must rally to defend. This framing is acceptable to many who are college educated, white and of color alike, but not to majorities of voters.

But, in Haney López's view, "Shor weds himself to the wrong conclusion. As the Ezra Klein piece reports, Shor 'and those who agree with him argue that Democrats need to try to avoid talking about race and immigration.' This is Shor's most dangerous piece of advice to Democrats. For Shor, this has become an article of faith."

Haney López argues that the best way to defuse divisive racial issues is to explicitly portray such tactics as "a divide-and-conquer strategy."

The main idea, he wrote, "is to shift the basic political conflict in the United States from one between racial groups (the right's preferred frame) to one between the 0.1 percent and the rest of us, with racism as their principal weapon. In our research, this race-class fusion politics is the most promising route forward for Democrats."

Steve Phillips, the founder of Democracy in Color (and, like Haney López, a frequent contributor to the *Times*), goes a giant step further. In an email, Phillips argued that for over fifty years, "Democrats have NEVER won the white vote. All of it is dancing around the real issue, which is that the majority of white voters never back Democrats." Even white college-educated voters "are very, very fickle. There's some potential to up that share, but at what cost?" The bottom line? "I don't think they're movable; certainly, to any appreciable sense."

Phillips wrote that his "biggest point is that it's not necessary or cost-efficient to try to woo these voters. A meaningful minority of them are already with us and have always been with us. There are now so many people of color in the country (the majority of young people), that that minority of whites can ally with people of color and win elections from the White House to the Georgia Senate runoffs," noting, "Plus, you don't have to sell your soul and compromise your principles to woo their support."

In his email, Phillips acknowledged that "it does look like there has been a small decline in that Clinton got 76 percent of the working-class vote among minorities and Biden 72 percent. But I still come back to the big-picture points mentioned above."

On this point, Phillips may underestimate the significance of the 4-point drop and of the larger decline among working-class Hispanics. If this is a trend—a big if, because we don't yet know how much of this is about Donald Trump and whether these trends will persist without him—it has the hallmarks of a new and significant problem for Democrats in future elections. In that light, it is all the more important for Democratic strategists of all ideological stripes to detail what specific approaches they contend are most effective in addressing, if not countering, the divisive racial and cultural issues that have weakened the party in recent elections, even when they've won.

Saying the party's candidates should simply downplay the tough ones may not be adequate.

43

The Moral Chasm That Has Opened Up between Left and Right Is Widening

There has been a remarkable erosion in public tolerance of "offensive expression about race, gender and religion," according to a paper Dennis Chong and Morris Levy, political scientists at the University of Southern California, and Jack Citrin, a political scientist at Berkeley, presented in September at the annual meeting of the American Political Science Association.

"Tolerance has declined overall," they add, particularly "for a category of speech that is considered unworthy of First Amendment protection because it violates the goal of equality."

The three authors cite the 2018 promulgation of new guidelines by the American Civil Liberties Union—which was formerly unequivocal in its defense of free speech—as a reflection of the changing views within a large segment of the liberal community. Under the 2018 guidelines, the ACLU would now consider several factors that might warrant a refusal to take on certain cases.

This article first appeared in *The New York Times* on October 27, 2021. Copyright © 2021 by Thomas Edsall and The New York Times Company. All rights reserved.

"Our defense of speech may have a greater or lesser harmful impact on the equality and justice work to which we are also committed" depending on "the potential effect on marginalized communities; the extent to which the speech may assist in advancing the goals of white supremacists or others whose views are contrary to our values; and the structural and power inequalities in the community in which the speech will occur."

Chong, Citrin, and Levy write, "Arguments for censoring hate speech have gained ground alongside the strengthening of the principle of equality in American society. The expansion of equal rights for racial and ethnic minorities, women, L.G.B.T.Q., and other groups that have suffered discrimination has caused a re-evaluation of the harms of slurs and other derogatory expressions in professional and social life. The transformation of social attitudes regarding race, gender, and sexuality has fundamentally changed the tenor of debate over speech controversies."

Traditionally, they point out, "the main counterargument against free speech has been a concern for maintaining social order in the face of threatening movements and ideas, a classic divide between liberal and conservative values. Now, arguments against allowing hate speech in order to promote equality have changed the considerations underlying political tolerance and divided liberals amongst themselves. The repercussions of this value conflict between the respective norms of equality and free expression have rippled far beyond its epicenter in the universities to the forefront of American politics."

In an email, Chong wrote that "the tolerance of white liberals has declined significantly since 1980, and tolerance levels are lowest among the youngest age cohorts." If, he continued, "we add education to the mix, we find that the most pronounced declines over time have occurred among white, college educated liberals, with the youngest age cohorts again having the lowest tolerance levels."

The Chong-Citrin-Levy paper focuses on the concept of harm in shaping public policy and in the growing determination of large swaths of progressives that a paramount goal of public discourse is to avoid inflicting injury, including verbal injury, on marginalized groups. In this context, harm can be understood as injury to physical and mental health occurring "when stress levels are perpetually elevated by living in a constant state of hyper-vigilance."

Proponents of what is known as moral foundations theory—formulated in 2004 by Jonathan Haidt and Craig Joseph—argue that across all cultures, "several innate and universally available psychological systems are the foundations of 'intuitive ethics.'" The five foundations are care/harm, fairness/cheating, loyalty/betrayal, authority/subversion, and sanctity/degradation.

One of the central claims of this theory, as described in "Mapping the Moral Domain"—a 2011 paper by Jesse Graham, Brian A. Nosek, Haidt, Ravi Iyer, Spassena Koleva, and Peter H. Ditto—is that "liberal morality would prioritize harm and fairness over the other three foundations because the 'individualizing foundations' of harm and fairness are all that are needed to support the individual-focused contractual approaches to society often used in enlightenment ethics, whereas conservative morality would also incorporate in-group, authority, and purity to a substantial degree (because these 'binding foundations' are about binding people together into larger groups and institutions)."

I asked Julie Wronski, a political scientist at the University of Mississippi, about the role of concerns over ideology and gender in the changing character of liberalism.

"I think we need to move beyond a simple 'gender gap' story to better understand how conceptualizations of womanhood impact politics," she replied. "The first way is to think about the gender gap as a 'feminist gap.'"

From this perspective, Wronski continued, men can hold feminist values and women can be antifeminist, noting that "the attitudes people have about gender roles in society have a bigger impact on political outcomes than simple male/female identification."

Wronski cited a paper, "Partisan Sorting and the Feminist Gap in American Politics" by Leonie Huddy and Johanna Willmann, which argues that feminism "can be distinguished from political ideology when construed as support for women's political advancement, the equalization of male and female power, the removal of barriers that impede women's success, and a strengthening of women's autonomy." Huddy and Willmann noted that in a "2015 national survey, 60 percent of women and 33 percent of men considered themselves a feminist."

There are substantial differences, however, in how feminist women and men align politically, according to their analysis: "We expect women's feminist loyalty and antipathy to play a greater role in shaping their partisanship than feminist affinity among men because feminist and anti-feminist identities have greater personal relevance for women than men, elicit stronger emotions, and will be more central to women's political outlook."

The authors created a feminism scale based on the respondent's identification with feminism, support for female politicians, perception of sex discrimination, and gender resentment. Based on survey data from the 2012 and 2016 elections, they found that "men scored significantly lower than women in both years (men: .55 in 2012, .46 in 2016; women: .60 in 2012, .54 in 2016). Nonetheless, men and women also overlap considerably in their support and opposition to feminism."

Personality characteristics play a key role, they found: "Openness to experience consistently boosts feminism." A predilection for authoritarianism, in contrast, "consistently lowers support for feminism," while "agreeableness promotes feminism," although its effects are strongest "among white respondents."

Demographic differences play an important role too: "Religiously observant men and women are less supportive of feminism than their nonobservant counterparts. Well-educated respondents, especially well-educated women, are more supportive of feminism." Single white women are "more supportive of feminism than women living with a partner."

Feminism, in addition, is strongly correlated with opposition to "traditional morality"—defined by disagreement with such statements as, "We should be more tolerant of people who live according to their own moral standards," and agreement with such assertions as, "The newer lifestyles are contributing to a breakdown in our society." The correlation grew from −0.41 in 2012 to −0.53 in 2016.

During this century, the power of feminism to signal partisanship has steadily increased for men and even more so for women, Huddy and Willmann found: "In 2004, a strong feminist woman had a .32 chance of being a strong Democrat. This increased slightly to .35 in 2008 and then increased more substantially to .45 in 2012 and .56 in 2016." In 2004 and 2008, "there was a .21 chance that a strong feminist male was also a strong Democrat. That increased slightly to .25 in 2012 and more dramatically to .42 in 2016."

In an email, Huddy elaborated on the partisan significance of feminist commitments: "It is important to remember that women can be Democrats or Republicans, but feminists are concentrated in the Democratic Party. Appealing to an ethic of care may not attract Republican women if it conflicts with their religious views concerning the family or opposition to expanded government spending. Sending a signal to feminists that the Democratic Party is behind them shores up one of their major constituencies."

In a 2018 paper, "Effect of Ideological Identification on the Endorsement of Moral Values Depends on the Target Group," Jan G. Voelkel, a sociologist at Stanford, and Mark J. Brandt, a professor of psychology at Michigan State, argue that moral foundations theory that places liberals and conservatives in separate camps needs to be modified.

Voelkel and Brandt maintain that "ideological differences in moral foundations" are not necessarily the result of differences in moral values per se, but can also be driven by "ingroup-versus-outgroup categorizations." The authors call this second process "political group conflict hypothesis."

This hypothesis, Voelkel and Brandt contend, "has its roots in research that emphasizes that people's thoughts, attitudes, and behaviors are strongly influenced by the ideological groups they identify with and is consistent with work suggesting that people's ideological identifications function like a group identification. According to this view, liberals and conservatives may selectively and flexibly endorse moral values depending on the target group of the moral act."

Voelkel and Brandt cite as an example the moral foundation of fairness: "The strong version of the moral divide account predicts

that liberals should be more likely to endorse the fairness foundation no matter the target group. The political group conflict account
makes a different prediction: Liberals will condemn unfair treatment
of liberal groups and groups stereotyped as liberal more than conservatives. However, conservatives will condemn unfair treatment
of conservative groups and groups stereotyped as conservative more
than liberals. Such a finding would suggest that the fairness foundation
is not unique to liberals, as both groups care about fairness for their
own political in-groups."

The surveys the authors conducted show that, "consistent with
the political group conflict hypothesis, we found that the effect of
ideological identification depended on whether moral acts involved
liberal or conservative groups. Consistent with the moral divide
hypothesis, we found the pattern identified by MFT [moral foundations theory] (liberals score higher on the individualizing foundations and conservatives score higher on the binding foundations) in
the moderate target condition."

Put another way: "We find evidence that both processes may play
a part. On one hand, we provide strong evidence that conservatives
endorse the binding foundations more than liberals. On the other
hand, we have shown that political group conflicts substantively contribute to the relationship between ideological identification and the
endorsement of moral values."

The debate over moral values and political conflict has engaged
new contributors.

Richard Hanania, president of the Center for the Study of Partisanship and Ideology and a former research fellow at Columbia's
Saltzman Institute of War and Peace Studies, argues that "women
are having more of a role to play in intellectual life, so we're moving
toward female norms regarding things like trade-offs between feelings and the search for truth. If these trends started to reverse, we
could call it a 'masculinization' of the culture I suppose. The male/
female divide is not synonymous with right/left, as a previous generation's leftism was much more masculine, think gender relations
in communist countries or the organized labor movement in the
U.S. at its peak."

The role of gender in politics has been further complicated by a controversial and counterintuitive finding set forth in "The Gender-Equality Paradox in Science, Technology, Engineering and Mathematics Education" by Gijsbert Stoet and David C. Geary, professors of psychology at Essex University and the University of Missouri, respectively.

The authors propose that, "paradoxically, countries with lower levels of gender equality had relatively more women among STEM graduates than did more gender-equal countries. This is a paradox, because gender-equal countries are those that give girls and women more educational and empowerment opportunities, and generally promote girls' and women's engagement in STEM fields."

Assuming for the moment that this gender-equality paradox is real, how does it affect politics and polarization in the United States?

In an email, Mohammad Atari, a graduate student in psychology at the University of Southern California and lead author of "Sex Differences in Moral Judgments across 67 Countries," noted that "some would argue that in more gender-egalitarian societies men and women are more free to express their values regardless of external pressures to fit a predefined gender role," suggesting an easing of tensions.

Pivoting from gender to race, however, the nonpartisan Democracy Fund's Voter Study Group this month issued *Racing Apart: Partisan Shifts on Racial Attitudes over the Last Decade*. The study showed that "Democrats' and independents' attitudes on identity-related topics diverged significantly from Republicans' between 2011 and 2020—including their attitudes on racial inequality, police, the Black Lives Matter movement, immigration, and Muslims. Most of this divergence derives from shifts among Democrats, who have grown much more liberal over this period."

The murder of George Floyd produced a burst of racial empathy, Robert Griffin, Mayesha Quasem, John Sides, and Michael Tesler wrote, but they note that poll data suggests "this shift in attitudes was largely temporary. Weekly surveys from the Democracy Fund + UCLA Nationscape project show that any aggregate changes had mostly evaporated by January 2021."

Additional evidence suggests that partisan hostility between Democrats and Republicans is steadily worsening. In their August 2021 paper, "Cross-Country Trends in Affective Polarization," Levi Boxell and Matthew Gentzkow, both economists at Stanford University, and Jesse M. Shapiro, a professor of political economy at Brown, wrote, "In 1978, according to our calculations, the average partisan rated in-party members 27.4 points higher than out-party members on a 'feeling thermometer' ranging from 0 to 100. In 2020 the difference was 56.3, implying an increase of 1.08 standard deviations."

Their conclusion is that over the past four decades, "the United States experienced the most rapid growth in affective polarization among the 12 O.E.C.D. countries we consider"—the other eleven are France, Sweden, Germany, Britain, Norway, Denmark, Australia, Japan, Canada, New Zealand, and Switzerland.

In other words, whether we evaluate the current conflict-ridden political climate in terms of moral foundations theory, feminism, or the political group conflict hypothesis, the trends are not favorable, especially if the outcome of the 2024 presidential election is close.

If the continuing anger, resentment, and denial among Republicans in the aftermath of the 2020 presidential contest are precursors of the next election, current trends, in combination with the politicization of election administration by Republican state legislatures, suggest that the loser in 2024, Republican or Democratic, will not take defeat lying down.

The forces fracturing the political system are clearly stronger than the forces pushing for consensus.

44

America Has Split, and It's Now in "Very Dangerous Territory"

Why did the national emergency brought about by the COVID-19 pandemic not only fail to unite the country but instead provoke the exact opposite development, further polarization?

I posed this question to Nolan McCarty, a political scientist at Princeton. McCarty emailed me back, "With the benefit of hindsight, Covid seems to be the almost ideal polarizing crisis. It was conducive to creating strong identities and mapping onto existing ones. That these identities corresponded to compliance with public health measures literally increased 'riskiness' of intergroup interaction. The financial crisis was also polarizing for similar reasons—it was too easy for different groups to blame each other for the problems."

McCarty went on: "Any depolarizing event would need to be one where the causes are transparently external in a way that makes it hard for social groups to blame each other. It is increasingly hard to see what sort of event has that feature these days."

Polarization has become a force that feeds on itself, gaining strength from the hostility it generates, finding sustenance on both

This article first appeared in *The New York Times* on January 26, 2022. Copyright © 2022 by Thomas Edsall and The New York Times Company. All rights reserved.

the left and the right. A series of recent analyses reveals the destructive power of polarization across the American political system.

The United States continues to stand out among nations experiencing the detrimental effects of polarization, according to *What Happens When Democracies Become Perniciously Polarized?*, a Carnegie Endowment for International Peace report written by Jennifer McCoy of Georgia State and Benjamin Press of the Carnegie Endowment: "The United States is quite alone among the ranks of perniciously polarized democracies in terms of its wealth and democratic experience. Of the episodes since 1950 where democracies polarized, all of those aside from the United States involved less wealthy, less longstanding democracies, many of which had democratized quite recently. None of the wealthy, consolidated democracies of East Asia, Oceania or Western Europe, for example, have faced similar levels of polarization for such an extended period."

McCoy and Press studied fifty-two countries "where democracies reached pernicious levels of polarization." Of those, "twenty-six—fully half of the cases—experienced a downgrading of their democratic rating." Quite strikingly, the two continue, "the United States is the only advanced Western democracy to have faced such intense polarization for such an extended period. The United States is in uncharted and very dangerous territory."

McCoy and Press analyzed the international pattern of polarization and again the United States stands out, with by far the highest current level of polarization compared with other countries and regions, as figure 44.1 shows.

In their report, McCoy and Press make the case that there are "a number of features that make the United States both especially susceptible to polarization and especially impervious to efforts to reduce it."

The authors point to a number of causes, including "the durability of identity politics in a racially and ethnically diverse democracy." As the authors note, "The United States is perhaps alone in experiencing a demographic shift that poses a threat to the white population that has historically been the dominant group in all arenas of power, allowing political leaders to exploit insecurities surrounding this loss of status."

Political polarization rating

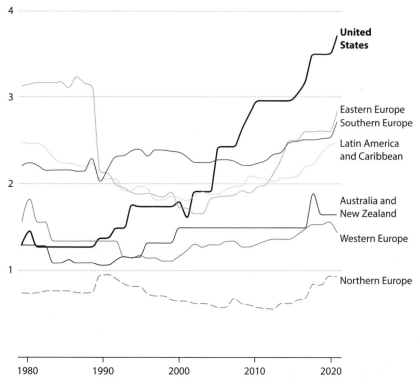

FIGURE 44.1. LEVELS OF POLARIZATION IN THE U.S. STAND OUT
Note: Polarization ratings are aggregated among countries by region, with not all regions shown. A rating of 0 indicates that opposing political groups tend to interact in a friendly manner, while a rating of 4 indicates that they tend to be hostile. *Source*: Varieties of Democracy Institute. From The New York Times. © 2022 The New York Times Company. All rights reserved. Used under license.

An additional cause, the authors write, is that "binary choice is deeply embedded in the U.S. electoral system, creating a rigid two-party system that facilitates binary divisions of society. For example, only five of twenty-six wealthy consolidated democracies elect representatives to their national legislatures in single-member districts."

Along the same lines, McCoy and Press write that the United States has "a unique combination of a majoritarian electoral system with strong minoritarian institutions."

"The Senate is highly disproportionate in its representation," they add, "with two senators per state regardless of population, from

Wyoming's 580,000 to California's 39,500,000 persons," which, in turn, "translates to disproportionality in the Electoral College—whose indirect election of the president is again exceptional among presidential democracies."

And finally, there is the three-decade trend of partisan sorting, in which "the two parties reinforce urban-rural, religious-secular and racial-ethnic cleavages rather than promote crosscutting cleavages. With partisanship now increasingly tied to other kinds of social identity, affective polarization is on the rise, with voters perceiving the opposing party in negative terms and as a growing threat to the nation."

Two related studies—"Inequality, Identity and Partisanship: How Redistribution Can Stem the Tide of Mass Polarization," by Alexander J. Stewart, Joshua B. Plotkin, and McCarty, and "Polarization under Rising Inequality and Economic Decline," by Stewart, McCarty, and Joanna Bryson—argue that aggressive redistribution policies designed to lessen inequality must be initiated before polarization becomes further entrenched. The fear is that polarization now runs so deep in the United States that we can't do the things that would help us be less polarized.

"The success of redistribution at stemming the tide of polarization in our model is striking," Stewart, Plotkin, and McCarty write, "and it suggests a possible path for preventing such attitudes from taking hold in future."

In a reflection of the staying power of polarization, the authors observe that "once polarization sets in, it typically remains stable under individual-level evolutionary dynamics, even when the economic environment improves or inequality is reversed."

In response to my emailed inquiries, Stewart explained: "A key finding in our studies is that it really matters when redistributive policies are put in place. Redistribution functions far better as a prevention than a cure for polarization in part for the reason your question suggests: If polarization is already high, redistribution itself becomes the target of polarized attitudes."

In other words, a deeply polarized electorate is highly unlikely to support redistribution that would benefit their adversaries as well as themselves.

In addition, Stewart wrote, polarization can arise independently from conditions of increasing inequality:

> We find that cultural, racial and values polarization can emerge even in the absence of inequality, but inequality makes such polarization more likely, and harder to reverse. We also find that the features of identity which are most salient shift over time, with the process of "sorting" of identity groups along political lines driven by similar forces to those that drive high polarization. And so cultural, racial and values polarization are a force independent of inequality, with inequality acting as a complementary force that points in the same direction, and redistribution a force that acts in opposition to both.

In "Polarization under Rising Inequality and Economic Decline," Stewart, McCarty, and Bryson argue that economic scarcity acts as a strong disincentive to cooperative relations between disparate racial and ethnic groups, in large part because such cooperation may produce more benefits but at higher risk: "Interactions with more diverse out-group members pool greater knowledge, applicable to a wider variety of situations. These interactions, when successful, generate better solutions and greater benefits. However, we also assume that the risk of failure is higher for out-group interactions, because of a weaker capacity to coordinate among individuals, compared to more familiar in-group interactions."

In times of prosperity, people are more willing to risk failure, they write, but that willingness disappears when populations are "faced with economic decline. We show that such group polarization can be contagious, and a subpopulation facing economic hardship in an otherwise strong economy can tip the whole population into a state of polarization. Moreover, we show that a population that becomes polarized can remain trapped in that suboptimal state, even after a reversal of the conditions that generated the risk aversion and polarization in the first place."

At the same time, the spread of polarization goes far beyond politics, permeating the culture and economic structure of the broader society.

Alexander Ruch, Ari Decter-Frain, and Raghav Batra studied the political and ideological profiles of purchasers of consumer goods in their paper "Millions of Co-purchases and Reviews Reveal the Spread of Polarization and Lifestyle Politics across Online Markets." Using "data from Amazon, 82.5 million reviews of 9.5 million products and category metadata from 1996–2014," the authors determined which "product categories are most politically relevant, aligned and polarized."

They write, "For example, after Levi Strauss & Co. pledged over $1 million to support ending gun violence and strengthening gun control laws, the jean company became progressively aligned with liberals while conservatives aligned themselves more with Wrangler. The traces of lifestyle politics are pervasive. For example, analyses of Twitter co-following show the stereotypes of 'Tesla liberals' and 'bird hunting conservatives' have empirical support."

Analyzing these "pervasive lifestyle politics," Ruch, Decter-Frain, and Batra find that "cultural products are four times more polarized than any other segment."

They also found lesser but still significant polarization in consumer interests in other categories: "The extent of political polarization in other segments is relatively less; however, even small categories like automotive parts have notable political alignment indicative of lifestyle politics. These results indicate that lifestyle politics spread deep and wide across markets."

Further evidence of the entrenchment of political divisiveness in the United States emerges in the study of such related subjects as "social dominance orientation," authoritarianism, and ideological and cognitive rigidity.

In a series of papers, Mark Brandt, Jarrett Crawford, and other political psychologists dispute the argument that only "conservatism is associated with prejudice" and that "the types of dispositional characteristics associated with conservatism (e.g., low cognitive ability, low openness) explain this relationship."

Instead, Crawford and Brandt argue in "Ideological (A)symmetries in Prejudice and Intergroup Bias," "when researchers use a more heterogeneous array of targets, people across the political spectrum express prejudice against groups with dissimilar values and beliefs."

Earlier research has correctly found greater levels of prejudice among conservatives, they write, but these studies have focused on prejudice toward liberal-associated groups: minorities, the poor, gay people, and other marginalized constituencies. Crawford and Brandt contend that when the targets of prejudice are expanded to include "conservative-associated groups such as Christian fundamentalists, military personnel and 'rich people,'" similar levels of prejudice emerge.

"Low openness to experience is associated with prejudice against groups seen as socially unconventional (e.g., atheists, gay men and lesbians)," they write, whereas high openness is "associated with prejudice against groups seen as socially conventional (e.g., military personnel, evangelical Christians)." They continue, "Whereas high disgust sensitivity is associated with prejudice against groups that threaten traditional sexual morality, low disgust sensitivity is associated with prejudice against groups that uphold traditional sexual morality."

Finally, "people high in cognitive ability are prejudiced against more conservative and conventional groups," while "people low in cognitive ability are prejudiced against more liberal and unconventional groups."

In "The Role of Cognitive Rigidity in Political Ideologies," Leor Zmigrod writes that the "rigidity-of-the-right hypotheses" should be expanded in recognition of the fact that "cognitive rigidity is linked to ideological extremism, partisanship and dogmatism across political and nonpolitical ideologies."

Broadly speaking, Zmigrod wrote in an email, "extreme right-wing partisans are characterized by specific psychological traits including cognitive rigidity and impulsivity. This is also true of extreme left-wing partisans."

In a separate paper, "Individual-Level Cognitive and Personality Predictors of Ideological Worldviews: The Psychological Profiles of Political, Nationalistic, Dogmatic, Religious and Extreme Believers," Zmigrod wrote, "When a series of cognitive behavioral measures were used to assess mental flexibility, and political conservatism was disentangled from political extremity, dogmatism or partisanship, a clear inverted-U shaped curve emerged such that those on the extreme right and extreme left exhibited cognitive rigidity on neuropsychological tasks, in comparison to moderates."

While the processes Zmigrod describes characterize the extremes, the electorate as a whole is moving further and further apart into two mutually loathing camps.

In "The Ideological Nationalization of Partisan Subconstituencies in the American States," Devin Caughey, James Dunham, and Christopher Warshaw challenge "the reigning consensus that polarization in Congress has proceeded much more rapidly and extensively than polarization in the mass public."

Instead, Caughey and his coauthors show "a surprisingly close correspondence between mass and elite trends. Specifically, we find that: (1) ideological divergence between Democrats and Republicans has widened dramatically within each domain, just as it has in Congress; (2) ideological variation across senators' partisan subconstituencies is now explained almost completely by party rather than state, closely tracking trends in the Senate; and (3) economic, racial and social liberalism have become highly correlated across partisan subconstituencies, just as they have across members of Congress."

Caughey, Dunham, and Warshaw describe the growing partisan salience of racial and social issues since the 1950s: "The explanatory power of party on racial issues increased hugely over this period and that of state correspondingly declined. We refer to this process as the 'ideological nationalization' of partisan subconstituencies."

In the late 1950s, they continue, "party explained almost no variance in racial conservatism in either arena. Over the next half century, the Senate and public time series rise in tandem." Contrary to the claim that racial realignment had run its course by 1980, they add, "our data indicate that differences between the parties continued to widen through the end of the 20th century, in the Senate as well as in the mass public. By the 2000s, party explained about 80 percent of the variance in senators' racial conservatism and nearly 100 percent of the variance in the mass public."

The three authors argue that there are a number of consequences of "the ideological nationalization of the United States party system."

For one, "it has limited the two parties' abilities to tailor their positions to local conditions. Moreover, it has led to greater geographic concentration of the parties' respective support coalitions."

The result, they note, "is the growing percentage of states with two senators from the same party, which increased from 50 percent in 1980 to over 70 percent in 2018. Today, across all offices, conservative states are largely dominated by Republicans, whereas the opposite is true of liberal states. The ideological nationalization of the party system thus seems to have undermined party competition at the state level."

As a result of these trends, Warshaw wrote me in an email, "it's going to be very difficult to reverse the growing partisan polarization between Democrats and Republicans in the mass public. I think this will continue to give ideological extremists an advantage in both parties' primaries. It also means that the pool of people that run for office is increasingly extreme."

In the long term, Warshaw continued, "there are a host of worrying possible consequences of growing partisan polarization among both elites and the public. It will probably reduce partisans' willingness to vote for the out-party. This could dampen voters' willingness to hold candidates accountable for poor performance and to vote across party lines to select higher-quality candidates. This will probably further increase the importance of primaries as a mechanism for candidate selection."

Looking over the contemporary political landscape, there appear to be no major or effective movements to counter polarization. As the McCoy-Press report shows, only sixteen of the fifty-two countries that reached levels of pernicious polarization succeeded in achieving depolarization and in "a significant number of instances later repolarized to pernicious levels. The progress toward depolarization in seven of 16 episodes was later undone."

That does not suggest a favorable prognosis for the United States.

Conclusion

Polarization now threatens the viability of the American constitutional system. The Republican Party has become an antidemocratic party. Elected leaders are engaged in a calculated effort to subvert election processes. Republican state legislators are taking power over elections away from secretaries of state and bipartisan election boards while granting themselves authority to determine election outcomes—a strategy more dangerous than the January 6, 2021, insurrectionists who sought by violent means to block the orderly transition from one president to another.

This threat has left the Democratic Party as the political institution obliged by default to defend democracy. The party is currently ill-equipped to restore order, however. By the very nature of its coalitional structure, the Democratic Party struggles to maintain an alliance of diverse, often conflicting interests, constituencies, and individuals, running the gamut from Joe Manchin to Alexandria Ocasio-Cortez.

And the severe constraints limiting the Democrats' capacity to defend democracy against Republican incursion show no signs of loosening.

While the Democratic Party is nominally the advocate of the least well-off Americans, the share of Democratic voters from the upper rungs of the socioeconomic ladder—often those with college and postgraduate degrees—has nearly doubled from 22 percent in 1996 to 41 percent in 2019, according to the Pew Research Center.[1] By 2019, 70 percent of Republican voters did not have college degrees—the pollsters' definition of working class—compared with 59 percent of Democratic voters.

Using income rather than education as a measure, voters, white and minority, who make less than $60,000 a year are 35 percent Republican, almost as many as the 42 percent who are Democrats, according to data supplied by the Cooperative Election Study at Harvard.[2] White voters making less than $60,000 are 47 percent Republican and 33 percent Democratic.

In sum, what the numbers show is that in terms of voting behavior and partisan allegiance, the Republican Party is now just as much the party of the working class as is the Democratic Party.

The Democratic Party, at the same time, is far more diverse in the demographic makeup of its voters as well as in the range of their beliefs. Pew found that 81 percent of the Republican electorate is white, compared with 59 percent of Democratic voters. By 2036, the Democratic electorate will be majority minority. Even more problematic, the white-minority divide within the Democratic Party is, in many respects, a class divide, with whites overwhelmingly college educated and relatively well-off, while Democratic minority voters, especially Blacks and Hispanics, face substantial hurdles competing in the contemporary workplace and earning a living wage.

The ideological diversity of the Democratic Party grows out of its role, since the mid-1960s, as the political home of the transformative rights revolutions. These movements have worked both to the advantage and disadvantage of the party, depending on the moment, but over time Democratic liberalism has been on the side of history in a nation steadily moving leftward on racial and cultural issues.

This may no longer be the case. The progressive wing of the party has adopted, and assertively advocated, policies concerning police power; white privilege; diversity, equity, and inclusion; critical race theory; and transgender rights that at times stretch mainstream tolerance. The reality is that the stances adopted by the party's progressive wing limit the Democrats' scope of appeal, endanger its margins of victory among aspiring minorities, and serve as roadblocks to working- and middle-class whites who support universal economic redistribution.

In other words, while the deterioration of the Republican Party has placed the burden of preserving our system of government on the Democratic Party, conflicts within the party—and between the party and voters who are ambivalent about often unfamiliar progressive initiatives—may prevent the party from fulfilling that role. As a result, a probable scenario for the near future is a continuing erosion of the democratic system of elections, especially in red states where Republican legislatures are transferring power to decide election outcomes to themselves in what has all the earmarks of corrupting election rules and procedures.

The Democratic Party suffers from systemic forces that severely restrict its capacity to win majorities. Democratic voters are highly concentrated in urban centers, which makes it difficult to spread the party's voting strength across multiple House districts, giving Republicans a built-in advantage in the decennial redistricting process. The Senate, in turn, gives disproportionate weight to small, generally rural states, guaranteeing the Republican Party a fixed lead in the competition to control the Senate and in the presidential contest to win the majority of the Electoral College. Given these obstacles, the Democratic Party cannot afford to align itself with the most controversial and divisive policies such as—at the moment— defund the police, abolish ICE, and critical race theory.

The tensions within the political system are potentially dangerous. An example: the election is close, and the Democrat (Joe Biden or a new nominee) appears to win, only to see Republican state legislatures shift enough Electoral College votes to give the Republican nominee, possibly Donald Trump, the victory. Trump's wholesale assault on political norms in the wake of his 2020 loss has left the nation vulnerable, especially when presidential elections are close.

Sanford Levinson captured an element of this in the *New Republic* in April 2022:

> I don't think that anybody seriously believes that he [Trump] could win a national popular vote election, simply because he would lose by many millions of votes in California and New York for starters, and even if he would take all the small states . . . he would still be losing by millions of votes. He won in 2016 only because of the Electoral College. He came close in 2020 only because of the Electoral College, and he would win in 2024 only because of the Electoral College. . . . The saving grace of Donald Trump is his incompetence. What we should really fear is a competent Trumpista, and there are some waiting in the wings who would cheer, at least privately, if Donald Trump died tomorrow. . . . A Republican ascendancy would mean even fuller capture of the federal judiciary than there is now . . . and so if you have a unified Republican government, then you would have to be terrified at what legislation they would pass.[3]

At this writing, polarization and partisan hostility are increasing, along with the likelihood of embittered, potentially violent, losers. This is not the America Americans want.

NOTES

Introduction

1. "'Welfare Queen' Becomes Issue in Reagan Campaign," *NY Times*, February 15, 1976, https://www.nytimes.com/1976/02/15/archives/welfare-queen-becomes -issue-in-reagan-campaign-hitting-a-nerve-now.html.

2. "Historical Highlights: Immigration and Nationality Act of 1965, October 3, 1965," History, Art & Archives, US House of Representatives, accessed July 8, 2022, https://history.house.gov/Historical-Highlights/1951-2000/Immigration-and -Nationality-Act-of-1965/.

3. Jerry Kammer, "The Hart-Celler Immigration Act of 1965," Center for Immigration Studies, September 30, 2015, https://cis.org/Report/HartCeller -Immigration-Act-1965; "U.S. Immigrant Population and Share over Time, 1850–Present," Migration Policy Institute, accessed July 8, 2022, https://www .migrationpolicy.org/programs/data-hub/charts/immigrant-population-over -time.

4. Josh Dawsey, "Trump Derides Protections for Immigrants from 'Shithole' Countries," *Washington Post*, January 12, 2018, https://www.washingtonpost.com /politics/trump-attacks-protections-for-immigrants-from-shithole-countries-in -oval-office-meeting/2018/01/11/bfc0725c-f711-11e7-91af-31ac729add94_story .html; Glenn Thrush and Maggie Haberman, "Trump Gives White Supremacists an Unequivocal Boost," *New York Times*, August 15, 2017, https://www.nytimes .com/2017/08/15/us/politics/trump-charlottesville-white-nationalists.html.

5. Thomas Byrne Edsall, *Chain Reaction: The Impact of Race, Rights, and Taxes on American Politics*, with Mary D. Edsall (New York: W. W. Norton, 1992); Thomas Byrne Edsall, "When the Official Subject Is Presidential Politics, Taxes, Welfare, Crime, Rights, or Values . . . the Real Subject Is Race," *Atlantic*, May 1991, https://www.theatlantic.com/past/docs/politics/race/edsall.htm.

6. Daron Acemoglu, "Harms of AI," NBER Working Paper 29247, Nation Bureau of Economic Research, September 2021, https://www.nber.org/papers /w29247.

7. Lawrence Mishel et al., *The State of Working America*, 12th ed. (Ithaca, NY: Cornell University Press, 2012), 173.

8. Ron Lesthaeghe and Lisa Neidert, "US Presidential Elections and the Spatial Pattern of the American Second Demographic Transition," *Population*

and Development Review 35, no. 2 (June 2009): 391–400, https://www.jstor.org /stable/25487671; "Batool Zaidi and S. Philip Morgan, "The Second Demographic Transition Theory: A Review and Appraisal," *Annual Review of Sociology* 43 (July 2017): 473–92, https://www.annualreviews.org/doi/10.1146/annurev-soc-060116 -053442.

9. Lesthaeghe and Neidert, "US Presidential Elections."

10. Ron Lesthaeghe, "The Second Demographic Transition: A Concise Overview of Its Development," *Proceedings of the National Academy of Sciences* 111, no. 51 (December 23, 2014): 18112–15, http://www.pnas.org/content/111/51/18112.full.

11. Ronald Inglehart, "The Silent Revolution in Europe: Intergenerational Change in Post-industrial Societies," *American Political Science Review* 65, no. 4 (December 1971): 991–1017, https://doi.org/10.2307/1953494.

12. Ronald Inglehart, *The Silent Revolution: Changing Values and Political Styles among Western Publics* (Princeton Legacy Library, 2016 [1977]), https://press .princeton.edu/books/hardcover/9780691641515/the-silent-revolution; Ronald Inglehart, *Culture Shift in Advanced Industrial Society* (Princeton University Press, 1990 [1989]), https://press.princeton.edu/books/paperback/9780691022963 /culture-shift-in-advanced-industrial-society; Ronald F. Inglehart, *Cultural Evolution: People's Motivations Are Changing, and Reshaping the World* (Cambridge University Press, 2018), https://www.cambridge.org/core/books/cultural-evolution /34F637928AB1AA87B6409C28B4DFC9F5.

13. Ronald Inglehart and Pippa Norris, "Trump and the Populist Authoritarian Parties: *The Silent Revolution* in Reverse," *Perspectives on Politics* 15, no. 2 (June 2017): 443, https://www.cambridge.org/core/journals/perspectives -on-politics/article/trump-and-the-populist-authoritarian-parties-the-silent -revolution-in-reverse/FE06E514F88A13C8DBFD41984D12D88D.

14. Inglehart and Norris, "Trump and the Populist," 444.

15. Inglehart and Norris, 447.

16. Sara McLanahan, "Diverging Destinies: How Children Are Faring under the Second Demographic Transition," *Demography* 41 (2004): 607, http://link .springer.com/article/10.1353/dem.2004.0033#page-1.

17. Morris Pearl, "It's Time for Congress to Close the Carried Interest Loophole," *Hill*, December 10, 2021, https://thehill.com/blogs/congress-blog/politics /585320-its-time-for-congress-to-close-the-carried-interest-loophole.

18. Nicholas Riccardi, "Democrats Keep Winning the Popular Vote. That Worries Them," AP News, https://apnews.com/article/democrats-popular-vote-win -d6331f7e8b51d52582bb2d60e2a007ec.

19. Ingrid Creppell, "The Concept of Normative Threat," *International Theory* 3, no. 3 (September 20, 2011): 450–87, https://www.cambridge.org/core/journals /international-theory/article/the-concept-of-normative-threat/A71D75503B033 876E74F54611B01A8FD.

20. *From Crisis to Reform: A Call to Strengthen America's Battered Democracy* (Washington, DC: Freedom House, March 2021), https://freedomhouse.org/sites /default/files/2021-03/US_Democracy_Report_FINAL_03222021.pdf.

21. Sarah Repucci, "From Freedom to Reform: A Call to Strengthen America's Battered Democracy," Freedom House Special Report, March 2021, 1, https://freedomhouse.org/sites/default/files/2021-03/US_Democracy_Report_FINAL_03222021.pdf.

22. Economist Intelligence Unit, *The Democracy Index 2021: The China Challenge* (New York: Economist Intelligence Unit, 2022), 3, https://pages.eiu.com/rs/753-RIQ-438/images/eiu-democracy-index-2021.pdf.

23. All columns retain their original titles, with the original publication dates listed, and readers interested in seeing the sources and other hyperlinks can view this in the versions that appear online.

Conclusion

1. "The Changing Composition of the Electorate and Partisan Coalitions," Pew Research Center, June 2, 2020, https://www.pewresearch.org/politics/2020/06/02/the-changing-composition-of-the-electorate-and-partisan-coalitions/pp_2020-06-02_party-id_2-03/.

2. Cooperative Election Study, Harvard University, accessed July 19, 2022, https://cces.gov.harvard.edu/.

3. Grace Segers and Daniel Strauss, "What If Trump Wins in 2024? Here's What 13 Famous Politicians and Pundits Said," *New Republic*, April 19, 2022, https://newrepublic.com/article/165986/what-if-trump-wins-2024.

INDEX OF NAMES

INDEX OF SUBJECTS

A NOTE ON THE TYPE

This book has been composed in Adobe Text and Gotham.
Adobe Text, designed by Robert Slimbach for Adobe,
bridges the gap between fifteenth- and sixteenth-century
calligraphic and eighteenth-century Modern styles.
Gotham, inspired by New York street signs, was designed
by Tobias Frere-Jones for Hoefler & Co.

MAY - - 2023

TWO WEEKS

MT PLEASANT

DISCARD